Podcasting

Dario Llinares • Neil Fox • Richard Berry
Editors

Podcasting

New Aural Cultures and Digital Media

Editors
Dario Llinares
School of Media, University of Brighton
Brighton, UK

Richard Berry
Faculty of Arts and Creative Industries
University of Sunderland
Sunderland, UK

Neil Fox
School of Film & Television
Falmouth University, Penryn Campus
Penryn, Cornwall, UK

ISBN 978-3-319-90055-1   ISBN 978-3-319-90056-8   (eBook)
https://doi.org/10.1007/978-3-319-90056-8

Library of Congress Control Number: 2018947795

Cover credit: Jhy Turley. Photography/Moment Open/Getty Images
Cover design by Henry Petrides

Printed on acid-free paper

This Palgrave Macmillan imprint is published by the registered company Springer International Publishing AG part of Springer Nature.
The registered company address is: Gewerbestrasse 11, 6330 Cham, Switzerland

Acknowledgements

The endeavour of editing a collection of essays is, by its nature, a collaborative process requiring the expertise, commitment, goodwill, patience and faith of a phalanx of contributors. Even after splitting the editorial duties between the three of us, the level of support we have received, both collectively and individually, is humbling and inspiring. In the context of publishing within higher education, fraught as it is with interminable obstacles for what can seem like questionable rewards, in an era where one's time and labour is as precious a commodity as can be bestowed, the constellation of scholars that have made this book a reality have our deepest and sincerest gratitude. Sharing one's valuable research in a nascent area of study is not an easy decision. We acknowledge and thank the authors for their trust and belief in the project as a whole and for juggling many other commitments to be able to meet the deadlines, respond to questions and comments, and deal with the raft of paperwork that is the necessary evil of publishing. We are proud of the work in this volume and hope that the authors feel their contributions to this book have been a rewarding experience resulting in a worthwhile outcome.

We are also extremely grateful to our network of international reviewers who took time to diligently read the submissions and offer detailed feedback on the chapters you are about to read. In all cases this work has been undertaken with true collegiality and a commitment to scholarship in its most fundamental sense. Our sincerest thanks go to Sarah Arnold, Paula Blair, Tiziano Bonini, David Brodbeck, Alec Charles, Lance Dann, Leighton Evans, Lucy Frears, Nele Heise, Rob Jewitt, Evi Karathanasopoulou, Rachel Leventhal-Weiner, Mia Lindgren, Alex Lockwood, Jason Loviglio, Caitlin Kight, Katy McDonald, Caroline Mitchell, Matthew Rogers, Jo Tyler and Abigail Wincott.

Thanks are also due to colleagues at Brighton, Falmouth and Sunderland, and the institutions themselves, for their support during the writing and editing process. Glenn Ramirez and Shaun Vigil at Palgrave have been extremely encouraging, efficient and accomodating in helping us develop the project and particularly sympathetic to our somewhat chaotic interpretation of 'final submission'.

Finally, and of course, we would all like to thank our families and friends without whose selfless and tireless support in inumerable ways, this project would never have seen the light of day.

Contents

Notes on Editors and Contributors

Editors

Richard Berry is a Senior Lecturer in Radio at the University of Sunderland. He has published work on different aspects of the intersection between radio/audio media and new technologies. His 2006 essay on Podcasting 'Will iPod Kill the Radio Star?' has become part of the foundation upon which subsequent studies of podcasting have been built.

Neil Fox is a Senior Lecturer and Course Coordinator in Film at Falmouth University's School of Film & Television. His research interests include film education, music documentaries and concert films. His debut feature film as writer/producer, '*Wilderness*' played over 15 international festivals, winning 11 awards including for Best Screenplay. He is also the co-founder and co-host of the *Cinematologists* podcast.

Dario Llinares is Principal Lecturer in Contemporary Screen Media at the University of Brighton. He has published work on a range of topics including the astronaut in American culture, British prison film, the cinema as time machine, and podcasting as academic practice. His current research focuses on the status and practice of cinema-going in the digital age. He is also the co-founder and co-host of the *Cinematologists* podcast.

Contributors

Danielle Barrios-O'Neill is a Lecturer in English and Publishing at Falmouth University. Her research is largely focused on emergent practices and intersections in narrative and technology, with particular attention to what might be described as the discourse 'sustainable worlds' and engaging in critical conversations between textual and human futures.

Kathleen Collins is a faculty librarian at John Jay College of Criminal Justice in New York. She is the author of *Dr. Joyce Brothers: The Founding Mother of TV Psychology* (2016) and *Watching What We Eat: The Evolution of Television Cooking Shows* (2009) and has written about television and media history for both popular and scholarly publications.

Stacey Copeland is a Communication & Culture MA student in the York–Ryerson University joint graduate program. She received her BA in Radio and Television Arts from Ryerson University. She currently resides in Toronto, Canada where she is actively involved in radio production and sound/art. Queer culture, community radio and feminist media are her areas of academic interest.

Danielle Hancock is a University of East Anglia PhD candidate whose research focuses on podcast horror. She has several publications forthcoming discussing: national identity and radio horror, podcasting communities, and podcasting's relationship to radio. She is a frequent contributor to *The Gothic Imagination Blog* and *Critical Studies in Television*.

Lieven Heeremans is a research masters student in Media and Performance Studies at Utrecht University, Amsterdam. His interests lie at the intersection of media archaeology and production studies. Lieven has hosted *Radio Swammerdam*, the weekly science programme at the local public broadcaster AmsterdamFM, and is currently establishing a podcast network in Amsterdam.

Leslie McMurtry is a Lecturer in Radio Studies at the University of Salford. Her research interests include podcasts, sound design, and empirical experiments on imagery generation through aural drama. Her work on audio drama has been published in the *Journal of Popular Culture*, *Palgrave Communications*, and the *Journal of Radio & Audio Media*.

Rebecca Ora is a scholar and artist whose work focuses on performance, comedy, and nonfiction/docufiction. She holds an MFA in Social Practice from California College of the Arts, where her performative nonfiction video *Watching Lillian* won the Toby Devan Lewis Award. Ora is currently working toward her PhD in Film and Digital Media at UC Santa Cruz on inappropriate representations of the Holocaust. She is the founder of the Rebecca Ora Award for Risk-Taking in the Arts.

Pille Pruulmann-Vengerfeldt is Professor of Media Studies in University of Tartu, senior lecturer in media and communication in University of Malmö and member of board for Estonian Public Broadcasting. Her research interests include cultural participation in museums and libraries, internet and social media user typologies and conceptualisations of privacy online.

Farokh Soltani is completing his PhD on the phenomenology of radio drama at the Royal Central School of Speech and Drama, where he is also employed as a visiting lecturer. His research is influenced by his professional background as a writer and sound designer in the Iranian theatre and television industries.

John L. Sullivan is Professor of Media & Communication at Muhlenberg College, Allentown, PA, USA. Sullivan's research explores the links between media industries and systems of social and economic power. He has published *Media Audiences* (Sage, 2012) and articles on US distribution of the British science fiction TV series *Doctor Who*, the development of a social movement around free, open source (F/OSS) software, and issues of artificial scarcity in digital software.

Lukasz Swiatek is a Lecturer in Communication and Public Relations in the School of Communication, Journalism and Marketing at Massey University, New Zealand. He has taught a range of undergraduate and postgraduate courses in New Zealand and Australian universities.

Johanna Willstedt Buchholtz has a master's degree in Art History focusing on Visual Studies from Lund University. She has worked for ten years as a process communication manager in telecom. She is currently pursuing a master's degree in Media and Communication Studies at Malmö University.

Robbie Z. Wilson studied drama at the University of Kent, specialising in stand-up comedy with Oliver Double, before training in acting at East 15 with Andrea Brooks. Now back at Kent for a PaR PhD, Robbie uses performance to facilitate ludic interactions between people and environments.

List of Figures

1

Introduction: Podcasting and Podcasts— Parameters of a New Aural Culture

Dario Llinares, Neil Fox, and Richard Berry

In adopting a new form of media practice, one might be forgiven for a certain level of naivety regarding the technological skills, creative applications, intellectual reflections and socio-cultural outcomes that would result. This is certainly true for two of the editors of this book. Dario Llinares and Neil Fox have produced *The Cinematologists* since 2015, the decision to start a podcast emerging from a fusion of the scholarly and personal pleasures of discussing all things cinema, allied with the sense that this relatively new audio medium could offer the potential to amalgamate the depth and rigour of academic research with the immediacy, openness and distribution power of the internet. Podcasting imbued in us the enthusiasm of possibility. Namely the possibility, in one 'space', to create a considered yet engaging conversation that merges criticality, scholarship, fandom and practice, not to mention the possibility of attracting an audience that found value in our conversations. We soon came to realise that working in audio was a different register to writing.

D. Llinares (✉)
School of Media, University of Brighton, Brighton, UK
e-mail: d.llinares@brighton.ac.uk

N. Fox
School of Film & Television, Falmouth University, Penryn Campus, Penryn, Cornwall, UK
e-mail: neil.fox@falmouth.ac.uk

R. Berry
Faculty of Arts and Creative Industries, University of Sunderland, Sunderland, UK
e-mail: richard.berry@sunderland.ac.uk

© The Author(s) 2018
D. Llinares et al. (eds.), *Podcasting*, https://doi.org/10.1007/978-3-319-90056-8_1

1

The processes of production and the creation of content affords new freedoms with regard to the communication of knowledge. The medium's hybridity of thought, sound and text perhaps even fosters a reinvigoration of the dialectic, an exchange of ideas beyond what is possible in purely written form—be it in a magazine or academic journal. Podcasting, for us, taps into something fundamental about oral communication, argument and even the tension between subjective and objective knowledge that has been amplified in the digital age. Perhaps our attitude to working in the medium is somewhat quixotic and idealised but podcasting seems to possess the advantages of the internet while expelling some of the pitfalls. The podcast 'space' engendering a forum for discussion that is not defined by the culture of instantaneous reaction, sound-bite reductionism and anonymous mudslinging.

Undoubtedly our fandom of podcasts more broadly, spanning a range of genres, subjects and formats, was instrumental in inspiring us to create our own. The flexibility of listening and the relative lack of editorial and formal scrutiny in production marks the medium as something different, more radical, and more culturally urgent than radio. Furthermore, the technological specifics of the medium cultivates an autonomy of approach that result in conversational, informal, personal, even supportive, atmospheres. Podcasting also exemplifies the maxim that 'the specific is universal' by creating spaces for niche and cult content that caters for the more idiosyncratic cultures of interest. This openness to specialism, works counterintuitively, imbuing a sense of inclusivity for both producers and listeners. No matter how deep or obscure your interests are, there is a podcast for you, or there is (relatively) little stopping you making your own. Podcasting culture thus manages to be both personal and communal, a sensibility that is related to the active choice the listener has to exercise, and the modes of consumption—through headphones, car sound systems, home computers, mobile phones etc.—which imbue a deeply sonorous intimacy. To be a private, silent participant in other people's interests, conversations, lives and experiences, relating to a subject you are passionate about, generates a deep sense of connection. Perhaps such immersion into a simultaneously interior and exterior sonic experience may be the essential reason why podcasts have become so popular: they offer the listener a means to explore the self while simultaneously providing anchoring points in the chaos of a digital and material experience that is increasingly blurred.

Our production and consumption of podcasts has had effects that have gone beyond what we had foreseen, provoking a range of questions related to the very ontology of the medium, its context in the current media landscape, and how it instigates a self-reflectivity regarding one's identity as a mediated and mediating subject. As academics working in the broad landscape of the humanities the overwhelmingly transformational force of 'the digital' predicates our work. Indeed, researching and teaching in media today requires both a search for apposite angles of analysis and modes of expression that capture the zeitgeist. Higher education is, of course, not immune to the effects of convergence culture, transmedia dissemination and the myriad reconfigurations of digital production, distribution and exhibition. Podcasting has, for us and for many of the authors in this book, inspired and enabled the creation of new avenues of research dissemination, expanding the sphere of influence across platforms and audiences. In this sense, podcasting is a significant part of the growing open-source ethos that challenges the structures of traditional academic publishing, and perhaps even offers the beginnings of a challenge to the hegemony of text and image as the primary communicative modes of the digital age.

We see that there is a level of irony in publishing a book focusing on an audio form that we advocate as disrupting, challenging and possessing the potential to reconfigure the traditions of academic discourse. However, there's no denying that while cultures are changing, they are not quite changed yet. The written word is not only dominant, but also a vital and rewarding way of engaging with all cultures, including new aural ones. In the spirit of being true to the form though, this book has an accompanying podcast that discusses the themes, issues and ideas thrown up by this written collection.

This is the first comprehensive interdisciplinary collection of academic work analysing the definition, status, practices and implications of podcasting within the broader context of digital media and cultural studies. It brings together the research of experienced and early career academics, along with practitioners of various types from a wide breadth of international contexts. Encompassing chapters that span a range of analytical and methodological approaches we envisage the entries here will be of interest to a range of scholars and students in what is an underdeveloped yet burgeoning area of enquiry. While the focus of chapters is diverse, the interrelationship between technological configuration, creative practice and conceptual understanding is an anchoring structure. Furthermore, for many of the authors, the digital milieu that has led to podcasting's current moment of mainstream cross-over has activated a philosophical interrogation of how information and knowledge is communicated. Many of the analyses here challenge the theorist/practitioner dichotomy and explore how podcasting facilitates autonomy and agency over one's mediated self.

The third editor of this book, Richard Berry, joined in the early stages of the process and is a key voice in defining podcasting in relation to its closest familial progenitor: radio. As with the other editors, consumption of podcasts generated a curiosity in the form, not least in the questions it posed for radio both academically and industrially. Indeed, as time has passed more and more students with an interest in audio are gaining that passion through podcasts. The next section of the introduction maps out some of the core arguments and contextual parameters regarding the radio/podcast relationship from which research into podcasting has emerged. This provides the springboard from which we suggest that podcasting has transitioned into a new phase, a 'new aural culture', with its applications and effects requiring wider interdisciplinary conceptual approaches. We introduce some of the formative research that constitutes the starting point of a 'podcast studies' before proceeding to set out how the chapters in this volume expand this nascent field. *Podcasting: New Aural Cultures and Digital Media* is not intended as an exhaustive account, rather it offers a series of starting points and trajectories of enquiry which wrestle with podcasting's technological, industrial, cultural and social dynamics in the context of digital media.

Podcast v. Radio: An Uneasy Paternalism

Despite podcasting being around for over a decade, there is still an uneasiness in defining it as a medium. Richard Berry has spent a lot of time thinking and writing about the contentious connecting tissue between podcasting and radio as the focus of his research. Whilst podcasting shares many auditory codes and production practices with radio, many of the chapters that follow outline the inherent differences that are beginning to emerge and be classified. In many ways, podcasting is a 'new' form in that it has facilitated entry into the creative production of audio for individuals and groups with no broadcasting background. In the UK, the monolith of the BBC, the specific structures of commercial radio, and the idiosyncrasies of community broadcasting, present myriad barriers to entry. In the US, public service radio has provided the breeding ground for some of the most popular titles such as *Radiolab, The Heart* and *Serial.* Whilst the affiliation between radio and podcasts continues, ideas and talent flowing freely between the two, within this book we examine the complexities, nuances and even distinctions that underlay the symbiosis. In terms of form, podcasts often demonstrate a distinctively different sound aesthetic where traditional rules around language, content, duration and structural conventions are bent if not completely broken. As podcaster and academic Adam Ragusea highlights, 'The lines between these mediums are both grey and fluid. But the lines do exist, and we need to reckon with them' (2015).

It is important to note that whilst the comparisons to radio are easy to make, the origins of the medium come from a desire to circumvent the mediated practices of the radio station and to deliver independent content directly to listeners. Whilst some podcasts are remediated radio content, not all podcasts could sufficiently be described as 'radiogenic', a term, which is itself under constant flux and contention (Chignell 2009: 93–94). Heise (2014) suggests that podcasting might build 'on the shoulders of giants' suggesting that rather than seeking to remediate, refashion or replace radio, podcasting pays homage to it. Indeed, whilst there is some evidence to suggest that podcast addicts listen to more podcasts than anything else (Edison 2017) radio listening remains buoyant (Ofcom 2017), which suggests practices of complementary listening, or replacement listening for audiences under-served by radio. In her work, Markman (2012) suggests that participants were drawn to podcasting out of a desire to 'do' radio, a theme she develops in her preface to a 2015 special issue on podcasting by adding that 'podcasts give producers the freedom to pick and choose those elements that they like about radio, and repackage them for the digital age' (241).

When discussing podcasting one inevitably has to reach a decision about what it is one is talking about. On the surface, podcasting is a delivery mechanism, a means of distributing MP3 audio files across the internet. However, as various chapters in this collection discuss, the outcome of this is 'a specific set of practices and cultural meanings' (Morris and Patterson 2015: 221) where modes of production, presentation, audience engagement and intention become factors through which we can delineate more clearly between podcasts and radio. Just as cinematic practice influenced television, radio practices have influenced podcasts, even if the resultant works bear little resemblance to contemporary forms of radio broadcasting. Excitingly, in this book the authors discuss their subjects as objects in an embryonic field of podcast studies, often without reference to radio at all.

As the chapters in this book outline, the practice of podcasting is not simply another iteration of radio, rather it is a collection of cultural work and practice that spans journalism, performance art, comedy, drama, documentary, criticism and education. We can further this discussion by considering the consumption behaviours (MacDougall 2011), where listeners make deliberate (and often narrow) decisions over what to listen to and consume intimately (McHugh 2016). It is, as McHugh concludes, 'much more than a delivery mode for audio content' (78). The question of how much more, and whether podcasting is an area of study or as we provocatively suggest, a new aural culture, is central to the enquiry of this collection of essays.

Podcasting Studies or 'New Aural Culture'?

This book emerges at a time when the notion of podcasting's 'golden age' is a prevalent discourse in both academic and wider cultural circles (Berry 2015; Bottomley 2015; Hempel 2015). This assertion derives from the contention that podcasting has crossed-over into mainstream consciousness in a way that has a new cultural significance. Perhaps the two most obvious examples of a heightened symbolic value were the appearance of President Obama on the *WTF with Marc Maron* podcast, and the phenomenal success of the podcast *Serial*, which the New York Times called 'arguably the medium's first breakout hit' (Carr 2014) elevating 'the podcast medium to astronomical heights' (Chaudry 2016: 263). A surge of journalistic interest in podcasting's cultural significance has morphed into a familiar and rather narrow interest in metrics and money (Cellan-Jones 2016; Boboltz 2016). Indeed, as we write this the announcement that iTunes, the digital infrastructure that has provided the basis for podcast distribution since its inception, has introduced analytics for the first time is proving a major talking point (Quah 2017).

Analyses that focus solely on audience numbers and economic potential ignores the vast spectrum of podcast culture, its forms and contexts, the reasons they are made, why they are listened to, and the complexity and diversity of their impact. In many ways, the podcast remains a curiosity sitting on the periphery of mainstream media, an esoteric offshoot of digital culture. Its interest and identity, for us, lay in its practical and conceptual liminality and the play of mediatory possibilities it provokes. However, currently discussions are generally shoehorned into existing narratives already cemented by other forms (although, as Brian Reed, creator of the 2016 hit *S-Town* notes: 'Podcasting is still so new, there aren't a lot of rules for how things should be done' (Reed in McGrane 2017). This kind of freedom makes podcasting, like all other 'new' mediums before it, confounding and therefore potentially dangerous for more conservative commentators who downplay its uniqueness and divert conversation into staid realms.

The research and analysis in these essays are in many ways a reaction to, and engagement with, a medium that has now reached a watershed moment, just over ten years after its inception. Positing the notion of a 'New Aural Culture' is somewhat of a provocation intended to symbolise the current zeitgeist as a flourishing of digital creativity in terms of aesthetic form, production context, cultural status and social relevance. Previous allusions to the importance of Radio Studies that foregrounded aurality from a broadly media/ humanities disciplinary standpoint are of course indicative, but one can also call upon the advocacy of 'auditory culture' by Michael Bull and Les Back which, among other things 'aims to counter the assumed supremacy of the 'visual' in accounts of the social' (2003: 3). There is certainly a cross-over of concerns with podcasting offering up new modes of sound utilisation which in turn has fostered novel socio-cultural effects. 'Auditory Culture' perhaps offers a socio-historic umbrella term that encompasses disciplinary sub-fields of sound studies, acoustic ecology and soundscape studies. The analyses contained in this book span anthropology, gender studies, philosophy, digital humanities and performance, suggesting that interdisciplinarity is fundamental to studies of podcasting. This results in the key question of whether podcasting demands its own specific disciplinary space—a 'podcast studies'—or is merely a digital media tool for understanding aspects of other cultural spaces in new ways. It's early days, but this collection and accompanying podcast is intended to open up pathways of enquiry as the medium matures and parameters of understanding become potentially less nebulous.

Academic study of the podcast does have various conceptual trends already in place and growing. The links to radio we have already touched upon (See also Menduni 2007; Sterne et al. 2008) but perhaps the most in-depth strand of podcasting research followed the medium's initial emergence in the mid-2000s and concerns the potential applications in pedagogic practice (Campbell 2005; Copley 2007; Frydenberg 2008; Lazzari 2009; Daniel and Woody 2010; Rosell-Aguilar 2013). More contemporary work has begun to examine the motivations of podcast producers/consumers (McClung and Johnson 2010; Chadha et al. 2012; Markman 2012; Markman and Sawyer 2014) and there are increasing textual and contextual analyses of individual podcasts with focus on *Serial,* as the landmark cross-over podcast, undoubtedly at the forefront of such work (O'Meara 2015; Meserko 2016; McMurtry 2016; McHugh 2017). Research has also begun to emerge, to which this edited collection adds, that explores the status of the medium in the contemporary media/cultural landscape (Berry 2015; Bonini 2015; Bottomley 2015; Markman 2015).[1] In the final section, we set out the content of this collection that we hope will contribute to expanding academic focus on podcasting as one of the key digital media cultures and practices of the new century.

The Scope of This Book

When inviting and compiling contributions to this collection we wanted it to reflect the diversity of podcasting as a form and practice. Podcasting is a welcome space for both the amateur and professional, for narrative and non-narrative, for performance and journalism, and we intend this collection to be a welcome space for the established and early-career academic, for cultural studies and ethnography, for interviews and empirical research, for industrial and textual analysis, and all areas in between. In this collection, there are discussions of blockbuster and supremely niche podcasts; articles by scholars and practitioners which represent in microcosm the range of voices and discourses that have emerged in podcasting's short history. The representation of theory and practice isn't merely through the contributions of scholars and producers but through investigations into how podcasting provides a productive space for reflections that actively theorise practice. We believe that a collection that seeks to argue for the fluid, interdisciplinary and diverse nature of podcasting needs to be reflective in its construction and output. The chapters do primarily focus on the United States podcast culture which, in output and listenership, dominates the landscape. Indeed, the international, national and regional dynamics of podcasting is undoubtedly a theme requiring further scrutiny.

Richard Berry begins our collection with an exploration into the doing and being of podcaster identity. Drawing from contextual analysis of the medium's structural development, allied to responses from an online survey of podcast producers, Berry contextualises the innovative outcomes of podcasting, as relative to, but distinct from radio, particularly in manifesting forms of mediated cultural identity. To this end Berry advocates for a discreet 'podcast studies' through which the myriad uses, outcomes and interpretations of the form can be theorized. In Chap. 3, John Sullivan posits the recent expansion of podcast production as a transitional moment in which the medium is morphing from specialist, amateur, niche sensibilities into a commercially viable media industry. The formation of podcast networks is a resultant phenomenon in which entrepreneurialism and monetisation is shifting the aspirations of formally independent producers. Sullivan explores developing tensions in the podcast ecosystem via an investigative analysis of the Podcast Movement Conference held in 2016 in Chicago.

On similar territory, Lieven Heeremans examines the development of podcast networks in the US using a comparative analysis of three case studies: *Radiotopia*, *Relay FM* and *The Heard*. He argues that an economic model has emerged slowly out of the radio infrastructure with individual and independent podcast titles increasingly joining fledgling networks in a move that has both similarities and differences from traditional broadcast commodification. Using interviews with executives from said networks Heeremans suggests that podcaster motivations for joining networks are borne out of a desire to forge gatekeeping mechanisms for the sector going forward, share resources, optimise audiences and create possibilities for monetisation.

Danielle Hancock and Leslie McMurtry give us our first engagement with the podcast phenomenon that is *Serial*. They explore *Serial's* status as not only a watershed moment for podcasting but how it helped define the parameters and possibilities for audio fiction in podcasting leading to a set of identifiers, particularly in terms of the thriller genre, that can be termed post-*Serial*. The seminal 2014 podcast comes under scrutiny again, this time its relationship to understandings of truth in documentary forms, as the focus of Rebecca Ora's contribution. *Serial* was notable for its mainstream success, the resultant press attention undoubtedly pulling in and gripping audiences, yet Ora argues that it failed to offer a satisfactory conclusion. Audiences therefore engaged in invitatory practices through avenues beyond the podcast itself which, Ora suggests, forces a reconceptualization of what we might understand as a 'live medium'.

In Chap. 7, Dario Llinares discusses how the infrastructure of podcast production and consumption has opened up aural practice to facilitate new possibilities of being and doing mediation. Forwarding the concept of liminal praxis, Llinares draws on his own experience and the reflections of other academics and writers, to explore how podcasting disrupts the hierarchy between written and sound communication. He goes on to analyse the discourse of self-reflexivity that underpins much of podcast creation, suggesting that production practices 'provide a mechanism by which producer/ consumers use the medium to define and enact their own agency within the highly fractured subjectivity of the internet age'. Through analysing the 'conversational science' of the *Stuff to Blow Your Mind* podcast, Danielle Barrios-O'Neill examines points of convergence between the sciences and the humanities and how the podcast form can break down complex relations and engage listeners in challenging ecological subject matter, blurring previously fought-over binaries regarding theory and practice, and hard and soft subject matter.

Analysing the *Nobel Prize Talks* podcast Lukasz Swiatek defines podcasting as an 'intimate bridging medium', which forges unique modes of connectivity that cross boundaries between producer and listener. Although, on the one hand, Swiatek suggests podcasting can transverse the knowledge boundaries and also barriers between individuals and group identities, he also suggests that the bridging potential is undermined by many of the traditional hierarchies that beset traditional media communication. Farokh Soltani furthers ideas put forward earlier by Hancock and McMurtry regarding the potential of podcast audio drama to become something distinct and evolved from its radio precursors. Using Merleau-Ponty's ideas around the phenomenology of perception, he argues that through its unique and intimate components podcast drama can become something sensory and embodied. Audio dramaturgy is thus conceptualised as potentially instigating 'a radical break with the limits placed on it by radio technology'.

Intimacy and the feminist voice in the, now disbanded, podcast *The Heart* is the focus of Stacey Copeland's entry. As a collection of work that explores intimate issues around sex, gender and sexuality, 'The Heart' has made great use of the intimacy of the podcast form. In her chapter Copeland explores this through discussion of a number of episodes and relates them to representations of the voice 'that can challenge visual-philic heteronormative and gendered expectations by engaging with the listener through the affective use of sound'. Kathleen Collins explores the rise of comedian-hosted interview podcasts, where comics mix personal conversations with comedic personas linking this to Graeme Turner's (2010) term the 'demotic turn'. Collins places this discussion in the context of her earlier work on television and radio confessionals, connecting our current focus on digital media with earlier broadcast iterations of similar formats.

Pille Pruulmann-Vengerfeldt and Johanna Willstedt Buchholtz discuss how collaboration, humour and multiple voices are key to accessing and delivering sensitive material in podcasting. Their analysis of the podcast *Sickboy* takes in audiences, production practices and funding structures as it deconstructs how myriad factors contribute to being able to discuss the lived experience of people with disabilities in ways that are inclusive and non-discriminatory. Following this, Robbie Wilson explores his own use of podcasting as a tool in performance art. Rather than considering podcasts as another iteration of traditional broadcasting, Wilson, using his own practice-based research, conceptualises the role of podcasts as a portable, personal medium, used to locate listeners in the environment once again exemplifying our assertion that podcasting is a liminal medium. In our final chapter Neil Fox interviews the high-profile, prolific British podcaster Richard Herring. Fox's interview is a revealing insight into the cultural development of the podcast from one of its early adopters and the interview covers the theorising of practice, funding structures, audiences, writing and form from the perspective of a committed practitioner with a diverse portfolio of shows.

This edited book is at once a reaction to podcasting's zeitgeist moment, an expansion of academic research and a collation of existing forms of discourse in this emergent area. In conceptualizing the podcast on its own terms, the chapters in this collection examine its liminal status perhaps even finally dissolving the rather archaic dichotomies of 'old' and 'new' media and 'professional' and 'amateur' production values, practices and identities. They deconstruct the podcast's reliance on mainstream industrial structures whilst attempting to retain an alternative, even outsider, sensibility. We believe that this collection has the potential to be positioned at the forefront of an expanding research area, acting as a gateway to what will undoubtedly develop over the coming years. We hope it becomes a seminal text for students, scholars and practitioners seeking to understand and further develop knowledge of the medium who will take this 'new aural culture' to heights and places we cannot imagine as we write this.

Note

1. Also, see other articles from the 2015 special symposium on podcasting www.tandfonline.com/toc/hjrs20/22/2

Bibliography

Berry, R. (2006). Will the iPod kill the radio star. Profiling podcasting as radio. *Convergence, 12*(2), 143–162.

Berry, R. (2015). A golden age of podcasting? Evaluating serial in the context of podcast histories. *Journal of Radio & Audio Media, 22*(2), 170–178.

Boboltz, S. (2016). 2016 was awful for pretty much everything except podcasts. *www.huffingtonpost.com* https://www.huffingtonpost.com/entry/2016-was-awful-for-pretty-much-everything-except-podcasts_us_58529c05e4b0732b82fefd74 [Internet]. Accessed 20 Sept 2017.

Bonini, T. (2015). The 'second age' of podcasting: Reframing podcasting as a new digital mass medium. *Quaderns del CAC, 41*(xviii), 21–30.

Bottomley, A. J. (2015). Podcasting: A decade in the life of a 'new' audio medium: Introduction. *Journal of Radio and Audio Media, 22*(2), 164–169.

Campbell, G. (2005). There's something in the air: Podcasting in education. *Educause Review, 40*(6), 32–47.

Carr, D. (2014). 'Serial,' podcasting's first breakout hit, sets stage for more. *The New York Times* https://www.nytimes.com/2014/11/24/business/media/serial-podcastings-first-breakout-hit-sets-stage-for-more.html [Internet]. Accessed 20 Sept 2017.

Cellan-Jones, R. (2016). Can podcasts turn a profit? www.bbc.co.uk [Internet]. Accessed 20 Sept 2017.

Chadha, M., Avila, A., & Gil de Zúñiga, H. (2012). Listening in: Building a profile of podcast users and analyzing their political participation. *Journal of Information Technology & Politics, 9*(4), 388–401.

Chaudry, R. (2016). *Adnan's story*. London: Penguin Random House.

Chignell, H. (2009). *Key concepts in radio studies*. London: Sage.

Copley, J. (2007). Audio and video podcasts of lectures for campus-based students: Production and evaluation of student use. *Innovations in Education and Teaching International, 44*(4), 387–399.

Daniel, D., & Woody, W. D. (2010). They hear, but do not listen: Retention for podcasted material in a classroom context. *Teaching of Psychology, 37*(3), 199–203.

Edison Research. (2017). The podcast consumer 2017. www.edisonrearach.com [Internet]. Accessed Dec 2017.

Frydenberg, M. (2008). Principles and pedagogy: The two Ps of podcasting in the information technology classroom. *Information Systems Education Journal, 6*(6), 1–11.

Heise, N. (2014). On the shoulders of giants? How audio podcasters adopt, transform and reinvent radio storytelling. *Transnational radio stories (Martin Luther University Halle- Wittenberg)*. https://hamburgergarnele.files.wordpress.com/2014/09/podcasts_heise_public.pdf [Internet]. Accessed 10 July 2017.

Hempel, J. (2015). If podcasts are the new blogs, enjoy the golden age while it lasts. www.wired.com [Internet]. Accessed 15 Sept 2017.

Lazzari, M. (2009). Creative use of podcasting in higher education and its effect on competitive agency. *Computers & Education, 52*(1), 27–34.

MacDougall, R. (2011). Podcasting and political life. *American Behavioral Scientist, 55*(6), 714–732.

Markman, K. (2012). Doing radio, making friends, and having fun: Exploring the motivations of independent audio podcasters. *New Media & Society, 14*(4), 547–565.

Markman, K. (2015). Considerations—Reflections and future research. Everything old is new again: Podcasting as radio's revival. *Journal of Radio and Audio Media, 22*(2), 240–243.

Markman, K., & Sawyer, C. E. (2014). Why pod? Further explorations of the motivations for independent podcasting. *Journal of Radio & Audio Media, 21*(1), 20–35.

McClung, S., & Johnson, K. (2010). Examining the motives of podcast users. *Journal of Radio & Audio Media, 17*, 82–95.

McGrane, C. (2017). 'S-Town' creator: Podcasting is so new, the rules are still being written. www.geekwire.com [Internet]. Accessed 10 Dec 2017.

McHugh, S. (2016). How podcasting is changing the audio storytelling genre. *The Radio Journal—International Studies in Broadcast and Audio Media, 14*(1), 65–82.

McHugh, S. (2017). Why S-Town invites empathy not voyeurism. *The Conversation Online*. https://theconversation.com [internet]. Accessed Apr 2017.

McMurtry, L. G. (2016). "I'm not a real detective, I only play one on radio": Serial as the future of audio drama. *The Journal of Popular Culture, 49*(2), 306–324.

Menduni, E. (2007). Four steps in innovative radio broadcasting: From QuickTime to podcasting. *Radio Journal: International Studies in Broadcast & Audio Media, 5*(1), 9–18.

Meserko, V. M. (2016). Going mental: Podcasting, authenticity, and artist-fan identification on Paul Gilmartin's mental illness happy hour. *Journal of Broadcasting and Electronic Media, 58*(3), 456–469.

Morris, J., & Patterson, E. (2015). Podcasting and its apps: Software, sound, and the interfaces of digital audio. *Journal of Radio and Audio Media, 22*(2), 220–230.

Nobel Prize Talks. (2013–). www.nobelprize.org/podcast/ [Internet]. Accessed 16 Sept 2017.

O'Connell, M. (2015). The 'serial' effect: Programmers ramping up on podcasts. *The Hollywood Reporter.* www.hollywoodreporter.com [Internet]. Accessed 16 Sept 2017.

O'Meara, J. (2015). 'Like movies for radio': Media convergence and the *Serial* podcast sensation. *Frames Cinema Journal, 8.* http://framescinemajournal.com/ [Online]. Accessed May 2016.

Ofcom. (2017). International communications market report 2017. www.ofcom.org.uk [Internet]. Accessed Dec 2017.

Quah, N. (2017). Apple's new analytics for podcasts mean a lot of change (some good, some inconvenient) is on the way. www.niemanlab.org [Internet]. Accessed 24 Sept 2017.

Ragusea, A. (2015). Three ways podcasts and radio actually aren't quite the same. *The Current.* www.current.org [Internet]. Accessed 18 Dec 2017.

Rosell-Aguilar, F. (2013). Delivering unprecedented access to learning through podcasting as OER, but who's listening? A profile of the externa iTunes U user. *Computers and Education, 67*, 121–129.

S-Town. (2016–). www.stownpodcast.org/ [Podcast]. Accessed 16 Sept 2017.

Serial. (2014–). www.serialpodcast.org [Podcast]. Accessed 16 Sept 2017.

Sickboy. (2015–). www.sickboypodcast.com [Podcast]. Accessed 16 Sept 2017.

Sterne, R., et al. (2008). The politics of podcasting. *The Fibreculture Journal, 13.* http://thirteen.fibreculturejournal.org/fcj-087-the-politics-of-podcasting/

The Heart. (2014–). www.theheart.org [podcast]. Accessed 20 Feb 2018.

Turner, G. (2010). *Ordinary people and the media: The demotic turn.* Los Angeles: Sage.

WTF with Marc Maron. (2009–). www.wtfpod.com [podcast].

2

'Just Because You Play a Guitar and Are from Nashville Doesn't Mean You Are a Country Singer': The Emergence of Medium Identities in Podcasting

Richard Berry

Introduction

The title of this chapter quotes a podcaster who responded to an author-conducted online survey that sought to explore how podcasters defined their own practice. The quote offers an insight into whether podcasters view their activities as another iteration of radio, or something else. Just as early journalistic reporting of podcasting used radio as a framing tool to help readers understand the new innovation, early academic studies of podcasting (Crofts et al. 2005; Berry 2006; Menduni 2007; Sterne et al. 2008; Sellas 2012) also made references to the relationship between podcasting and radio. For these academics, podcasting was either a bridge between internet radio on a PC and a wireless future (Menduni), or a new form of broadcasting (Sterne). In each case, radio was a useful (often cultural) reference point. In their 2005 article Crofts et al. (2005) concluded that 'Just as podcasting poses a risk to the radio industry, it also promises many opportunities', suggesting that whilst podcasting (as a platform) offered new routes of distribution, podcasting (as a medium) created opportunities for competitors without transmitters. As a medium, radio evolved from offering a simple solution for point to point to communication, through to its current status as a one-way medium of mass communication. If we follow that trajectory, it is then only logical to suggest

R. Berry (✉)
Faculty of Arts and Creative Industries, University of Sunderland, Sunderland, UK
e-mail: richard.berry@sunderland.ac.uk

© The Author(s) 2018
D. Llinares et al. (eds.), *Podcasting*, https://doi.org/10.1007/978-3-319-90056-8_2

that podcasts form part of that tradition as both forms are auditory experiences distributed over a wide area in a process we still might call broadcasting. However, it is my assertion here that contrary to this view, podcasting should not be understood as an attempt to replace, radicalise, or reinvent radio; rather it is a complementary arena that shares production practices.

Whilst programmes from traditional broadcasters are often amongst the most popular on podcasts charts, podcasting was a distribution system developed to share work that wasn't made by radio professionals. The RSS developments that made podcasting possible were developed by Dave Winer, who asserts that it was intended as 'a space for amateurs' and not professionals (Winer 2015), even if initially some early advocates came from the world of radio (Walker 2015). Whilst podcasts such as *Welcome to Night Vale* celebrate and refashion traditional forms, (Bottomley 2015: 186) the medium also presents formats that might challenge traditional notions of what radio should sound or behave like (Meserko 2015). Rather than considering podcasts as a reinvention or rejuvenation (cf Marshall 2004) of radio, we can instead reflect upon it as a process of innovation. Just as Pedersen and Have (2012) suggest that the audiobook should be reviewed as 'a new medium experience that calls for a new theoretical framework' (93), podcasting should also be disconnected from the past to help make sense of the current. In this framework, then, podcasting ought to be reviewed as a medium in its own right, rather than an extension, or a reconfiguration of other media.

Podcasting is a medium that is sonically influenced by radio, and whilst in places it is *institutionally* the same, it should not be seen as *actually* the same. This all suggests that it inhabits a liminal space between broadcast media and online media practices, and such draws traits from each. Within this space podcasting is developing an increasingly distinct identity as it is moves slowly away from these antecedents into a new arena that is increasingly self-defined, economically established, moves driven in part by developing this sense of identity. Definitive understandings of podcasting can, however, be complicated by its dichotomous status as both a delivery system and a medium. It is not my intention to fully explore (or resolve) this issue now, and for the purposes of this chapter the focus will be on defining podcasting as a medium, and not a technology.

In this chapter, I intend to reference business models, survey data, and examples from other disciplines to explore the development of the medium and the ways in which podcasters are asserting their own sense of medium (and cultural) identity. In their book on YouTube Burgess and Green (2009) highlight the problem of studying new media forms, suggesting that to reach a shared understanding of a medium each work must make choices, 'in effect recreating it as a different object each time' (7) in which each choice can present a different understanding. Throughout this chapter, it is my argument that we must consider podcasting on its own terms in what we might call podcast studies as in doing so, we might reach a better understanding of its inherent qualities as a medium. Podcasters themselves feel they are engaged in a very different form of media production: in a survey conducted for this chapter one respondent noted that podcasting is 'very different to radio' as although 'you use your voice, the creation and distribution process and business can be very different' (Respondent 35) In other words, just because podcasts might sound like radio it does not necessarily mean that they always *are* radio.

Hype Cycle to Understand Podcast Histories

As indicated above it is my intention here to reflect on the nature of podcasts as a distinct media practice. To begin this exploration, it is worth reflecting on how audiences have responded to it. Using Google Trends, we can see that interest in the word 'podcast' peaked in January 2006 (Google 2017). Google Trends allocates a value of 100 to the peak of any search term and all points below that with a lower value, where a result of 50 indicates that the search term is half as popular as it was. The interest in 'podcasting' holds for a further year, with values of more than 80 throughout this period. Then, slowly, interest (or at least searches) started to fall away. The listeners who were interested did not need to search and the medium was no longer generating the new interest it once did. Between January 2008 and June 2014 searches fell to almost half of their peak with values between 72 (January 2009) and 53 (December 2013), at which time interest had almost halved. Whilst this does not suggest a decline in usage, it does suggest that popular interest had waned. This is a pattern that fits trends illustrated by the *Hype Cycle* – an innovation trends tool developed by the technology-monitoring company, Gartner, and detailed by Fenn and Raskino (2008). They describe the process as one where an 'innovation comes along that captures people's fancy, and everybody, including the media, joins the parade with great fanfare and high expectations... Then, when it fails to deliver the promised bounty right away, everyone starts bailing out' (2008: 7). The model, whilst not scientific, offers a basic framework which measures factors such as visibility, share price, or in this case, audience interest. As a medium (or a business) podcasting must compete in what James Webster (2014) has described as the 'Marketplace of Attention', where different media forms must compete for the attention of an audience who have access to more media than they can possibly consume. In this regard, searches are a reasonable indicator of that 'attention'.

The Hype Cycle talks about five key stages: 'the innovation trigger' (the point at which interest starts to build); 'the peak of inflated expectations' (the peak of interest that rises sharply on a tidal wave of hype) which is rapidly followed by the 'trough of disillusionment' (where interest drops away almost as quickly as it grew). However, this nadir is followed by a slower more sustainable growth marked by the 'slope of enlightenment' (where interest returns) and the 'plateau of productivity' (Fenn and Raskino 2008: 8)—a period which, I would argue, podcasting now finds itself in. For podcasting there was a definite 'hype' around the opportunities during 2004, growing from the original article in *The Guardian* by Ben Hammersley (2004) that acted as the trigger for those initial searches. By the time the *Ricky Gervais Show* debuted in 2005, many listeners who had never heard of podcasting were searching and listening. However, for them the technical interface was difficult and the opportunities to listen on the move were limited to those who owned an iPod, or something similar. It was neither a fluid nor a convenient process. Perhaps, as Menduni suggests, podcasting was a 'mid-term technology' offering a bridge between the radio of the past and new forms of mobile digital distribution. As I will discuss we can connect this decline in searches with both the technological problems which Menduni describes, but also the time it has taken for podcast creators to understand the medium they were working in. In her discussions with producers McHugh (2016) offers several examples where practitioners with a radio background suggest that both the demands and the practices are different, but our experiences with other media suggest that such realisations take time (see Gates 1996).

Amid the newness of these possibilities, the technology magazine *Wired* splashed the headline 'The End of Radio?' across its cover in March 2005. In one of several articles, the magazine focussed on Adam Curry, a former MTV VJ and a podcaster who had achieved near-cult status in this new field, through his podcast *The Daily Source Code* (2004–2013). Still podcasting today, Curry was central to the dissemination of the new medium (see Berry 2006), with the *Wired* article noting 'Every new medium needs a celebrity, and Curry is happy to fill that role' (Newitz 2005). Any medium that appeared to offer radical opportunities, will naturally garner attention, as Gilmor (2006) suggests in the preface to the second edition of his book *We the Media*, where he notes that searches for the word 'podcasts' went from a standing start to over 100 million Google hits in just over a year, adding: 'can you say velocity?' (xiv).

One might have expected that upward cycle to continue and for home-produced podcasts to start competing with radio. However, as Fenn and Raskino note, things are more complex than simply consumers adopting an idea as 'human nature drives people's heightened expectation, while the nature of innovation drives how quickly something new develops genuine value. The problem is, these two factors move at such different tempos that they're nearly always out of sync. An innovation rarely delivers on its promise when people are most excited about it' (2008: 25–26). In the case of podcasting, the hype didn't reflect either the potential appeal of the content or the convenience of access that a wider audience might require, for the technical reasons already outlined. Their concerns are echoed by Friedman (2005) and Wolfe (2008) with the latter closing an article with 'is podcasting dead? My answer is, yes, I think it is.' (np).

Early academic work on podcasting might offer some insights to what went on here, as whilst podcasting promised fresh opportunities to content creators, it was not a finished solution. It was, as Menduni suggests, an interim solution for audio delivery; as 'it is difficult to think of mass podcasting given that it requires a component of specialised computer work' (2007: 16). Podcasting was a tool that followed in a tradition of radio listening, music personalisation, file sharing and internet radio, in what Friedman (2005) refers to as 'one of the most revolutionary forms of collaboration in the flat world [because] More than ever, we can all now be producers, not just consumers' (94–95). For Friedman and others, the power of podcasting lay in the ability of the public to 'become producers and 'not just passive listeners and viewers' (Friedman 2005: 120). This hyperbole around the convergence culture that podcasting exemplified might go somehow to explain a flourish of excitement followed by a period of sluggish growth and stagnation. We all *could* be podcasters, and we all *could* listen to whatever we want but the reality is that during these early phases both tasks presented technical challenges for the vast majority of people. It took the development of the smartphone and further integrations to create the more fluid system that the audience described by Rogers (2003) in *The Diffusion of Innovations* as the 'early majority' demand.

Serial, the 'Early Majority', and the Return of the Podcast

Although interest in podcasting has seen steady growth since 2006 (Vogt 2016), if we consider media coverage of the podcast *Serial* in 2014 it seemed as through podcasting was a medium that had been forgotten. Journalists wrote about a renaissance (Roose 2014) and a new golden age of audio from a medium that had been neglected. Produced by Sarah Koenig and other members of the *This American Life* production team, *Serial* has become a benchmark for narrative journalism podcasts (McHugh 2016) and established Koenig as an advocate of the podcast medium. Whilst *Serial* was emblematic of change, podcasting was already entering a more confident era, which is well illustrated in the podcast *Start-Up* which documents the creation of Gimlet Media, a full six months before *Serial* debuted. However, it did highlight the importance of distinctive and attractive content in the development of a medium.

Prior to *Serial,* it seemed that whilst a hard-core group of early-adopters had continued to support their favourite podcasts, the wider population were less engaged in the medium. Technology was a factor, but as I will discuss, so was the lack of a sense of a medium. In what might be emblematic of the root problem, we can turn to the origins of Twitter. The social media platform emerged in 2006 from the remnants of the podcasting platform Odeo; where the founders abandoned their project and went looking for a new opportunity (Carlson 2011). Where Odeo struggled, more recent start-ups such as Acast, are enjoying considerable success (Wang 2016) due in no small part to the development of mobile applications and a more coherent content offer. This new app-based environment not only assists the flow of listening but, as Morris and Patterson suggest, it is also 'increasingly performing the cultural work of filtering and constructing niche audiences by directing listeners towards content' (2015: 227). This addresses two of the key problems of podcasting: access and discovery. In an early consumer book on podcasting, Herrington (2005) spends the best part of two chapters discussing where to find podcasts and how to download them, including building your own application. We can connect this to a process the Hype Cycle calls synchronization, through which it is possible to reflect on the journey podcasting has been going through. A 2006 podcast listener might be expecting a simple process that offers a wealth of content but find that, as a *USA Today* article from 2005 notes, 'Subscribing to your favorite podcasts can be tricky, as the steps can vary' (Acohido 2005: np). In this technical hurdle lies the synchronisation problem, as whilst the desire to consume was there and some of the content was there the listeners' means to access it were restricted.

Whilst the Hype Cycle might offer some insight into the processes of adoption and the progression into assimilation into daily life other models of innovation might also offer some perspectives on the development of podcasting. The greatest challenge and the greatest asset for podcasting is the fact that it is (like the internet) a decentralised space deploying open-sourced tools without organisational structure. There is no international committee of podcast standards and, unlike YouTube, there is no-one who can remove you from the platform or inform all users of your presence. In technological terms podcasting had a single point of innovation (the development of RSS enclosures) followed by a series of user-experience enhancements (the integration into iTunes and then apps) and whilst distributors have been able to make servers faster or insert advertising dynamically, the overall ecology of the platform is unchanged. This means that any growth must be linked to either user-end enhancements, or the availability of compelling content rather than medium-led technical enhancements, like 4 K TV or DAB digital radio.

The development of podcasting was driven then, not by technology itself, but by the popularity of the uniqueness of the content and the simplicity of the applications used to capture and the consume that content. As Morris and Patterson argue 'Podcasting is neither limited to nor defined by its technologies. Rather, it is a specific set of practices and cultural meaning' (2015: 221) which is entwined with technologies for distribution and consumption. In their article, they suggest that the mobile app adds a new layer of intermediaries, capable of affecting the listening experience in a positive way, helping listeners navigate the space and find new content. This is where we might be able to draw comparisons between the Gartner model and Rogers. In his model, Rogers identifies a chasm between visionaries and the early majority, a chasm which we might describe as the period of disillusionment suggested by the Hype Cycle a period between the early stages of innovation. Early adopters (in this case podcast listeners), 'expect a radical discontinuity between the old ways and new; and they are prepared to champion this cause against a tide of entrenched resistance. Being the first, they also are prepared to bear with inevitable bugs and glitches that accompany any innovation coming to market' (Moore 2014: 24–25). Moore adds that 'to cross into the mainstream market – you have to first meet the demands of the pragmatist customers' (134). In other words, in order to attract a more mainstream audience, media content must deploy more mainstream technical solutions. As Bergström suggests, 'users are driven to adopt an application primarily because of the functions it performs for them, and secondarily for how easy or hard it is to get the system to perform those functions' (2015: 6). This might explain that in the research for this chapter a managing editor of a podcast network (author interview) told me he felt there had been a slump in engagement, but a producer for a 'tech' podcast said he had experienced continued and steady growth (personal correspondence). In other words, there are different audiences within the same platform, all with different needs and expectations, which highlight the dual tempo rate of development discussed earlier in the chapter.

This period of medium development and technical improvement brings us to a period described by Bonini (2015) as a 'second age of podcasting'. A period which, he says is characterised by 'the transformation of podcasting into a commercial productive practice and a medium for mass consumption' (22). Bonini argues that the rhetoric of the first age was giving way to a period where we might consider podcasting to be 'not merely as an alternative to broadcasting but as a renewed form of it, with emerging new markets as well as a growing number of listeners and practitioners' (23). For Bonini, the movement of podcasting from innovative upstart to mainstream is driven by the triad of economy, technology and creativity, where '…the more wide-spread use of smartphones, the popularity of new crowdfunding sites and the artistic and creative growth of a legion of professional radio producers trained in public radio have brought about a new phase for podcasting' (25). This second age begins at the point where the Hype Cycle has bottomed out and is climbing out of the 'trough of disillusionment', as both listeners and practitioners find formats that work, funding methods that aid sustainability, and technologies that remove the barriers that were once there. This is an era where the processes and practices of podcasting have been professionalised and institutionalised, often presenting a more distinctive form of production practices which have allowed podcasters to differentiate their work (usually from radio) in a more confident manner.

The second age of podcasting can be characterised as a stage where the innovation developed into a fully-fledged medium; Gartner's Cycle describes this stage as a period of productivity. In developing Moore's Diffusion of Innovations, Rogers (2003) describes this transitory phase and uses the term 'early majority' to describe those who adopt innovations after the early adopters. This early majority are characterised as being pragmatic and vertically orientated 'meaning that they communicate more with others like themselves' (57). There are the Serial listeners who revitalised the attention around the medium in 2014. In other words, whilst early adopters of podcasts might look outside their own communities for new ideas, later listeners favour a more coherent offer with established, formalised, accessible networks of distribution and recommendation.

Just as the early radio listeners were happy to build their own radio sets, the very early adopters of podcasts were enthusiastically willing to create their own software, drag files from computers to iPods and to connect their devices each morning to download fresh content. The majority of people, though, have less patience, less time, and less technical skill to find, access, and consume content. This is where the development of the smartphone, in particular, the iPhone, (the so-called 'Jesus phone' – see Campbell and La Pastina

2010) proved to be so important in carrying podcasting across the 'trough of disillusionment' and into the wider markets of casual media consumers. Whilst technology was clearly a fundamental driving force behind the evolution of podcasting, the development of content and economic strategies should also be acknowledged. For public broadcasters podcasting was an additional platform, in a process that has not been so much about creating new forms of content 'but rather about podcasting as a form of time-shifting or creating archives to be listened to in whatever time sequence the listener chooses' (Madsen 2009). This is a mode of production and consumption that Cwynar (2015) has described as 'VCR for the radio' In mapping, the experience at CBC Radio Cwynar illustrates how the corporation shifted approaches between a podcasting as platform approach towards one that paid attention to the qualities of the medium. In the first instance, Cwynar notes that podcasts were seen as 'promotional paratexts for their source radio programs' (191). Whilst other modes were deployed, Cwynar concludes that the 'recent resurgence in interest has prompted new discourses about the format's nature and potential' however for many media institutions 'the format continues to be more about extension than disruption' (197). This 'podcasting-as-platform' approach has slowly given to a greater sense of remediation 'where older media refashion themselves to answer the challenges of new media' (Bolter and Grusin 2001: 15). In podcasting, programmes are no longer constrained by programme schedules and listeners are more able to put aside time to give intricate content more of their attention. In what might be called the Pantone of podcasts, there is a spread of content that ranges from content that is merely a redistributed radio programme, through to content that is honed for the space. From podcasts made by radio professionals for whom the podcast is a by-product, to podcasts made by podcasters for sole distribution online.

Podcasts such as *99% Invisible* and *Radiolab* were able to grow both new audiences but also scale and duration when freed from the live schedule. In each case, podcasting offered producers the opportunity to spin off projects or businesses with a podcast, rather than a broadcast, focus. In the case of *99% Invisible* this led to independent Kickstarter projects and the development of the Radiotopia collective, and in the case of *Radiolab* the creation of WYNC studios, a venture intent on 'leading the new golden age in audio with high-quality storytelling that informs, inspires and delights millions of intellectually curious and highly engaged listeners across digital, mobile and broadcast platforms.' (WNYC). Such developments are key elements to Bonini's discussion of the 'Second Age' of podcasting where the political economy of the most successful podcasts has moved from cross-funded ventures to 'economic systems that are alternative to public services such as crowdfunding, sponsors and advertising' (2015: 27). It is a model where not only do podcast 'studios' and networks emerge, but also the financial models to support them. This occurs because of an accumulation of technological, economic and aesthetic factors. It is within this final criterion that we may find a further and more insightful rationale behind the development of the podcast movement since 2014.

Podcasts as a Distinct Medium

In her survey and analysis of podcasters in 2012 Markman notes that many of those she surveyed talked of their desire to 'do radio', via the online on-demand delivery system that podcasting offered them. This, she suggests, reflects the difference between the practices and protocols of a medium (in this case radio) and the system used to deliver content to audiences. These podcasters were adhering to 'the traditional protocols associated with broadcasting (DJ banter, back announcing, talk show formatting etc.,) while at the same time being divorced from the *delivery technology*' (2012: 561, her emphasis). This suggests that, in some regards, podcasters were doing radio by another route and so purposely retained the same cultural, social and discourse practices seen in linear broadcast radio as a means of culturally identifying their practice. Therefore, podcasting appeared to offer producers democratic access to the media and offer listeners a means to consume media in a way that engendered a degree of control not previously available. In my own survey, respondents also spoke about the way in which podcasting appeared to pass control to them, rather than decisions resting with commissioners, editors or media owners. The respondents also confirmed that whilst they did not necessarily see their practice as radio, it is a useful cultural shorthand that listeners and potential guests understood, 'since we have a cultural understanding of what is "radio", it makes things easier for those who are trying to understand what we do' (Respondent 25), 'We call podcasting "radio" to give an easy analogy to a new form of media' (R32) with another adding 'Calling it 'radio' also gives it more credibility with guests and listeners' (R19). Whilst some felt that radio was a sufficiently broad term, when asked what they make, just 3 per cent of the sample self-identified as someone who makes 'radio', whilst half (49 per cent) described their activity as making podcasts specifically, as opposed to making media content (32 per cent) or being an entrepreneur (14 per cent). This suggests that whilst externally and stylistically podcasters might use radio as a frame of reference, culturally and industrially they might situate their economic or cultural practice within podcasting as a distinct practice.

As one podcaster put it 'Podcasting to me is very different to radio. Simply because you use your voice, the creation and distribution process and business can be very different. Just because you play a guitar and are from Nashville doesn't mean you are a country singer. Similarly, podcasting and radio can be very different' (R26). We can take this to mean that just because it superficially appears to sound like radio, it does not necessarily mean that it is radio. This reinforces the proposal that podcasting is somehow a different medium, capable of presenting inherent qualities that define it as being different to our current understanding of radio.

Studies from other forms of new media can assist us here in framing a debate around podcasting. In 2006 the academic danah boyd spoke to bloggers about their practice, asking them how they defined themselves and the artefacts they produced, but she also reflected on how a medium comes to be defined. She suggests that one should seek to understand what media are through a web of sources—academics, the mass media and the participants themselves. This approach posed a question for boyd as to whether blogs were a genre, (like news), or a medium in their own right, concluding that 'blogs are not a genre of communication, but a medium through which communication occurs' (np). In discussing this, boyd adds that whilst metaphors are 'valuable for introducing the concept to newcomers, it complicates both evaluation and identification' and that a medium is defined by practice and the ways in which participants identify with that practice. We can link this idea to Burgess and Green's proposal of a 'continuum of cultural participations' (2009: 57) where anyone who uploads, consumes, or comments is a participant with equal value. Therefore, the manner in which podcast listeners review shows on iTunes, or create lists of 'top' podcasts suggests that they too have a role in medium definition.

As in boyd's study, the respondents to my survey noted both the correlations and the disparities between their practice and those of legacy media. Interestingly, whilst there was a correlation between those from broader media backgrounds and a desire to use podcasting as a platform, there was no significant difference in attitude about what to call their activity between those who had experience of radio and those who did not. Some noted that whilst the practices were often interchangeable, inherent differences existed; not least because the lack of mediating factors (producers, editors, corporate policies, etc.) offered 'The freedom of telling the story the way you like it without having to follow editor or radio station guidelines' (R19). In a larger study, Markman (2012) noted that podcasts were part of a wider pattern of convergence culture and Pro-Am publishers, where previous of notions of producers and consumers begin to blur, creating what Bruns (2006) calls 'prosumers'. However, amid this newness, the tag of 'radio' remains a popular definition of what podcasts do, perhaps used as a cultural shorthand. When reflecting on the development of the medium and our current understanding of its ontological status, it is worth reflecting briefly if this remains a useful position. Whilst radio scholars such as Kate Lacey (2008) suggest that radio has no edges, as it continues to adapt as technologies shift around it, podcasting continues to throw up challenges to this assertion. For Lacey, the term 'radio' is not only one that is subject to change but ultimately difficult to pin down, not least because streaming services have adopted the term to draw upon our own our previous experiences of listening to the radio. These are issues that Black reviewed in 2001 when considering whether internet 'radio' services were justified in their use of the term. He suggests that 'calling an internet practice "radio" puts a lid on some of the options as to where it can go and what it can become' (403) and may even make the dominance of the radio industry in that space inevitable. For this reason, any claims that podcasting is radio must be treated cautiously, not least because it abandons the origins of the medium as a place for amateurs but also because of the reductive nature of that discourse.

From a convergence perspective, podcasting can be presented as merely another iteration of radio, one that might demonstrate its own cultures and practices but remains part of the radio family. As Meikle and Young (2012) suggest, in media convergence ideas are contested through a process of constant negotiation and change. Just as YouTube videos are capable of being different to television, podcasts are capable of demonstrating differences to radio. It is important to recognise that podcasting is an ecosystem that is shared between varying, but not necessarily competing, auditory forms that span entertainment, education and amateur audio work. Whilst the moniker of 'radio' might be an accurate description of some this work, it may be hopelessly inaccurate when describing, say, a university lecture, a language course or a podcast about serial killers made at home. Many podcasts also demonstrate content that defies our previous experiences of radio or presents formats that would not meet the economic, political or legal standards that many broadcast systems demand. Just as the bloggers boyd spoke to suggest that we know a blog when we see one, there is a strong argument to suggest that we know a podcast when we hear one; so just as Lacey discusses 'radioness' (24) we could think about our ability to identify *podcastness,* even if we cannot (yet) reach agreement over what that might be. As Lotz observes, 'A "medium" derives not only from technological capabilities, but also from textual characteristics, industrial practices, audience behaviors and cultural understanding'. (2017: 3). As a medium, podcasting draws on each of these criteria, demonstrating not only defined delivery system but also industrial, textual and cultural distinctiveness.

In what is now regarded as a prophetic work Microsoft founder Bill Gates explored the impending digital world in *The road ahead* (1996), in which he suggests that early iterations of new media transfer content over from other media. However, Gates argues, to make the best use of the capabilities of the medium, content must be authored for the space. This is what we have seen in podcasting. Whilst remediated radio forms dominated during the early phases, the most popular podcasts of today have been created with the podcast listener in mind. These are podcasts made by podcasters. As Bonini notes 'Whereas, in their first ten years, the most downloaded podcasts with the greatest following were produced by European and American public radio broadcasters, today many of these same podcasts ... are starting to be funded through economic systems that are alternative to public services such as crowdfunding, sponsors and advertising' (2015: 27). In effect, the economic centres of podcasting have shifted from traditional media (using podcasting as a platform) to independent businesses for whom podcasting is distinct media form, with different rules for production and advertising. Bonini further argues that the development of podcasting coincided with a shift in dominance from traditional media outlets to specialist podcast businesses or divisions. In essence, what we might be talking about here is *credibility*, where the Hype Cycle applies to both attention and medium identity, as whilst audiences continued to grow, the sense that podcasting presented itself as a distinct medium for storytelling, entertainment or sustainable commercial activity grew much more slowly. The 2014 podcast *Serial* was largely credited for establishing this medium maturity but, as its co-creator, Ira Glass has acknowledged, the success was emblematic of the shift, rather than the cause of it (Kocher 2015) a point echoed in 2017 by this analysis in *The National*, where Bristow-Bovey notes 'As the networks gather strength by developing new shows and experimenting with new forms, podcasting is approaching a creative and economic tipping point, similar to the evolution of network television in the 1950s and 1960s. Production values increase, shows are more exquisitely produced, quality rises in the search for new ears' (np). The podcasters in my survey also noted that they felt that this sense of 'quality' was a factor in development and growth. One podcaster notes that 'Great sound quality, attention to detail, and the emotional investment of the listener, are the most important contributory factors' (R9) for success. A thought echoed by a Canadian producer, who states that 'Being featured by iTunes can give you a hit. But our biggest growth moment was making an Imgur list of top ten audio dramas. We believe writing is the single most overlooked element in the audio drama podcast world. Second is recording technique' (R34). This self-driven sense of improvement exhibited here and in the comments in podcaster groups on Facebook is significant. There is sense in the latter of a community where other cultural works in their own space are the reference points, rather than work from legacy media.

It is this amalgam of developing technologies, steady audience growth and a stronger skill base that created what became known as a 'golden age' of podcasting in 2014 (see Roose 2014). Roose suggests that whilst technology played a role here so did the development of production skills and techniques as 'today's podcasts are simply better. Most podcasts used to be pretty amateurish – two people talking about sports for an hour, say, or a businessman ad-libbing MBA lessons. And some still are. But today's top podcasts … are full-scale productions with real staffs, budget, and industry expertise behind them' (np). However, whilst not all podcasts have such aims there is a definable sense of podcastness on display. As an ecosystem, podcasting is a porous space where traditional media and newcomers share a platform, where produsers are able to exploit their experience and their cultural capital by adopting commercial models or moving into other media forms, such as books or broadcast media. It is also an environment where expertise has migrated into podcasting from public radio services such as the BBC or NPR, but also where what was once an entirely amateur activity has been professionalised through a web of participants experimenting with different approaches and concepts. We can see the economics of the shifts by briefly considering the evolution of *This American Life*, a syndicated public radio programme initially produced and supported by WBEZ in Chicago. The programme first embraced podcasting as a delivery platform to extend the reach offered by the public radio system. In 2014 the programme launched the podcast *Serial*, a series only ever intended for online distribution. Such was the success, that the programme launched Serial Productions, to manage this new enterprise, which grew into the podcast *S Town*, a project born of an email to *This American Life* but one which in finished form has uniquely podcast aesthetic (McHugh 2017). Whilst deploying traditional radiogenic techniques highlighted by Spinelli (2006) there is also a claustrophobic intimacy here that lends itself to listening on headphones in a single sitting (Berry 2016; McHugh 2016). This is audio production that shares a common heritage, a common media language, and shared practices, but through trial, error, and experience, podcast producers have successfully created a mesh of their own practices which exploit the innate characteristics of the listening practices, flows and capabilities of podcasting as a medium.

Conclusion

It has been my aim in this chapter to present an argument that as the economic and cultural centres of podcasting move away from radio, we can also migrate (at least some of) the debate from radio studies into podcast studies. We are able to do this because, as a teenaged medium, podcasting has been able to assert its own identity, just as real teenagers do. The most recent phase of podcast history described by the media as a renaissance was, in fact, the Hype Cycle in practice; a paradigmatic shift where technologies and identities coalesced in a revitalised and distinct medium. A medium that is self-defined culturally, sonically and technically; rather than a form of radio. Whilst work within radio studies (Freire 2007; Lacey 2008) suggests that radio constantly remediates itself, there is much within podcasting that is distinct. Just as 'radio' still provides a useful cultural shorthand to explain audio content, the term 'podcast' is now so established that it too has useful cultural capital, with the music platform Spotify commissioning speech content that it describes as 'podcasts'; even though they are not available outside of the Spotify platform and, as such, are not podcasts in a technical sense.

Whilst some forms of podcasting can be located industrially, economically or institutionally within the radio sphere, it can be argued that it is (mostly) culturally different, and over time it is likely that this ideological difference and sense of cultural independence will become more pronounced—even if technologies ultimately render the delivery system invisible to the consumer. As with blogs, those boundaries are often set by the participants themselves, as boyd notes (of blogs), 'The medium is defined by the practice it supports and the ways in which one identifies with that practice... The boundaries of blogs are socially constructed, not technologically defined' (2006: np). Podcasts are more than downloaded MP3 files, they are a cultural product that is defined by participants and listeners, and demonstrates practices that are distinct from other media. Although podcasters may not identify themselves as being part of the radio industry, the radio industry did seek to embrace them. Perhaps this was driven by a sense of kinship, one where fellow audio creatives sought to embrace and celebrate their shared passions, technologies and ideas. But perhaps also this was an act of political economy, where radio services sought to embrace the new opportunities as evidence of their digital achievements, at a time when the internet was slowly eroding their business. Whilst podcasts do form part of the new ecology of radio, they do so in a way that subjugates podcasting to the role of a distribution platform. In 2001, Black asked the same questions of internet radio, suggesting that that the discussion has significance beyond the semantic (398). There are further parallels here to YouTube, of which Burgess and Green note: 'each scholarly approach to understanding how YouTube works make choices… in effect recreating it as a different object each time' (2009: 6). In the same way, we should consider podcasting differently depending on the lens through which we use to view it. For example, a lens of political economy might tell a story of the professionalization of the space and the continued relevance of radio stations (as institutions) in generating and financially supporting podcasting. If the lens used is one of radio then whilst it might allow explorations to delineate between content which sounds like radio (recorded in a studio etc.) and those which acoustically appear different, it may not truly help understand the nature of podcasts. It also draws us further away from the origins of the medium as a means for the wider population to make media.

By reflecting on the feedback from the podcasters who responded to my survey, then it is clear that many podcasters culturally and economically identify themselves as podcasters, which is a view that should inform how we regard the content they create. In an interview with McHugh, Julie Shapiro an Executive Producer at PRX (the organisation behind the successful Radiotopia network) notes that 'podcasting doesn't have to be different but I think makers do feel a little more liberty with the form, thinking of themselves as podcaster versus radio producers' (2016: 17), suggesting that experienced audio professionals see inherent differences between the forms. As with YouTube, there are branches of podcasting that are economically interwound with broadcast media, offering broadcasters a simple means to distribute remediated or un-broadcast content. However, in the larger (numerically, at least) independent and amateur space there is an increasing rationale to suggest that podcasts are ontologically and culturally different. Podcasts are made by podcasters, not radio producers, and for mobile listeners, in search of niche content, who listen on-demand. It is this sense of purpose, combined with improvements to technologies, funding mechanisms, talent development and profile, that has helped podcasting to mark out its own cultural space. As Markman (2015) warns, 'if podcasting is in danger of being colonized by the mainstream, it is vital that our research does not fall into this same trap' (243) and so miss the diversity, and the podcastness exhibited by content in the farthest reaches of this new medium. It is for this reason that future research should not only consider podcasting as a self-identifying medium, but it should do so under the banner of 'podcast studies' as this will truly allow such work to fully explore the meanings and practices of the medium.

Bibliography

Acohido, B. (2005). Radio to the MP3 degree: Podcasting. *USA Today*. https:// usatoday30.usatoday.com/tech/news/2005-02-09-podcasting-usat-money-cover_x.htm. Accessed May 2017.

Bergstöm, A. (2015). The contexts of internet use: From innovators to late majority. *Participations, 12*(1), 3–18.

Berry, R. (2006). Will the iPod kill the radio star? Profiling podcasting as radio. *Convergence, 12*(2), 143–162.

Berry, R. (2015). Serial and ten years of podcasting: Has the medium finally grown up? In M. Oliveria & F. Riberio (Eds.), *Radio, sound and internet*. Braga: University of Minho Press.

Berry, R. (2016). Part of the establishment: Reflecting on 10 years of podcasting as an audio medium. *Convergence, 22*(6), 661–671.

Black, D. A. (2001). Internet radio: A case study in medium specificity. *Media, Culture and Society, 23*(3), 397–408.

Bolter, J. D., & Grusin, R. (2001). *Remediation. Understanding new media*. Cambridge, MA: MIT Press.

Bonini, T. (2015). The 'second age' of podcasting: Reframing podcasting as a new digital mass medium. *Quaderns del CAC, 41*(18), 21–30.

Bottomley, A. (2015). Podcasting, Welcome to Night Vale, and the revival of radio drama. *Journal of Radio & Audio Media, 22*(2), 179–189.

boyd, d. (2006). A blogger's blog: Exploring the definition of a medium. *Reconstruction 6*(4). https://www.danah.org/papers/ABloggersBlog.pdf. Accessed May 2017.

Bristow-Bovey, D. (2017). Are we entering the golden age of podcasts? *The National* n.p. http://www.thenational.ae/arts-life/music/are-we-entering-the-golden-age-of-podcasts. Accessed Apr 2017.

Bruns, A. (2006). *Blogs, Wikipedia, second life and beyond*. New York: Peter Lang.

Burgess, J., & Green, J. (2009). *YouTube. Online video and participatory culture*. Cambridge, UK: Polity Press.

Campbell, H. A., & La Pastina, A. C. (2010). How the iPhone became divine: New media, religion and the intertextual circulation of meaning. *New Media and Society, 12*(7), 1191–1207.

Carlson, N. (2011, March 13). The real history of twitter. www.uk.businessinsider.com. Accessed Mar 2017.

Crofts, S., Fox, M., Retsema, A., & Williams, B. (2005). Podcasting: A new technology in search of viable business models. www.firstmonday.com, *10*(9) [Internet]. Accessed Apr 2017.

Cwynar, C. (2015). More than a "VCR for radio": The CBC, the radio 3 podcast, and the uses of an emerging medium. *Journal of Radio and Audio Media, 22*(2), 190–199.

Fenn, J., & Raskino, M. (2008). *Mastering the hype cycle: How to choose the right innovation at the right time*. Boston: Harvard Business Press.

Freire, A. M. (2007). Remediating radio: Audio streaming, music recommendation and the discourse of radioness. *The Radio Journal – International Studies in Broadcast and Audio Media, 5*(2 & 3), 91–112.

Friedman, T. L. (2005). *The world is flat: The globalized world in the twenty-first century*. London: Penguin Books.

Gates, B. (1996). *The road ahead*. London: Penguin.

Gilmor, D. (2006). *We the media. Grassroots journalism by the people for the people*. Sebastopol: O'Reilly Media.

Google. (2017). Google trends data for "Podcast". https://trends.google.co.uk/trends/explore?date=all&q=podcast [Internet]. Accessed Mar 2017.

Hammersley, B. (2004, February 12). Audible revolution. *The Guardian*. http://www.theguardian.com/media/2004/feb/12/broadcasting.digitalmedia. Accessed April 2014.

Herrington, J. (2005). *Podcasting hacks: Tips and tools for blogging out loud*. Sebastopol: O'Reilly Media.

Kocher, C. (2015). This American life' host Ira Glass returns to Ithaca. *Ithaca Journal*. http://www.ithacajournal.com/story/entertainment/2015/02/10/american-life-host-ira-glass-returnsithaca/23175157/. Accessed Jan 2015.

Lacey, K. (2008). Ten years of radio studies: The very idea. *Radio Journal: International Studies in Broadcast & Audio Media, 6*(1), 21–32.

Lotz, A. D. (2017). *Portals. A treatise on internet-delivered television*. Ann Arbor: Maize Books.

Madsen, V. (2009). Voices-cast: A report on the new audiosphere of podcasting with specific insights for public broadcast. *A paper to ANZAC09 Conference*, Brisbane.

Markman, K. (2012). Doing radio, making friends, and having fun: Exploring the motivations of independent audio podcasters. *New Media and Society, 14*(4), 547–565.

Markman, K. (2015). Considerations – Reflections and future research. Everything old is new again: Podcasting as radio's revival. *Journal of Radio and Audio Media, 22*(2), 240–243.

Marshall, P. D. (2004). *New media cultures*. London: Arnold Publishers.

McHugh, S. (2016). How podcasting is changing the audio storytelling genre. *The Radio Journal: International Studies in Broadcast and Audio Media, 14*(1), 65–82.

McHugh, S. (2017). Why S-Town invites empathy not voyeurism. www.theconversation.com [Internet]. Accessed Apr 2017.

Meikle, G., & Young, S. (2012). *Media convergence. Networked digital media in everyday life*. Basingstoke: Palgrave Macmillan.

Menduni, E. (2007). Four steps in innovative radio broadcasting: From QuickTime to podcasting. *The Radio Journal – International Studies in Broadcast and Audio Media, 5*(1), 9–18.

Meserko, V. (2015). The pursuit of authenticity in Marc Maron's WFT podcast. *Continuum: Journal of Media & Cultural Studies, 29*(6), 796–810.

Moore, G. A. (2014). *Crossing the chasm: Marketing and selling disruptive products to mainstream consumers.* New York: Harper Collins.

Morris, J. W., & Patterson, E. (2015). Podcasting and its apps: Software, sound, and the interfaces of digital audio. *Journal of Radio and Audio Media, 22*(2), 220–230.

Newitz, A. (2005). Adam Curry wants to make you an iPod radio star. archive.wired.com, *13*(3) [Internet]. Accessed Mar 2017.

Pedersen, B. S., & Have, I. (2012). Conceptualising the audiobook experience. *Sound Effects, 2*(2), 88–95.

Rogers, E. (2003). *The diffusion of innovations.* New York: The Free Press.

Roose, K. (2014). What's behind the great podcast renaissance. www.nymag.com [Internet]. Accessed Jan 2015.

Sellas, T. (2012). A two-dimensional approach to the study of podcasting in Spanish talk radio stations. *The Radio Journal – International Studies in Broadcast and Audio Media, 10*(1), 7–22.

Spinelli, M. (2006). Rhetorical figures and the digital editing of radio speech. *Convergence, 12*(2), 199–212.

Sterne, J., Morris, J., Brendan Baker, M., & Moscote Freire, A. (2008). The politics of podcasting. *Fibreculture* Issue 13 (FCJ – 087) np. http://thirteen.fibreculture-journal.org/fcj-087-thepolitics-of-podcasting. Accessed Dec 2015.

Vogt, N. (2016). Podcast fact sheet. Pew Research Center [Internet]. http://www.journalism.org/2016/06/15/podcasting-fact-sheet/. Accessed Mar 2017.

Walker, B. (2015). Secret histories of podcasting. *Benjamen Walker's Theory of Everything* https://toe.prx.org/2015/10/secret-histories-of-podcasting/ [Podcast]. Accessed Oct 2017.

Wang, S. (2016). Acast wants to get new audiences "in the podcast door" with more diverse shows and better data. www.niemanLab.org [Internet]. Accessed Oct 2017.

Webster, J. G. (2014). *The marketplace of attention. How audiences take shape in a digital age.* Cambridge, MA: MIT Press.

Winer, D. (2015). A podcast about podcasting. www.scripting.com [Blog]. Accessed Oct 2017. Also see associated podcast: http://scripting.com/2015/09/30/daveCast2015Sep30.m4a

WNYC. (undated). Reinventing audio for a new generation of listeners around the world. http://wnycstudios.wnyc.org/#wnyc-studios [Internet]. Accessed Apr 2017.

Wolfe, A. (2008). Is podcasting dead? www.informationweek.com [Blog]. Accessed Oct 2017.

3

Podcast Movement: Aspirational Labour and the Formalisation of Podcasting as a Cultural Industry

John L. Sullivan

Alex Blumberg's podcast entitled *Start Up* tells the story of his halting and sometimes comically inept efforts to start his own fledgling podcast production company, Gimlet Media. A public radio producer and refugee from National Public Radio's (NPR) hit series *This American Life*, Blumberg struggles to grasp the basics of startups, such as drafting a business model, courting sceptical venture capitalists, finding a financial partner, and cultivating his own personal brand. Blumberg's experiences—packaged self-referentially as a podcast series produced by the very production company that is the subject of his show—offer a revealing window into some of the profound changes currently under way in the podcasting ecosystem. The launch of Gimlet Media is symptomatic of a broader trend in podcasting: the slow transformation of an amateur medium into a new vehicle for commercial media content.

While podcasting has thrived since its creation in 2004 as a bastion for homegrown, amateur media production, in the past several years, entrepreneurs and so-called 'legacy media' companies (those with commercial interests in broadcast radio and television) have rapidly expanded their interests in podcasting as a business, bringing professional standards and the logics of capital with them. In the United States, well-resourced public radio stations like New York City's WNYC, for example, have started their own podcasting divisions (Sisario 2015), and advertising firms like Midroll have specialised in bundling popular podcasts for sale to advertisers. E.W. Scripps, a traditional

J. L. Sullivan (✉)
Muhlenberg College, Allentown, PA, USA
e-mail: johnsullivan@muhlenberg.edu

© The Author(s) 2018
D. Llinares et al. (eds.), *Podcasting*, https://doi.org/10.1007/978-3-319-90056-8_3

media company which owns a diverse portfolio of legacy media such as newspapers, broadcast radio and television stations, bought Midroll in 2015 for $10 million and recently purchased podcasting app company Stitcher for $4.5 million. *Washington Post*-owned Slate Group (publisher of online magazine *Slate*) launched its own podcasting 'network' entitled Panoply in 2015, which features podcasts produced by corporate media giants such as *The New York Times, Huffington Post*, and HBO (The Slate Group 2015). These companies are motivated not simply by the creative possibilities of the medium, but also by the potential to cultivate mass audiences. A market survey conducted in 2015, for example, reported that 45 million Americans had listened to a podcast in the previous month (Edison Research 2015). Breakout hits such as 2014s *Serial* (with nearly 40 million downloads) and *This American Life* have demonstrated to both programmers and advertisers the potential for podcasting to emerge as a commercially viable media industry (O'Connell 2015). Thus, despite podcasting's roots as a forum for user-generated content, the recent expansion of the podcast audience and interest from traditional media has begun to transform it 'from a do-it-yourself, amateur niche medium into a commercial mass medium' (Bonini 2015: 27).

The entrepreneurial fervour surrounding podcasting in the wake of the cultural phenomenon of *Serial* is fuelling what scholars call *formalisation*. Formalisation describes the process by which

> media systems become progressively more rationalised, consolidated and financially transparent. It can happen as a result of increased state intervention in a particular industry, which finds itself dragged into the light of regulation and accountability. Alternatively, it can occur when formerly small-scale media concerns become integrated into larger-scale structures. (Lobato and Thomas 2015: 27)

In the case of podcasting, amateur podcasters with sizeable audiences are being recruited to join podcast networks, lured by the potential for a larger percentage of advertising sales revenue and the ability to expand their audience via cross-promotion with other shows on the same network. Additionally, existing media producers—many of them from legacy media such as commercial or public radio—are entering the podcasting space and directly competing with those amateurs. As a consequence, the commercial-style production values, audio quality, content genres, distribution methods and monetisation structures are beginning to inform the production practices of independent podcasters. Presented with the potential opportunity to pursue podcasting as form of gainful employment, podcast producers and hosts can be increasingly identified as an 'aspirational labour' force. Aspirational labour describes free labour offered in the hope or expectation of future (monetary) benefits. Independent podcasters' dreams of future commercial success are not fleeting, either. Blumberg's podcasting company Gimlet Media, for example, recently raised $15 million from venture capital investors thanks in part to deals with traditional media companies to create new films and television series from some of its more popular podcasts (Abbruzzese 2017; Locke 2017). The success of podcasting networks like Gimlet Media demonstrates that the process of integrating podcasting into the commercial media ecosystem is well underway.

This chapter explores industry formalisation in podcasting by examining the entrepreneurial discourses found at Podcast Movement (PM) convention in 2016. PM was the brainchild of veteran podcaster Gary Leland and CPA Dan Franks, and launched in 2014 as a result of a successful Kickstarter campaign (Corcoran 2014). It has since grown to become the largest annual convention of podcast producers, distributors and technology providers, with over 2000 attendees. PM attendees represent a broad cross-section of the podcasting universe, from independent, amateur podcasters to radio station executives, advertisers, podcast-hosting companies, equipment manufacturers, podcast network professionals and crowdfunding companies, among others. Since PM attracts such a wide variety of players in the podcast ecosystem, it is an ideal venue to observe the process of formalisation up close. Based upon my own participant observation of PM16 in Chicago, along with a review of trade press articles, this chapter explores some of the deep tensions that have resulted from podcasting's recent rise in popularity. As I outline below, discourses of podcast formalisation at PM16 co-existed with more utopian discourses of self-expression, authenticity, democratisation and media diversity. The uneasy tension between these two discourses is indicative of the struggle for identity at the heart of the podcast ecosystem.

What Is Podcasting in 2017? A Short History of a Long Tail Medium

Podcasting has emerged as a pop culture phenomenon in the past several years due largely to the success of *Serial* in 2014. That podcasting should suddenly occupy such a prominent place in our cultural zeitgeist is curious, since the technology is hardly new; it has been around since the early 2000s. Podcasting can be understood as 'a technology used to distribute, receive, and listen, on-demand, to sound content produced by traditional editors such as radio, publishing houses, journalists, and educational institutions… as well as content created by independent radio producers, artists, and radio amateurs' (Bonini 2015: 21). The term 'podcasting' was coined by journalist Ben Hammersley back in 2004 (he also floated the term 'audioblogging') as a means to describe a mode of distribution similar to radio broadcasting, but delivered via portable digital devices, of which the Apple's iPod was the most well-known (Hammersley 2004). At the time, podcasting's popularity was limited due to the relative niche status of portable digital audio players like iPods and the necessity for those devices to be connected to computers in order to access new downloaded content.

The idea for podcasting relies not just on the internet for distribution, but in particular upon the technical infrastructure of RSS, known colloquially as 'really simple syndication.' Podcasting was built upon the open framework of RSS, and the idea to leverage the ease of the system to assist the distribution of online content was originally hatched by RSS creator Dave Winer and independent radio broadcaster Adam Curry. RSS allows online listeners to reliably find podcasts and to discover new podcasts with relative ease (Markman and Sawyer 2014: 20). Similar to the impact of the videocassette recorder with television, podcasting afforded listeners greater control and autonomy over when they listened to recorded content. In one of the first scholarly treatments of podcasting, Richard Berry (2006: 140) argued that podcasting represented an 'empowered' type of radio listening because it allowed listeners to time-shift and to carry their radio content with them thanks to the portability of digital audio players like Apple's iPod. Sterne et al. (2008) observed that this leveraging of RSS as the mechanism for distributing new content also 'creates an expectation of seriality which shapes both production and consumption practice: podcasts are supposed to repeat over time, so listeners subscribe to "shows" and podcasters make "shows"'. Thus, the notion of podcast 'shows' with updated 'episodes' with new content is a consequence, at least in part, of the underlying technology for distributing the content.

Podcasts are widely available as either via streaming or direct downloading to digital devices via helper software (such as podcatchers like iTunes, Google Play or other third-party desktop and mobile applications). Podcatchers have made it relatively simple to locate, subscribe and listen to on-demand audio files. When Apple decided to include RSS aggregation into their iTunes Music Store in Spring 2005, their market dominance in digital audio sales opened the floodgates for millions of iTunes users to easily locate and download podcasts (Sterne et al. 2008). The key benefits of podcasts over traditional broadcast media are their portability and their ability to time-shift other forms of media (such as radio broadcasts). Given its on-demand structure, podcasting is also very much in line with media consumption habits of most twenty-first-century audiences who have come of age in an era of streaming platforms such as YouTube, Spotify, Netflix and Pandora. Podcasting has evolved considerably since the early 2000s, becoming more popular especially after the 2008 introduction of the iPhone, which allowed audiences to access and consume digital media on mobile devices anywhere and anytime. Thus, podcasting's rise in popularity is at least partially due to its technological features: its availability, convenience and near ubiquity thanks to global adoption of mobile smartphones.

To say that podcasting is essentially a method for easily distributing audio files online, while technically accurate, doesn't really capture how it has evolved as a medium with its own unique culture. As Markman and Sawyer (2014: 21) have noted, while the 'podcasting as distribution' model is a good description of how broadcast radio networks like National Public Radio (NPR) essentially allowing for easy time-shifting of programs, the popular fascination with podcasting stems mainly from the home-grown, grassroots nature of its content. Thanks to independent and amateur podcasters creating new podcast episodes on a continual basis, podcasting has developed a powerful ethos of authenticity. Since the economic and technological barriers to podcast production are low, tens of thousands of podcast shows have mushroomed, covering extremely small 'niche' topics such as 'The Pen Addict' (about the finer points of writing pens: fountain vs. ballpoint), 'Gilmore Guys' (two friends watch the entire series of *Gilmore Girls* with commentary), and 'Witch, Please' (two literature professors discussing the Harry Potter books from a feminist perspective) (Basu 2017). Listeners have discovered in podcasts what they may have found wanting in commercial media content: compelling, real stories about people from all walks of life, unburdened by the necessity to cultivate large, mainstream audiences.

Podcasting is thus a prime example of what Anderson (2006) has called a 'Long Tail' market. Online storage and distribution, argues Anderson, has made narrow, niche content economically viable which, in turn, is re-shaping how content providers imagine audiences. The richness and diversity of the podcasting ecosystem offers us a glimpse into a quintessential Long Tail media environment. Indeed, podcasters often proudly proclaim their creative independence from the strictures of the mainstream, and this newfound abundance of content options has promised to mark the 'death of the blockbuster economy' (Freedman 2012). As Ben Hammersley (Ulanoff 2015) noted, 'I don't think there is a mainstream anymore... Mainstream success is really a 20th century artifact.' As a distinctly Long Tail medium, the audiences for each show are tiny in comparison to legacy media like television and radio. For example, market research firm Edison Research has reported that podcasting's 'Share of Ear' (the percentage of American audio consumers who listen) is a marginal 2 per cent. AM/FM Radio share of ear, by contrast, is 56 per cent (Ulanoff 2015). The sheer diversity of podcasting content, coupled with the enthusiasm from independent podcasters to jump online and explore tell their own stories, has fuelled podcasting's reputation as a uniquely home-grown, authentic medium.

Podcasting's status as an amateur medium began to shift in 2012 at the start of what Bonini (2015) has termed the 'second age' of podcasting. However, beginning in 2012, some of the most popular podcasts that were produced by American public radio broke away from public broadcasting to finance themselves through venture capital and crowdfunding. One of the earliest such efforts was the podcast *99% Invisible*, a podcast about architecture, which separated from KALW public radio of San Francisco to crowd-fund over a half million dollars over two years. The breakout success of the investigative journalism program *Serial* in 2014, which garnered over a million downloads per episode, captured the imagination of advertisers and content producers (O'Connell 2015). *Serial* provided yet another evolutionary inflection point for podcasting (Berry 2016), moving it into the mainstream and encouraging traditional media players as well as entrepreneurs to regard podcasting as the next great frontier for online media. Conventions like Podcast Movement aim to push this evolution of podcasting in the direction of traditional media markets by encouraging and bringing about the formalisation of the medium.

Entrepreneurialism at PM16: Discourses of Artistry, Authenticity and Autonomy

Upon descending the escalator into the cavernous basement conference centre of the downtown Hyatt in Chicago, one notices the familiar trappings of a typical technology-related convention: a registration desk, a large main stage room for keynotes, smaller conference rooms for panels and breakout meeting sessions, and a large area with vendors selling technology-related products and services. Amidst the chino-clad professionals from traditional media companies were a motley collection of largely amateur podcasters milling about. Since the entry fee of several hundred dollars is prohibitive for most (though presenters were able to attend for free or at a reduced rate), amateur podcasters went to PM with the implicit promise of improving the reach and professionalism of their podcasts in order to gain an entrée into the world of advertising support. These are the 'pro-ams', or media creators who 'pursue an activity as an amateur, mainly for the love of it, but [who] set a professional standard. Pro-Ams are unlikely to earn more than a small portion of their income from their pastime but they pursue it with the dedication and commitment associated with a professional' (Leadbeater and Miller 2004: 20).

If they are not already semi-professional in their orientation, the unstated goal of Podcast Movement was to encourage amateurs to become professionals: by giving 'how to' seminars on the mechanics of high quality audio production and editing, by educating amateurs about the fledgling business of audience metrics, by introducing them to terminology in the advertising business, and by facilitating networking opportunities with key decision-makers working in media companies. While Leadbeater and Miller's definition was meant to describe a new class of media producers who have voluntarily adopted the content formats and production routines of commercial media, in the case of podcasting, it is more accurate to state that commercial media techniques and industry standards are being consciously grafted onto what was hitherto a largely amateur, user-generated media form.

The key to this pro-am transformation at PM16 was the discourse of *entrepreneurialism* that suffused the conference. Paraphrasing the influential Austrian economist Joseph Schumpeter, Lobato and Thomas (2015: 45) describe this historical figure of the entrepreneur as 'a risk-taker, the harbinger of creative destruction, a visionary who creates value where it did not previously exist.' Entrepreneurs, according to Schumpeter, are a 'revolutionary force' in otherwise static economic systems. The image of the modern entrepreneur has been heavily influenced by popular myths surrounding celebrity CEOs like Richard Branson of Virgin Group, Mark Zuckerberg of Facebook, and Steve Jobs of Apple: individuals who started small with a brilliant concept or prototype, who then went on develop multi-billion dollar corporate powerhouses. The popular image of the prototypical entrepreneur is also closely intertwined with Silicon Valley tech startup culture. In her investigation of Silicon Valley startups, Marwick (2013: 257) notes that entrepreneurs 'personify individualism, technological innovation, creativity, and intelligence – all characteristics that reinforce the myth of meritocracy.' Podcast Movement celebrated these qualities in the presentations and keynotes. The convention itself also served as a broader stage upon which entrepreneurialism was enacted by participants.

Artistry and Authenticity

The entrepreneurial ethos was evident in the keynote speeches given at PM16. These sessions featured recognisable, successful podcasters offering up their own narratives about how they got started, how they developed content for their podcast, and how their own commitment to the medium had paid off for them in both figurative and literal ways. The keynote speakers were popular luminaries in the podcasting world, some of whom had spent a decade or more producing podcasts. Others had relatively recently stepped into the role of podcast hosts. The thread that tied all of these speakers together, however, was the fact that they had cultivated large audiences (or, at least large enough to garner the conspicuous attention of major national advertisers).

The keynotes explored some key themes surrounding podcast production—namely, that podcasts are a form of deeply personal, intimate form of creative expression that has unique power to connect listeners to stories. For example, Glynn Washington, host of WNYC radio show and podcast *Snap Judgment* roved the keynote stage with a kind of religious fervour, urging amateur podcasters in the audience to think about their productions as nothing less than the next frontier of narrative, noting:

> I don't care about podcasting! [audience laughter] I don't! I don't care... What I care about is storytelling, and passion, and energy, and magic [audience applause] and that's what you care about as well... There's not enough money here to make us care about anything else. We are here because of that magic, that storytelling, that passion. Because there are easier ways to get paid [audience laughter]. I'm feeling some things as a storyteller. This is a storytelling craft.

Throughout his keynote, Washington explicitly identified podcasting as an immediate, almost visceral form of narrative, something he noted that public media was sometimes lacking. Here podcasting was linked explicitly to other forms of narrative creativity: to novels, to poetry, and to music. Discourses of creativity and passion were paramount in Washington's keynote, and he generally eschewed mass media production models, noting that the best 'inspiration is from amateurs.'

Another common refrain among the keynote speakers was that podcasts were set apart from the typical constraints of commercial or mass-produced media, making them a uniquely *authentic* form of cultural expression. Authenticity is a cornerstone concept within the practice of entrepreneurialism. Among Silicon Valley entrepreneurs, one form of 'authenticity' is being true to your own ideals and 'following your passion.' As podcaster Kevin Smith enthused in front of a crowd of podcasters at his keynote: 'The medium belongs to you!' Another aspect of authenticity, as Marwick (2013: 251) discovered, involves the 'creation and promotion of intimate knowledge.' In other words, the manner in which Silicon Valley entrepreneurs communicate to others about their efforts should convey not just a desire to start a business and get rich, but to reveal something deep about themselves and their own identity in the process. In the case of podcasting and other Web 2.0 media, the pursuit of authenticity has emerged as a possible remedy to the mass-produced, over-commercialised, cookie-cutter culture of commercial media.

All of the keynote presenters at PM16 described their own version of a 'personal epiphany' moment when they realised that they wanted to pursue podcasting as either a full-time or part-time vocation. This epiphany was typically the result of listening to other podcasts (most if not all podcasters admitted to being heavy podcast listeners as well). Integral to all of these origin narratives was their inspiration to add their own unique voice and perspective to the cultural conversation. Tracy Clayton, co-host of the Buzzfeed podcast *Another Round with Heben and Tracy* explained the transformative effects of podcasting's ability to channel unique, authentic voices and experiences:

> One of the benefits of podcasting is [that] you get to listen. And if you choose to listen to people who live a different life than you do, a different reality than you do, you can learn so much. And when you learn you can start admitting changes in the real world, and we need a lot of those. So, find some Black podcasts, shut up and listen to them. Tell your friends about them. It's a good start [audience applause].

Similarly, Anna Sale, host of the WYNC podcast *Death, Sex, and Money* took the keynote stage to explain that her interest in podcasting sprang from her dissatisfaction with the types of stories that she was able to tell about the people she interviewed as a traditional NPR journalist. She pursued podcasting because she felt that the everyday Americans she covered on the radio had an 'urge to feel heard, the urge to feel connected', and that their authentic stories could be completed told only through the long-form medium of podcasting.

The concept of authenticity was also deployed in other sessions in the PM16 schedule, mainly as a kind of rhetorical bulwark against the argument that podcasters who introduced advertising into their shows would be branded as 'sell outs.' For example, Farnoosh Torabi, host of the *So Money* podcast and a CNBC financial expert, outlined her initial anxiety about introducing an advertising sponsor on her podcast:

> I had been doing a daily show, literally Monday, Tuesday, Wednesday, Thursday, Friday, Saturday, Sunday – for over six months, seven months at this point and I felt like I'd given so much good content for free to my audience that I was worried. I thought, 'Will they disrespect me if I start having sponsors? Am I going to "sell out"? And I thought, no, you know what. In fact, one listener said to me, "Farnoosh, when are you going to have sponsors, because doesn't that legitimise you in some ways? You must not be doing that well if you don't have a sponsor."'

Here the potential anxiety over betraying the authenticity of the host's perspectives on personal finance is neatly dispatched by the deployment of a counter-narrative: that without some sort of commercial validation of her podcast, her content is perhaps less 'legitimate'. As I explore later, the notion of legitimation through monetisation was a strong undercurrent at the largely industry-centred panel discussions.

Other panel sessions emphasised how specific word choices and vocal style of the individual podcast host should be preserved during 'on air' advertising pitches in order to make the pitch request less forced or jarring to the listener. Being 'authentic' in this context meant that podcasters should attempt to use their own words and, if necessary, to manufacture a more homespun enthusiasm for a sponsor's product instead of reading stale and stilted advertising copy. The mantra in these sessions was to 'be true to yourself', all within the context of the commercialisation of the podcast. These discourses of authenticity surrounding podcasting are similar to those uncovered by Duffy (2015) among female fashion bloggers in that any sign of overt commercialism threatens the perceived integrity and originality of amateur-produced media.

Autonomy

Integral to the entrepreneurial ethos of PM16 was the recurring theme of podcasting as a gateway to greater personal *autonomy* in media production careers. Autonomy here refers to the professional liberation of podcasters from the (largely commercial) forces that typically circumscribe creative labour in a market economy. Podcasters taking the stage across PM16 noted that they were fortunate to do this kind of work because they had finally found a career path that allowed them to pursue their passion while also 'paying the bills.'

Even the logo for the conference itself (see Fig. 3.1), a clenched fist with a microphone, served to underscore the ethos of personal empowerment that dominated the convention. The packed keynote by Hollywood actor, producer and podcaster Kevin Smith encapsulated many of these claims. Smith argued that everyone now had access to technologies that allowed them to 'self-express', which allowed for podcasting to be enjoy the status of a uniquely democratic medium. Given his previous experiences as a motion picture

Fig. 3.1 Podcast Movement 2016 logo. (Image taken by the author at the conference)

writer, producer, and actor, Smith focused heavily on the liberation of podcasting from traditional gatekeepers in commercial media. He noted:

> [In] every other medium of self-expression in this world, if you want to say something, you can say it, but if you want to say it on a grand scale, or if you want to write large on a massive canvas that everyone can see, there *will* be a gatekeeper. You can make any TV show you want, but if you want to put it on a network, you're going to encounter someone who'll say, 'Let me see if this is good enough for us.' You can write any book you want and self-publish, but if you want to publish through a label or something like that, there *will* be a gatekeeper. You can make any movie you want, but if you want to put it in a movie theatre, a legit movie house, sooner or later, someone will say, 'Let me see if this is good enough. Let me see if your self-expression counts.' *This medium* had none of that. There's no gatekeeper, man.

Underlying Smith's narrative about the absence of gatekeepers is the notion that online labour can act as liberation from the drudgery of traditional creative work.

Myths of autonomy via entrepreneurial online labour are a recurring theme in Silicon-Valley-style discourses. Indeed, the goal of tech entrepreneurs today has shifted somewhat away from becoming the next tech giant like Apple or Facebook, and instead toward 'having pride in a small business that gives them autonomy' (Heller 2013). Yet, as others have found, the much-vaunted autonomy of Web 2.0 is often accompanied by under-compensated work, wage insecurity, copious amounts of overtime and personal stress (Terranova 2000; Andrejevic 2013; Duffy 2015; Scholz 2016; Duffy and Pruchniewska 2017).

Formalisation of Production Practices: Self-Branding and the Politics of Aspirational Labour

While the keynotes at PM16 celebrated podcasting as an authentic, liberating and uniquely creative practice, the numerous 'how to' demonstrations problematised many of these claims. These sessions, many of which were hosted by 'solopreneur' podcasters, promised attendees a backstage look at specific production practices, covering both mundane topics such as the optimal types of podcasting equipment (microphones, sound mixers, editing software), the mechanics of cultivating advertising sponsors, and audience metrics, as well as more intangible topics such as how to harness one's personal experiences and creativity to create compelling audio content. These sessions featured provocative titles such as 'Go From Podcaster to Media Superstar', 'Brutally Honest Storytelling', and 'How to Get Off the Plateau and Create a Hit Episode that will Skyrocket your Downloads.' Podcast practitioners and representatives from podcast networks actively socialised attendees into professional production practices that were required to attract advertising support. These 'how to' sessions, then, were the front lines of the broader formalisation effort.

The most prevalent of these discourses was that podcasting was a uniquely meritocratic medium. Consistently, podcasters in the 'how to' sessions emphasised that anyone who put in the hard work required to connect with their listening audience (and, incidentally, who subscribed the speaker's podcast or signed up for exclusive content on their website) would grow the size of their audience. For example, podcaster Daniel J. Lewis held sway with a large audience at his session entitled 'How to make your podcast stand out'. Lewis, the host of his own show entitled *The Audacity to Podcast*, began his session with a series of questions: 'Do you want more listeners? [Audience responds: Yes!] Do you want more money? [Audience responds: Yes!]... Do you want more hard work? [Audience responds: No! Laughs] But here's the truth: You say you don't want more hard work, but it takes work. Don't believe the people who tell you it's super easy.' Lewis went on to describe a number of labour-intensive steps he recommended for podcasters to grow their audience, including managing multiple social media accounts for their podcast (Facebook, Twitter, etc.), engaging in email marketing, producing 'bonus' content in addition to the podcast to send out to email subscribers, and more. 'The secret to getting more,' noted Lewis, 'is giving more.' This was echoed by podcaster, newspaper columnist, radio host and comedian Josh Elledge in his session called 'Go from podcaster to media superstar'. Elledge emphasised that high online visibility was the key to audience engagement:

A lot of us, I think unfortunately, get into the trap where we end up spending so much time on the nuts and bolts of podcasting that we're not growing our business. And so, one thing I would recommend that you do is that you spend twice as much time – this is a good litmus test—*twice* as much time building the business of your podcast than actually working on your podcast.

Elledge noted that the key for independent podcasters was to find ways to market yourself through other media (including more popular podcasts), since cross-promotion was the only way to get known by audiences. As these and other independents urged, podcasting success was found in a mixture of social media omnipresence and self-branding prowess.

The foregrounding of this type of intensive relationship-building labour as part of podcasting entrepreneurship is similar to what scholars have found in other forms of digital content production. In interviews with self-employed female bloggers, for example, Duffy and Pruchniewska (2017) found that these entrepreneurs felt compelled to present themselves continually on social media in ways that reinforced traditional notions of femininity. Specifically, their interviewees felt a need to: (1) engage in 'soft self-promotion' to brand themselves in 'subtle' and 'organic' ways; (2) continually engage in relationship-building activities online ('interactive intimacy'); and (3) maintain 'compulsory visibility' on social media by putting their private lives on display as a means to cultivate an audience. In the largely masculine world of entrepreneurial podcasting, the promotion techniques being advocated at PM16 were certainly not 'soft', but some of the same strategies were emphasised such as: compulsory online visibility, the push to generate 'extra' content in order to entice listeners to subscribe, and developing a long-term relationship with listeners by addressing them directly and personally through multiple online media.

The ultimate goal, of course, was to attract a larger listener base so that podcasters could begin to attract sponsorship and begin to earn money. The 'how to' sessions therefore encapsulated the notion of what Kuehn and Corrigan (2013) term 'hope labor' in podcast production. Hope labour refers to 'un- or under-compensated work carried out in the present, often for experience or exposure, in the hope that future employment opportunities may follow' (Kuehn and Corrigan 2013: 10). Duffy (2015) refers to this intensive labour done in the belief that future economic benefits may follow as 'aspirational labor.' In the emerging commercial podcast ecosystem as discussed at PM16, amateurs were being enticed by the promise of autonomy and creative freedom, yet were also being encouraged to work for long hours with little realistic hope of achieving commercial success.

Podcast Metrics and Monetisation: The Dynamics of Formalisation

The looming, existential question that hung over every session and hallway conversation at PM16 was how to mould podcasting into a reliable revenue-generating medium. Even the conference's wifi password ('getmoney') pointed unequivocally to this goal. Away from the keynote stage, where optimism about the unique authenticity of podcasts held sway, almost all of the panel discussions revolved around the intricacies of attracting advertising revenue.

The key sticking point for many industry representatives (and, by extension, for advertisers) was the lack of common metrics for assessing audience size. Throughout these panels, the message to amateur podcasters was clear: without any data about the size and character of your listeners, or without the visibility and cross-promotion that came with carriage on one of the podcast networks, advertisers would likely pay them little attention. Assuming that podcasters had compiled sufficient data, however, even the lowest bar for minimal advertiser support was still likely out of reach for most independent podcasters. As PM16 demonstrated, the stirrings of interest by advertisers in the podcasting space has begun the process of regularising the use of metrics as well as the adoption of other typical industry practices (such as 'upfront' sales). In these discussions about advertising, the personal, unique nature of podcast production was eclipsed by the standardisation and formalisation of audience metrics.

Podcast Metrics

In my conversations with hosting service representatives and industry professionals at PM16, it became clear that the process of generating, interpreting, and touting data about podcast audiences was a paramount issue. Indeed, a number of panel sessions hosted by professionals working for networks and hosting companies were designed to educate independent podcasters about various measurement techniques and the necessity for quantifying their audience in order to pursue transactions with advertisers. While all PM16 presenters and panellists agreed on the importance of metrics to the development of podcasting as a viable media industry, the definition of those metrics was highly contested terrain. In one session, Edison Research President Larry Rosin outlined a positive outlook for podcasting based upon his company's survey research data. Rosin noted that 21 per cent of a nationwide sample of respondents in 2016 (an estimated audience of 57 million) reported listening to a podcast in the previous month. While Edison's data were referenced often in basic 'proof of concept' pitches from independent podcasters to potential investors, representatives of podcasting hosting firms (like Blubrry, Libsyn and PodBean, among others) to whom I spoke on the convention floor were largely dismissive of Edison's survey data, arguing that only 'hard' data such as subscriber counts and episode download totals (as measured by server log data, which the podcast hosting firms controlled) gave a truly accurate picture of the listening audience. Additionally, the ability to provide varying types of server-based measurements to their podcaster-users was one technique of hosting companies to differentiate themselves from one another in the competitive market for the business of individual podcasters.

At several industry-specific panels, representatives from podcast hosts, media buying firms, NPR and advertising agencies presented a somewhat united front, noting that the industry was moving in the direction of standardised audience metrics. Many cited the work of the Interactive Advertising Bureau (IAB), which had convened a large working group of companies to hammer out an agreed-upon set of standards (Interactive Advertising Bureau 2017). Steve Mulder, Senior Director of Audience Insights at NPR, laid out this common interest in one panel discussion when he observed that 'without deliberate and thoughtful measurement, without improvements in measurement, the podcast industry won't mature as fast as we want it to'. Despite this mutually understood necessity for standardisation, there is a considerable amount of jockeying among different industry players about which measurement standards should be adopted. NPR, for example, released a 'working document' on podcast measurement in February of 2016, hoping to be the first to influence future discussions about podcast metrics (Wang 2016). NPR's effort was denounced days later by Todd Cochrane (2016), CEO of RawVoice/Blubrry, who labelled NPR's document 'fraught with measurement shortfalls and an inflammatory statement that threatens to undermine the credibility of podcasting and podcast measurement.' At PM16, PodTrac CEO Mark McCrery explained that he and his fellow hosting companies had identified 'unique downloads per episode [a]s the industry standard,' noting that these numbers were 'analogous to numbers that Nielsen and ComScore put out for other media types.' Here the notion that podcast metrics should be roughly analogous to metrics utilised for other online media is an attempt to synchronise podcast measurement with these other forms, allowing advertisers to compare the efficiency of their buys across these forms. The intensity of the debates at PM16 over the establishment of a commercially viable system of audience measurement indicates its importance to the formalisation of podcasting.

Monetisation and Advertising Support

There were many sessions at PM16 devoted to the monetisation of podcasts, many with similar titles such as 'Under the hood: How podcast monetization really works', 'How to sell out while keeping it real: Taking the revenue step', 'How to build an audience and revenue for your podcast', and 'Podcast monetization: The economics of podcasting'. While multiple modes of monetisation were mentioned throughout the panel sessions, including crowdfunding and 'in kind' sales (through t-shirts and other branded merchandise), the dominant model discussed was on-air advertising. The centrality of advertising as the 'default' funding mechanism for podcasting has invited other structural shifts as well. For example, for the first time in 2015, the Interactive Advertising Bureau (IAB) began hosting an 'upfront' session for advertisers to purchase time on upcoming shows and for podcasters to pitch new podcast series to advertisers (Johnson 2016).

The needs of advertisers for a systematic, predictable environment for pitching products has begun to shift the balance of power away from hosting services and toward podcast networks. Based upon their comments at PM16, advertisers have come to regard podcast networks (like Panoply, NPR or Gimlet Media) as reliable 'tastemakers' for quality podcasts. Advertising sales company executives at PM16 also noted that it was simpler to make deals for sponsorship with networks than with individual podcasters because networks offered them groups of listeners across a number of different podcasts for broader exposure and reach. Due to this new business reality in podcasting, Chris Yarusso, Associate Media Director Mediavest/Spark actively urged independent podcasters to seek carriage on networks, noting that 'being part of a network is probably a smart thing to do so you can get access to brands that won't otherwise find you'. One panel even discussed an emerging subgenre of 'sponsored' podcasts, wherein a sole-sponsored program (General Electric was one example) underwrites and assumes editorial control over the content of the podcast. These types of public relations-oriented podcasts become a kind of 'native advertising' for their sponsor. It is important to note here that the increasing centrality of networks to the podcast ecosystem essentially formalises these networks as distribution gatekeepers, in direct opposition to the kind of freedom and autonomy that Kevin Smith celebrated in his keynote. Likewise, the introduction of fully sponsored content formats challenges the very notion of authenticity that was so central to the utopian discourses about podcasting at PM16.

The industry-oriented panels at PM16 also underscored the instability and precarity of emerging advertising-supported revenue models in the podcasting ecosystem. This precarity was felt by independent podcasters and industry watchers alike. Solo podcasters remarked that their efforts to secure sponsors were stymied until they were able to demonstrate to advertisers that their shows received an average of fifty thousand downloads per episode. A representative from Libsyn noted that *less than 1 per cent* of their hosted podcasts met this minimum episode download threshold. A number of attendees who posted reflections on their own blogs after PM16 expressed some skcepticism about the viability of an advertiser-supported ecosystem for podcasting. For example, podcaster and entrepreneur Matt Cundill (2016) reflected after the conference that 'no one has figured out how to monetize the medium; which leads to many shared ideas about marketing, promotion and revenue opportunities. A number of podcasters are resigned to not making any [revenue]; satisfied with the branding and exposure for themselves, guests and clients.' Another post-mortem by sports broadcaster and sometime podcaster Jason Barrett noted the one statistic that stood out to him the most: that the broadcast radio industry is a $2 billion annual industry, while podcasting is currently a $100 million annual industry. He offered the following 'reality check' for podcast enthusiasts:

> The world isn't all sunshine and rainbows, and the economic returns in the podcasting world are low compared to radio. If the financial numbers echoed throughout multiple sessions are accurate, that would make the radio industry 20× more profitable than the podcasting business. That's enormous. (Barrett 2016)

More recent digital advertising data has underscored the market difficulties facing digital content producers like podcasters. According to the recent Group M 'Interaction 17' report, while 77 cents of each new advertising dollar in 2017 is expected to be spent on digital advertising, 'more than two-thirds of global ad spend growth from 2012 to 2016' came from just two online services: Google and Facebook (Davies 2017). This type of 'reality check' about the potentially murky future of podcast monetisation was largely muted at PM16, however. Most industry presenters focused on podcasting's huge potential for growth instead of the rather slim chance that most podcasters would be able to eke a living wage out of their hobby.

Conclusion: Formalisation and the Future of Podcasting

The presentations and discussions at Podcast Movement 2016 revealed that podcasting is in the midst of a significant transformation. The professional discourses at Podcast Movement 2016 were characterised by two contradictory impulses: one was a sunny entrepreneurial fervour, while the other was the hard-nosed realism of industry formalisation. On the surface, Podcast Movement celebrated podcasting as an authentic medium that offered a welcome respite from the stale content and rigid professional structures of mainstream broadcast media. Through the keynotes and the on stage 'how to' sessions, PM presenters largely ignored or downplayed the often-conflicting aims of creativity and commerce. Instead, their presentations captured the entrepreneurial spirit by emphasising the creative freedoms offered by pod-casting, the sense of personal and professional autonomy it offered as opposed to a traditional '9-to-5' job, and the joys of creating original content that represented one's true, 'authentic' self. There was a strong counter-narrative within PM16, however. This narrative was prominent on the stages of the panel discussions, most of which were peopled by media professionals work-ing for radio broadcasters, podcast networks, technology companies and advertisers. These panel sessions served to socialise amateur podcasters into the routines and structures of mass media production, to emphasise the impor-tance of audience metrics, and to firmly establish the centrality of advertising sponsorship as the most viable form of revenue support. These efforts are part of a broader effort of formalisation that is currently underway in podcasting.

As scholars of other forms of user-generated digital content have noted (Terranova 2000; McChesney 2013; Duffy and Pruchniewska 2017), the net effect of the formalisation of podcasting may be to effectively curtail many of the imagined freedoms of digital entrepreneurialism. While podcasting net-works, hosts and advertisers have brought an influx of capital into the ecosys-tem, they have also begun to establish themselves as professional gatekeepers for new content and curators of existing content. Some of these companies, like E.W. Scripps, have created synergies across different power roles. Podcasters working with Scripps, for example, have access to the following services all within the same corporate umbrella: an extensive network of other podcasts for revenue sharing and cross-promotion (Earwolf and Wolfpop), an in-house advertising firm specialising in podcasting (Midroll) and a mobile platform for distributing those podcasts (Stitcher, purchased by E.W. Scripps in June 2016). These synergies work to concentrate the resources available to support podcasting into a few companies with deep pockets, creating scarci-ties that will make it more difficult for amateur, start up podcasters to be able to cultivate a large base of listeners (a prerequisite for advertising support). The effects of formalisation will be felt not just in the economic structure of the industry, but in the content as well. For example, talent scouts for the larger networks will search for podcasts that are similar in style or content to other popular podcasts. This will encourage amateurs to adopt similar formats and content for their own podcasts in an effort to attract the attention and resources that these networks can provide.

Looking to the future, scholars would do well to explore how the shifting dynamics of the medium are shaping individual producers' creative decision-making. How do individual podcasters perceive their own labour within the shifting context of formalisation, for example? Additionally, once the industry settles upon a set of agreed-upon metrics for measuring audiences, how will this affect the development and continued existence of the hundreds of thousands of podcasts that do not meet the fifty thousand download threshold? Since most of the major podcast distributors such as Apple, Google, and Spotify are US companies, it is possible that the push toward industry formalisation will ripple out to the podcast ecosystems of other countries as well, though this question requires more extensive study. If the discussions taking place at PM16 are a harbinger of the future, then podcasting as a forum for unique and independent cultural expression is at a historic crossroads. On the one hand, podcasting still enjoys a reputation as a home-grown, authentic cultural form created primarily by unpaid amateurs. On the other hand, the increased focus on effective methods of audience monitoring, monetisation via advertising, standardisation of production techniques, and maintaining one's own 'brand' may fundamentally challenge the democratic ethos of podcasting.

Bibliography

Abbruzzese, J. (2017). The latest trend in podcasts? Making them into movies. www.Mashable.com [Internet]. Accessed 4 Aug 2017.

Anderson, C. (2006). *The long tail: Why the future of business is selling less of more.* New York: Hyperion Books.

Andrejevic, M. (2013). Estranged free labor. In T. Scholz (Ed.), *Digital labor: The internet as playground and factory* (pp. 149–164). New York: Routledge.

Barrett, J. (2016). Takeaways from the Podcast Movement conference. *Barrett Sports Media.* http://sportsradiopd.com/2016/07/takeaways-from-the-podcast-movement-conference/ [Internet]. Accessed 4 Apr 2017.

Basu, S. (2017). The delightful world of Super-Niche podcasts. www.WNYC.org [Internet]. Accessed 12 Apr 2017.

Berry, R. (2006). Will the iPod kill the radio star? Profiling podcasting as radio. *Convergence: The International Journal of Research into New Media Technologies, 12*(2), 143–162.

Berry, R. (2016). Part of the establishment reflecting on 10 years of podcasting as an audio medium. *Convergence: The International Journal of Research into New Media Technologies, 22*(6), 661–671.

Bonini, T. (2015). The 'second age' of podcasting: Reframing podcasting as a new digital mass medium. *Quaderns del CAC, 41*(18), 21–30.

Cochrane, T. (2016). RawVoice/Blubrry responds to the public radio podcast measurement guidelines. www.powerpress.com [Podcast]. Accessed 29 Mar 2017.

Corcoran, J. (2014). How the first national podcasting conference launched with a $30,000 Kickstarter campaign. www.huffingtonpost.com [Internet]. Accessed 22 Apr 2017.

Cundill, M. (2016). The Podcast Movement is indeed a thing. www.mattcundill.com [Internet]. Accessed 4 Apr 2017.

Davies, J. (2017). The global state of digital advertising in 5 charts. www.Digiday.com [Internet]. Accessed 8 May 2017.

Duffy, B. (2015). Amateur, autonomous, and collaborative: Myths of aspiring female cultural producers in Web 2.0. *Critical Studies in Media Communication, 32*(1), 48–64.

Duffy, B. E., & Pruchniewska, U. (2017). Gender and self-enterprise in the social media age: A digital double bind. *Information, Communication & Society, 20*(6), 843–859.

Edison Research. (2015). Monthly podcast listeners grow to 46 million Americans 12+. www.edisonresearch.com [Internet]. Accessed 28 Jan 2016.

Freedman, D. (2012). Web 2.0 and the death of the blockbuster economy. In J. Curran, N. Fenton, & D. Freedman (Eds.), *Misunderstanding the internet, Communication and society* (pp. 74–94). New York: Routledge.

Hammersley, B. (2004). Audible revolution. *The Guardian.* https://www.theguardian.com/media/2004/feb/12/broadcasting.digitalmedia [Internet]. Accessed 22 Apr 2017.

Heller, N. (2013). Bay watched. *The New Yorker* http://www.newyorker.com/magazine/2013/10/14/bay-watched [Internet]. Accessed 13 Apr 2017.

Interactive Advertising Bureau. (2017). *Podcast technical working group* https://iabtechlab.com/working-groups/podcast-technical-working-group/ [Internet]. Accessed 28 Mar 2017.

Johnson, L. (2016). With second 'podcast upfront,' IAB hopes brands will buy into audio advertising. www.adweek.com [Internet] (21 July, 2017). Accessed 6 Apr 2017.

Kuehn, K., & Corrigan, T. F. (2013). Hope labor: The role of employment prospects in online social production. *The Political Economy of Communication, 1*(1) http://www.polecom.org/index.php/polecom/article/view/9 [Internet]. Accessed 12 Aug 2013.

Leadbeater, C., & Miller, P. (2004). *The pro-am revolution: How enthusiasts are changing our economy and society.* London: Demos.

Lobato, R., & Thomas, J. (2015). *The informal media economy* (1st ed.). Cambridge/Malden: Polity.

Locke, C. (2017). Where is Hollywood looking for the next hit? Podcasts. www.wired.com [Internet]. Accessed 20 July 2017.

Markman, K. M., & Sawyer, C. E. (2014). Why pod? Further explorations of the motivations for independent podcasting. *Journal of Radio & Audio Media, 21*(1), 20–35.

Marwick, A. E. (2013). *Status update: Celebrity, publicity, and branding in the social media age* (1st ed.). New Haven: Yale University Press.

McChesney, R. W. (2013). *Digital disconnect: How capitalism is turning the internet against democracy.* New York: The New Press.

O'Connell, M. (2015). The 'serial' effect: Programmers ramping up on podcasts. www.hollywoodreporter.com [Internet]. Accessed 18 Aug 2015.

Scholz, T. (2016). *Uberworked and underpaid: How workers are disrupting the digital economy* (1st ed.). Cambridge/Malden: Polity.

Sisario, B. (2015). WNYC to open new podcast division. www.nytimes.com [Internet] (12 October, 2015). Accessed 30 June 2016.

Sterne, J., et al. (2008). The politics of podcasting. *The Fibreculture Journal,* (13). http://thirteen.fibreculturejournal.org/fcj-087-the-politics-of-podcasting/ [Internet]. Accessed 16 Mar 2017.

Terranova, T. (2000). Free labor: Producing culture for the digital economy. *Social Text, 18*(2), 33–58.

The Slate Group. (2015). The Slate Group announces Panoply, a podcasting network for media brands and authors. www.slate.com [Internet]. Accessed 24 Aug 2016.

Ulanoff, L. (2015) Podcasting: A decade outside the mainstream. www.mashable.com [Internet]. Accessed 7 Mar 2017.

Wang, S. (2016). Public radio staffers across the U.S. lay out new guidelines for podcast audience measurement. www.niemanlab.com [Internet]. Accessed 29 Mar 2017.

4

Podcast Networks: Syndicating Production Culture

Lieven Heeremans

Introduction

The past two decades have seen developments in distribution technology, economic models and production and consumption cultures that have affected all facets of the media industry profoundly. The relative lack of attention paid to theorising contemporary audio production cultures leaves many questions open, especially with regard to podcasts. This chapter sets out to investigate the production culture of podcasts both with regard to the broadcast radio industry (which producers compare it to) and as an emerging media industry.[1] The focus will be on a specific phenomenon of contemporary podcasting production culture: the formation of podcast networks.

Podcast networks of various shapes and sizes, and with different origins, organisational structures and goals, have emerged across the globe in the past decade. Though not analysed in this chapter, the diversity and quantity of podcast networks seems as big outside of the United States as within it. This is not to say, however, that podcast networks constitute a strictly new phenomenon.[2] Traditional broadcast media use their own proprietary distribution systems as well as the services of much larger digital-first commercial platforms such as iTunes to publish their regular content through podcast

The author would like to thank Sarah Arnold, Linda Duits, Amanda Lotz and William Uricchio for their insightful comments on earlier versions of this chapter.

L. Heeremans (✉)
Utrecht University, Utrecht, The Netherlands
e-mail: lieven@heeremans.eu

© The Author(s) 2018
D. Llinares et al. (eds.), *Podcasting*, https://doi.org/10.1007/978-3-319-90056-8_4

catalogues. For instance, CBS does this with their *Play.it* podcast network, and NBC has the *NBC Sports Podcast Network*. Other print or digital media publishers also gather together different podcasts under the aegis of a podcast network; for example, the *Panoply* podcast network falls under the production of *Slate* magazine. Among the bigger and older 'native' podcast networks—i.e. those who produce their content for and publish mainly through an online podcast distribution platform—that originated out of the efforts of podcast producers are *Earwolf* (comedy) and *Quick and Dirty Tips* (education). Other instances of smaller, non-commercial podcast networks, like *Phantom Haus* or *The Heard*, are a conglomeration of amateur or semi-professional podcasts under one network (Phantom Haus 2016). My interest here lies with the economic circumstances and motivations that drive individual podcast producers to form networks; therefore the object of this chapter is to consider native podcast networks only. However, to make sense of these relatively young types of networks, they are disambiguated from traditional broadcast networks.

Unlike the centralised broadcast network era, podcasting developed on the back of relatively open, accessible, and democratising internet distribution technologies. Making the assertion that the technology of podcasting was built on open-source code, Richard Berry notes that the medium of podcasting is 'a convergence of technologies that already existed and, in many cases, that users already owned' (2006: 145). This convergence of technologies leads to 'a move in power from programmers to listeners' (ibid.): not only can podcasts function as a VCR for radio, but anyone can produce and publish a podcast. Ten years ago, these promises made it understandable for Berry to proclaim podcasting as a disruptive technology that would ultimately democratise radio, since it made possible 'grassroots radio' instead of top-down broadcasting. Indeed, more recently, Berry stated that 'it would seem fair and logical to consider podcasting as an extension of radio' (2016: 8).[3] If one accepts Berry's earlier observation that podcasting allows for grassroots production cultures combined with his more recent notion that the institutionalisation of the medium has turned it into an extension of traditional broadcast radio, an analysis of the emergence of podcast networks becomes relevant. Can the formation of podcast networks be conceptualised as a category of grassroots production, or does it follow the logic of earlier broadcasting institutions and their business models?

By analysing three different native podcast networks originating in the United States, this chapter aims to provide an account of the spatio-temporal situation of podcasting production culture in that country which gives rise to podcast networks of different shapes and sizes, but that have common intentions and strategies. This analysis is relevant because despite the diversity of podcast networks, they have tended to develop similar institutional practices, thus negotiating between grassroots initiatives to more conventional business models. To find out the motivations behind the formation of podcast networks, three podcast networks are compared: *The Heard, Radiotopia*, and *Relay FM*. The analysis is based on the few existing primary and secondary sources about these networks, but relies predominantly on interviews with the podcast networks' executives—I elaborate on the rationale for this later in Section 4. Before discussing the results, previous academic literature is reviewed in order to situate the critical yet overlooked aspect of podcasting production culture that this chapter examines. Second, it considers classic commodification models in order to conceptualise the (financial) motivations behind the formation of podcast networks. Third, the analysis of these podcasts networks shows how they can be characterised differently, but share common interests and strategies. Finally, I show how motivations for networked podcast production—vis-a-vis dominant cultural practices and business models in this realm of audio content creation—are evidence of developing tactics for producers and platforms in a fledgling podcasting industry.

Research and Friction in Podcasting Production Cultures

I will first provide an overview of the relatively little academic work that focuses on podcasting.[4] Perspicacious analyses on the level of individual podcasters, a broadcast-institutional level and (historical) media industry studies situate the argument that follows.

Insightful surveys conducted by Markman (2012) and Markman and Sawyer (2014) have shown that podcasting communities are populated by predominantly tech-savvy older males, who, through podcasting, create and serve an online community. With regard to the practices of podcast producers, these observations insinuate a tension between grassroots podcast communities and traditional broadcast radio, especially seeing as the producers take advantage of and are highly motivated by the affordances of the technology of podcasting as syndication over the internet. Although Markman and Sawyer's studies provide valuable insights into grassroots podcast productions, they do not provide any suggestions as to why podcasters would start to work together in podcast networks. Other insights as to the motivation of producers can be found by approaching the object the other way round: that is by looking at how traditional broadcast organisations adapted podcasting.

On a broadcasting institutional level, there is evidence of both technical and regulatory tensions in the emergence of podcasting practice within radio broadcasting. Cwynar's (2015) analysis of the Canadian Broadcasting Company shows that when the traditional radio broadcaster ventured into podcasting, unique technological features of podcasting were often neglected, thus making it 'more similar to radio' (Cwynar 2015: 191). In the short history of the CBC Radio 3 podcast, we can see how podcast production practices conflict with larger, broadcast-institution-wide interests. Taking into consideration several public broadcaster services' values, Murray (2009) deepens this analysis by considering the enthusiastic adaptation of podcasting technologies by the BBC, PRX, the Australian Broadcasting Company, and Special Broadcasting Service. Murray shows how the charters and ethos of these broadcasters often conflict with the technological affordances of podcasting. Allowing more experimental, user-generated productions to appear under the name of the broadcaster makes the 'public' broadcaster more accessible, but at the same puts the quality of the content at risk, thus highlighting a gatekeeping issue (ibid. 212–213). These conflicts, the contrast between the promise of Web 2.0 media production and the hegemony of broadcast radio institutions, can inform our understanding of contemporary podcasting practices in the emerging podcast industry. From these insights into podcasters and broadcasters, I argue we can see how a new distribution system—digital audio delivered through RSS feeds—allows for new affordances, types of content, accessibility and ways of reaching audiences. At the same time this technology leads to a struggle over conceptions of 'radio', which brings forth iterations of older cultural practices—for instance the usage of the network jingle, as we will see with *Radiotopia*. Additionally, the institutions that previously dominated the realm of audio are faced with existential challenges in terms of (but not limited to) the claim to authority they are able to enforce in a democratised distribution system. As we will see, the new podcast networks take on the 'seal of approval' function which broadcast institutions formerly had unique access to. The technology underlying podcasting, combined with the emergence of developing cultural practices, enables the arrangement of a new media industry that brings these players, grassroots podcast producers, and public broadcast radio institutions into contact and perhaps at odds with one another.

Media industries studies, such as those of Amanda Lotz and Eleanor Patterson, provide a framework for understanding the frictions that appear when new distribution methods are introduced. These frictions can have an effect on industry wide practices, such as the conceptions of audiences and approaches to generating revenue. Broadcast radio can function as a prime example to historically situate issues that are still at stake today with the growing popularity of podcasts. With a keen eye for historical precedent Patterson argues that 'radio was the first broadcast medium whose industry and reception underwent massive transformation after the introduction of new domestic broadcast technology, and also, it was the first broadcast medium to exploit the potential of audience segmentation and narrowcasting' (2016: 4). Thus, radio history shows that shifts in distribution technology brought forth new conceptions of audiences and cultural practices. Researching a more proximate historical period, Lotz's examination of the media industry 'during periods of institutional uncertainty [...] reveals the way [in which] new possibilities can develop from emerging industrial norms' (2014: 21). As can be read in Lotz' s analyses and in the literature specific to traditional broadcast radio and podcasting as discussed above, industrial norms are generally established at the executive level, take effect throughout large sections of the industry, and are a result of legal, technological-material, and commercial struggles. Central to the analysis of industrial reformations is a distinction made between the cultural practices—for both consumers and producers—surrounding the medium on the one hand, and the technology that makes the medium possible on the other (Lotz 2014: 3). New technological affordances provided to audiences, such as podcasting, allow for new cultural practices in consuming media. Especially in the case of audio-visual media, this revolves around end-user control over what content is consumed at what time.[5] This development ties into the conception of niche audiences, in which content is tuned toward specific types of individual consumers. Fragmentation meant a threat to the massive audiences the bigger traditional broadcasters were used to, instigating a shift from exposure to engagement as metrics of value (Napoli 2011; Lotz 2014). These factors all centre around the models used to create revenue in media industries.

Commodification Models for Cultural Products

To understand why podcast networks form, we need to understand the interplay between the business strategies on an industry level for the podcast networks and the conditions of labour for individual podcast producers. In this section I problematise Lotz's analysis of contemporary revenue generating practices against the situation found in podcasting.

To arrive at a conception of contemporary media business models, Lotz refers to Bernard Miège's commodification models in different forms of media (Lotz 2017). Miège puts forward three different models that make the commodification of media products possible: the 'publishing model', 'flow logic', and the 'logic of the written press' (Miège 1989: 12). Of these, 'flow logic' suited broadcast media such as radio and television.[6] In this model, revenue for producers is constituted by the incentive to produce 'regular broadcasting of programs [in order] "to create an audience", because the financing is entirely assured by means of advertising or by public or institutional funds' (ibid.). Now, Lotz argues, distribution of content over the internet problematises the models provided by Miège. In her reassessment of Miège's models, Lotz shows how services such as Netflix fall in between the flow model and the publishing model (Lotz 2017: 22). In the contemporary situation, consumers access a wider ranging but still limited set of content which lacks a broadcasting schedule: it is available on demand. Lotz conceptualises these services as 'portals', defined as 'the crucial intermediary services that collect, curate, and distribute television programming via internet distribution' whose 'primary task might be [...] regarded as that of curation—of curating a library of content based on the identity, vision, and strategy that drive its business model' (ibid., 8). Crucial for the portal business model (or at least the services Lotz analyses) is a required paid subscription for unlimited access to a limited set of cultural goods. Though Lotz's iteration of Miège's business models certainly helps us to understand how changes in distribution technology can bring changes to the order of the means of production and its surrounding cultures (this being especially apt to the realm of television), her concept of 'portals' does not neatly fit onto the current commodification model in podcasting.[7]

Where the strategies of portals revolve around the acquisition, management and creation of intellectual property (Lotz 2017: 8; 48–49), podcast producers and, as we will see, podcast networks generally publish their content across a variety of publishing platforms without getting any financial compensation from those platforms. iTunes, Stitcher, and Soundcloud cannot be considered a portal according to Lotz's definition because they do not curate or fight for exclusivity over content (yet). Since no-one is paying for the content, these publishing platforms, outside of technical specifications, do not enforce any quality thresholds to make use of the distribution platform.[8] Using the concept of capitalisation models, we will be able to evaluate the practices of the young podcast networks studied in this chapter in the conclusion. It is my assertion that podcasting and current revenue strategies should be understood differently in terms of the commodification models Miège provides.

Subscribers, lack of broadcasting schedule and unlimited access to content are key in podcasting. Every time a new podcast episode is published, the edition gets synced to subscribers through RSS. Therefore, the distribution technology shares characteristics with Miège's written press model. The revenue model—if podcast producers need one, since production costs are generally relatively low—however, is more akin to Miège's flow model because of the exceptional inability to complete a financial transaction for a podcast (paid subscription). For example, iTunes has a payment system in place for every type of content available through its store, except for podcasts. The same goes for other podcasting publishing platforms such as Stitcher and Soundcloud.[9] This forces podcast producers to make money through advertisements, or by asking listeners to support them financially, which fits to Miège's written press model. The case studies that follow are representative of the different forms podcast networks take and their accompanying strategies in the contemporary podcasting industry.

Three Young Podcast Networks: Selection and Method

The podcast networks that are the object of study in this chapter were chosen because of their comparable characteristics: they are relatively young, have a low number of member podcasts, and produce somewhat comparable type of content. The networks are:

- *The Heard*, launched March 2015 on the initiative of independent producer Jakob Lewis.
- At the time of writing the network has eight member shows, all storytelling based.
- *Radiotopia*, launched in 2014 as a collaboration between independent podcast producer and radio host Roman Mars and Public Radio Exchange (PRX) (Matheson 2014). At the time of writing, the network is comprised of 16 storytelling shows.
- *Relay FM*, launched in 2015 by podcast hosts Myke Hurley and Stephen Hackett, at the time of writing has 24 member shows, all of which are talkshows that revolve around technology.

All three podcast networks originate in the same country and share a common publication language, thus they compete with each other and other types of media for the same potential audience. Most importantly, all discussed networks were started by native podcast producers as a way to gain a steady foot in the podcasting industry. Thus, the podcast networks should be conceptualised differently from production companies of comparable age and size like Gimlet Media.

In terms of method, interviews with executives of the networks can be considered the main source for this study. Getting access to the strategies and practices of media productions is tricky as it can be of great value. Interviews with media producers allow for insight into the development of the industry as well as a deeper analysis concerning the challenges and positions of these podcast producers. Not only can interviewees at media productions provide unique insights into motivations among producers, speaking to producers often also invokes access to their professional network.[10] The semi-structured interview method used for this chapter is straightforward and common in production studies (Mayer 2008). Preliminary research was done by listening to various podcasts and by online research. All respondents were approached via email, and 20- to 30-minute semi-structured interviews were conducted and recorded through Skype in spring 2016. Additional correspondence provided answers to follow-up questions in the review and rewriting process. After a detailed description based on data acquired through the interviews and from online research, the three podcast networks will be analysed based on shared characteristics, such as the origins and social functions of the network, gatekeeping mechanisms, and the way in which, on a network-wide level, the combination of these factors can be exploited to benefit the members and the podcast network.

The Heard

The Heard can be considered the least formal, least commercial and thus most 'grassroots' network examined in this chapter. The network was initiated in 2014 by Jakob Lewis, producer of the *Neighbors* podcast. Living in Nashville, Tennessee and relatively inexperienced as an audio producer, Lewis found himself frustrated at not having the connections or resources to grow his podcast into a full-time job. After visiting the Third Coast International Audio Festival he found other individual producers to connect with (initially Jonathan Hirsch from the *ARRVLS* podcast and Rob McGinley Myers from the *Anxious Machine* podcast). After a short period of acquiring other potential members through personal or professional connections, *The Heard* officially launched with six member shows in March 2015 (Lewis, J. 28 June 2016 personal communication). Most current members have a background in media or other creative industries but are relatively new to producing podcasts. Little involvement from positions 'higher up' in the podcasting or radio industry—i.e. solely organising the Third Coast International Audio Festival as an event where the producers could meet—underlines the grassroots characteristic of the network.

As the youngest network discussed in this chapter, *The Heard* is a collective of 'indie' podcast producers whose individual productions are focused on 'sound-rich, finely-crafted storytelling' (*The Heard* 2016). *The Heard* is comprised of individual producers that operate as a collective (Lewis, J. personal communication, 28 June 2016). As of February 2017, the network encompasses eight shows, one of which is currently in development (*The Heard* 2016). The network has a website that lists all member shows, a general statement about the network and links to the individual shows' online presence. Each individual podcast publishes new episodes at their own pace, ranging from one to three or four episodes per month. Since the age, pace and number of episodes varies per podcast, it is difficult to pinpoint the overall reach of the network.[11] Every individual podcast has a different approach to generating income, and no effort is made to bring in funding for the entirety of the collective. Some of the podcasts' content gets broadcast by local public radio stations, albeit usually in a shorter form. Others reach out to their audience for financial support. Advertisements are also sold, either by brokering ad deals individually or by signing up to sell ads via advertisement networks like *Midroll*. There is no centralised organisation structure, nor are there shared financial responsibilities. Within the network activities are undertaken in a collaborative spirit and decisions are made on a consensus basis. Since all the members are located in different locations across the US, the members conduct a weekly Skype meeting and communicate via other digital channels such as Slack. Gathering individual shows under the aegis of a network or collective strengthens individual producers and has various advantages for both the collective and its constituent elements.

The producers who are part of *The Heard* form a podcast network or collective to mutually benefit from each other: sharing knowledge, resources, and reach is the central motivation. Since *The Heard* defines itself as a collective, the activities undertaken under the guise of the collective are taking place on the basis of cooperation, less formal than in other networks. For example, some producers provide others with editing and sound design support, financial and promotional advice, or do recordings on location. Thus, the benefits of being part of the network mostly pay out in the form of social or cultural capital, or at least the exchange of other forms of capital (such as time and gear) is organised along these lines. Most prominent to listeners are references to other shows in the network. By doing this the producers aim to share their reach and audience with each other, which benefits the collective as a whole since it stimulates the growth of the total number of listeners for the network. Moreover, being part of the network also helps to add status value to the individual podcasts: producers are able to leverage their membership of *The Heard* against advertisers, since it provides credibility in terms of quality control. As advertising and selling content to broadcast radio stations are the main sources of income for the producers in the collective, they can be considered to stay within Miège's 'flow' model. However, this strategy plays a prominent role on the level of the individual producers, less on the level of the network. Lastly, the organisational structure of *The Heard* allows for a lot of freedom and experimentation, which Lewis considers to be a unique advantage over more formal types of networks (Lewis, J. 28 June 2016, personal communication).

To benefit from the advantages of the network, some selection mechanisms are put in place. Curation of the podcasts eligible for the network is based primarily on the status of the individual producer and secondly the content or quality of the show:

> We have several people who have reached out to us from time to time and are like 'Hey, I think I've got a good show, I'd be a good fit,' and they might have a great show, but they might not be a great fit for what we we're doing. Either because of their philosophy and what they're looking for, because they might be looking for a traditional network and somebody that can really boost them up whereas this is more like: bring what you can to the table and let's see how we can help one another succeed. (Lewis, J. 28 June 2016, personal communication)

In terms of quality, the network tries to format itself in a 'palatable way to people' by bringing together shows that have 'a certain vibe or aesthetic' (Lewis, J. 28 June 2016, personal communication). The diversity among the podcasts and their producers, both in terms of topics and their geographic locations, is considered to be a strength of the network by the members. Up to now no producers have left the network to join other collectives or more formal networks.

To summarise: *The Heard* podcast network operates as a collective in order to bypass the gatekeeping mechanisms of broadcast radio and other networks (Murray 2009). The network was initiated out of shared frustrations with the accessibility of professional audio storytelling to allow previously unacquainted members to help each other on a usually voluntary basis. Working together under the aegis of a podcast network increases the amount of knowledge, reach and resources for the individual producers. The network takes shape on the basis of implicit common characteristics, both in terms of the status of individual producers and the type of content they present in their podcasts. Though the individual reach, pace, and subject matter of the podcasts in the network varies widely, bringing together the shows in *The Heard* strengthens the collective. By bonding together, *The Heard* can profile themselves against other podcasts or podcast networks and at the same time remain autonomous in their effort to become full-time podcast producers.

Radiotopia

Radiotopia can be characterised a grassroots network, but has very strong ties to broadcast public radio institutions. The network officially launched in 2014 as the result of a successful initiative by Roman Mars, host and producer of the *99% Invisible* podcast and radio program on KALW. His personal and professional connections to the independent radio community in the US enabled Mars to get together the first seven shows to form the network. Julie Shapiro, co-founder of the Third Coast International Audio Festival, was also involved from the beginning. After an initial gathering in the fall of 2013, a fundraising campaign was started on crowdfunding website *Kickstarter*. In the online post describing the need for the network, Mars writes: 'The hardest part of creating a new show is getting started and then getting enough audience and support to move into regular production. We want to provide a platform where the best producers can find an audience and flourish' (2013). As a platform, *Radiotopia* is able to provide support for individual audio producers, functioning as an ecosystem to grow talent. The approach of financing through crowdfunding introduced a third party in the constitution of the podcast network: the audience were involved in the innovation of the public radio landscape.[12]

Radiotopia describes itself as a 'curated network of extraordinary, cutting-edge podcasts. The network allows independent producers to do their best work, grow their audiences, and increase their revenue. At its core, Radiotopia cultivates community—for both listeners and makers alike' (*Radiotopia* 2016). Though the format and topic of each podcast differs widely, all member shows can be described as 'storytelling-based, creative-audio-production-driven' (Shapiro, J. 23 June 2016, personal communication). The network has a website, gathers all shows under an 'artist' page in the iTunes podcast repository, and is active on Soundcloud (*Radiotopia* 2017b).[13] All member podcasts open with a mention of their Radiotopia membership and close with the *Radiotopia* jingle. All podcasts are English-spoken and produced in the United States, except for *The Bugle* and *The Allusionist*, which originate in the United Kingdom. Publishing schedules differ per podcast, generally ranging from biweekly to weekly. This publishing range finds its origin at the level of the network: the podcast network generally asks shows to produce 24 new episodes per year, with a minimum of 20 shows per year. This practice, combined with the strong ties to broadcast radio institutions and the dominance of its advertising revenue model show the perseverance of Miège's 'flow' model for the network. At the time of writing the *Radiotopia* network is comprised of 16 podcasts, with over 15 million downloads per month. In the period of May to November 2016 the total number of downloads was at least 84,650,000 (*Radiotopia* 2016; Shapiro, J. 3 January 2017, personal communication).

Radiotopia is run by media company PRX, which is part of an effort by public broadcasting to venture into the digital realm. It produces and distributes radio content across the United States and different publishing platforms, including broadcast, web and mobile (Loviglio 2013: 57; Shapiro, J. 3 January 2017, personal communication). Out of the 20 employees that work at PRX, approximately six staff work part time on *Radiotopia* regularly, and in 2015 Julie Shapiro was hired to be full-time executive producer—note that the individual producers are not hired by *Radiotopia* (Shapiro, J. 3 January 2017, personal communication). Because 'it is quite different from being a company that works in a building together', the role of executive producer includes helping form solidarity within the network (Shapiro, J. 23 June 2016, personal communication) in addition to carrying out network wide initiatives across all the member podcasts—like producing network-wide live shows—and presenting *Radiotopia* as a distinct podcast network. Other general daily operations include managing the individual podcast feeds across the major podcast publication platforms and providing technical, editorial, and marketing support. Sponsorships and sales are managed on a network-wide level, as is data gathering and analysis, including audience surveys. In addition, PRX has developed a system for advertisement insertion which allows back catalogues and archives to be opened for ads. Systems like these and the many ties into the traditional broadcasting industry set *Radiotopia* apart from the other podcast networks—though Miège's 'flow model' stays dominant. There is constant contact between *Radiotopia* staff and individual podcast producers over instant messaging platforms.

In terms of curation, the producers of the first seven shows 'knew each other well enough to stay on the same page: being independent but value the collective sense of being together and being a team' (Shapiro, J. 23 June 2016, personal communication). Curation for later additions was mainly steered by

Mars. Central considerations involved in the selection of individual members are based on both an individual, 'entrepreneurial', and 'public radio' spirit: the former comes down to approaching audio production in a 'cutting edge' or 'indie' way and having the ambition to grow audience numbers and revenue, so as to making podcasting a full-time job for the individual producers; the latter refers to the values of American Public Radio as perceived by the *Radiotopia* network, 'bringing in voices that are not traditionally heard on commercial broadcast, a more intellectual approach to entertainment but at the same time reaching out to understand the world' (Shapiro, J. 23 June 2016, personal communication). According to the *Radiotopia* initiators, the traditional broadcast public radio has 'a lot of gatekeepers' whereas podcasting 'is a very open, "make the most you can of it" sort of situation now', even though 'a lot of those [public radio] values definitely transfer over to the motivations of the producers working in this field' (ibid.). Recent additions to the network have been primarily based on decisions from within the network, where the network's executives open up their ears for podcasts that 'suit our tastes for innovative and adventurous storytelling' and where they 'sense a lot of talent and where we can help that show [reach a wider audience]' (ibid). From the outside, the network gets pitched a lot and also involves its listener community. In 2016 *Radiotopia* organised *Podquest*, an open call for story-driven podcasts which received 1537 submissions to which crowdfunders got to listen and judge. The winner of this contest, *Ear Hustle*, launched in 2017 (*Radiotopia* 2017a).

For the members in the network, both a sense of independence and collectivity is important. The podcast network provides the independent members the advantage of making use of the collaboration happening within the network whilst at the same time remaining autonomous and having full creative control over the content and form of their podcast. Collaboration among the producers in the network is 'kind of self-perpetuating': some help out more than others but there is a lot of cross-pollination in many different ways (Shapiro, J. 23 June 2016, personal communication). Producing shows under the aegis of the *Radiotopia* network not only benefits the producers, but helps develop the digital audio distribution industry as well. Outside the affordance that RSS and time-shifting technology provides for individual producers, Shapiro sees how podcast networks are able to differentiate themselves and their practices against those of traditional broadcast radio:

> Conceptually *Radiotopia* is like a framework that all these shows operate in, and so we are not tied to a broadcast clock and we can be a little bit more open to content that might be too edgy for broadcast. I think the form of podcasts is slowly evolving beyond what the radio waves have been able to accommodate. (Shapiro, J. 23 June 2016, personal communication)

As well as having similar tensions as *The Heard* concerning gatekeeping mechanisms in traditional broadcasting radio, we are able to signal a second tension here: for *Radiotopia* specifically there is a wish to be free from the restrictions of traditional broadcast radio. By providing a platform in the form of a podcast network *Radiotopia* aims to innovate and stimulate the production processes around digital audio storytelling. In order to help audio storytelling evolve, the network promotes talented creative audio producers by making use of new distribution affordances.

Relay FM

The *Relay FM* podcast network can be characterised as the most commercial and biggest of the three case studies. Co-founded in July 2014 by Myke Hurley and Stephen Hackett, *Relay FM* describes itself as 'an independent podcast network for people who are creative, curious and maybe even a little obsessive—just like its hosts' (*Relay FM* 2016). As of February 2017, the network is comprised of 24 individual shows, covering a wide range of consumer-technology-related topics, from Apple-related products and news to *The Pen Addict*, a show exclusively about all sorts of pens and related products. The website lists seven 'retired shows', most of whose formats have been retitled or rebooted into an active show (*Relay FM* 2016). The network has a website, gathers all shows under an 'artist' page in the iTunes podcast directory, and has a master feed that gathers the twenty most recent episodes of the network in one feed (*Relay FM* 2016). Publishing schedules differ per show, though the majority of the shows publish on a weekly or biweekly schedule. All shows are hosted by writers for popular tech websites who individually have a relatively high online following or influence (Dillet 2015). Including Hurley and Hackett, there are 32 hosts, most of whom are US-based (Hurley himself is based in London).

Historically, the *Relay FM* network organically grew out of a collaboration between individual podcasters in an earlier technology-centred podcast network called *5by5*. Hurley and Hackett got to know each other and other individual hosts through podcasting (see also Markman and Sawyer 2014), and shared the ambition to start an independent podcast network. At the initial five-show launch in 2014, several sponsors were involved. Some of these sponsors were already familiar with the hosts that were on the network, others were new. Over the past two years the network has grown, adding new shows, hosts and sponsors to the network, providing enough income to support Hurley and Hackett to both work full-time on the network. Sales of the advertisements in the network has moved from ad-broker *Midroll* to a pure in-house activity. The pair undertake the network's daily tasks which include handling incoming payments from sponsors, paying bills to the hosts and other administrative tasks, but also the development of new and existing shows. Incidental editorial and graphic design help is provided by freelancers. Next to this, both Hurley and Hackett host and produce their own shows on the network (personal correspondence with Hackett 2016).[14]

The curation and gatekeeping of the network's shows is executed exclusively by Hurley and Hackett. New shows can enter the network from different angles: Hurley and Hackett actively develop ideas for shows, sometimes new collaborations or topics arise from the hosts already in the network, and people from outside the network pitch their show ideas to them. In the latter case, individual producers apply to join the network with their shows to take advantage of the marketing and sales department of *Relay FM*, and to be able to delegate infrastructure and hosting to those working for the network. Hurley and Hackett have several considerations for allowing shows to be on the network: 'it needs to be a fit content-wise and it needs to make sense business-wise and it needs to be somebody that we feel we can have a good relationship with and we can work with long term' (Hackett, S. 28 June 2016, personal communication). Apart from keeping the graphic and audio design streamlined, the network enforces no editorial control over the shows. Hosts come up with their own content, topics and special series.

As the tagline of *Relay FM* and the topics of the shows indicate, the podcasts in the network explicitly focus on niche subjects. This attracts niche audiences for each show, which are a valuable asset for the network. In selling advertisements on the shows, *Relay FM* targets the community of listeners that exists around the individual shows. Because the individual shows cover such niche topics, the interest level and attention span of the listeners is considered to be higher. For advertisers, this creates a relatively concentrated audience per podcast to target their promotions on. The network exists mainly as a means of collectively engaging with advertisers, as advertising is the main source of income for the network. Hackett puts this quite explicitly:

> I think the reason podcast networks exist is, even though [the] podcast can be considered a relatively new medium, it exists in an old media world, especially when it comes to advertising. [...] We can mix and match purchases across the different shows, [which gives us] power and a platform, that a single individual person [does not have]. (Hackett, S. 28 June 2016, personal communication)

What is discernible here is that next to being an independent podcast network, the network functions as a platform that operates between the shows and the advertisers, as is the case in Miège's 'flow model'. In contradistinction to centralised broadcast media networks, the history of *Relay FM* shows how the network organically grew out of an online community of podcasters. Thus *Relay FM* can be regarded as a grassroots podcast network. Most importantly, the network uses their niche audiences as an asset to leverage against advertisers. It is clear that although the origins of the networks can be considered grassroots, the advertising model is still very dominant.

Now that we have examined the podcast networks in detail, I will turn to comparing the strategies that they have in common.

Comparing the Networks

Even though the origins, size, aims, and production or organisational structures of all three examined networks differ, some generalisable practices and affordances can be recognised. In this section, the three podcast networks are compared to deduct common strategies regarding three topics: the origins and social functions of the network, gatekeeping mechanisms, and the way in which on a network wide level the combination of these factors can be exploited to benefit both members and collective. Distilling strategic motivations behind and in the formation of these podcast networks allows us to resituate these practices in the contemporary situation, which can provide provisional insights into the arrangement of the means and practices of production in a nascent industry. In the conclusion, these practices will serve as evidence for the tensions and incentives already hinted at above.

Starting from the observation that all discussed podcast networks were started by bringing individual podcast producers together in a network or collective, it should be noted that the networks find their origin in social and professional networks or institutions. *Relay FM* originated from a previous podcast network and draws its members from a bigger online community of technology journalists (see also Markman 2012). *Radiotopia* was formed out of a collaboration with PRX, an institution that is nearest to traditional broadcast public radio (Mars 2013; Hilmes 2013a, b). Lastly *The Heard* members did not have prior connections to each other, but found initial members partly through the Third Coast International Audio Festival (Lewis, J. 28 June 2016, personal communication). These original connections function as pools of resources—such as social and professional acquaintances tied to institutions like festivals and public radio—that the podcast networks can draw from. At the same time, the podcast networks not only take shape in the form of voluntary collectives (*The Heard*), content specific networks (*Radiotopia*), and companies (*Relay FM*), but also form new social and professional connections themselves.

The flexibility and reliability that social networks provide are also at the core of the podcast networks researched in this chapter. Within all three podcast networks, freedom and room for experimentation is a central value for the producers. Operating within a network enables producers to work together, helping each other out with production assistance, and editorial or business advice. At the same time the podcast networks can function as the source for new experimental collaborations that sometimes lead to new content being created. Key to the cross-pollination of resources is the mutually beneficial character on which these collaborations thrive: the formation of networks is a zero-sum game for the individual producers. Being able to stay independent and working together at the same time is a crucial drive for member producers. This flexibility points towards the forging of strategies for the best ways to go about navigating the nascent podcast industry.

Issues with gatekeeping mechanisms are most explicit in the cases of *The Heard* and *Radiotopia* because of their ties with traditional broadcast public radio. Both networks formed out of a frustration with the gatekeeping mechanisms in traditional broadcast public radio: producers and their shows often need to reach a certain level of quality to be allowed into this system. As we have seen argued by Lotz (2017), this gatekeeping mechanism is a result of the regulatory limitations of radio broadcast technology.[15] Limited time and bandwidth created a strict and complex institution that was (and still is) hard to penetrate. At the same time the podcast networks can be seen as producing their own gatekeeping system. In the contemporary podcasting publishing situation this can, to some extent, also be tied to limitations in technology. Search functionality is far from optimal in most podcast catalogues, and no algorithmic recommendation systems (such as Netflix has) are yet in place. Still, I would argue that podcast networks are mostly a deployment of social and aesthetic configurations. Not only are members selected on the type of content they produce in terms of creativity, quality, and approach to niche audiences; their status as individual producers and the opportunities for improving their podcasts also play a role. These gatekeeping practices allow the producers within podcast networks to stand out from other, fully independent podcasters. Selecting and shielding who joins the podcasting networks is important not only for professional and social cohesion, but also because, on the outside, the podcast networks make use of their specific social constellations.

The syndication of individual producers manifests itself in several ways. Although each network is organised differently, every podcast network facilitates and motivates internal communication between members and coordinates meetings, either through online platforms such as Slack or Skype, or face to face at festivals. Practical and financial matters like administration, managing the podcasts' feeds, data analysis, and selling advertisements for the slots on the shows are tasks undertaken by the networks themselves, in the cases of *Relay FM* and *Radiotopia*. Here the double-edged sword of the podcast networks is most clear: taking these production tasks out of the hands of the individual producers allows them to focus on producing content, and additionally the growth of the individual podcasts' niche audiences provide better leverage in brokering advertisement deals. This increase in the division of labour once again testifies to the maturation of podcasting as a medium (see Becker 2008). Moreover, podcast networks create economies of scale by cross-promoting shows within the network and accumulating the same types of shows. Finally, this allows the network to brand itself as a go-to network for specific types of content, which improves discoverability and attracts niche audiences who are more valuable to advertisers (Lotz 2014: 27). It would appear that the old saying 'one for all, all for one' also applies to podcast networks and their strategies in the contemporary advertising-supported (Miège's flow model) podcast business. Even though other forms of podcast networks can emerge, the formations and practices discussed in this chapter could well be regarded as sketches for a newly forming industry.

Concluding Remarks

This chapter set out to examine why podcast producers syndicate in the contemporary podcasting industry. The motivations of the podcast producers were examined from the point of view of three independent network executives. These motivations can be sketched out around several incentives and offer a small but palpable insight into the workings of what can be considered an emerging podcasting industry. Here we return to answer the question of whether the formation of podcast networks is best conceptualised as a category of grassroots production, or if it follows the logic of earlier broadcasting institutions and their business models. One has to conclude that both can be seen taking place at the same time.

Firstly, individual podcast producers organically bond together in networks out of frustration with the gatekeeping mechanisms of broadcast radio. Forming a podcast network provides advantages of sharing resources, accumulating audiences, and enhancing credibility. Being part of a network gives status to the individual podcasts and their producers, who in turn give face to the podcast network. This creation of gatekeeping mechanisms on the podcast network's own terms has an important advantage: in the vast sea of available content, discoverability is increased through cross-referencing and branding. Secondly, it is the objective of podcast networks to take advantage of the affordances that podcasting as a distribution system provides. Not only does distribution via podcasting bypass broadcasting schedules and the limitations on reach via airwaves; it also allows for more freedom in approaches to audio storytelling both in terms of form and content. In the podcast networks studied in this chapter, producers retain full creative control over their productions. Finally, podcast networks offer podcast producers advantages for creating revenue. It can be argued that the contemporary situation operates according to the logic of the dominant 'flow' commodification model. Under these conditions, the podcast networks take advantage of their ability to attract niche audiences as leverage against advertisers. It must be noted that this conclusion is relatively speculative since not enough statistics could be shared and it is based on an analysis of a fraction of the podcast network landscape. Thus, although podcast networks might start and develop as grassroots collectives of individual producers, when aiming to get a steady foot in the developing podcasting industry the podcast networks adopt some of the strategies of centralised broadcasting institutions by forming platforms that facilitate the execution of the incentives delineated above.

Seeing how changes in the production, distribution and consumption of non-musical audio content is undergoing gradual but far-reaching changes, some considerations for future research into podcasting are in order. Observations made in this small-scale study show how, if we are to understand changes in production cultures, focussing on commodification models can bring underlying motivations most clearly to the fore. I have argued that Lotz's recent conceptualisation of 'portals' as a business model for internet-distributed content does not fit the contemporary state of affairs in podcasting. Though this may change, these circumstances also point to areas of interest for further research. One complex but crucial area of interest is the relation between advertisement networks and podcast networks, since this chapter has argued that revenue models are a central motivation behind the formation of podcast networks. Additionally, the implicit gatekeeping mechanisms discussed in this chapter could benefit from both a more detailed and inclusive analysis. Finally, since the scope of this chapter was limited to US-based podcast networks, it will also be valuable to compare how podcast networks from other contexts operate within the organisation of their national media production cultures.

Notes

1. Since 2014, an increase in attention paid to podcasting has brought in new listeners and, promptly following, advertisers and venture capital. *Nieman Lab* has been providing consistent in-depth coverage on developments within the podcasting industry. See for instance Nicholas Quah's *Hot Pod* newsletter (Doctor 2016a; Quah 2017).
2. Earlier US podcast networks are *Rooster Teeth* (founded in 2003) and *This Week in Tech* (founded in 2005). These networks, however, take the form of a multi-media production platform rather than focusing solely on audio productions. An example of a non-US network is *The Podcast Network* in Australia. For an overview of podcast production and distribution companies and their alliances see https://en.wikipedia.org/wiki/List_of_podcasting_companies. Accessed 27 March 2017.
3. To be clear: when talking about 'radio', I am talking about the institutionalized form of broadcast radio which usually uses freely accessible media to disseminate audio content in a one-to-many system (see Hilmes 2007; Peters 1999), whether this be online or via the airwaves. This excludes other forms of radio, such as police or traffic radio, and even new iterations such as RFID chips. The phenomenon of streaming 'internet radio', I would argue, should also be set apart from the technology of podcasting, predominantly because of delivery over RSS.
4. This lack of attention has been explicitly articulated in the *Journal of Radio & Audio Media* (2015, second issue), *The Radio Journal – International Studies in Broadcast & Audio Media* (2016) and by Michele Hilmes (2013).
5. As we are speaking of gradual developments, we can see changes being set into motion earlier, for example in cable distribution and the introduction of the VCR and cassette tapes—see Hilmes (2007) and Uricchio (2004).
6. In each model, the financial transaction is arranged differently: publishers create material goods that carry cultural productions (such as books, albums, DVDs) which are sold directly to consumers. Flow logic is determined by the ability of an audio-visual product to create an audience that can be sold to advertisers. Finally, the logic of the written press combines the previous elements, for it creates an audience that should repeatedly buy a material product, such as a newspaper (Miège 1989: 12). Though related, the 'flow model' should not be confused with Raymond Williams's more textual approach to the construction of flow in broadcast media (Williams 1990 [1975]; also Uricchio 2004).
7. I say 'current' because approaches with portals for (non-musical) audio content are being developed, see Doctor (2016b).

8. Despite the arrival of competitors, iTunes still accounts for 60 per cent of the total amount of podcasts downloaded (Doctor 2016a). Stitcher does offer a paid subscription service that offers premiums such as early listening, which only makes it a partial portal because parts of its content can be accessed freely but with advertisements.

9. A notable exception to this is Spotify, which since 2016 has been adding curated podcasts to their library based on these qualifications: 'That appeal to millennials. That it's evergreen content. That it's tech oriented. That it's story-telling' (Lybsin 2016). Note that Spotify, like Stitcher, is a partial portal as its content can be accessed for free, but with advertisements.

10. Through this last 'snowball' type of connection *The Heard* was found via the *Radiotopia* respondent, for example.

11. Since *The Heard* did not have these numbers readily available, each individual producer was approached to share their overall download numbers in order to estimate network-wide reach. However, the producers were not able to provide the numbers either due to issues of confidentiality or the lack of technical expertise required to measure their reach. Reliable tracking of podcast audience numbers can be seen as an industry-wide problem, which was addressed by NPR directly in 2016 (NPR 2016).

12. Prior to the campaign for *Radiotopia*, Mars had successfully funded a couple of campaigns with the support of the *99% Invisible* audience. Funding productions through listener support is neither a new nor an uncommon practice in the history of American public radio (see Loviglio 2013). In relation to Miège's commodification models, the practice of financing through audiences falls within the publishing model and the written press model, since material products such as branded t-shirts are often obtained as reward for providing financial support. For more on the cultural practices surrounding fan-based support, see D'Amato (2014).

13. Of the three networks discussed in this chapter, *Radiotopia* is the most explicitly active on the popular audio publishing website *Soundcloud*. Besides publishing network-related audio stories exclusively, every individual podcast publishes their episodes on Soundcloud, which get promoted by *Radiotopia*'s account. See <https://soundcloud.com/radiotopia/tracks> accessed 14 February 2017.

14. *Relay FM* could not share reach or listener numbers for confidentiality reasons. In 2015 the network delivered about 1.5 million downloads per month (Dillet 2015).

15. Of course, there are more historical factors that produced the current form of broadcast radio, such as social and governmental factors. For an extensive overview, see Hilmes (2007).

Bibliography

Becker, H. (2008). *Art worlds* (25th anniversary ed.). Berkeley: University of California Press. Originally published in 1982.

Berry, R. (2006). Will the iPod kill the radio star? Profiling podcasting as radio. *Convergence, 12*(2), 143–162.

Berry, R. (2016). Podcasting: Considering the evolution of the medium and its association with the word "radio". *The Radio Journal – International Studies in Broadcast & Audio Media, 14*(1), 7–22.

Cwynar, C. (2015). More than a "VCR for radio": The CBC, the radio 3 podcast, and the uses of an emerging medium. *Journal of Radio & Audio Media, 22*(2), 190–199.

D'Amato, F. (2014). Investors and patrons, gatekeepers and social capital: Representations and experiences of fans' participation in fan funding. In L. Duits, K. Zwaan, & S. Reijnders (Eds.), *The Ashgate research companion to fan cultures* (pp. 135–148). Farnham: Ashgate.

Dillet, R. (2015). How relay FM proves that podcasts aren't an overnight success. www.techcrunch.com [Internet]. Accessed 21 July 2016.

Doctor, K. (2016a). An island no more: Inside the business of the podcasting boom. www.niemanlab.org [Internet]. Accessed 28 Mar 2017.

Doctor, K. (2016b). Are you ready to pay for a Netflix for podcasts? www.niemanlab.org [Internet]. Accessed 28 Mar 2017.

Hilmes, M. (2007). *Only connect. A cultural history of broadcasting in the United States* (2nd ed.). Belmont: Thomson Wadsworth.

Hilmes, M. (2013a). The new materiality of radio. In J. Loviglio & M. Hilmes (Eds.), *Radio's new wave. Global sound in the digital era*. New York: Routledge.

Hilmes, M. (2013b). On a screen near you: The soundwork industry. *Cinema Journal, 52*(3), 177–182.

Lotz, A. (2014). *The television will be revolutionized* (2nd ed.). New York: New York University Press.

Lotz, A. (2017). *Portals: A treatise on internet-distributed television*. Ann Arbor: Michigan Publishing.

Loviglio, J. (2013). Public radio in crisis. In J. Loviglio & M. Hilmes (Eds.), *Radio's new wave. Global sound in the digital era* (pp. 24–42). New York/London: Routledge.

Lybsin. (2016). How to get your podcast into spotify! www.blog.libsyn.com [Internet]. Accessed 23 Feb 2017.

Markman, K. M. (2012). Doing radio, making friends, and having fun: Exploring the motivations of independent audio podcasters. *New Media & Society, 14*(2), 547–565.

Markman, K. M., & Sawyer, C. E. (2014). Why pod? Further explorations of the motivations for independent podcasting. *Journal of Radio & Audio Media, 21*(1), 20–35.

Mars, R. (2013). Radiotopia. www.kickstarter.com [Internet]. Accessed 13 Feb 2017.

Matheson, W. (2014). Radiotopia: Plug in to this new podcast network. www.USAToday.com [Internet]. Accessed 21 July 2016.

Mayer, V. (2008). Studying up and f**cking up: Ethnographic interviewing in production studies. *Cinema Journal, 47*(2), 141–148.

Miège, B. (1989). *The capitalization of cultural production*. London: International General.

Murray. (2009). Servicing 'self-scheduling consumers', public broadcasters and audio podcasting. *Global Media and Communication, 5*(2), 197–219.

Napoli, P. M. (2011). *Audience evolution. New technologies and the transformation of media audiences*. New York: Colombia University Press.

NPR. (2016). Public radio podcast measurement guidelines. bit.ly/podcastguidelines. Accessed 22 Feb 2017.

Patterson, E. (2016). Reconfiguring radio drama after television: The historical significance of Theater 5, Earplay and CBS Radio Mystery Theater as post-network radio drama. *Historical Journal of Film, Radio and Television, 36*(4), 649–667.

Peters, J. D. (1999). *Speaking into the air*. Chicago: The University of Chicago Press.

Phantom Haus. About Us. www.phantomhaus.org [Internet]. Accessed 25 July 2016.

PRX. About PRX. www.prx.org [Internet]. Accessed 25 July 2016.

Quah, N. *Hot Pod*. A Newsletter about Podcasts. www.hotpodnews.com [Internet]. Accessed 11 Sept 2017.

Radiotopia. About. www.radiotopia.fm [Internet]. Accessed 25 July 2016.

Radiotopia. (2017a). Radiotopia Podquest. www.radiotopia.fm [Internet]. Accessed 13 Feb 2017.

Radiotopia. (2017b). Radiotopia iTunes artist page. itunes.apple.com/nl/artist/radiotopia/id850139119?l=en&mt=2 [Internet]. Accessed 9 Feb 2017.

Relay FM. (2016). Relay FM iTunes artist/network page. itunes.apple.com/nl/artist/relay-fm/id908489268?l=en&mt=2 [Internet]. Accessed 28 Dec 2016.

Relay FM. About. www.relay.fm [Internet]. Accessed 25 July 2016.

Stimson, L. (2016). Nielsen adding podcast/on-demand to ratings. *Radio and Television Business Report*. www.rbr.com [Internet]. Accessed 22 July 2016.

The Heard. Who. www.theheardradio.com [Podcast]. Accessed 21 July 2016.

The Heard About. www.theheardradio.com [Podcast]. Accessed 21 July 2016.

Uricchio, W. (2004). Television's next generation: Technology/interface culture/flow. In L. Spigel & J. Olsson (Eds.), *Television after TV: Essays on a medium in transition*. Durham: Duke University Press.

Wikipedia. (2016). List of podcasting companies. en.wikipedia.org [Internet]. Accessed 21 June 2016.

Williams, R. (1990). In E. Williams (Ed.), *Television: Technology and cultural form* (2nd ed.). London: Routledge Originally published in 1975.

5

'I Know What a Podcast Is': Post-*Serial* Fiction and Podcast Media Identity

Danielle Hancock and Leslie McMurtry

Introduction

The Black Tapes Podcast, TANIS, Rabbits, The Message, Limetown, Archive 81. What do all of these fictional podcasts have in common? In the simplest terms, all of them are popular post-*Serial* podcast thrillers. But what does it mean, to be a post-*Serial* podcast thriller? Let us take each term one at a time. If podcasting arose in 2004, it can be said to have become 'mainstream' in 2014. This is partly due to the phenomenon of *This American Life's Serial* (2014). As podcast-advertising specialist Måns Ulvestam explains, *Serial* 'completely changed people's perceptions of podcasting' from being techno-centric and niche (cited in Bergman 2017). Hosted by long-time *This American Life* audio-journalist Sarah Koenig, *Serial* is the emphatically 'true life' investigation of a 1990s murder case: a week-by-week re-evaluation of the evidence that saw 18-year-old Adnan Syed imprisoned for the murder of his ex-girlfriend Hae Min Lee. While self-admittedly far from unique or pioneering in its underpinning concepts of either serialisation, or stylised audio-documentary

D. Hancock (✉)
University of East Anglia, Norwich, UK
e-mail: Danielle.hancock@uea.ac.uk

L. McMurtry
University of Salford, Salford, UK
e-mail: l.g.mcmurtry@salford.ac.uk

© The Author(s) 2018
D. Llinares et al. (eds.), *Podcasting*, https://doi.org/10.1007/978-3-319-90056-8_5

(Snyder cited in Biewen et al. 2017: 78), and although a number of previous podcasts had achieved cult success (Hancock and McMurtry 2017), *Serial* stands alone as the first 'mainstream' podcast.

Serial undeniably broke records: the fastest-ever podcast to reach 5 million downloads (within its first month); 40 million downloads in its first two months (Dredge 2014); holding the #1 rating on iTunes' download chart for three months; the first podcast to win a Peabody Award. By Christmas 2014, *Serial* claimed such broad popularity, and iconic status, as to warrant a (highly praised) *Saturday Night Live* parody, the significance of which is epitomised in *Time* magazine: "'No way", some people thought, "a podcast could never be big enough to get the SNL treatment"' (Grossman 2014). For many commentators, *Serial* breathed new life into an otherwise niche, and somewhat dwindling media form (Zurawik 2014). As podcasting authority Richard Berry notes, ten years after podcasting debuted, 'the world was suddenly talking about podcasting again' (2015: 170).

Defining the Post-*Serial*

The post-*Serial* brings with it more elements than simply following *Serial* in chronological terms. Alongside bringing non-fiction podcasting to the public eye, and despite being explicitly built around notions of truth and reality, *Serial* represents the most influential force upon podcast *fiction* since Old Time Radio drama (OTR).[1] Since its release, *Serial* has been accredited with a wave of 'copycat' fiction: a developing sub-genre of highly popular fiction podcasts which seem consciously to follow what podcast veteran Alasdair Stuart terms '[t]he *Serial* model; "bad thing happens, crusading journalist investigates, interviews and discussion ensue"' (2016). These programmes have received mainstream media attention, as much due to questions of media identity as to their popularity. As Nino Cipri (2016) observes:

> There seems to be a growing subgenre of 'intrepid female journalist uncovers a supernatural conspiracy.' Well, if not a subgenre, then at least a trope in the making. *The Black Tapes, Limetown,* and *The Message* all share this same basic premise: *Serial* goes full-on *X-Files*.

Never before has podcast fiction, as a genre rather than a one-off hit, been so visible. Yet while numerous press commentators have branded such podcasts derivative, or as 'trying too hard to be like *Serial*', (McFarland 2015) we argue this overlooks the crucial fact that *Serial* is not just an extension of effective radio journalism aesthetic and form, but rather offers an inherently and importantly successful, sympathetic utilisation and expression of its unique podcast media identity. Furthermore, this ignores the extent to which such shows expand upon *Serial*'s blueprint. From *Serial*, we may see audio-drama take a new and critically important shape as the first explicitly podcast-oriented audio-fiction form.

Some audio scholars anticipated the podcasts above, as fictional thrillers, identifying *Serial* as having 'component parts [which] break down to form the spine of a recipe that audio dramatists can use', while Berry asserts it 'presented podcasting as a viable alternative platform for content creators and storytellers' (McMurtry 2016: 320; Berry 2015: 176). This chapter expands such predictions, arguing that what in fact appeals so much in *Serial*'s 'blueprint' is its understanding and exploitation of its own podcast medium. If, previously, fiction podcasts often depended upon radio's frameworks, conventions and even aesthetics (Hancock and McMurtry 2017), *Serial* established a narrative style which was informed by, and exploratory of, podcast media identity, and its properties of mobility, fragmentation, and integrated multi-platforming. That *Serial* perhaps emerges as the most notable podcast to date may be less to do with its 'rubbernecking spectacle' (Livingstone 2017), and more that it was among the first podcasts to recognise and harness the distinctive narrative potentials of its own media form: to show us the new ways which podcasting enables us to tell and hear stories.[2] This chapter thus explores a range of post-*Serial* podcast fictions, asking to what extent these utilise and develop *Serial*'s model to offer a new audio-fiction form explicitly built around, and exploratory of, podcasting's unique media properties. Specifically, we example the Pacific Northwest Stories (PNWS) podcast network (whose output comprises of *The Black Tapes Podcast, TANIS* and *Rabbits*); *The Message* (General Electric Podcast Theater); *Limetown* (Two Up Productions); and *Archive 81* (Dead Signals). After briefly exploring the deeper significance of aesthetic and formulaic repetition, we will address three main aspects of these programmes: distribution, platforming and mediation.

Repetition

The similarities between *Serial* and those fictions which follow it are often acknowledged by their creators, if not directly, then through reference to the show's 'parent-figure' *This American Life* as a strong influence (McFarland 2015; Powell cited in Prina 2016). Indeed PNWS' co-creator Terry Miles depicts *Serial* as a creative time-bomb: '[w]e thought when we were doing this that someone else was going to do it … I remember calling Paul and being like, 'Man we have got to hurry, do you understand?'' (cited in Shaw 2016). Shortly after, *The Message* was commissioned as '*Serial* with aliens' (Sims 2015). However, not all post-*Serial* fictions follow from *Serial* in their conception: despite its later release, *Limetown* was reputedly envisioned roughly 'a year before *Serial* debuted', suggesting an almost inevitability to the programme's structure and style (McFarland 2015). Perhaps then there is something more meaningful at play in the podcasts' emergent conventions— a formula, of sorts, in whose understanding we may glean an insight into the unique potentials and properties of podcast media as a narrative medium. 'Radio is rich in conventions' as Guy Starkey observed (2004: 29), and while podcasting as a form has proved far more flexible than much of traditional radio, conventions still abound to frame audience expectations. This is highly evident when performing close comparisons between *Serial* and post-*Serial* podcast fiction thrillers. This is more than mere slavish mimicry. The conventions of Ira Glass' *This American Life* give the WBEZ Chicago/American Public Media an aural signature, which Glass likens to two basic components, of plot and moments of reflection (2017: 70). The terms Glass uses for non-fictional storytelling are not unique—plot, story—but they do suggest an affinity with fictional narrative. 'I think the biggest thing is that people responded to this journalism as if it were entertainment,' something writers Sarah Koenig, Julie Snyder and producer Dana Chivvis consciously constructed, suggests Koenig as regards *Serial* (cited in Bernard 2017). While several of the post-*Serial* fiction podcasts respond explicitly to the *Serial* script and style, none of the podcasts is more explicit in its emulation than *The Black Tapes Podcast (TBT)*.

Cipri (2016) defines *TBT* as referential 'possibly to the point of parody: even the show's theme song is extremely similar to *Serial*'s, with a voicemail in the place of the announcement of a collect call'. Indeed, *TBT* emulates *Serial* throughout its opening audio-collage: a mash-up of 'found-footage' style soundbites and voices interspersed with a catchy, moody theme tune which both establishes narrative trajectory and aesthetic. *Serial*'s opening segue reads almost as a TV transcript, with a sponsor segment, and a theme song 'so catchy and distinct that just a few notes of it set the mood and a level of expectation in the listener', interspersed with a 'previously on *Serial*' clips section, and a richly textured 'hallmark' opening sequence comprised of Syed's and the prison automated call system's voices (DeMair 2017: 29). If *TBT* mirrors *Serial*'s opening 'sounds', it also borrows almost literally from *Serial*'s script, with the hosts' self-explanatory establishing frames echoing one another:

Koenig:	For the last year, I've spent every working day trying to figure out where a high school kid was for an hour after school one day in 1999 ... ('The Alibi')
Alex Reagan:	For the last two months, I've been immersed in the fascinating world of paranormal investigation. ('A Tale of Two Tapes: Part 1')

Although *TBTs'* initial near-perfect reproduction of *Serial*'s aesthetics dissipates as the show progresses, a clear duplication of form is maintained throughout the seasons.

This emulation of form and acoustic style is present throughout post-*Serial* fiction; indeed all of the shows discussed employ near-identical opening sequence sounds and structures, featuring 'found-footage', theme and audio-clips of the show. Through emulating *Serial*'s recognisable form, podcast fiction becomes intelligible to an unfamiliar audience: '[w]hen a fiction podcast uses a nonfiction form, there's a set of contexts that makes sense to you, as a listener,' explains *Archive 81* creator Dan Powell (cited in Locke 2016). Comparing *Serial* to the popular 'real life' murder dramatisation TV programme *Dateline*, David Letzler posits that, 'for the broader audience captivated by *Serial*, its appeal rests in the narrative construction, not the events of the murder' (2017: 39–40). This recollects 'television's sequence of diverse fragments of narrative, information and advertising [which] defines the medium's fundamental structure during the network era' (Butler 2012: 17). However, there are also recollections of radio and audio-book form. Salvati (2015) characterises fan (non)fictional podcast *Dan Carlin's Hardcore History* (2006–) as using a combination of broadcast liveness/paratextual flow and the narrative voice familiar from audio-books as well as the use of Web syndication (if not outright serialisation) in its Web 'pull' (Butler 2012: 233). This sequence may be TV-like in structure, but acoustically it asserts the vividness of sound, and the podcast's pre-recorded, 'time-shift' properties. The rich, kaleidoscopic sounds of *Serial*'s opening frames emphasise that '[t]he documentary genre within audio's renaissance of storytelling has striven to make sound an *experience*' (Salvati 2015: 234, italics original). In seconds, the sequence establishes a sense of varied locations and times, a continuity of programming, and, in Glass's authoritative broadcast voice and the introductory advertising segment, a defined listener positioning of anticipation and attentiveness. The opening sets the scene for an hour or so of devoted listenership, more akin to TV's 'primary' entertainment position than radio's long-held secondary status.

As *Serial*'s iconic structures become applicable to, and recognisable within, podcast media more generally, a new media identity emerges. The podcast no longer operates merely as re-played radio, wrenched from another media form, or as an assortment of eclectic one-offs, but rather as a media form which is increasingly recognisable as consciously self-contained, pre-recorded, play-on-demand acoustically complex, and formally sponsored. The repetitions of post-*Serial* fictions make bold steps toward forming a unified podcast media identity.

Distribution

What ultimately distinguished podcasting from Internet radio was its portability, its user-control options, its lack of overarching gatekeeper or censorship system/s, and its accessibility (in terms of distribution). It is this last feature that reached its zenith with *Serial*. Besides aping *Serial*'s style and public radio context, post-*Serial* fiction further appropriates the show's groundbreaking use of serialised release. Of course, serialization has always exerted a strong pull on audiences. What John Cawelti calls 'resistance to closure' (2004: 347) characterises the 'endlessly deferred narrative' that Matt Hills identifies in *Fan Cultures* (2002: 128). Though far from the first podcast to tell a single story through instalments, *Serial* is among the first to promote this aspect as beneficial: important enough, even, to earn its namesake. Nathan Matisse asserts, 'Serialization may have always existed, but [*Serial*] demonstrates that an audio-only audience is not only open to it, they crave it' (Matisse 2014).

'Crave' is an apt term. *Serial*, and the fictions which succeed it, have been described as 'addictive', 'drug-like' and with listeners needing their next 'fix' (McCracken 2017: 54; Locker 2015). There is an obvious parallel with Netflix binge-watch culture: when interviewed in 2017, *Serial*'s writers/producers Sarah Koenig and Julie Snyder noted that they pushed the 'previously on' tag in *Serial*, which they said they had acquired from TV (cited in Biewen et al. 2017: 78). However, unlike television fiction, which is created as a block series, and/or traditional radio, which must adhere to wider broadcast scheduling issues, podcasting allows for genuinely up-to-the-minute delivery of extra material, divergence and update, as fast as the producers can mix and upload it. This all appears on the subscriber's podcast RSS feed immediately, ready to be heard on any mobile listening device, from the moment of release. Moreover, as podcasts are increasingly accessed through personally integrated (technologically convergent) devices like Smartphones, the concept of 'listening time' becomes less constrained. The podcast medium enables a serialised story that may be heard anytime, anywhere, that may be added to almost instantaneously that delivers itself and any updates to its audience, and often to its audience's most intimate and often-utilised technologies, and which in doing so continually reminds listeners of its presence. A podcast can tell a never-ending story that follows listeners anywhere.[3]

However, what post-*Serial* fiction does is develop *Serial*'s unsustainable 'reality-audio' model. As *Serial* attempted extended if not eternal life, aping the endlessly deferred narrative, (with Season One's ending being repeatedly 'prolonged' with audio-updates on Syed's ongoing legal battle) audience attentions dwindled. This occurrence teaches much about the importance of pace and dependent anticipation. Though *Serial* Season One continued to release material, such information was no longer drawn from the ever-available well of the past: it was contingent upon events beyond the *Serial* team's control, and thus could not meet the same steady, reliable, just-fast-enough release schedule of the podcast's regular episodes. Koenig iterated that her journalistic integrity precluded her making the conclusions that furnish satisfying drama (cited in Biewen et al. 2017: 78). Some fans disagreed; they complained, lost interest, and branded Season Two a flop.[4] A Reddit post summed up the fan response: 'I, like pretty much everyone else, loved S1. But I got an episode or two into S2 as they were coming out and I just didn't like it as much' (MorboReddits 2017). For many, the season's central mystery was upstaged by 'more tenuous' ethical conversations, 'riveting for some and dull as dry toast for others' (Locker 2016).

In the realms of fiction, however, such complaints never need be. Post-*Serial* fictions evidence an understanding of the need for both continuance, control and conclusion. In fiction, hyperdiegetic universes provide a sense of breadth and depth in the text's setting, a sense that any one story being told is only the tip of the iceberg in a larger universe. In a seminal study, Ien Ang called the TV soap *Dallas* 'television fiction without end', (1985: 6) an apt categorisation of *Serial*'s fictional progeny. Found-footage horror *Archive 81* develops specifically around this concept. The show tells the story of missing archivist Dan, who has recently disappeared after being hired to record himself listening to a collection of audio-cassette tapes titled 'Archive 81', ostensibly to digitise the collection, but with the unsettling caveat that he must never turn his recorder off. As one of an unspecified but seemingly vast collection of audio-tape archives, 'Archive 81' holds a potentially inexhaustible trove of mysteries to investigate and can feed its audience's insatiability in ways that *Serial* cannot. Furthermore, the show's serialised, steady drip-feed format is intentionally mirrored in its narrative premise: the archives being broadcast are, in fact, the re-embodiment of a demonic entity, who is seeking to find form through an unending, and compelling, story. This point is emphasised frequently, as when, on realising the archive's unsettling nature, protagonist Dan attempts to abandon the project. Herein Dan's 'project manager' explains:

> when a natural storyteller like you hears something as powerful as what's on those tapes, you get invested. And because you care so much about what happened, well, it's difficult for you to leave without hearing the whole story. ('A Body in a New Place')

The 'binge-listen' audio-culture that *Serial* tapped into is darkly mirrored: just as Dan is compelled to continue listening to the supernaturally charged recordings, so too are his listeners seemingly compelled to listen to him listening.

Similarly, the 'black tapes', from which the eponymous Pacific Northwest Stories show derives its name, are in fact a shelf of VHS cases, each containing the details of an unsolved paranormal case. When radio journalist Alex Reagan first discovers the tapes, there is a strong inference of a 12-part programme structure coming to fruition, as she explains:

> Dr. Strand eventually agreed to let me take a look at one of the unsolved, he would say unsolved yet, cases from that mysterious row of plastic black VHS containers ... It looks like there were around a dozen or so VHS cases on that shelf. This birthday party is from what we're calling tape number one. ('A Tale of Two Tapes: Part 1')

In numbering the tapes, and dealing with the first of the twelve in the show's first episode, Reagan sets in motion a measured 'monster-of-the-week' system which suggests a twelve-episode limit to the show. In one sense, this is delivered, as each of the first season's episodes orients itself around the opening of the next 'black tape', and the season finale offers a clear sense of denouement in the opening of all of the tapes. There is a narrative satisfaction in this conclusion which *Serial* could never supply. However, when Reagan asks paranormal sceptic Richard Strand, 'Are the Black Tapes all connected?' she unconsciously reaches out to the longevity of *TBT*'s narrative; Seasons 2 and 3 will not detail more tapes, but tap into the rationale behind their connections to one another and to Strand's personal life (*The Codex Gigas*). As *Limetown* creator Zack Ackers notes:

Serial had to stay nonfictional. At the end of the show, it didn't necessarily mean that it had a conclusion. That's the biggest advantage we have: We're making it up. So we can give you an ending. (Cited in Owen 2015)

Unlike *Serial*, post-*Serial* fiction can have its cake and eat it, offering listeners a clear sense of narrative culmination, while extending the same story's life onto an equally plentiful, and methodically-released, new season.

This appropriation of the podcast's fluidity and intimacy of distribution is continued, as post-*Serial* podcasts frequently send listeners diegetic updates and teasers, building on *Serial*'s initially effective delivery of Adnan's trial updates in a more reliably sustainable, and dramatic, manner. In *Limetown*, podcasting's unique distribution method allows a unique realism, with the show's creators enforcing an unpredictable release schedule:

> We need to get them out at a pace where people don't forget what's happening, but at the same time, I do think the consistency [of traditional public radio] is a little archaic ... Having an inconsistent release schedule is more like what happens in the real world. If Lia is exploring this story in present day, well, sometimes an episode might just be 40 seconds of breaking news. (Bronkie cited Owen 2015)

Yet while, in the immediate delivery of such material to subscribed listeners, the podcast may develop a 'real-time' narrative tension and pace that radio may not, there is also notable fan appreciation for, and adaptation to, the more individualistic 'listen-on-demand' podcast format. Many post-*Serial* fiction fans report 'hoarding' episodes for a binge listen, and indeed, several report feeling that the shows' narratives are designed for such engagement:

> I suspect I'd enjoy them all a lot more if I'd waited a year and listened to them all in one sitting, rather than trying to keep up with them in serial form. Hopefully in a couple years I'll have forgotten enough to do that with fresh ears. (eotvos)

Beyond being merely long-running, post-*Serial* fictions are demanding of listener attention. Just as *Serial* requires 'our fullest mental commitments to parse what we can and cannot understand' (Letzler 2017: 160), post-*Serial* podcasts require full, immersive audience attention, in a way that radio has seldom been credited with since the Crystal set's demise. As David Chang (2016) observes:

Tanis ... demands your full attention. Let your mind wander for just a minute, and you may miss a vital clue. Skip an entire episode, and you could be lost at sea ... listening to this podcast is like drinking out of a wonderful, amazing yet very powerful fire hydrant. Your brain is FLOODED with information.

Information-overload is indicative of the broader genre. Joseph Farrar of *Archive 81* similarly explains: 'It all gets a little *Inception*-esque, and if you space out during podcasts you're likely to get tripped by the rabbit holes.' (2016) Sandy Tolan notes, '[t]he documentary functions best when it is not merely a long piece of fact-jammed journalism but a nonfiction drama set on an audio stage with scenes, characters, narrative arc, dramatic tension, and even silence' (2017: 195). Increasingly, as a facet of new modes of engaging with podcasting, it seems that 'soundwork' (to use Michele Hilmes' phrase) requires some level of careful listening: this is not confined to *Serial*, but, again, was popularised by it. Whereas traditional radio was ephemeral and fleeting, podcasts may be paused and replayed, allowing listeners to follow more complex plots. Rather than passing from one story to the next, the listener must juggle many strands of the same story, over 12 or so installments.

The complexity of these shows is a source of listener fascination, with Reddit fan communities producing detailed plot-maps, and many listeners admitting to pausing, re-playing, and repeating episodes or even entire seasons to maintain their understanding. The required listening skills are now entering mainstream digital culture, a reminder of a time when radio was the solo broadcasting medium. This tendency is highlighted, and encouraged, as in all opening sequences when both Reagan *TANIS*' Nic Silver direct new listeners to head to the shows' first episodes and catch up before continuing listening (as does Koenig in *Serial*).

Thus with the mobile MP3 player's revival of headphone listening (Bull 2007) comes a renewed emphasis on complex and demanding audio-fiction—a far cry from the BBC's '[p]lays to hoover to' (Scotney cited Wade 1981: 222). This is also a far cry from the multi-tasking, mobilised, on-the-go listening culture which new audio-media has thus far been tied to. It would be difficult to navigate city streets, or busy traffic, and not fall into 'rabbit holes'. Perhaps post-*Serial* fictions are built for less taxing mobility; headphones do allow for a more directed, undisturbed listening experience and certainly many listeners report catching up during commutes. However, this overlooks a concurrent rise in domestic and shared listening, reported both in the 2017 Next Radio Conference held in London (Lazovick 2017), and by post-*Serial* fiction listeners themselves. In direct opposition to Michael Bull's depictions of lonely listeners, many post-*Serial* fans report listening at home, either alone or with friends and family. In 2017, due to the use of Smart Speakers, audio is now being consumed in group settings (Lazovick 2017). While Smart Speaker use is currently confined to about 7 per cent of the total US population, 40 per cent of those who own a Smart Speaker use it to listen to podcasts (NPR/Edison Research 2017). In a digital take on radio's Golden Era families grouped at the wireless, listeners are now gathering around the digital speaker, and such focussed attentions are increasingly being met. Rather than continued adherence to a form of radio most closely associated with formatted music (with chatty DJ hosts), which are often affiliated with radio's 'secondary' media status, in post-*Serial* fiction, podcasting's properties of temporal manipulation and isolated listening are finally harnessed. Thus we find more complex, vast and demanding narratives than audio-drama has, by and large, previously undertaken.

Platforming

A crucial means by which post-*Serial* podcasts further maintain such complex serialised narratives is through the development of audio-visual narrative. Podcasting is often conceptualised similarly to radio, which was originally defined as a solely auditory media bearing no visual identity. Hilmes (2013) has rechristened podcast/ radio as 'soundwork' and 'screen medium', suggesting that podcasting is accessed through screens 'both mobile and static, using tactile and visual and textual interfaces' (p. 44). Visibility plays an important role within podcasting, with website imagery, logos and show/episode 'posters' comprising integral aspects of a podcast's reception.

Pre-*Serial*, such visual paratexts frequently shaped and informed a podcast-listening experience, imbuing the listening material with a particular aesthetic or solidifying an otherwise 'invisible' space or appearance (Hancock and McMurtry 2017: 4–5; Jaynes 2017) Yet *Serial* evolves this, using its website as a 'base-camp' of sorts for the show's investigation and integrating its audio form with the materials displayed there. On the website, listeners may peruse evidence and information pertaining to Syed's case (such as phone records and trial transcripts), labelled the 'visual stuff *in* this story'. To consider *Serial's* visual material as additional rather than composite overlooks the extent to which Koenig refers to and directs listeners to the website material, and the extent to which having such material allows the podcast to tell such a complex story. As Erica Haugtvedt notes, Koenig is 'sometimes monotonously pedantic about the details of the years-old case [*Serial*] chronicles'; without making the records available to the listener, *Serial* risks losing its intelligibility (2017: 26). Only by appropriating the podcast's audio-visual properties and creating a multi-sensory, multi-platform narrative, may the story function adequately, as the website 'has taken peculiar pains to present corporeal evidence, as if the story as presented aurally by Koenig is not enough; there must be physical, written, seen traces' (McMurtry 2016: 308). Indeed, the extent to which this is true is evidenced in the website's 'introduction' to its documents section as 'This is the place where we'll collect all the visual stuff in this story' ('Maps, Documents, etc.'). Herein, the audible voice is reconciled with the visible 'voice'. Koenig's presentation style contrasts strongly with 'the ingrained style of most NPR-ish features, a style that could be characterized as largely disembodied, as if reporters are merely a pass-through, a conduit' (Michel 2017: 213). Acknowledging this, *Serial* must be understood as an audiovisual experience, with Koenig's spoken narrative being intertwined throughout with various visual elements.

Just as *Serial* displays phone records and blueprints for the audience's scrutiny, so too does *TBT* offer audiences visual testimony on its website. Captioned: 'FOUND BEHIND A PAINTING IN A HOTEL IN VICTORIA, B.C., CANADA,' is a handwritten list of number configurations on a (perhaps digitally) sepia-ed piece of paper. *TANIS* and *Rabbits* both significantly extend this trope, dutifully displaying email correspondence, news-clippings, photographs, artworks and screen-grabs referenced in each episode, and creating a story form which is throughout dualistically audiovisual. These visual elements take audio drama from the highly individualistic, nebulous realms of the imagination, and into the more concrete, shared realms of the object. Post-*Serial* fictions further replicate *Serial*'s audio-visual narrative by including 'real', 'findable' materials alongside fictional storylines, forging a narrative form 'which is acutely aware of the audience's ability to fact-check and research that which is presented as true-life' (Hancock and McMurtry 2017: 6). That listeners may Google the artifacts, news stories, characters and histories discussed in the shows underpins narrative tension in such scenes as *TBT*'s *Codex Gigas*, wherein Reagan Googles 'The Devil's Bible':

Carmichael:	You can look [The Devil's Bible] up online.
Reagan:	Really?
Carmichael:	Yes. It's called *The Codex Gigas*. You should Google it. I'll stay on the line.
Reagan:	You don't mind?
Carmichael:	Not at all.
Reagan:	Okay, great. [pause] Oh, wow. There's a huge drawing of the devil in it.
Carmichael:	Quite something, yes?
Reagan:	Yeah, that's... something.

While initially this may seem an over-long segue to Reagan's discovery of a Satanic image, in fact by delaying such discovery the scene allows, and encourages, the listener to Google alongside Reagan, reinforcing the notion that soundwork and podcasting are extensions of screen media. In doing so, the listener will discover reams of information on the factual *Codex Gigas*, and may examine the book's illustration alongside Reagan's subsequent description of it. Here we find a fruitful exampling of Henry Jenkins' 'convergence media', wherein 'consumers are encouraged to seek out new information and make connections among dispersed media content' (2006: 3).

If 'convergence occurs within the brains of individual consumers and through their social interactions with others', then we may further argue post-*Serial* fictions to complicate 'first wave' concerns regarding new audio-media's antisocial properties (Jenkins 2006: 3). In allowing audiences to double-check, study and dissect, such materials, audio-visual podcast narratives coax acts of armchair detective-work and interactivity, as listeners not only discuss and argue the various podcasts' mysteries, but, on fan forums like Reddit, work collaboratively to solve them. Furthermore, many post-*Serial* fictions operate upon the premise of their respective journalist/ narrator characters having chosen the podcast media form specifically because of its potential to allow uncensored collaboration and communication between speakers and audience. *Archive 81*'s host (missing man Dan's friend), Mark Sollinger, explicitly aligns his choice of mediation with the podcast's ability to allow him to reach out to the world for help, saying, 'I will be releasing all of his audio to everyone, to *everyone*' ('A Body in a New Place'). Sollinger further suggests the podcast medium's word-of-mouth culture and its integration with screen cultures, asking listeners to contact him if they have any knowledge of his friend's whereabouts, or of 'Archive 81'. Likewise— in a playful narrative/ marketing device— Solinger implores listeners to help and 'just get the word out' by sharing the story of Dan's disappearance on social media, and through boosting the podcast's iTunes' rating (ibid). *Rabbits* operates upon a similar awareness of the podcast medium's sociability and connectivity, and openly encourages listeners to join in the hunt for 'reporter' Carley Parker's missing friend Yumiko. Parker explains that 'I started this podcast because I want to find out what happened to my friend', further qualifying the show as 'a way of eliciting assistance, engaging the hive mind, a way of asking you, our listeners, for help.' ('Game On'; 'Concernicus Jones').

That listeners are kept almost on an even-score with the investigations again springs from *Serial*'s innovations of form, which crucially used the podcast medium's immediacy of distribution and reception to further assert a temporal immediacy between listener and speaker which podcasting has previously been considered to deny. 'Koenig … wanted the podcast to sound different than *This American Life* and have a live vibe' (Koenig cited in Anonymous 2014). *Serial* episodes were thus written and produced no earlier than a week before broadcast, and were subject to constant last-minute change and update, creating a story which was constantly developing and seemingly self-directing. Herein pre-ordained narrative and biases were supposedly denied, as Koenig emphasises: 'I don't know where it will end actually' (cited in Raptopoulos). Responding to listener-requests for block-release, Chivvis explains:

> We're reporting this story as we write it. We're still pinning down information, doing interviews, following leads. So when you listen each week, the truth is that you're actually not all that far behind us. ('A Question of Binge Listening')

The show's on-the-go construction is further presented as bringing listeners almost as close to the story as the producers and reporters. As Glass sold it: 'each week, we will go with Sarah on her hunt to figure out what really happened. And we will learn the answers as she does' (cited in Larson 2014). Podcasting's fast production and unrestricted distribution process are thus pivotal to narrative, allowing the story to be updated and diverted at any minute and enabling a more immersive and interactive narrative than traditional media might allow.

The emulation of such pace and supplementation is integral to post-*Serial* fictions, with all of the shows presenting their episodes as airing alongside ongoing, unscripted and unpredictable investigations. *TBT* purportedly begins as an anthology-documentary of various 'interesting lives, remarkable occupations and amazing stories' before 'unexpectedly' focusing on Dr. Strand and his black tapes. Like *Serial*, the story is suggested as organically self-directed, as an 'interesting, confusing, and occasionally macabre story that had started spilling out around the edges' of Reagan and her producers' 'original vision' ('A Tale of Two Tapes: Part 1'). Thus, rather than presenting a sculpted, 'designed' documentary series, Reagan explains:

> … we decided that we would let things play out exactly as they happen to us. You will experience the events just as we experience them. I'll step in every once in a while to help guide you through it. But other than those interruptions, we're going to let things play out exactly as they happened. ('A Tale of Two Tapes: Part 1')

Like Koenig and Chivvis, Reagan suggests an almost shoulder-to-shoulder closeness between her investigation, and the listener's reception. In *Limetown*, even the show's production methods promote a sense of co-discovery between narrator/journalist and listener. Annie-Sage Whitehurst (Haddock) is given little plot-information before her recordings, describing herself as 'learning along with Lia', and— like Koenig— having no idea how the show would end (cited Framke 2015).

The extent to which the listener is co-opted into the post-*Serial* detective narrative recollects Jenkins' discussion of massively multiplayer online games (MMPOGs), in which '[g]ame designers acknowledge that their craft has less to do with prestructured stories than with creating the preconditions for spontaneous community activities' (2006: 164). Given the extent to which PNWS in particular facilitates and prompts online collaborative detective 'game-play', it is all the more significant that *Rabbits* explores a mysterious (eponymous) MMPOG, in which players disappear. A common fan-theory is that the podcast is developed its own MMPOG or Alternate Reality Game, which listeners may join if they decipher the show's clues correctly (blanktracks; pnb0804; LPLoRab 2017). As post-*Serial* fictions weave together fiction and fact, the podcast's social potential and aspects of multi-platform and integrated-media listening are brought to narrative fruition.

Mediation

Throughout *TBT*, *TANIS* and *Rabbits*, preoccupation with media form is an explicit, even thematic, concern—this is also the case with *Limetown* (conceived before *Serial* was released) and *The Message*, and remains leitmotif throughout *Archive 81*. If *Serial* gave podcasting a mainstream identity, then this is a concept of which these podcast fictions are particularly (sometimes painfully) aware. *TBT* acknowledges explicit dependence upon *Serial* for identity as one interviewee responds: 'Cool, I love podcasts—have you listened to *Serial*?' (cited in Hancock and McMurtry 2017: 6). Likewise, in *Rabbits*, interviewee Harper Billings links *Rabbits* to *Serial*, and to *TANIS* and *TBT*:

Billings: This is for one of your radio stories?
Parker: A podcast, yeah.
Billings: You know Ira Glass?
Parker: You know I don't.
Billings: You know Nic Silver and Roman Mars?
Parker: I don't know Roman Mars.
Billings: Roman Coppola? ('Concernicus Jones')

In querying whether Parker knows Glass, Billings clearly connects the notion of podcasting with *Serial/ This American Life*, before conflating PNWS with both Glass' work and with public radio network KALW's popular podcast *99% Invisible* (presented by public radio podcast visionary Roman Mars).[5] Furthermore, Billings conflates radio and podcasting--a point which Parker subtly 'corrects'. Throughout *their* shows, Reagan and Silver frequently define podcasts for their interviewees, often having to extrapolate podcasting from other media types, and usually framing podcasting as an extension of radio:

Tina Stephenson:	So this is for the radio?
Nic Silver:	It's a podcast, actually.
Stephenson:	A what?
Silver:	It's a kind of radio on demand.
Stephenson:	I don't know what that is.
Silver:	It's basically the radio. (*TBT* 'Name That Tune')

In *Rabbits*, Parker explains podcasting as radio's digital incarnation:

Parker:	I'm producing a podcast.
Aimee X:	What's that?
Parker:	It's kind of like radio on demand.
Aimee X:	On the internet?
Parker:	Exactly. ('Concernicus Jones')

Interestingly, both interviewees' confusion, and Silver and Parker's somewhat simplified explanations – 'it's basically the radio'; 'it's kind of like radio on demand'—respond to a key debate within radio studies—how elastic *is* the term radio? Radio, some would argue, 'perpetually sidesteps the question of definition' (Dubber 2013: 10); Hilmes has comprehensively defined it as a litany of forms (2013: 44) which include podcasting, both fictional and non-fictional.

A sense of exasperation often underlies these moments, suggesting the fragility and apparent anonymity of podcasting's identity in the face of mainstream media. However, *TANIS* suggests an alternate picture. Herein Silver begins his podcast-explanation spiel only to be quickly, almost jokingly, rebuffed for its redundancy:

Silver:	It's actually a podcast. ... like radio and the Internet.
Geoff Van Sant:	I know what a podcast is. (*TANIS*, 'Radio, Radio')

Clearly, listeners know that *TANIS* knows that they know what a podcast is. This reflects changing US listening habits; of those surveyed in Edison Research's 2010 *Infinite Dial* study, only 23 per cent had ever listened to a podcast (Arbitron/Edison Research, p. 40). By 2017, 40 per cent of those surveyed reported listening to a podcast that *month* (Edison Research/Triton Digital 2017: 40). Indeed, the extent to which the shows explain their media identity to an almost-implausibly clueless American and Canadian public generates frequent parody on the shows' Reddit fanforums:

gttlb:	... TBT is easily my favorite podcast right now!
tedsmitts:	A podcast?
Mehmeh111111:	You know, like radio for the internet.
TheEpiquin:	Oh, like radio on demand... (BigBassBone)

Such Reddit jokes, and the exasperation of characters like *TANIS*' Van Sant, highlight that podcasting may have become mainstream to a certain group, identifiable by its relative youth, tech savvy and affluence—but not to the population as a whole. This is suggested in a presentation made by Megan Lazovick of Edison Research, which ostensibly frames podcasting consumption by ethnically diverse consumers interested in a wide variety of podcast content—yet likely from a similar socio-economic background (2017).

By contrast, *Limetown's* host Lia Haddock (Annie Sage-Whitehurst) draws less attention to working in the podcast medium, but she remains a radio journalist in the mould of Sarah Koenig, Ira Glass, and many reporters working in public service broadcasting in the United States. For example, Katie Davis, whose work has appeared on NPR's *All Things Considered, This American Life* and *The Story,* suggests that a certain kind of journalistic, socially conscious reporter emerges as a 'commentator' once his or her sense of self is more deeply invested within a story—a new kind of journalistic identity which stresses the personal and eschews neutrality (2017: 99). This identity describes Haddock, whose investment in her journalistic quest is apparent from the start of *Limetown:* Haddock is a podcast commentator, to use Davis's term. Haddock works for the quasi-fictitious American Public Radio (APR). APR was a Minnesota-based group of stations from which *A Prairie Home Companion* arose in the 1970s, financed by the Radio Fund on a model based on PBS. However, the group changed its name to Public Radio International (PRI), under which it operates today. While the US public service broadcasting tapestry is threaded through with many elements (including American Public Media, NPR, PRI and Public Radio Exchange), public service radio has gained a cachet for trustworthy reporting, usually conflating all PSB radio journalism into NPR and its credibility. As De Mair notes, 'Listeners who associate [*Serial*] with the journalistic endeavours of NPR would be likely to start with the assumption that the narrator is reliable and unbiased' (DeMair 2017: 107), despite the fact that *Serial* and its parent-show *This American Life* emerged from Chicago Public Media and is distributed by PRX, not NPR. PRX began in 2003 'as a means of encouraging and enabling independent producers to place their material on public radio stations' (Mitchell and Sterling 2010: 62). Moreover, PRX bypasses network gatekeepers in a way similar to podcasting (Tolan 2017: 202).

Serial thus emerged from a US PSB environment often conceptualised as monolithic (emanating from NPR) but in fact threaded through with many strands. While Lia Haddock's home network (American Public Radio) does not explicitly connect her with *Serial,* they were perceived as emanating from the same tradition (Framke 2015). Haddock's foray into podcasting with regard to her 'parent' network is somewhat unclear, though the relationship with the network is tied to Haddock's ability to present more 'daring' content in her podcast, content that evidently endangers not only her life but results in others' deaths as well. This prompts formal rebuffs from station management ('Scarecrow'), which Haddock promptly ignores—something that could never be countenanced on real-life PSB. Haddock reinforces that part of her podcast's appeal is her reporting freedom: she is a lone commentator on an offshoot project, taking a story into her own hands.

Nicky Tomalin (Annapurna Sriram), the podcast host of *The Message,* pushes this idea even further from its radio journalism/ *Serial*-prompted roots. Indeed, the diegetic title of Tomalin's podcast is not *The Message* but *CypherCast,* and it is more closely related to fan podcasts than PSB networks (fictitious or otherwise). As a quasi-'revival' of OTR branded sponsorship by the company General Electric, *The Message*'s roots are both with historical radio drama and with *Serial* (Francisco cited in Toonkel 2015; Rogers 2015). There are many layers to Tomalin's character as 'amateur' podcaster, removed from journalistic ethics debates unlike the *Serial* and *TAL* teams (Barnwell 2014). *CypherCast,* in its storyworld, would appear to compete with PSB radio programming/ podcasting of journalistic integrity; Tomalin's integrity is called into question several times, not without justification.

Yet Tomalin's fan podcasting, even without its explicit link to legitimising journalistic frameworks like American Public Radio (Haddock), PNWS (Reagan and Silver, see below), and Chicago Public Media/PRX (Koenig), is tolerated, even encouraged. As the host of a fan podcast for Cypher Center for Communications (a fictitious cryptography consultancy), Tomalin's presence is accepted by the resident cryptographers, who are analysing a mysterious message from space, as part of the documentation process and even as a public relations venture. Cypher Center and General Electric are both for-profit entities using, respectively, *CypherCast* and *The Message* as extensions of their brand; this is a one-upmanship from commercial sponsorship of the OTR era. Tomalin's reporting prowess is an illustration, less of her journalistic integrity, her sterling ability to discover and present stories, than being at the right place in the right time, and yet the fact that she is a podcaster and very much on trend legitimises her presence within a corporate environment, where podcasts are an expected paratext (Geiger Smith 2017).

To conclude this section, the podcasts of the fictitious PNWS network (*TBT, TANIS*) return to a more PSB-based notion of the journalist host. The presentation of PNWS as an NPR (or PRI, or Chicago Public Media)-like network, with real offices and real staff, is an important aspect of these podcasts. The real-life *This American Life* is famously hosted and produced by Ira Glass, who mentored Koenig (a former *TAL* staffer) through *Serial*'s first season. Indeed, during its creation, *Serial* identified itself through its association with *TAL*, as Koenig explains:

> For a lot of the interviews, I was just saying, 'I work for a public radio show called *This American Life*,' because *Serial* didn't exist yet and frankly, until a few weeks before we existed, I wasn't sure it was going to exist! ... And I figured the harder thing to tell people is, 'Look, you might be on the national radio.' I wanted people to be prepared for that versus explaining 'There's this podcast, it [sic] on the internet ... '. (Cited in Raptopoulos 2014)

Serial maintains a pervasive sense of a parent/child relationship between the show's radio roots, and its podcast offspring. Although *Serial* sought throughout to establish its unique, novel podcast identity, it was bound inextricably to the media form which financially and creatively enabled it, both for economic viability and public recognition. *Serial*'s 'debt' to WBEZ Chicago and *This American Life* was acknowledged at each episode's start, and this is aped with *TBT*'s fictitious networks and shows. The PNWS network symbolises WBEZ and PRI, recollecting the institutional-like gravitas engendered by *TAL/Serial*'s parent companies. Tellingly, interviewees in *TBT* and *TANIS* often express enjoyment/recognition of (fictive) PNWS-produced shows. While this extended invention may provide verisimilitude, or character background, it also[6] serves, as in *Serial*, not to undermine the podcast's unique identity, but rather to highlight it as emergent from, but distinct to, 'traditional' radio media.

The relationship between radio and podcast form develops through *TBT*'s real-life mirroring of *Serial*'s in-house podcast production. Like *Serial*'s off-shoot podcast *S Town*, *TBT* produces *TANIS*, and *Rabbits*. This generation of brand identity and network distribution is a key aspect of podcast history, and the method is highlighted and formalised as Reagan names it: '[w]e launched as a podcast. Well, a podcast network, actually' ('Their Satanic Monastery's Request'). In self-identifying not simply as a podcast, but as 'a podcast network', *TBT* gives credence to podcasting's developing media identity. The podcast is no-longer a side project of radio, but a self-regulating and generating media form in its own right. Both 'in-universe' and out, *TBT* and *TANIS* example well *Serial*'s provision of a blueprint by which podcast fiction may eschew radio drama's shadow, and begin to develop a unique audio narrative-form constructed around, and developmental of, its own media identity.

Conclusion

In identifying and investigating *Serial*'s development in podcast fiction, we assert podcasting's claim to a distinct, and rapidly evolving, form of audio-fiction storytelling. The post-*Serial*, we posit, is not just a genre of spin off copycat fictions, but rather an exploratory, and highly fruitful, creative cycle which develops a new form of audio fiction based consciously within the podcast media form. Post-*Serial* represents a crucial evolutionary step in audio fiction. The properties of podcast media are not simply used to deliver narra-tive, but also to shape and inform the storytelling mode itself. Through acts of repetition and appropriation of *Serial*'s structure and acoustic style, we con-tend post-*Serial* fictions have developed a recognisable, unique, podcast form. Through assertion of podcast media's independent, immediate, and on-demand properties, new understandings of podcasting's unique properties of narrative pace, tension and immersion emerge. Furthermore, detailed and prolonged audio-narrative forms which traditional radio-drama seldom allowed also surface. In emulation and extension of *Serial*'s multi-sensory and multi-platformed design, we assert audio-drama for the convergence era has resulted in post-*Serial* fiction. Finally, in their self-reflexive reference and dis-cussion of form, post-*Serial* fictions assert themselves openly to *be* podcast fiction. More than mere extensions of *Serial*'s success then, the post-*Serial* represents the next movement in audio-fiction form.

Notes

1. See Hancock and McMurtry (2017) for a more detailed discussion of fiction podcasting's genealogy.
2. Indeed, it is worth noting that the show's Peabody was awarded on the grounds of its 'innovations of form and its compelling, drilling, account of how guilt, truth and reality are decided' (Peabody Awards 2014).
3. This companionability of the podcast is, for Ulvestam, a key component to its future development: 'We see a future where you can start listening to a podcast on your walk to work, get into your car and have it immediately start playing from where you left off and get home and have your Amazon Echo continue. It'll learn with you and continuously play content that it knows will interest you, in different formats. That's how we'll make podcasts as easy to listen to as radio, and that's why we'll continue to grow.'
4. According to Snyder, the difference in storytelling (and indeed, a different way of relating to Koenig as a character, is due to the fact that 'The structure of the story didn't necessitate it [in series 2], so Sarah is not as much of a character' (cited in Biewen et al. 2017: 82).
5. Similarly, in *Archive 81,* Dan's new boss compares the audio-archive to both NPR, and perhaps *This American Life* more specifically, stating, 'You like NPR, right? They're like these little radio-documentaries, the uplifting ones' ('A Body in a New Place').
6. This technique is not new per se; take, for example, *The Columbia Workshop's War of the Worlds* (1938) whose creation of verisimilitude was second-to-none. The journalist Carl Phillips, played by Frank Readick, represented the CBS network's respected news staff, even if never formally identified as a CBS correspondent. Indeed, CBS's reputation as a respected chronicler of news was only reinforced during World War II and in particular, with the techniques of Edward R. Murrow. It seems only CBS could believably offer a programme where its news team went back in time to cover important events in history, play-by-play, minute-by-minute, sometimes not even surviving as in the Pompeii episode of *You Are There* (1947–50). Now, the new kind of radio journalist voice, transposed to podcasting, is signified by Koenig and her imitators.

Bibliography

Ang, I. (1985). *Watching Dallas: Soap opera and the melodramatic imagination* (trans: Couling, D.). London: Methuen.

Anonymous. (2014). *Serial the highly addictive spinoff podcast of this American life.* www.NBCNews.com [Internet]. Accessed 23 Oct 2017.

Arbitron/Edison Research. (2010). *The infinite dial 2010: Digital platforms and the future of radio*. http://www.edisonresearch.com/the_current_state_of_podcasting_2010/ [Internet]. Accessed 26 Apr 2014.

Arnold, R. (2008). Podcrastination. In E. Wittkower (Ed.), *iPod and philosophy: iCon of an ePoch, D* (pp. 215–228). Illinois: Carus Publishing.

Barnwell, A. (2014). "Unpacking the complexities" of authorship on *This American Life*. *Continuum: Journal of Media and Cultural Studies, 28*, 709–719.

Bell, S. (2013). *Internet saved the radio star*. www.popmatters.com [Internet]. Accessed 30 Apr 2017.

Benedictus, L. (2010). *Don't touch that dial: The threat to radio drama*. www.theguardian.com [Internet]. Accessed 30 Apr 2017.

Bergman, S. (2017). Podcasts were guys talking about tech, then along came *Serial*. *The Guardian*. https://www.theguardian.com/small-business-network/2017/jul/31/acast-founders-podcasts-industry-tech-serial [Internet]. Accessed 23 Oct 2017.

Bernard, S. (2017). *Serial* onstage. www.seattleweekly.com [Internet]. Accessed 24 Oct 2017.

Berry, R. (2015). A golden age of podcasting? Evaluating *Serial* in the context of podcast histories. *Journal of Radio and Audio Media, 22*(2), 170–178.

Biewen, J., et al. (2017). One story, week by week: An interview with Sarah Koenig and Julie Snyder. In J. Biewen & J. Snyder (Eds.), *Reality radio: Telling true stories* (pp. 74–96). Chapel Hill: University of North Carolina Press.

BigBassBone. (2017). Is TBT dead? reddit.com [Internet]. Accessed 30 Apr 2017.

blanktracks. (2017). Comment on aroes '[RABBITS] Episode 101 discussion thread' reddit.com [Internet]. Accessed 30 Oct 2017.

Bull, M. (2007). *Sound moves*. Oxon: Routledge.

Butler, J. G. (2012). *Television: critical methods and applications*. London: Routledge.

Cawelti, J. (2004). *Mystery, violence, and popular culture*. Madison: University of Wisconsin Popular Press.

Chang, D. (2016). *Those creepy and disturbing shoes with severed feet still inside them*. www.podcastenthusiast.com [Internet]. Accessed 22 Feb 2017.

Chirico, K. (2014). *This parody of the "Serial" podcast is so ridiculously on point*. www.buzzfeed.com [Internet]. Accessed 24 Apr 2017.

Chivvis, D. (2014). *A question of binge listening*. www.serialpodcast.org [Internet]. Accessed 30 Apr 2017.

Cipri, N. (2016). *The black tapes podcast*. www.strangehorizons.com [Podcast]. Accessed 22 Feb 2017.

Davis, K. (2017). In J. Biewen & A. Dilworth (Eds.), *'Covering home', reality radio: Telling true stories in sound* (2nd ed., pp. 97–105). Chapel Hill: University of North Carolina Press.

DeMair, J. (2017). Sounds authentic: The acoustic construction of *Serial's* storyworld. In E. McCracke (Ed.), *The serial podcast and storytelling in the digital age* (pp. 75–122). London: Routledge.

Dredge, S. (2014). *Serial podcast breaks iTunes records as it passes 5M downloads and streams*. www.theguardian.com [Internet]. Accessed 30 Apr 2017.

Dubber, A. (2013). *Radio in the digital age.* Cambridge: Pollity.

Edison Research. (2016, May 26). *The podcast consumer 2016.* edisonresearch.com. Accessed 20 Apr 2017.

Edison Research/Triton Digital. (2017). *The infinite dial 2017.* http://www.edisonre-search.com/infinite-dial-2017/ [Internet]. Accessed 3 Aug 2017.

eotvos, comment on FanFare.com. (2016). *Archive 81: Episode 2: A night at an Opera.* https://fanfare.metafilter.com/6606/Archive-81-Episode-2-A-Night-At-An-Opera [Podcast]. Accessed 23 Oct 2017.

Farrar, J. (2016). *Archive 81 and the rise of "soft-horror" podcasting.* wwwDailyDot.com [Internet]. Accessed 23 Oct 2017.

Framke, C. (2015). Limetown, a chilling new podcast, is your paranormal serial replacement. *www.vox.com* [Internet]. Accessed 23 Oct 2017.

Geiger Smith, E. (2017). *Welcome to the podcast. First a world from our celebrity.* www.nytimes.com [Internet]. Accessed 3 Aug 2017.

Glass, I. (2017). Harnessing luck as an industrial process. In J. Biewen & A. Dilworth (Eds.), *Reality radio: Telling true stories in sound* (2nd ed., pp. 64–76). Chapel Hill: University of North Carolina Press.

Grossman, S. (2014). *This Hilarious SNL serial parody is the ultimate Christmas present.* www.time.com [Internet]. Accessed 23 Oct 2017.

Hancock, D. (2016). Welcome to w*elcome to night vale*: First steps in exploring the horror podcast. *Horror Studies Journal, 7*(2), 219–234.

Hancock, D. (2018, Autumn). Our friendly desert town: Alternative podcast culture. In J. Weinstock (Ed.), *Between Weather and the void: Critical approaches to welcome to night vale.*

Hancock, D., & McMurtry, L. (2017). "Cycles upon cycles, stories upon stories": Contemporary audio media and podcast Horror's new frights. *Palgrave Communications, 3,* 17075.

Haugtvedt, E. (2017). The ethics of serialized true crime: Fictionality in *Serial* season one. In E. McCracken (Ed.), *The serial podcast and storytelling in the digital age* (pp. 24–74). London: Routledge.

Hills, M. (2002). *Fan cultures.* London: Routledge.

Hilmes, M. (2013). The new materiality of radio. In J. Loviglio & M. Hilmes (Eds.), *Radio's new wave: Global sound in the digital era* (pp. 43–61). New York: Routledge.

Jaynes, L. (2017). *Thumbnails for radio.* London: The Next Radio Conference.

Jenkins, H. (2006). *Convergence media.* New York: New York University Press.

Larson, S. (2014). *What serial really taught us.* www.newyorker.com [Internet]. Accessed 23 Oct 2017.

Lazovick, M. (2017). *Podcast research.* London: The Next Radio Conference.

Letzler, D. (2017). Narrative levels, theory of mind, and sociopathy in true-crime narrative – Or, how is *Serial* different from your average *dateline* episode? In E. McCracken (Ed.), *The serial podcast and storytelling in the digital age* (pp. 123–169). London: Routledge.

Livingstone, J. (2017). *With S-Town, podcasts come of age.* www.newrepublic.com [Internet]. Accessed 30 Oct 2017.

Locke, C. (2016). *Fiction podcasts are finally a thing! thank you Sci-fi and horror.* www.wired.com [Internet]. Accessed 20 Apr 2017.

Locker, M. (2015). *How Tanis podcast keeps mystery alive in the digital age.* www.theguardian.com [Internet]. Accessed 20 Apr 2017.

Locker, M. (2016). *Serial season two: Why did the must-listen show suffer a sophomore slump?* www.theguardian.com [Internet]. Accessed 20 Apr 2017.

Lombardo, M. (2008). Is the podcast a public sphere institution? In E. Wittkower (Ed.), *iPod and philosophy: iCon of an ePoch* (pp. 215–228). Peru: Carus Publishing.

LPLoRab. (2017). Comment on aroes '[RABBITS] episode 101 discussion thread. reddit.com [Internet]. Accessed 30 Oct 2017.

Manjoo, F. (2015). Podcasting blossoms, but in slow motion. www.nytimes.com [Internet]. Accessed 20 Apr 2017.

Matisse, N. (2014). *Serial*'s transformation of audio journalism is just beginning. www.wired.com [Internet]. Accessed 22 Feb 2017.

McCracken, E. (2017). The *Serial* commodity: Rhetoric, recombination, and indeterminacy in the digital age. In E. McCracken (Ed.), *The serial podcast and storytelling in the digital age* (pp. 170–220). London: Routledge.

McFarland, K. M. (2015). Fiction podcasts are trying too hard to be like *Serial.* www.wired.com [Internet]. Accessed 30 Apr 2017.

McMurtry, L. (2016). "I'm not a real detective, I only play one on radio": *Serial* as the future of audio drama. *Journal of Popular Culture, 49,* 306–324.

Meserko, V. M. (2015). The pursuit of authenticity on Marc Maron's *WTF* podcast. *Continuum: Journal of Media & Cultural Studies, 11*(2), 796–810.

Michel, K. (2017). Adventures in sound. In J. Biewen & A. Dilworth (Eds.), *Reality radio: Telling true stories in sound* (2nd ed., pp. 212–217). Chapel Hill: University of North Carolina Press.

Miller, V. (2011). *Understanding digital culture.* London: Sage.

Mitchell, J., & Sterling, C. H. (2010). Public radio since 1967. In C. H. Sterling, C. H. O'Dell, & M. C. Keith (Eds.), *The concise encyclopedia of American radio* (pp. 615–622). New York: Routledge.

MorboReddits. (2017). Is Serial 2 worth listening to? *Reddit.* https://www.reddit.com/r/podcasts/comments/5w4wcg/is_serial_season_2_worth_listening_to/ [Internet]. Accessed 5 Aug 2017.

NPR/Edison Research. (2017). *The smart audio report.* https://nationalpublicmedia.com/wp-content/uploads/2017/06/The-Smart-Audio-Report-from-NPR-and-Edison-Research-2017.pdf [Internet]. Accessed 24 Oct 2017.

Owen, L. (2015). Serial meets the X-Files in Limetown, a fictional podcast drawing raves after just one episode. Nieman Lab, 28 August 2015. http://www.nieman-lab.org/2015/08/serial-meets-the-x-files-in-limetown-a-fictional-podcast-drawin-graves-after-just-one-episode/. Accessed 30 Oct 2017.

Pacific Northwest Stories. (2015a). www.theblacktapespodcast.com. [podcast].

Pacific Northwest Stories. (2015b). *TANIS.* www.tanispodcast.com [podcast]. Accessed Dec 2016.

Peabody Awards. (2014). Winner 2014 – *Serial*/this American life/Chicago public media. www.thepeabodyawards.com [Internet]. Accessed 30 Oct 2017.

Pnb0804. (2017). Comment on aroes '[RABBITS] episode 101 Discussion Thread. reddit.com [Internet]. Accessed 30 Oct 2017.

Prina, D. (2016). From foundfootage horror movies to foundfootage stories in audio: Listen to (and be scared by) a new project on audio storytelling. www.sound-design.info [Internet]. Accessed 30 Oct 2017.

Raptopoulos, L. (2014). This American life's first spin-off podcast: "I don't know where it will end". www.theguardian.com [Internet]. Accessed 30 Apr 2017.

Rogers, M. (2015). Writing Sci Fi for the stage – And the ears. www.slate.com [Internet]. Accessed 30 Oct 2017.

Salvati, A. (2015). Podcasting the past: Hardcore history, fandom, and DIY histories. *Journal of Radio and Audio Media, 22*(2), 231–239.

Shaw, R. (2016). Vancouver Duo enjoys success with popular *black tapes* and *TANIS* podcasts. www.vancouversun.com [Internet]. Accessed 30 Apr 2017.

Sims, D. (2015). The radio-age genius of the message. www.theatlantic.com [Internet]. Accessed 30 Oct 2017.

Starkey, G. (2004). *Radio in context*. London: Palgrave.

Steuer, E. (2015). Roman Mars: The man who's building a podcasting empire. www.wired.com [Internet]. Accessed 23 Oct 2017.

Stuart, A. (2016). Podcast review: Archive 81. www.gwdbooks.com [Internet]. Accessed 23 Oct 2017.

Tolan, S. (2017). 'The voice and the place', *Reality Radio: Telling True Stories*. In J. Biewen & A. Dilworth (Eds.), *Reality radio: Telling true stories in sound* (2nd ed., pp. 194–203). Chapel Hill: University of North Carolina Press.

Toonkel, J. (2015). General electric producing science fiction podcast series. www.reuters.com [Internet]. Accessed 23 Oct 2017.

Wade, D. (1981). British radio drama since 1960. In J. Drakakis (Ed.), *British radio drama* (pp. 218–244). Cambridge: Cambridge University Press.

Whitman, H. (2016). Why serial season 2 was such a flop. www.ordinary-gentlemen.com [Internet]. Accessed 20 Apr 2017.

Young, M. (2016). *Serial* podcast's creator Julie Snyder talks of the fallout from *Saturday Night Live* parody: "It was shocking". www.News.Com.Au [Internet]. Accessed 23 Oct 2017.

Zurawik, D. (2014). A brilliant byproduct of Sarah Koenig's storytelling in "*Serial*". *Z on TV*. www.baltimoresun.com [Internet]. Accessed 30 Apr 2017.

6

Invisible Evidence: *Serial* and the New Unknowability of Documentary

Rebecca Ora

According to Lyotard, postmodernism might be defined, 'simplifying to the extreme,' as an 'incredulity toward metanarratives (1984: xxiv).' Lyotard's exploration of changes in knowledge and knowability in the contemporary age generated serious consideration of representations of the lived world across media formats, and the ways by which audiences engage with new technological forms. The podcast, despite many formal semblances to the radio show, emerges within a postmodern landscape that arguably places it within a different theoretical framework. This medium is not only a sonic broadcast; the podcast is also an intervention staged within a specific (and obsessive) largely image-based documentary media landscape. The podcast, when viewed within the trajectory of documentary media theory, through eschewing the evidentiary image, can speak wryly to the very thing it is *not,* as well as to larger ideas around knowledge-building, believability and representability. Whereas there are so many possible access-points into the ontology of the podcast, this text is interested specifically in considering the podcast in relationship to trajectories of documentary cinema and its theoretical landscape.

Sarah Koenig and Julie Snyder's *Serial,* an investigative murder whodunnit, speaks to the development of postmodern theories of documentary film whose seeds were planted in the 1990s with the work of Bill Nichols, Michael Renov, Linda Williams and Brian Winston. These conversations, which laid the foundation for what is now known as 'documentary theory,' are concerned

R. Ora (⊠)
University of California, Santa Cruz, CA, USA

© The Author(s) 2018   **107**
D. Llinares et al. (eds.), *Podcasting*, https://doi.org/10.1007/978-3-319-90056-8_6

with the modes and degrees of mediation of the lived world as presented to an audience through aesthetic conventions of authority. *Serial* pushes these conventions to their extremes, thereby testing the capacity of media to engage with new audiences cultivated within a hyperactive and hyperlinked media landscape.

A spinoff of *This American Life, Serial* follows a single story over the course of twelve episodes. In the first season, aired in 2014, creator Sarah Koenig investigates the case of Adnan Syed, a young man serving a life sentence in a Maryland prison after having been found guilty, at age 17, of the murder of his ex-girlfriend, Hae Min Lee. Koenig assumes the role of amateur investigator and attempts, through journalistic interventions, to tell Adnan's story by sorting through the 'facts' of the case. In returning to Lee's 1999 murder, Koenig pulls from the dregs of the twentieth century, posited as a moment of technological and social flux (the murder occurs the same week the primary suspect purchased his first cell phone), examining one of the last plausibly invisible crimes before a generation of teenage amateur cell phone documentarians would emerge. Unlike most traditional documentary that attempts to build toward an argument, rather than to inch toward conclusive proof of guilt or innocence, Koenig breaks down any claims made by her interview subjects and all material evidence and, in the process, questions the very notion of knowability and its representation. She traces the shift, technologically and socially, from the undocumented to the undocumentable.

Serial is, significantly, set in the 1990s, on the cusp of the representational change that sparked renewed conversations around documentary as a category and its relationship to the mysteries surrounding knowing that obsess Koenig's project. At this time, Linda Williams' pivotal 1993 essay 'Mirrors without Memories' discusses 'new' trends in documentary and their indication of a shift in valence regarding truth-telling (Williams 1993). Williams observes a rising tension between earlier 'naive' perceptions of documentary truth and a 'new' postmodern flattening of the image to the point of unbelievability (13). In her words,

> The contradictions are rich: on the one hand the postmodern deluge of images seems to suggest that there can be no a priori truth of the referent to which the image refers; on the other hand, in this same deluge, it is still the moving image that has the power to move audiences to a new appreciation of previously unknown truth (10).

Williams urges her readers to define documentary not as a Manichean dichotomy between 'idealistic faith' and cynicism, but rather a set of strategies from among 'relative and contingent truths' (14). Williams' conception of postmodernism comes through Jameson, who expands on Lyotard by describing the 'cultural logic of postmodernism' as a 'new depthlessness, which finds its prolongation both in contemporary 'theory' and in a whole new culture of the image or the simulacrum,' indicated, in part, by a 'weakening of historicity' (6). Unlike modernist articulations of the world, postmodernism refuses traditional representations through narrative and history and instead subscribes to an inseparability of reality from its cultural representation. Jameson analogises this relationship with the world to schizophrenia, in that 'the schizophrenic is reduced to an experience of pure material signifiers, or, in other words, a series of pure and unrelated presents in time' (27). In postmodernism, there is no reality outside of cultural representation, whose relationship to anything outside of itself is broken down along the chain of signification (34).

According to Williams, these postmodern and post-truth attributes are exemplified by Errol Morris's *The Thin Blue Line*. Morris, whose 1988 film takes on Randall Adams's death sentence for the murder of a Dallas police officer, employs representational strategies that depict visually the litany of conflicting testimonies around the Adams case. Repeatedly, we see scenes of a police officer stopping the driver who will ultimately shoot and kill him, each a different permutation of the same incident. Whereas there is clearly theatricality behind the crispness of Morris's stylised visualisations, his repeated tropes—the seemingly trivial footsteps of the officer, the spilling of the milkshake—give a sense of plausibility that bolster the efficacy behind each enactment (Barthes 1989), while also equalising the Rashomon-like accumulation of versions to the point that all run together as impossibly *equally* plausible. According to Bill Nichols, 'The necessary awareness of a gap between past event and present reenactment remains altogether vivid, as it gradually becomes in *The Thin Blue Line* in which the series of reenactments of the original murder of a policeman constructs an Escher-like impossible space of conflicting narratives' (Nichols 2008: 83).

Morris aesthetically offers the likelihood that, barring incontrovertible evidence, because all versions of the past are equally representable onscreen, all could have occurred with equal plausibility; the resulting world of the film, which is also shared by the documentary viewer, becomes slippery to the point of aporia. This is the ultimate weakening in historicity, and the assertion that there may be no clear path to knowledge. This is, as I will show, also the territory explored by Koenig's *Serial*.

The Thin Blue Line, paradoxically, is lauded as the prime example of a documentary that has materially affected the world both we and its characters inhabit by bringing about justice; the film reopened the case of Randall Adams and resulted in his eventual acquittal. While the film does, as mentioned, stage a series of possible scenarios that cultivate the ambiguity on which Williams bases her argument, it is difficult to contend that Morris does not take a definite stance in the film. It is impossible, too, for the audience to emerge without a single opinion as to what definitively happened on the night in November 1976 when the Dallas police officer was shot. At the film's close, the postmodern crisis Morris has built is toppled by his acquisition of the taped phone conversation in which Harris essentially confesses to the murder of the officer. Since the start of the film, Morris has had the key to the unassailable truth; we have not been flying without a net.

It is important to revisit Morris's film at this moment not only because we have clearly reached a saturation point with copycat re-stagings intercut with interview testimony, but also because we are at a moment parallel to that of the 1990s, when a shift in the perception and representation of truth is taking place; that shift can be 'seen' in *Serial*. Despite the scholarship published around *The Thin Blue Line* insisting upon its embrace of unknowability, the work more aptly being described by Williams is perhaps not *Thin Blue Line*, but rather Koenig's *Serial*. Whereas Morris's intervention is the reopening of a crime whodunnit through the visualised aggregation of possible scenarios, Koenig does him one better by refusing the image altogether, and, ultimately, rebutting all accounts offered. *Serial* contributes to the shattering of 'the grand narratives' of modernity originally instigated by the postmodern non-indexical image without any image at all.

Serial's form and content point at *absences*—of image, of evidence and of truth—and underscores our paradoxical visual dependency alongside the understanding that the image is no longer tied to knowing. This displacement of learning 'the truth' from the centre to the periphery in favour of different types of evidence-gathering with different aims of understanding is a renewal of the indexical panic of the 1990s, when the digitalisation of cinema called into question the relationship of the image to the lived world (and, concurrently, the ability of an image to speak truth), but in more social terms; *Serial* marks a renewal of these tensions within a new media climate, where a shift in widespread availability of documentation and its ubiquitous use for online social media purposes have altered the reception of the visual document. On the one hand, *Serial* is comparable to *The Thin Blue Line* and adds considerably to documentary considerations of truth and believability within postmodernism. On the other hand, *Serial* also divulges changes in the way documentation manifests online and within the podcast format.

Whereas there is certainly a history of documentary sound that has taken up questions of verisimilitude and authority—the emotion behind non-diegetic music, the capacity of sync sound to enhance believability, the slippage between studio and field recordings—the majority of what we hear in *Serial*, like so many podcasts, is actually testimonial account. The trajectory of testimonial authority is intermingled with particular concerns of documentary, as well as the recouping of traumatic history more generally.

Testimony, as it is presented in Morris's work and so much subsequent documentary, is not to be taken at face value and is framed as often having an uneasy relationship to truth. According to Felman and Laub's *Testimony: Crises of Witnessing in Literature, Psychoanalysis and History,* 'the frailty of the witness, the unreliability and even at a certain point the impossibility of bearing witness, had become the decisive aspect of testimony, its power to register and convey the horror of events' (Keenan and Weizman 2012). The very ambiguity of traumatic testimony is, to an extent, one of the markers of believability assigned to 'true' witness testimony. Morris performs this ambiguity of testimony alongside the insertion of concrete (and contradictory) imagery on which the viewer might (problematically) base a decisive narrative.

Even amid this foreknowledge that testimony is fraught or even paradoxical, *Serial* treats testimony, from the onset, with an eye toward further contraverting. The series begins, fittingly, with a sequence of quick interviews with a collection of teenage voices—those likely born around the year of Lee's murder—inquiring where they were and what they were doing on a given day six weeks prior. Keonig narrates:

> I just want to point out something I'd never really thought about before I started working on this story. And that is, it's really hard to account for your time, in a detailed way, I mean. How'd you get to work last Wednesday, for instance? Drive? Walk? Bike? Was it raining? Are you sure?
>
>   Did you go to any stores that day? If so, what did you buy? Who did you talk to? The entire day, name every person you talked to. It's hard. (Koenig 'The Alibi' 2014)

Her nephew responds:

> No. Not at all. I can't remember anything… No. I can't remember anything that far back. I'm pretty sure I was in school. I think—no?
>
>   Not a clue. In school, probably. I would be in school. Actually, I think I worked that day. 'Yeah, I worked that day. And I went to school. That was about it… I don't think I went to school that day…'

Koenig concludes, after this introductory experiment, that 'if nothing significant happened, then the answers get very general. I most likely did this, or I most likely did that. These are words I've heard a lot lately. Here's the case I've been working on' (Koenig 'The Alibi' 2014).

Koenig, before even detailing Adnan's case, attempts to prove the near impossibility of recalling the past. Before a single witness in Adnan's story has spoken, Koenig has already established the deep fallibility of memory, and, therefore, an uneasiness surrounding the attempt to piece together moments from the distant past: 'Now, imagine you have to account for a day that happened six weeks back. Because that's the situation in the story I'm working on in which a bunch of teenagers had to recall a day six weeks earlier…' (Koenig 'The Alibi' 2014).

Just as her nephew cannot recall whether he saw a movie or attended classes or went to work several weeks earlier, the teenagers central to the murder case in question are equally fallible in their statements about a winter day well over a decade prior; if it could be this difficult to recount and describe events a few weeks in the past, how much murkier must the memories of these characters be now, fifteen years later, about events that, at the time, seemed inconsequential.

This treatment of testimony as already flawed is indicative of Koenig's performance of the documentary tradition as only ever ironic. Whereas, according to Williams, it is the role of documentary to reveal 'some kinds of partial and contingent truths' even as an 'always-receding goal' (Williams 1993: 14), *Serial* seeks less to prove its case than it does to disprove all cases. *Serial* performs as a documentary, but, in doing so too knowingly, breaks down the elements of this documentary tradition in the process.

Serial responds to larger questions around possibilities of knowing about the past and about the world through mediated offerings by disputing, in whole or in part, the testimonies of its interview subjects, ultimately settling on no easy ground in its investigation of what happened in Baltimore in 1999. As a sonic medium, *Serial* refuses, all the while, to transfer evidentiary power onto the forensic image/object, another potential site of establishing proof. The 1990s returns, in this conversation, as the immediate aftermath of yet another shift in the presentation and reception of 'proof.' In 1988, Errol Morris's film performed an analogy to the controversy surrounding the unearthing of a set of bones in a mis-marked grave outside Rio de Janiero. According to Eyal Weizman and Thomas Keenan, the location and analysis of Josef Mengele's skull marked the end of the age of testimony epitomised by the trial of Adolf Eichmann, wherein the performance of traumatic repetition took the form of the verbal revisiting of a past trauma, to one in which return to the past takes the form of a forensic object or image (Keenan and Weizman 2012). 1985 marked the end of an 'era of witness' and the beginning of the evidentiary *thing*.

In 'Episode 12: What We Know,' the final instalment of *Serial*, Koenig addresses one of the most glaring problems with Adnan's alibi, which is displaced not only by contradicting testimony but also by cell records—the most substantial focus on forensic evidence in the series. Though Adnan had claimed that Jay, the prosecution's main witness who claims to have helped Adnan bury Lee's body, had Adnan's new cell phone on the day of the murder, a call placed by this phone to Nisha, a friend of Adnan's, who did not know Jay, would attest to Adnan's having the phone. Koenig, in her exhaustive investigations, expert interviews, analyses of cell phone contracts and their use in similar court cases, asks whether an unanswered call of this duration would show up on a phone bill; could this possibly be a butt-dial? Koenig's approach is, again, ironic in that she seeks to prove *not* whether Adnan had the phone, but rather whether it is equally possible that he either had or did not have his phone.

> Koenig:
> But now, I think the Nisha call might be moving from the 'no way around it, this looks bad for Adnan' column into 'eh, now I'm not so sure.' It means the Nisha call could conceivably have been a butt-dial that no one answered. *It means there isn't only one explanation for the Nisha call. There are alternative scenarios.* It could be that Adnan called Nisha, or it could be that Jay was with somebody else who called Nisha, or maybe Jay or someone else called Nisha by accident. A butt-dial and no one was ever the wiser because no one ever picked up. *If there are alternative scenarios, then that means the list of things we know, actually definitively know, facts we can show about the evidence against Adnan, that list just got shorter.* (Koenig 2014, 'Episode 12: What We Know')

After opening further possibilities—disproving the one piece of evidence that would seem to indisputably incriminate Adnan—Koenig performs a series of conclusions that actually, effectively, do the opposite of tying up loose ends. She draws conclusions that decrease, rather than increase, the list of knowable facts.

> She continues:
> If the call log does not back up Jay's story, if the Nisha call is no longer set in stone, then think about it. What have we got for that file? All we're left with is, Jay knew where the car was. That's it. That, all by itself, that is not a story. It's a beginning, but it's not a story. (Koenig 2014, 'Episode 12: What We Know')

Like the testimonies she seeks to disprove, Koenig erodes the theories she herself has attempted to construct, and the very endeavour of this investigative media journalism. Koenig, whose podcast is predicated in large part on testimonial interview, offers the possibility that memory is fallible in the first episode, then later acknowledges that witnesses lie; after exhaustively attempting to recreate the discordant accounts of Adnan and Jay, Koenig offers a previously unconsidered possibility:

> My original question going into this whole endeavor, this whole story, was: either Jay's lying or Adnan's lying. But what if it's not either/or; what if it's *both/ and*? (Koenig 2014, 'Episode 12: What We Know')

The twist in this final instalment, ironically titled 'What We Know', is the unsurprising surprise that '*we don't know*', this imageless experience that has gained so much popularity and traction in an era of the dominance of the recorded image *possibly necessarily* lends itself to an *impossibility* of evidence. Koenig's exercise is not one of building a case, but rather one of tearing down all cases, the breakdown of narrative cohesion, and the opening of a series of gaps in certainty. She has sought to show us *nothing*. Koenig performs the extreme 'flattening' of documentary (Jameson's 'new depthlessness'), disputing the truth-seeking endeavours of so many prior documentary projects.

Koenig takes her doubt to the extreme, offering the possibility that no one, not even the murderer, may know the truth about the case. In 'Episode 11: Rumors,' Koenig explores the potential that not only is the truth unknowable to her and her audience through the attempt to resurrect this case, but, moreover, that *no one* knows the truth, that Adnan is insane, and that he has (in a scenario that builds upon Felman and Laub's writings on the erosion of memory with trauma) possibly forgotten his own involvement in Hae's death altogether. In an interview with Charles Ewing, a forensic psychologist and lawyer, Koenig explores this theory:

Ewing: People can go into what's called a dissociative state where they're really psychologically not where they are physically. Probably half of the people I've evaluated who have killed other human beings have some degree of amnesia for what they've done.

Koenig: Did you say half? Half the people?

Ewing: Yeah.

Koenig: Wow.

Ewing: About half. Yeah. And it's not total amnesia usually, although I've seen some people who have a complete amnesia for killing. But it can be partly, 'I don't really recall the details, I don't recall doing this.'

Koenig: Because literally, like the memory isn't in their brain anymore, or it never was in their brain?… Do you think it's, is there another scenario where it starts out as a lie, a sort of cognizant lie, like, 'I didn't do this, I had nothing to do with this,' and then, over time, you truly believe that lie? Like you kind of erase the fact that you're lying and it just becomes the truth of it for you? (Koenig 2014, 'Episode 11: Rumors')

Koenig offers the explanation that not only is the past unprovable by forensic or image-based evidence, and not only are memory and its testimonial representation faulty, but, moreover, history may be lost to the ether amid psychotic breakdown and loss of time. After a year of research and approximately ten hours of programming, Koenig proposes that her primary subject and the main opposition to his account (and innocence) may both be lying, and asserts the possibility that Adnan, and possibly Jay and/or other characters, may not even know they are doing so. The memory of that day in the winter of 1999 may no longer exist at all, and, as such, may be entirely materially and mentally irretrievable and unrepresentable in image or language.

The Lacanian schizophrenic, according to Jameson, suffers from a 'breakdown of the signifying chain' until 'the schizophrenic is reduced to an experience of pure material signifiers, or, in other words, a series of pure and unrelated presents in time' (Jameson 1992: 27). This lack of coherent timeline resembles Koenig's reconstruction(s) of past events, as well as the inability of its participants to speak of it coherently within the casual interview structure, which leaves in all interstitial 'umm's' and 'like's' and 'hmmm's.' In 'Episode 8: The Deal With Jay,' Koenig presents the interview excerpt that, in her own estimation, articulates perfectly her sentiments around the case.

Koenig introduces the recording of Laura, a high school friend of Adnan's.

Koenig: This piece of tape I'm about to play you, it's my favorite piece of tape from all my reporting so far, because I relate to it so precisely. It could be me talking to Laura, instead of the other way around.

Laura: Well then who the fuck did it, like, why would—it doesn't make sense. Why would—(stuttering) Hae was—I can't—I'm probably just as confused as you are. (Koenig 2014, 'Episode 8: The Deal With Jay')

These losses—of timeline, of memory and of language—are themselves the appropriate articulations of Koenig's impressions of the case and her intentions behind this podcast. What remains, however, after the erosion of objective truth and knowledge, is a style and personal signature that allows for a second consideration of the podcast not only as an extension of documentary theory, but more specifically as a performative mode. This mode, like the crisis of truth in documentary, has roots in the 1990s, but is also deeply embedded within current media and technological landscapes.

In Koenig's first episode, after challenging her collection of teenagers to recall a given Friday's events as a comparison to Adnan's case, she astutely adds, '*and* it was 1999, so they had to do it without the benefit of texts or Facebook or Instagram' (Koenig 2014, 'The Alibi'). From the start, Koenig concedes that this case is a mystery that might be impossible right now, since self-documentation has overtaken the experience of the lived world. One need only mine an Instagram account, a Facebook timeline or a series of Google Calendar invites to piece together one's whereabouts on a given day; the accumulation of social media and phone-camera documentation of a cadre of teenagers would certainly yield a plausible scenario, or at least discount many. *Serial* documents (or, rather, *un*-documents) a lost world on the cusp of becoming our current one.

The 1990s, in *Serial,* is the waning glimmer of a past that has not been accounted for by camera phones, social media, Google Calendars and GPS. The mining of Adnan's case and its retrieval within a 'new' and 'real time' medium (the episodes were each created after the airing of the last, and were materially affected by the prior instalments' broadcast and popularity) is the failed hubris that modern eyes and technologies might unearth that which has been overlooked by the past. The key to this gap between 1999 and the world of social networking in which *Serial* exists is not, however, the answer to the question of who killed Hae Min Lee, or an analysis of the personalities of Adnan and Jay, but rather the ways by which the self is performed and preserved within this new medium. The podcast, in this particular iteration, is a frustrated representational form attempting to give evidence not through on-site sound recording, but, rather, through second- and third-hand testimony that, ultimately, yield the self more than the content of the interview.

In 'Episode 6: The Case Against Adnan Syed,' Koenig and her producer Dana Chivvis attempt to retrace the car route from Woodlawn High School that Adnan claims is impossible within the time allowed by the prosecutor's account. They attempt to drive through the city while narrating their moves.

Koenig: Yeah (laughs) it doesn't make any sense. Plus—it's like trying to—I'm trying to think of an analogy of what the uselessness of what we're trying to do by recreating something that doesn't fit, it's like a—like trying to plot the coordinates of someone's dream or something where it's just like 'but wait! That doesn't—as if we're going to be surprised every single time but it didn't—it doesn't because it's not prop—
Chivvis: I think they call that a fool's errand.

The pair, while discussing the effort to recreate partially remembered moves from fifteen years prior, might also be discussing the process of their documentation within the medium and its arguable futility. On the one hand, we have no reason not to take Koenig and Chivvis at their word; on the other, hearing their pratfalls and frustrations in attempting to retrace Adnan's speculative steps is a less than satisfying form of proof around what might have occurred in Baltimore a decade and a half ago. Indeed, the experience being documented is less comprised of the events of the past—the murder, the trial, Adnan's incarceration—so much as it is Koenig's encounters with these characters and with their statements. Despite the exhaustive research conducted through interviews, the primary testimonial subject in *Serial* is Koenig herself.

Serial, like so many podcasts (as well as documentaries such as Morris's), takes the form of the *discussion* of ideas or events rather than the documentation of the events themselves. While, in the effort to explore the podcast as a form of documentation, I might have culled from a history of sound in documentary, the podcast, particularly as typified by *Serial*, relies heavily on testimony rather than on-site sound, and is overtly a second-hand accounting. *Serial* has very few *verité* moments, and emphasises voice over other types of sound.

In a series of follow-up instalments covering hearings debating the reopening of Adnan's case, Sarah Koenig discusses that day's court proceedings with her producer from within a hastily-soundproofed closet in her hotel room. Whereas the subject of conversation is Adnan and the evidence presented in court, the most vivid descriptions, and the space that is represented sonically during the podcast is the closet where Koenig is flanked by insulating animal-print bathrobes. Indeed, throughout the series, the voice heard physically and metaphorically is Koenig's, and the experience documented is hers—not Adnan's and certainly not Hae's.

As a document formed within the digital internet milieu, *Serial* partakes in the 'selfie' culture of documenting not so much a place or an event, but rather an accumulation of personal responses to an event sourced from the 1990s. Bill Nichols, whose work favours ontological approaches to documentary modes, parses some of these types in his *Introduction to Documentary*. According to Nichols, there are six possible documentary modes: the poetic, the expository, the observational, the participatory, the reflexive and the performative (Nichols 2001: 33–34).

The Performative Mode, in his words, 'emphasizes the subjective or expressive aspect of the filmmaker's own engagement with the subject and an audience's responsiveness to this engagement. (It) rejects notions of objectivity in favour of evocation and affect' (Nichols 2001: 33–34). Williams, likewise, defines the performative as a rise in prominence in the overt and avowed presence and perspective of the documentarian and/or her persona:

> Coincident with the hunger for documentary truth is the clear sense that this truth is subject to manipulation and construction by docu-auteurs who, whether on camera (Lanzmann in *Shoah*, Michael Moore in *Roger and Me*) or behind, are forcefully calling the shots... the documentarian's role in constructing and staging these competing narratives thus becomes paramount. In place of the self-obscuring voyeur of verité realism, we encounter, in these and other films, a new presence in the persona of the documentarian. (Williams 1993: 12)

Serial, as a podcast, might be viewed as a commentary not only on documentary's search for truth, but also of this performative mode that admits to truth's fungibility as well as its subjectivity. Williams discusses the interrelationship of filmmaker persona and truth in Morris's case; he withholds evidence from the audience in order to construct a tense plot, revealing only at the end of the film that he knows who the actual killer is. According to Williams, 'what Morris does, in effect, is partially close down the representation of Adams' own story, the accumulation of narratives from his past, in order to show how convenient a scapegoat he was to the overdetermining pasts of all the other false witnesses' (Williams 1993: 13). Morris's hand is palpable throughout the film, in his reconstructions and his consciously doled-out facts, and ultimately as the saviour of his falsely-accused subject. Sarah Koenig's role is far more visible in that her voice is so prominent, but also in the analogous orchestration of what knowledge is imparted and when. Koenig, unlike Morris, does not hold any key to understanding, any 'aha!' moment at the work's culmination. Whereas Morris concludes his investigation with a clear path to knowledge, Koenig gives us only her confusion.

What we *are* given, in ample amounts, is a narrative always inseparable from the self and one's impression of it. *Serial* is, ultimately, a series of conversations, after-the-fact or from a bird's-eye-view, of the lived world through a specific and highly personal vantage. The podcast, if viewed through this lens, might be the sonic analogue of the selfie; it is a portrait of the world as always inseparable from the self and one's impression of it. The podcast is only ever a second-hand document, a collection of impressions and overtly curated discussion *of* __, just as the setting or context of a selfie—the social environment, the location—will never, in the image, exist apart from the subject's reaction.

The podcast, so often a second-hand narrative embedded firmly in personal voice, can be a probing and interrogative medium that happens to be frank about its imbrication within the personal experience, rather than to be summarised as narcissistic portraiture. In this instance, Koenig's is the dominant voice and the guiding persona for our entree into the world of *Serial.* Her doubt is transferred to the audience, and becomes *our* doubt, just as every selfie-mediated scene is filtered through the expression of the person facing the camera; this is the tone by which we should experience this material. Like Jameson's schizophrenic, who lacks a personal identity as differentiated from any outside world, Koenig's persona is inseparable from all other elements within this audio-selfie format. Just as the selfie background is only ever presented through the presence of 'me,' *Serial's*[1] worlding revolves around Koenig, her voice, and her crises of knowing.

While so many sat glued to their iPhones, at the edge of their seats, listening to what they would (or wouldn't) learn next, the public, by and large, received *Serial* with great dissatisfaction. People were not sated by this postmodern unknowing. Koenig's confusion, consequently, opened the door for the participation of so many audiences to engage, as amateurs, either through asserting opinions or even physically seeking answers. Many, despite Koenig's insistence otherwise, *did* form a single theory around Adnan Syed's guilt, stuck with it, and went out into the world attempting to prove this as the 'right' truth. And they blogged about it. The internet was set afire with home-detective work from desktops and beyond. 'Characters' were stalked, parking lots were photographed, schools were scouted out.

Whereas this participatory phenomenon may seem to counter claims that this unknowability is endemic of current media forms—that the thirst for knowledge is, above all else, still of primary concern—the ways by which this engagement occurred, as though 'real people' were mere characters in a teleplay, indicates more readily the inseparability of the lived and represented world. Jay, whose testimony was most antagonistic to Adnan's claims to innocence, found strangers wandering around searching for 'clues' on his lawn, and had his personal photographs and contact information made public online. The internet was set ablaze with professional and amateur assessments of the information from the podcast and its attendant website, each attempting to put forth a narrative no one had yet realised. Engagement with the material, as such, constituted less a concern for truth and justice than an effort to reframe Koneig's world as one's own; like 'reaction videos' populating YouTube around trending memes, the way to 'properly' respond to *Serial* is to offer one's own selfie to the mix.

This interactivity is critical to the podcast format as a live medium and as a transparently replicable format. The assertion of the self is possible only through self-performance enacted through absorption by media. These are impressionistic art-forms, structurally disinterested in standing alone as 'objective' documents. Perhaps, then, 'truth' is less an achievable goal in this equation than is believability, and how what we want to believe tells a story about who we are.

To add a third moment to this timeline, which has so far dealt with the connective tissue between the 1990s and 2014. I would like to submit 2016–2017 as a moment of particular scepticism toward images, information, and evidence. Whereas a version of this paper was presented at the Visible Evidence XXII conference in Toronto in August 2015, in that read of Koenig's project, I *did* try to use *Serial* to usher in the new era of unknowability, and to discuss our transcendence of any notion of truth as a noun (singular), compared to which this initial shift in documentary practice marked by Morris's film pales. This was the paper I initially wanted to write. 2018, however, is not 2015.

Incredulity, while central to a savvy and informed audience capable of pulling apart ideology from knowledge, has run rampant. Whereas I have, for so long and like so many other scholars and documentary practitioners, advocated for an expansive use of the documentary image and a sceptical reception of images claiming to speak the truth, the evacuation of all value systems by which to distinguish among possibilities—rendering all theories equally plausible—has led us to Fake News. In Fake News, all ideas are equally plausible and equally preposterous; all political candidates are equally damaging; and all actions are equally useless in response. This neologism is the political arm of the cultivation of unknowability performed partially by Morris, extremely by Koenig, and dangerously by political powers.

Alex Juhasz, one practitioner and theorist of wry media, describes media fakery as 'a powerful tool for self-aware estrangement, "good-humored cheek," or critical distance and (post)modernist attention to form' (Juhasz 2016). Writing recently, she, too, places Fake News on the spectrum of experimental forms that have sought to break down media's watertight, authoritative role. Fake News is both the insertion of 'alternative facts' into the contexts normally reserved for truth-telling, as well as the blanket accusation, based on scepticism both founded and unfounded, of all media as peddling fakery. Practitioners like Juhasz whose work lies between airtight authority and savvy or ironic use of documentary media, while hoping to build a healthy scepticism of those wielding the mainstream image with agenda, have helped to teach incredulity to their audiences. Neologisms such as 'docufiction,' 'mockumentary' and 'mock-doc' describe entire sub-sets dedicated to questioning the sobriety of documentary and the reliability of visual and testimonial claims as presented through media. Koenig, whose work relishes the impossibility of certainty (she never once, in the course of the podcast or its follow-up instalments, claims her main character's innocence—or guilt), is another member of this increasingly sceptical relationship to media. Through its confusion of stymied knowledge-seeking, *Serial* teaches the possibility that words, images, and objects may all be equally, and dangerously, evacuated of meaning.

Jameson, whom I have generously used, wrote about postmodernism within the context of capitalism; Fake News is the extension of postmodern depthlessness and doubt that most obviously, at the moment of my writing, cultivates political confusion and paralysis. Whereas *Serial*'s audience 'participants' are seemingly active, their conspiracy-theory speculation and treatment of the lived world as spectacle (and of spectacle as reality) make these less gestures of activism so much as they are pastiche, re-performance, and self-presentation. The fact that, fifteen years ago, a young woman was evidently brutally murdered and disposed of has taken a backseat to widespread interest in participating in public zeitgeist and the search for a new and exciting story.

Recently, Adnan Syed's case has been reopened, and, due in large part to the doubt 'proven' by Koenig—the only certainty she maintains is doubt itself, which, in juridical terms, is sufficient—he will face a new trial, over fifteen years later. Maybe *Serial* is, in the end, intended as an activation of the audience and as a renewed search for justice. Perhaps, as an audience, we are intended to react against the flattening of information as equally plausible or implausible. Perhaps we should be frustrated by the possibility that no one may be held responsible for a woman's murder because facts are seldom indisputable. In postmodernism, we can only ever come to truths wryly; perhaps Koenig's irony runs deep, to the point that she proves, through performances of unknowing, our vestigial and reactionary lust for the truth.

Note

1. When *Saturday Night Live* parodied *Serial*, it chose not to take on the case of Adnan Syed and the subject matter of the series, but rather Koenig's style and tone, as its comedic fodder. Even as interest in the case at hand was certainly at the forefront of audience interest and reception of the series, Koenig's persona, her profound introductions and interactions with 'facts' and opinions, were the emblems of this podcast that would read most clearly to an audience. The resulting sketch, a giggle-worthy Christmas mystery ('I interviewed Chris, a thousand-year-old toymaker who lives up north…'), mimics Koenig's approach without any mention of Adnan's case. Whether we were aware or not, Koenig was the main character in this series.

Bibliography

Barthes, R. (1989). The effect of reality. *The Rustle of Language* (trans: Howard, R.). Berkeley: University of California Press.

Jameson, F. (1992). *Postmodernism, or, the cultural logic of late capitalism*. Durham: Duke University Press.

Juhasz, A. (2016). *Four hard truths about fake news*. www.daily.jstor.org, [Internet]. Accessed 2017.

Keenan, T., & Weizman, E. (2012). *Mengele's skull: The advent of a forensic aesthetics*. Berlin: Sternberg Press.

Koenig, S. (2014). Serial. www.serialpodcast.org [Podcast]. Episode 1: 'The Alibi', Accessed 20 May 2017. Episode 5: 'Route Talk', Accessed 20 May 2017. Episode 6: 'The Case Against Adnan Syed', Accessed 20 May 2017. Episode 8: 'The Deal With Jay', Accessed 20 May 2017. Episode 11: 'Rumors', Accessed 20 May 2017. Episode 12: 'What We Know', Accessed 20 May 2017.

Koenig, S. (2016). Serial. www.serialpodcast.org [Podcast]. '*Adnan Syed's Hearing: Day 1*'. Accessed 20 May 2017.

Lyotard, J. F. (1984). *The postmodern condition: A report on knowledge*. Minneapolis: University of Minnesota Press.

Morris, E. (1988). *The Thin Blue Line* [Film]. American Playhouse.

Nichols, B. (2001). *Introduction to documentary*. Bloomington: Indiana University Press.

Nichols, B. (2008). Documentary reenactment and the Fantasmatic subject. *Critical Inquiry, 35*, 72–89.

Williams, L. (1993). Mirrors without memories: Truth, history, and the new documentary. *Film Quarterly, 46*, 9–21.

7

Podcasting as Liminal Praxis: Aural Mediation, Sound Writing and Identity

Dario Llinares

> You realise a world in which the principle mode of communication is oral is a very different kind of world in which the principle form of communication is written. It's something I hadn't thought about until I did a podcast. (Malcolm Gladwell)

The above quote from Malcolm Gladwell (*Longform*, 3 August 2016), about the writer's first venture into podcasting—a series entitled *Revisionist History*—encapsulates a philosophical interrogation and self-examination that emerges from working within this still relatively new sound medium. The question of what is the principle mode of communication in today's media-saturated world is itself a debateable one. However, I doubt whether sound would trump text or image in anyone's hierarchy of importance. Yet Gladwell is one of an increasing number of writers, artists, film-makers, critics and academics who have turned their hand to podcasting as an adjunct, subsidiary or development of their primary area of expertise. Such moves are perhaps a result of the desire to accrue economic, cultural or social capital, by diversifying into a medium that is arguably going through a 'golden age' (Berry 2015; Ganesh 2016), but which retains an edgy, alternative aura. Yet, when listening to the experiences of podcasters discussing the form, a sense of self-reflection around the processes and effects of mediation is often apparent. Gladwell, being a journalist and non-fiction writer, is interested in the relationship, or disparity,

D. Llinares (✉)
School of Media, University of Brighton, Brighton, UK
e-mail: d.llinares@brighton.ac.uk

© The Author(s) 2018
D. Llinares et al. (eds.), *Podcasting*, https://doi.org/10.1007/978-3-319-90056-8_7

123

between oral and written communication. He ruminates on how the form of communication one uses is inherent to the production and ontology of knowledge therein and, later in the interview, points to the ways in which podcasting even revealed his own shortcomings as a writer.

Gladwell is not alone in suggesting that podcasting engenders a process of self-reflection. Engagement in the diverse range practices required in the production of podcasting, and an attendant effect of critical (self)interrogation as a mediated subject, is a phenomenon that I have experienced in my own venture into the medium. *The Cinematologists* podcast emerged from the fundamental pleasure of discussing film with my colleague Dr Neil Fox, along with various other related subjects: the rigid strictures of academic production and dissemination, the mill of research and publication, the possibilities and pitfalls of the internet as a space for debate, and the transformational effect of the digital age on all aspects of cinema. Both Neil and myself had also become avid podcast listeners, sensing that some of the most articulate, insightful and relevant conversation was taking place in this independent and idiosyncratic audio space. In developing the format for *The Cinematologists*— recorded in a live venue, around a specific film screening, with audience debate the central component—we attempted to explore and utilise the characteristics of an audio medium to capture the sensibility of the cinema-going experience, and the enjoyment of discussing a film after you have watched it.

Becoming a podcaster has meant I have learned a range of technical skills – sound production and editing, online distribution, social media marketing and audio presentation—which, beyond their instrumental value, have provoked a reexamination in my own mind as to the relationship between the architecture of mediation and the ontology of knowledge. Furthermore, my experience of podcasting has also fostered a spirit of community, a forum for reasoned and informed debate, and even a space and time for academic discourse that is arguably becoming more marginalised in the university itself. An amalgamation of creative audio experimentation with the fundamental spirit of intellectual curiosity and the idealised aspects of the internet's communicative potential, I have also found hugely satisfying through podcasting. This experience I conceive of as a kind of positive destabilisation; an exciting and potentially revelatory disruption of the boundaries that tie disciplines and fields of inquiry to specific forms of expression and institutional norms. In this sense, I have come to think of podcasting as a 'liminal praxis': a mediatory practice that emerges out of an idiosyncratic yet fluid set of technological, economic, creative, social and disciplinary conditions, and which, concomitantly, imbues a questioning of the logics and effects of mediation itself.

Drawing upon the self-reflexive discourse of podcasters (including myself) who have come to this sound medium from other disciplines—using interviews on published podcasts and my own recorded interviews—this chapter is an exploration of mediated communication of knowledge and identity through podcasting. I begin by anchoring podcasting within the concept of liminal praxis, schematising the interrelationship between technological, industrial, socio-cultural and aesthetic parameters which has facilitated a unique, and perhaps contingent, creative context for podcasting to emerge. Subsequently, I explore the relationship between written and sound communication, arguing that the oral and aural mechanics of the podcast offer a potential disruption to logocentric biases in knowledge creation and dissemination. This leads on to an analysis of the parameters of autonomy and self-articulation experienced by podcasters through their sonic practices of being and doing. I argue that podcasting thus offers freedoms from disciplinary regimes and traditions, and from sanctioned modes of communication and knowledge production. This leads to the counter-intuitive assertion that podcasting provides a mechanism by which producer/consumers use the medium to define and enact their own agency within the highly fractured subjectivity of the internet age.

Sound Mediation Praxis in Context

Despite the inception of podcasting being back in the mid-2000s there are still questions as to its definition and identity as a discreet media form (Bottomley 2015). The most obvious ambiguity derives from easily made, yet problematic, correlations with radio regarding infrastructure of production, forms of sound content creation, and practices of listening (See Berry 2006 and Chapter 1 of this volume). Understanding podcasting as distinct from radio initially lies in the technological and distributive shift from the broadcast signal to the digital dissemination of individual audio files situated on an internet host site and sent out to podcast-catcher software such as iTunes or PlayerFM.[1] Yet, Nele Heise (2016: 1) drawing on work of Markman and Sawyer (2014), highlights the complexity of defining podcasting beyond its 'technological features (RSS-based distribution and subscription, downloadable audio files), because it can be understood "as both a simple distribution channel for existing content and an emerging programming vehicle", as well as "a new or hybrid media form that is accessible to amateurs as well as to media professionals (2014: 21)"'. The medium is often utilised as a secondary platform whose technological specificity allows the transference of content produced through established media forms and institutions. Yet simultaneously, that technology has also forged new creative possibilities of production, distribution and exhibition which, in turn, has given rise to an independent cadre of producer/consumers who have arguably forged a new sound media culture. The 'hybridity' mentioned above, echoed by Middleton's (2013) characterisation as 'a flexible medium', reflects an ontology of podcasts and podcasting which sits at the nexus of production and consumption technologies, practices and identities. Through the concept of liminal praxis I offer a development of this tradjectory of analysis in conceptualising the being and doing of podcasting.

Praxis is a salient term (which has a philosophical history that is beyond the scope of this article) in that it posits how knowledge is realised through the experience of practice. As Cowley outlines, tracing back to Aristotle, praxis is a move to overcome the fissure between mind/body, theory/practice dualisms that created a fundamental hierarchy where: 'any form of practical activity is seen as "base", and is carried out by the "average man", while sublime theoretical life becomes confined to the elite, resulting in a general depoliticization of the "average" people as they concern themselves with practical activity and everyday needs' (2008). The echoes of this fissure still reverberate through the history and philosophy of Western thought. Hierarchical distinctions between theory and practice are at the heart of the stuctural organisation of the academe and, in turn, society at all levels—think of the perceptions of status difference between theoretical and vocational knowledge in higher education. However, Cowley discusses the deployment of praxis by Hegel, Marx, Nietzsche and Sartre as a productive dialectic that synthesises theory and practice as the very underpinning of the ontology of knowledge. This approach to praxis has been adopted in pedagogic research with the work of Paulo Freire (1970) being particularly influential in advocating for the primacy of lived experience; with knowledge formulated through reciprocal dialogue between equal subjects rather than a top down hierarchy of teacher/student. The emergence of digital media technologies has of course had wide-ranging implications with regards to how knowledge is conceived, created and communicated, forging new possibilities of synthesis between theory and practice. Podcasting's specific technological structure, its essential interconnection with the transformative applications of the internet, has created new audio practices and experiences that can and should be understood instrumentally, artistically and socio-culturally. Underpinning this is the medium's liminality—its ontology of inbetweenness—facilitating a praxis in which podcasters are challenging boundaries and conventional approaches to mediation.

At the centre of the correlation between podcasting's technological function and its mediatory effects is Apple's iTunes. The default home for capture and dissemination since Steve Jobs first announced podcast integration with iTunes 4.9 in 2005,[2] its ubiquity and dominance as podcasting's foundational architecture is undeniable.[3] However, long-standing gripes with Apple's commitment to podcasting are manifold: lack of digital infrastructure development, uncertainty around download and subscription metrics, erroneous methods by which podcast charts are measured, and Apple's overarching reputation for clandestine decision-making, to name but a few.[4] Yet the specific parameters of the iTunes framework, which makes it free for anyone to upload their audio content, doesn't allow producers to charge, and has no embedded hierarchy to distinguish between institutional and independent production, has, perhaps accidentally, facilitated an environment in which a specific, even unique, creative culture has emerged.

Podcasting as liminal praxis intuitively lends itself to being contextualised in terms of Jenkins's (2006) theoretical lineage of convergence culture, transmedia storytelling and the dynamics between so-called 'old' and 'new' media. The notion of convergence is, as Matt Hills suggests, concerned with multi-platforming: 'where media texts and audiences perhaps start to move almost seamlessly across different platforms such as television, online on-demand radio, podcasts, user-generated content, digital video, and so on' (Hills 2011: 107). Convergence culture certainly buttresses the assertion that podcasting is 'just another distribution channel' offering consumers access points to content that is increasingly produced with such mobility in mind. There are many examples of podcasts that are explicitly designed around such practice—such as *Welcome to Nightvale* or *Blood Culture*—however they are not by any means, the dominant mode of output. Convergence asserts a reduced importance of platform specificity instead privileging the homogenous notion of content, where audiences engage in what de Certeau (1988) calls nomadic media consumption.

The RSS syndication method has given the listener control and with the arrival of the iPod, followed by the cultural ubiquity of the smartphone, audiences possess even greater autonomy with regards to choice, time, location, length and frequency of engagement. For McElearney and Middleton:

> podcasting can be thought of as time and location neutral due to the asynchronous nature of the downloaded media involved and the way it can be distributed to multiple devices, whether fixed, mobile, connected or stand-alone; hence the use of terms such as 'time shifting' (Donnelly and Berge 2006) and 'space shifting' (Meng 2005, 2013: 24)

Mobility, in a temporal and spatial sense, puts the onus on the listener, whose jurisdiction over the when, where and how of podcast engagement, on the one hand suggests a highly liberated, even democratised consumer experience, but on the other hand, is indicative of the atomisation of the audience in the digital age. The abundance and availability of content, increasingly niche sensibilities and a saturated media landscape, creates an intense battle for audiences who have limited attention yet almost unlimited choice (Webster 2014). A central preoccupation of producers, the who, when, where, why and how of the atomised audience, is often articulated as the key problem of digital production. Journalist Anna Sale discussing her show *Sex, Death and Money*, highlights how podcasting is beholden to the labour of choice:

> I love podcasting because when I started this show the thing that gave me terror was, you're not gonna just run into my show. Every time someone listens to the show they are going to have to make the choice to press play, so every episode has to be an argument in favour of them pressing play. (*The Ezra Klein Show*, 9 May 2017)

Sale's comments here, and later in the interview, reiterate the assumption around podcasting's subordinate relationship to radio, in terms of the broadcast infrastructure distribution, economic viability and historical dominance. Yet her awareness of the choice that is afforded to the podcast listener, the very labour implicit in selecting and consuming from an expansive range of possibilities, she suggests, adds value to the content that is selected for consumption. In a choice economy, infrastructure, marketing and distribution are all important factors, as they always were, in getting a media product out there and noticed. But consumer-led demand means that for every podcast, or series, that wants to grow an audience, the interest and quality of the content (however you might define that) has to stand for itself.

The idiosyncrasies of iTunes, along with the extensive possibilities of listening and sharing offered by smartphone software applications, which have amplified fundamental listener mobility and autonomy (Morris and Patterson 2015), are the basis of further formal and cultural outcomes that have shaped podcasting as a form. Principal among these is a dilution of distinctions, or more accurately, a levelling of distribution accessibility, between what Millette (2011) distinguishes as 'independent' and 'institutional' podcasting. The democratizing potential of digital media was one of the central utopian claims for the internet. As with other strands of digital creativity, podcasting's independent sector has undoubtedly grown due to the relative cheapness and ease of use regarding hardware and software for sound recording, editing and online housing. Millette, in her research on Montreal's independent podcast community argues the podcasting has a 'subcultural logic' that demarcates it from the institutional and production structures of radio and argues that 'independent' rather than 'amateur' should be used because of the considerably 'advanced communicational and technical expertise' demonstrated by practitioners (2011: 5). Liminal praxis is therefore intertwined with podcasters self-conception of being independently able to control their mediation, in terms of podcasting production skills and the autonomy of content, but in a context which offers a sense of status and even power.

The iTunes platform is again central in helping to create the sense that small producers can compete alongside major brands, if not on a totally level playing field, at least on a fairer footing. As podcaster and academic Lance Dann states, 'At the moment actually we do still have a delicious situation where you can have very established highly funded programming appearing and charting alongside stuff done from people's back rooms' (Interview 5 May 2017a). For independent podcasters, this sense of an anarchistic frontier in which the distribution possibilities present a demarcation from, but equality with, the mainstream, even if this is somewhat illusory, is one of the attractions of podcasting. Perhaps in this regard podcasting is not so far from blogging, YouTube, social media, and elements of internet-facilitated creativity, which amalgamate production, distribution and exhibition, bypass institutionally enforced censorship, and perhaps even point towards the promise of an effective public sphere. However, from my own experience, and from talking and listening to other podcasters, the specific possibilities that podcasting presents in terms of independent practice through audio has forged a creative and cultural uniqueness.

The discourses imbued through independent podcasting thus often reflect a sense of earnestness, serious vocation, community and even high-brow idealism. For journalist Michelle Dean, writing in *The New Republic,* this attitude permeates not only production but is also indicative of the podcast audience:

> Even though podcasts share no particular style and very few conventions, a sense of high purpose lingers around them. Podcast listening carries with it a faint aura of cultural snobbery, a notion that to cue up an episode is to do something highbrow and personally enriching, whether it's a history lecture broadcast from a university, or an amateur talk show recorded in someone's garage. (28 March 2017)

Apple's lack of development of the podcasting infrastructure may be primarily technological, but crucially, it is also economic. iTunes remains to this day set up as a system without any direct facility for monetisation. An independent podcasting ethos has therefore developed through individuals and organisations built out of a passion and love of creating audio content. Dean rightly goes onto suggest that the 'essence' of podcasting is 'esoteric' and 'specialised', a form perfectly suited to the niche individualism of the internet age. Without doubt the levels of obsessive detail and depth can push podcasting towards the worst excesses of pretentiousness, self-indulgence and navel-gazing. Yet this milieu also produces some of the most imaginative, distinctive and relevant 'media content' (for want of a better phrase).

Clearly the very nature of 'independence' is itself contestable in terms of how it is understood and enacted by podcasters, and whether audiences demarcate their listening choice according to independent v mainstream is questionable. However, podcasting's shift into mainstream consciousness is partly caused by its adoption as a secondary platform; another avenue for diversifying commercial potential of already existing content. Perhaps, producers' rejection of the charge that podcasting is just a 'channel' is the clearest demarcation between independent and institutional sensibilities. Psychologist, academic and early adopter of podcasting Dave Brodbeck is vociferous in his independent ethos:

> I am proudly independent about it. This is my hobby. I don't do this for money. A bunch of us, in fact, have a facebook group mostly we are Canadian and it's confined to people who are indie people who are not trying to make money… Bob Goyetche[5] one day at conference called *Podcasters Without Borders* was asked about monetising and he said: "it's like asking me how I'd monetise fishing". This is my hobby. This is fun for me. (Interview 27 April 27, 2017)

Despite this allusion to an anti-commercial purity, as with many other aspects of internet content production, many independent podcasters are fervently looking for ways to monetise either through advertising, membership, sponsorship and patronage. One cannot deny the relationship between 'independent' and 'institutional' podcasting is not as clear cut as 'purists' might claim or desire. Indeed, now that the medium is reaching higher levels of mainstream cross-over the issues that create traditional media hierarchies are increasingly influential. Despite the freedom of creativity afforded by the relative cheapness and ease of use of recording equipment and editing software, the potential global distribution platform the internet provides, and the dynamics of social media as a marketing tool, the power of corporate organisation, production values and 'star' name recognition are becoming increasingly significant in the supposedly cult world of the podcast. If iTunes is supplanted (or reconfigured) as the default distribution platform for podcasting one can imagine that a more explicitly economic infrastructure could fundamentally change how we see the impact and role of podcasts in the media landscape.

The dynamics of podcasting as liminal praxis, although perhaps not explicitly named as such, are explored in myriad ways throughout this book. In the remainder of this chapter I discuss how the fundamental element of sound is central to how podcasters reconceive of the relationship between thought and communication. This may seem like a blaringly obvious statement however it is fascinating to listen to podcasters, especially those who have come to the medium from using writing as their primary form of expression, ruminate in a philosophical way about how podcasting opened up new understandings around how the form of mediation absolutely shapes the meaning and effect of the content. Of course, it is possible to argue that most audio formats are in some way based on a structural blueprint laid down in the written word. Audio-books and radio plays are obvious examples and many podcasts are scripted to one degree on another. Interestingly, we have reached a point where certain podcasts are being turned into books: Marc Maron has recently released a book based on his seminal *WFT* podcast entitled *Waiting for the Punch* (2017), *The Smartest Book in the World* (2015) is based on comedian Greg Proops' irreverent podcast *The Smartest Man in the World*, and a book based on the hugely successful *Philosophy Bites* podcast, produced by David Edmonds and Nigel Warburton, is a selection of transcribed interviews with leading philosophers. This could be read simply as another avenue of monetisation, indicative of podcasting's increasing cross-over into mainstream sensibility or, as I postulate now, as suggestive of a shifting interrelationship between sound and writing in the context of digital media communication.

Sound Communication and the Conditionality of Meaning

In his interview on *Longform*, Malcolm Gladwell reveals his anxieties about podcasting and the unforeseen outcomes of moving from the textual to the sound medium:

> I also had all these misapprehensions in the beginning cos I thought that it was just writing articles and saying them because these episodes are scripted... I sort of realised halfway through the process that it's actually a different kind of storytelling. And that's when I got really excited because I feel like I had discovered this thing that I hadn't known which is that when you're dealing in sound there's all kinds of things you can't do but there's all kinds of things you can do... The

kind of emotions you can evoke are so much more powerful... I'm limited as a writer as I'm not good at eliciting strong emotional responses. (3 August 2016)

Gladwell's allusions to the storytelling distinctions between written and oral communication are a discovery that transmedia practitioners, or those working specifically with sound, know well. Yet his realisation concerning the aural 'materialisation' of the written word goes further, provoking the question of how the form of communication actually shapes meaning. Gladwell points out that even though his podcast is scripted – which of course implies the root of knowledge production as textual—articulation through sound evokes an emotionality that would not be produced if one was simply reading the words on a page. Implicit in Gladwell's comment is the effect that sound has in vivificating his own brand of non-fiction writing, which is heavily reliant on scientific research, statistical analysis, and arguably aspires to objective truth.

One might suggest that through podcasting Gladwell is encountering the contours of an ancient question with regards to language communication and the relationship between speech (oral) and writing (textual). Plato's critique of writing, or more specifically the use of written text as a basis for knowledge production and the process of learning, is implicit in what he calls 'stasis': a text's deadness or stillness. As John H. Fritz points out the Socratic contention is that writing cannot stand in for the activation of memory, or the rhetorical articulation of argument, that is produced by orated knowledge. Furthermore, the stasis of the written text precludes the possibility of dialectical challenge or subsequent synthesis, and thus any knowledge imparted depends on what may be the narrow or even misconceived interpretations of the reader: 'written discourse is merely an image of the spoken discourse of the one who knows and who writes in the soul of the learner' (2015: 173). Of course, one cannot escape the irony that our access to the Socratic dialogues is dependent on the written record. Furthermore, when one considers the dominance of textualised language forms, deployed as the assumed framework of knowledge structures in Western modernity (before we even get to the internet age), oral dialogue has the aura of the ephemeral.

Derrida's controversial intervention regarding the dichotomy between oral and written discourse asserts that language is an 'abstract possibility', a phenomenon of cognitive processes that subsequently finds outlet through the communication tools we learn (1976). His concept of archi-writing reflects the notion that language structure is based on a present absence: the fixity of the written form is a priori implicated within language's ontology, and thus writing is a kind of deep blueprint that is the foundation of communication. Western modernity, even if it acknowledges the oral traditions, has, through the formalised structures of textual recording and dissemination, come to be fundamentally defined as the architectural underpinning of thought. Furthermore, the primacy of rationality is anchored to the doctrine of modern philosophy and science by the written text as a kind of evidentiary guarantor. Think of how much we take for granted as fact that which is written down, and the inherent suspicion attributed to hearsay. Yet Derrida's conceptions could be contrasted with Walter Ong's work on the relationship between orality and literacy, based on research into the thought and history of primary oral societies. He suggests that Western culture's focus on textual formation of language 'have clamoured for attention so peremptorily that oral creations have tended to be regarded generally as variants of written productions or, if not this, as beneath serious scholarly attention' yet 'written texts all have to be related somehow, directly or indirectly, to the world of sound, the natural habitat of language, to yield their meanings' (Ong 2002: 8).

Coming back to Gladwell's assertion then, the effect of textual words materialised in sound is implicit in his use of the word 'emotion': 'The kinds of emotions you can evoke are so much more powerful' he states. Such emotional effects of the spoken word are perhaps ubiquitously assumed to the point of being taken for granted, yet a specific philosophy of sound, drawing upon epistemological and phenomenological approaches, is a relatively niche disciplinary area in which debates around intellectual versus emotional responses to music are a key focus (Gabrielsson 2001; Meyer 2008). Augoyard and Torgue analyse the impact of sound as akin to a 'sonic effect' in which 'sound has always been a privileged tool to "create an effect," to astonish (*étonner*, in its etymological sense). Sound undeniably has an immediate emotional power that has been used by everyday culture' (2005: 11). In terms of articulating written text the voice is the essential instrument for both nuancing meaning and conveying emotional profundity. The resonance of speech operates both in the dramatising of a story – injecting a sense of emotional texture to a narrative whether fictional or non-fictional – and as the vital component of public discourse, debate and argument. 'As many radio and audio producers who work regularly with voices as material object know, words alone do not do this; the voice—with all its tones, pauses, pitch changes, tremors, and stutters—can be highly revealing. A voice can be caught off guard no matter how well trained; inauthenticity detected; artifice and fabrication unmasked' (Madsen and Potts 2010: 48–49).

Of course, forms such as poetry and theatre scripts negotiate a position between textual fixity and material articulation in which the emotional evocation is paramount. It is therefore interesting that a non-fiction writer like Gladwell puts so much emphasis onto storytelling and emotion as one of key advantages of podcasting and knowledge dissemination through sound. In many ways, disciplinary structures and practices of Western philosophy have sidelined or even sought to purge troublesome and messy emotion (Williams 1998). This is something picked up on from different angle in another interview with Malcolm Gladwell, this time on *The Ezra Klein Show*. Comparing the intellectual space of the podcast to that of the academic conference, he suggests they both serve as a forum for testing out ideas in condensed presentational format:

> There is a reason why there is so much emphasis in academia on person to person oral presentation of arguments, data, what have you, because when it is presented in oral form it's so much easier to *honour the conditionality of the work* [my emphasis], to argue with it, to fix, to backtrack, to amend, to do all those things. The minute that it's on paper it has a kind of permanence and authority that maybe it doesn't deserve. (*The Ezra Klein Show*, 23 August 2016)

This notion of *honouring the conditionality of the work* implicit within oral communication, is central to the rules of engagement in the public sphere. The parallel between the academic conference, which is meant to foster a fluid and pliable sense of knowledge transfer, and the podcast is an apposite one. Indeed this sense of conditionality of meaning is also, echoed by Ezra Klein— Gladwell's interviewer – when he suggests a foundational connection between the 'spirit' of podcasting being in line with blogging:

> I will say the thing about podcasting and I do not understand this exactly but one reason it is easier to talk about some of these issues in a way that feels similar to me to early blogging, people are a little more generous to the idea that you might be wrong and that might be OK, that might be part of searching on these issues. (*The Ezra Klein Show*, 23 August 2016)

This correlation between the ethos of podcasting and the more open, unruly written form of blogging, both deriving from the creative expression facilitated by the internet, is commented upon by Madsen and Potts who suggest that 'the broader social context of podcasting includes the culture of weblogging into which the new audio platform, and a rhizomatic "links" culture helping to extend the podcast through time and space' (2010: 36). For Klien this parallel is both contextual and formal:

> There is a subtle but very powerful incentive towards coherence imposed by most of the formats in which we write… one reason this format (podcasting) is nice is that you can be a little rambling, it doesn't have to be one point, people are open to you making just a bunch of points and then at the end just kind of moving on. (*The Ezra Klein Show*, 23 August 2016)

Implicit in these reflections of podcasting, I argue, is again the possibilities of praxis. The form and structure of this medium creates a positive destabilisation of the hierarchy between text and sound in the conception of it proponents, reminding us of a more actively Socratic method of argument and learning, and perhaps even a framework of engagement, that is more productive in synthesising ideas and positions than textual communication in the era of the internet.

The appeal of the openness and flexibility of podcasting, particularly in terms of this sense of implied conditionality, could also, paradoxically, have become imbued with a greater sense of weight and veracity. It would be easy and churlish to appropriate the discourses *du jour*—post-truth and fake news—here, but podcasting's cultural significance has arisen concomitantly with digital superseding print, the attendant crisis in publishing, and collapse of the separation between professional and amateur writing. Indeed, podcasting arguably brings us up to boundaries of what of Walter Ong defines as today's 'secondary orality of present-day high-technology culture, in which a new orality is sustained by telephone, radio, television, and other electronic devices that depend for their existence and functioning on writing and print' (2002: 11). Ong's notion of secondary orality was postulated well before the arrival of the internet and though I am not suggesting we are moving towards anything approaching a culture where orality becomes primary, podcasting praxis is a reminder and application of the communicative possibilities of language materialised through sound.

The Podcasting Self

The research of Markman (2012) and Markman and Sawyer (2014) represents an initial scholarly gambit into the motivations of independent podcasters, revealing that the development of technical skills, locating a community through reciprocal relationships with other podcasters, and receiving positive reinforcement from the audience, were all factors. There is a paucity of research into the motivation and self-identification of podcasters which, even in the time since Markman and Sawyer's study, may have changed markedly considering the expanded cultural visibility of the medium (the aspiration to monetise audio content, I would hypothesise as more prevalent). In my own conversations with podcasters coming from different disciplines (and listening to podcast interviews) the specific move to identify oneself as a podcaster is infused with a range of purposes and motivations, but if a fundamental discourse exists it relates to a desire to forge independent, autonomous control and self-determination in shaping what might be termed the mediated self. For myself, adopting the audio form as mean of expression has undoubtedly instigated self-reflection regarding how I want to engage and enact my scholarship. Learning the technical aspects of production, building an audience whose feedback gives a strong sense of recognition, and working directly and indirectly within a podcast community, were layers of the process that shaped my sense of working in a specific form of mediation. Further elements such as the recording, production and structuring audio material, the approach to and shaping of research, understanding the dynamics of interviews, and the role of social media, have all factored into what has ostensibly been a reimagining of how I understand the relationship between practice and theory. This is again indicative of a liminal praxis facilitated through podcasting; the symbiosis of the 'instrumental' and the 'conceptual' have forged a unique circumstance that has reframed how I think of my role, practice and identity as an academic. Indeed, podcasting through its very liminality, particularly with regards to the fusing of material and digital ontologies—the centrality of physical presence, conversations with others, the use of the voice, all of which are captured, shared and listened to digitally—offers a profoundly valuable approach to understand mediated subjectivity.

In the internet era, the deployment of multiple definitions or categorisations of self, or even a refusal of them altogether, reflects the disseminated, fractured subjectivity we experience today. Looking at my own self-declared online biography, repeated across various platforms, I currently claim the titles of 'writer, podcaster and academic'. In my mind, these subjectivities are interrelated but I am certain that the order of them was a subconscious (perhaps even conscious, I can't quite remember) assertion of hierarchy. These are not just statements of fact, such self-definitions revolve around complex concerns about who you are, what you do, and how you want to be perceived as a social actor. Rachel Leventhal-Weiner, producer and host of *Boy v Girl: A podcast*, has a website biography that reads, 'I balance the responsibilities of associated wife, parent, college professor turned policy analyst, storyteller, podcaster, sister, and friend with relative grace and poise (and lots of coffee)'. This proliferation of selves, allied to a stylistic knowningness and self-deprecation, is almost a celebration of a complex multiplicity that crosses the boundaries of work, family, lifestyle, citizen and personality. Clearly how we define ourselves, whether it is a conscious biography like this, or the myriad forms of self-presentation we engage in daily, the determination of being is an inherent process of, increasingly interrelated, online and offline labour.

When I interviewed Leventhal-Weiner we discussed how her sense of self fed into the development of her podcast:

> We started October 2015, back then I was a little nervous to call myself a sociologist and a writer on the podcast, but now that is who I am, that's the lens I

bring to it. I was worried a little bit about putting those two things together and using that in the medium to share any kind of idea no matter how deep. (Interview, 5 May 2017b)

Clearly in this statement Leventhal-Weiner foregrounds the sociologist and writer aspects of her identity as the primary drivers behind the podcast that she produces. Indeed, it is implied that her podcast is merely a secondary platform through which her primary vocations are extended, explored and combined. She even questions the viability of podcasting to explore the relationship between the two fields. But she adds to this:

What's wild is that, as an academic, and I think some of this is as a woman, and I think some of it is that I came to the academic space at a non-traditional age, I didn't come straight through university like some of my colleagues did. I was dealing with a lot of imposter syndrome... and so for a while I felt like an imposter in every space I was in. Like, I'm not really a podcaster... but now I really identify with it and after learning at least the nuts and bolts, and I'm still always learning, I see it as a form that I can use in so many different ways. If I was ever to become a capital A academic again, or to have my toe in both worlds, that would be my medium. I almost wouldn't waste my time with journal publishing. (Interview, 5 May 2017b)

Here other elements of identity are combined (academic, woman, imposter) in a narrative of self-definition, followed by the assertion that learning to podcast actively enabled these strands of identity and practice to coexist in a form of positive evolution. Overcoming 'imposter syndrome' by finding the confidence to inhabit the identity of an 'academic', and using the medium to question traditional academic research dissemination, are achieved through the praxis enabled by podcasting. The technical aspects of this are implied rather than explicit (learning the nuts and bolts), but the outcome is evocative of praxis in that the active experience of podcasting is ingrained into a production of knowledge. Certainly, I recognise both these outcomes from my own experience of podcasting (indeed I address the question of academic podcasting in *Knowing Sounds* (2018) as a space where multiple aspects of the self are an inherent part of the praxis). As another of my interviewees, Dave Brodbeck, puts it, 'disparate parts of me get put together that wouldn't have been put together before' (Interview April 27 2017). One might argue that podcasters, through the medium, feel able to synthesise aspects of the self that may, because of disciplinary norms, be kept isolated.

Another element of identity that Leventhal-Weiner alludes to above is gender. She specifically reflects on how one is judged and treated as a woman in an academic environment, the impact this can have on self-perception, and the positive effect of podcasting in negotiating those issues. Gender is also at the centre of both the form and content of Sarah Williams' *Tough Girl Podcast*, a show which explicitly uses the medium to share experiences and stories of achievement from a female perspective:

> When I started going into local schools to talk about challenge and change, raising aspirations and having goals I became very aware that there weren't enough female role models out there and initially I was going to blog about it but then actually podcasting was just an incredible way to share these women's stories but also through the power of their voice and when these women are talking you can hear the passion in their voice, the drama, or when they went through challenging times and you can hear that emotion. I think it's an incredibly powerful medium. (Interview 5 May 2017b)

Williams reiterates a link between sound and emotion as fundamental to storytelling particularly with the articulation of female subjectivity as the driving force. Pointedly, she makes the distinction in terms of impact between blogging and podcasting with the power of the female voice the key parameter. It this sense it is the materiality and specificity of the female voice, articulating the stories of achievement, that imbue an emotional resonance and significance. Williams' advocacy of podcasting thus relates to a specific potential to for the medium represent women:

> At the moment for me mainstream media just does not represent women you just don't get to hear their voices. So, you have so many women out there who are starting their own blogs, starting their own podcasts, starting their own YouTube channels and there is almost this groundswell and the fact that I can be part of it is amazing. (Interview, 5 May 2017b)

Williams highlights how she sees podcasting as an opportunity, again relating to the medium's perceived non-mainstream sensibility, to explore the issues and stories of women, specifically here with the intention of inspiring action in other fields. This throws up an interesting incongruity (worthy of further study) when considering Markman and Sawyer's assertion that podcast production is 'dominated by technologically savvy, educated, older, professional males' (2014: 30). Williams also suggests that podcasting should be understood as part of a broader online community of practice, perhaps implicitly alluding to online or 'fourth wave' feminism (Munro 2013).

An association between emotional response and sound, particularly the practice of listening over visual communication, is something that is alluded to by Lena Dunham. In discussing podcasting in relation to her (then) new show *Women of the Hour* she states:

> There is something amazing about removing the visuals and this kind of beautiful experience of really listening, that is so, not to get too primal and deep, but there is something really primal and human about listening. It has like attuned me in a new way. Listening to the cuts you send me, interviewing people, listening to the speech patterns, I feel like it's given almost like a new super sense. (*Longform* October 28 2015)

Most obviously identified as creator of the TV show *Girls*, Dunham attests a new-found appreciation of the 'deep' experience of listening as actually having impact on her understanding of mediation though sound as a practice. Interestingly, Dunham connects this specifically to the omission of visuals, suggesting that images distract from the possibility of deep listening. Furthermore, there is an allusion here to the effect of the editing process itself—again, an element of the praxis of podcasting—in this case audio editing is asserted as enhancing Dunham's understanding of the way 'speech patterns' influence communication. She defines this as becoming more 'attuned', a concise and apt way describing of how working in the podcast medium shapes ones understanding of mediated practice and subjectivity.

   In listening to podcasters talk about identity through their praxis, the voice is clearly of central importance. This is a complex issue because of the often interchangeable allusion to the acoustics of the voice (how the sound of the voice defines both the material and the identity of the speaker), and the ideological questions around who has a voice, who gets to speak and which voices are listened to. When producing podcasts in which you are also a host, one of the principle elements that you become 'attuned' to is the sound and affectation of your own voice, its idiosyncrasies, and the inaccuracies of your own speech. Certainly, misgivings about my own speech and accent influenced my self-perception and, in turn, how I want to present myself through the podcast (Llinares, May 11 2016). For female podcasters, the politics of the voice is urgent as it links to a potential for podcasting to challenge gender hierarchies in media. But this is much easier said than done. Indeed, a discourse around the gendered voice, conceptions of authority, and the phenomenon of vocal fry as an affectation of younger female voices, have accompanied podcasting's more recent mainstream visibility (Miller 2015; *Fresh Air* 2015; Wolf 2015; Tiffe and Hoffmann 2017). Interestingly, Christine Mottram acknowledges that the gendering of vocal authority suggests that traditionally lower-pitched voices are associated with authority, yet argues that podcasting represents a 'shift in audience and speaker dynamics' in which 'finding vocal authority in podcasts is not about achieving the traditional Western aesthetic of the low, deep voice, but about sounding like a "real" person: individually authentic' (2016: 66).

Conveying through the voice a sense of individual authenticity rather than an omnipotent authority arguably correlates podcasting with the egalitarian ideals of the internet age. The resonance of a passionately authentic voice, rather than a more objectively dispassionate delivery, could reflect a cultural shift away from the paternalism of traditional structures of the public sphere and the reliance on 'expert' (usually white, male) voices. Pointedly, for the academics I have talked to (myself included), the decoupling of knowledge from a highly formalised, austere, even deliberately dull forms of delivery, is a central advantage to podcasting related to the creative use of sound to articulate knowledge. Rachel Leventhal-Weiner argues that podcasting has been the mechanism through which she has found her voice:

> In podcasting, I have found a definitive voice and viewpoint, something I have always struggled with in writing and in advocacy. I learned to be more forceful with the case I was making, with the evidence I provide, with the drama I use to convey my ideas. I have learned to be less measured and more passionate. Podcasting is a special medium—you can't rely on body language or facial expressions to reach an audience. It's just you, the microphone, and your voice. (March 31, 2017)

Leventhal-Weiner alludes here to an interconnection between the ideological paradigms of having a voice, and the importance of the aesthetic use of that voice in evoking what one wants to get across. This idea has a philosophical ancestry in Barthes notion of the 'Grain of the Voice' (1977), but perhaps an even more pertinent alignment is with Karpf's (2006) research on the gendered voice and more recently Rodero's analysis of prosodic features of speech and the impact on perceptions of audio content (2015). But what, one might ask, is the difference between podcasting and other mediums in suggesting form has an impact on the perception of content, or that there are ideological hierarchies that perpetuate the dominance of certain identities and groups. Podcasting obviously puts a premium on the voice as the central tool of expression and communication. Furthermore, the liminal infrastructure of production, distribution and exhibition instils a sense of independence and autonomy and, within a new listening context in which audience choice is a defining parameter, podcasting engenders a move away from authorial, top down dissemination of information to a more conversational, personal and subjective tone. Therefore, through podcasting praxis, personality, identity, experience and knowledge are intrinsically articulated, not just through the words spoken or ideas expressed, but within the very sound of the voice in all it textures, complexities uncertainties and emotional valences.

Conclusion

In writing this chapter I have been acutely aware of the irony of setting down assertions about the idealised possibilities of podcasting praxis in written form. If you lend any credence to my arguments around sound versus writing, the mediation of identity, or the potential effects on how we understand the communication of knowledge, the very act of reading exposes the fundamental epistemological flaw gnawing at very purpose of this chapter (and book). What continues to emerge through my theoretical and practical engagement with podcasting are a range of potential avenues of enquiry related to what as been defined in this book as new aural cultures. In the context of higher education, podcasting's value as a primary method of research dissemination could be a fundamental strand of the open access movement, challenging the problems of the academic publishing industry and, in the process, providing a way of bringing research out of the ivory tower. Podcasting can even be deployed as a research method in and of itself, as an archive of primary audio data, its praxis helping to challenge disciplinary silos within and across academia. Clearly, the interrelationship between sound, text and image is open to new explorations in the context of podcasting and, as the last section of this chapter points towards, podcasting fosters the communication of research in modes where the identity of the researcher is not exorcised in name of objectivity, but understood as a key parameter in the communication of knowledge.

There are fundamental caveats to the assertions and arguments I have explored here. My own experiences have influenced a positive understanding of the applications of the medium, both its individual effects but also its status and significance in wider media culture. A sense of what podcasting offers through its liminal praxis, and the dynamics of that praxis in challenging disciplinary and communicative boundaries in a way that offers a freedom and autonomy, has the potential to be explored, and challenged, much further. Indeed, this would undoubtedly have to be central to a future 'podcast studies'. However, in a media age which often seems completely chaotic and arbitrary, and governed by immediate, ephemeral and often superficial communication modes that seem to ferment individualisation and polarisation, the very liminality of podcasting—its flexibility, transcendence of boundaries between media which may be conceived as 'old' and 'new' and across practices of production, distribution and consumption—offers a coherent space where thought, identity and practice find common purpose.

Notes

1. This is further complicated by related forms and concepts of digital audio dissemination such as DAB, streaming radio and netcasting.
2. You can see this on YouTube: https://www.youtube.com/watch?v=IzH54FpWAP0
3. Estimates as to the percentage of podcasts obtained through Apple's iTunes are difficult quantify accurately but this 2015 report by Clammr suggests that 82 per cent of mobile listening happens on iOS devices and 78 per cent of iOS listening occurs through Apple's podcast app: http://rainnews.com/report-apples-importance-in-podcast-delivery/
4. Various (unnamed) luminaries in podcasting reportedly met with iTunes executive to air grievances (Herrman. *The New York Times*, 7 May 2016).
5. Bob Goyetche was a Canadian podcasting pioneer who 'co-organized the grassroots *Podcasters Across Borders* conference, and an early podcasting network'. [Internet] http://www.cbc.ca/radio/spark/335-the-lonely-generation-and-more-1.3853837/tribute-to-podcasting-pioneer-bob-goyetche-1.3857832 Accessed 5 May 2017.

Bibliography

Augoyard, J.-F., & Torgue, H. (2005). *Sonic experience: A guide to the effects of sound*. Montréal: McGill-Queen's University Press.

Barthes, R. (1977). *Image music text*. London: Fontana Press.

Berry, R. (2006). Will the iPod kill the radio star? Profiling podcasting as radio. *Convergence, 12*(2), 143–162.

Berry, R. (2015). A golden age of podcasting: Evaluating serial in the context of podcast histories. *The Journal of Radio and Audio Media, 22*(2), 170–178.

Bottomley, A. J. (2015). A decade in the life of a "new" audio medium: Introduction. *Journal of Radio and Audio Media, 22*(2), 164–169.

Brodbeck, D. (2017). [Interview] April 27, 2017.

Cowley, N. (2008). What is praxis? Discussed in relation to Hegel, Marx, Nietzsche and Sartre. *TKKA: Graduate and PostGraduate E-Journal, 4*. https://www.waikato.ac.nz/__data/assets/pdf_file/0005/149261/NatalieCowley.pdf [Internet]. Accessed 1 Nov 2017.

Dann, L. (2017a). [Interview] May 5, 2017.

Dann, L. (2017b–). *Blood culture*. www.blood-culture.com [Podcast] Accessed 4 Sept 2017.

de Certeau, M. (1988). *The practice of everyday life*. Berkeley/London: University of California Press.

Dean, M. (2017). Voices of America: Can podcasts tell more than stories of individual expression? www.newrepublic.com [Internet]. Accessed 25 May 2017.

Derrida, J. (1976). *Of grammatology* (trans: Spivak, G. C.). Baltimore: The Johns Hopkins University Press.

Donnelly, K. M., & Berge, Z. L. (2006). Podcasting: Co-opting MP3 players for education and training purposes. *Online Journal of Distance Learning Administration, 9*(3). https://www.westga.edu/~distance/ojdla/fall93/donnelly93.htm [Internet]. Accessed 11 May 2017.

Dunham, L. (2016–). Woman of the hour. www.art19.com [Podcast]. Accessed 26 Sept 2017.

Edmonds, D., & Warburton, N. (2012). *Philosophy bites*. Oxford: University Press.

Freire, P. (1970). *Pedagogy of the oppressed*. London: Continuum.

Fritz, J. H. (2015). *Plato and the elements of dialogue*. Lanham: Lexington Books.

Gabrielsson, A. (2001). Emotion perceived and emotion felt: Same or different? *Musicae Scientiae, 5*(1), 123–147.

Ganesh, J. (2016). Podcasts create golden age of audio. www.ft.com [Internet]. Accessed 19 May 2017.

Gladwell, M. (2016–). Revisionist history. www.revisionisthistory.com [Internet]. Accessed 2 June 2017.

Gross, T. (2015). From Upspeak to vocal fry: Are we 'policing' Young Women's Voices. *Fresh Air podcast*. https://wwwnprorg/programs/fresh-air/ [Podcast]. Accessed 5 Sept 2017.

Heise, H. (2017). On the shoulders of giants: How audio podcasters adopt, transform and reinvent radio storytelling. *MOOC Transnation Radio Stories*. https://hamburgergarnele.files.wordpress.com/2014/09/podcasts_heise_public.pdf [Internet]. Accessed 26 Apr 2017

Herrman, J. (2016). Podcasts surge, but producers fear apple isn't listening. www.nytimes.com [Internet]. Accessed 11 May 2017.

Hills, M. (2011). Participatory culture: Mobility, interactivity and identity. In G. Creeber & R. Martin (Eds.), *Digital cultures: Understanding new media* (pp. 117–121). Maidenhead: Open University Press.

Jenkins, H. (2006). *Convergence culture: Where old and new media collide*. New York: NYU Press.

Karpf, A. (2006). *The human voice: How this extraordinary instrument reveals essential clues about who we are*. London: Bloomsbury.

Kight, C. (2017). [Interview] May 4.

Klein, E. (2016). Malcolm Gladwell on the danger of joining consensus culture. www.vox.com [Podcast]. Accessed 8 June 2017.

Klein, E. (2017). Tim Ferris on suffering, psychedelics and spirituality. www.vox.com [Podcast]. Accessed 11 June 2017.

Leventhal-Weiner, R. (2017a). Podcasting. www.roguecheerios.com [Internet]. Accessed 12 May 2017.

Leventhal-Weiner, R. (2017b). [Interview] May 5, 2017.

Leventhal-Weiner, R., & Dix, M. Boy v girl: A podcast. http://boyvgirlpodcast.libsyn.com [Podcast]. Accessed 14 June 2017.

Llinares, D. (2016). The anxiety of the speech act-podcast editing and the shaping of meaning. www.dariollinares.com [Internet]. Accessed 2 May 2017.

Llinares, D., & Fox, N. (2015–). The cinematologists podcast. www.cinematologists.com [Podcast]. Accessed 25 Mar 2017.

Llinares, D., & Fox, N. (2018). Knowing sounds: Podcasting as academic practice. *Journal of Media Practice, 9*(1), 50–53.

Longform Podcast. (2015). Lena Dunham. www.longform.com [Internet]. Accessed 6 Sept 2017.

Longform Podcast. (2016). Malcolm Gladwell. www.longform.com [Internet]. Accessed 10 June 2017.

Madsen, V., & Potts, J. (2010). Voice-cast: The distribution of the voice via podcasting. In N. Neumark, R. Gibson, & T. van Leeuwen (Eds.), *Vø1ce: Vocal aesthetics in digital media* (pp. 33–59). Cambridge, MA: MIT Press.

Markman, K. M. (2012). Doing radio, making friends, and having fun: Exploring the motivations of independent audio podcasters. *New Media & Society, 14*(2), 547–565.

Markman, K., & Sawyer, C. E. (2014). Why pod? Further explorations of the motivations for independent podcasting. *Journal of Radio & Audio Media, 21*(1), 20–35.

McElearney, G., & Middleton, A. (2013). Podcasting and RSS – The changing relationship. In E. Middleton (Ed.), *Digital voices – A collaborative exploration of the recorded voice in post-compulsory education* (pp. 18–17). Media-Enhanced Learning Special Interest Group and Sheffield Hallam University. https://melsig.shu.ac.uk/melsig/files/2017/10/Digital-Voices.pdf [Internet]. Accessed 2 May 2017.

Meng, P. (2005). Podcasting and vodcasting: Definitions, discussions and implications. *A white paper by IAT services at University of Missouri.* http://www.tfaoi.com/cm/3cm/3cm310.pdf [Internet]. Accessed 11 May 2017.

Meyer, L. B. (2008). *Emotion and meaning in music.* Chicago: University of Chicago Press.

Middleton, A. (2013). *Digital voices – A collaborative exploration of the recorded voice in post-compulsory education* (pp. 28–32). Media-Enhanced Learning Special Interest Group and Sheffield Hallam University. https://melsig.shu.ac.uk/melsig/files/2017/10/Digital-Voices.pdf

Miller, K. (2015, May 19). Why do these women's voices bother you so much? *Refinary290.* https://www.refinery29.com/2015/05/87351/female-podcast-voices-vocal-fry [Internet]. Accessed 12 May 2017.

Millette, M. (2011). Independent podcasting as a specific online participative sub-culture: A case study of Montreal's podcasters. IR12 Association of Internet Researchers. Conference proceedings. https://spir.aoir.org/index.php/spir/article/viewFile/24/26 [Internet]. Accessed 10 June 2017.

Morris, J. W., & Patterson, E. (2015). Podcasting and its apps: Software, sound, and the interfaces of digital audio. *Journal of Radio & Audio Media, 22*(2), 220–230.

Mottram, C. (2016). Finding a pitch that resonates: An examination of gender and vocal authority in podcast. *Voice and Speech Review, 10*(1), 53–69.

Munro, E. (2013). Feminism: A fourth wave? *Political Insight, 4*(2), 22–25.

Ong, W. (2002). *Orality and literacy: The Technologising of the word.* Suffolk: Routledge.

Pierce, D. (2014). The new radio stars: Welcome to the podcast age. www.theverge.com [Internet]. Accessed 14 May 2017.

Proops, G. (2013–). The smartest man in the world podcast. www.gregproops.com [Podcast]. Accessed 17 Apr 2017.

Proops, G. (2015). *The smartest book in the world.* New York: Touchstone.

Rodero, E. (2015). The principle of distinctive and contrastive coherence of prosody in radio news: An analysis of perception and recognition. *Journal of Nonverbal Behaviour, 39*, 79–92.

Tiffe, R., & Hoffmann, M. (2017). Taking up sonic space: Feminized vocality and podcasting as resistance. *Feminist Media Studies, 17*(1), 115–118.

Webster, J. G. (2014). *The marketplace of attention: How audiences take shape in a digital age.* Cambridge, MA: MIT Press.

Williams, S. (1998). Modernity and the emotions: Corporeal reflections on the (ir)rational. *Sociology, 32*(1), 747–769.

Williams, S. (2017a). Tough girl podcast. www.toughgirlchallenges.com [Podcast]. Accessed 25 Apr 2017.

Williams, S. (2017b). [Interview] May 5, 2017.

Wolf, N. (2015). Young women, give up the vocal fry and reclaim your strong female voice. www.guardian.co.uk [Internet]. Accessed 14 June 2017.

8

Wild Listening: Ecology of a Science Podcast

Danielle Barrios-O'Neill

In recent years, there has been a growing area of research focused on points of convergence between scientific and humanities discourses, with methods of interpreting cultural products drawing increasingly on other disciplines and vice versa. Ecological readings of cultural materials would be included here, *ecological* not in the traditional sense of environmental criticism, but rather focused on the elements of network relations as they play out within the living systems of cultural works. This chapter will examine the ways in which podcasts can share structural and epistemological affinities with ecological processes, engaging the conversational science podcast *Stuff to Blow Your Mind (STBYM)* as a case study.[1] I will argue that *STBYM,* known for its elegantly produced discourse around complex material, with episodes like 'Meet Your Bacterial Masters' and 'The Habitable Epoch', exemplifies a growing trend toward epistemologically complex methods of approach to cultural processes (Norman 2010: 39). This chapter will explore how this kind of conversational podcast can work as a delivery channel for complex material, a 'wild' approach to knowledge-making, with attention to its format, aims and medial contexts (Tierney 2015; Morton 2016). I pose this mode as one with surprising potential to challenge top-down and linear logics, and to diverge toward a more complex ecological epistemology: audio discourse compelled in large part by expressions of compound and networked forms of knowledge, where any node of dialogue is emphatically represented as part of a larger ecosystem of information.

D. Barrios-O'Neill (✉)
Falmouth University, Falmouth, UK
e-mail: Danielle.BarriosONeill@falmouth.ac.uk

© The Author(s) 2018
D. Llinares et al. (eds.), *Podcasting*, https://doi.org/10.1007/978-3-319-90056-8_8

On Wildness

Ecological metaphors for cultural processes, now relatively commonplace, have taken on interesting new dimensions in the age of network-fluency. In the arena of popular science, cultural critic George Monbiot (2013a, b, c) drew on existing approaches to environmental ecology to build the cultural concept of *rewilding,* extending it from a method of restoring biodiversity to actual physical spaces, to a way of describing the deliberate activation of chaotic, 'wild', processes in human lives.[2] In ecological contexts, rewilding approaches environmental health through the introduction or reintroduction of living elements into local ecosystems—a particular species, for example—where there is then a cascading network effect that leads to greater biodiversity over time.[3] 'Wildness' in this context is a measure of biodiversity: the more rich, diverse and interconnected the species network, the wilder the environment. Likewise, cultural rewilding as posed by Monbiot is about the restoration of the 'wildness' of human nature, an extrapolation that links environmental health to cultural health: championing a broader re-involvement with nature in modern life, Monbiot advocates a human 'escape from ecological boredom' through experiences of 'fiercer, less predictable' ecosystems.[4] This involves the adoption of strategies of living that take into account the vast network of relationships composing environments, of which humans are but a single element. The ethos underlying the concept of rewilding is fairly non-anthropocentric, entailing a super-broad view on natural and cultural processes. As I explore *STBYM*, cultural and environmental rewilding are useful touchpoints for exploring how contemporary media express our changing relationships to our environments, where understanding the complexity of network processes has an increasingly important role to play. As I prepared to write this chapter, Joe McCormick and Robert Lamb, both writers and producers of *STBYM*, were kind enough to offer their own perspectives on how podcasting fits into contemporary knowledge ecosystems. This discussion of the podcast will focus on elements of its approach and contexts that amplify its capacity to express complexity; among these are an 'open field' approach that leads to a cumulative and collaborative structure, particular aspects of embodiment inherent in mobile listening, and (bio)diversity as an embedded production value.

How *Stuff to Blow Your Mind* Works

The format of a single episode of *STBYM* is deceptively simple. Typically, two hosts introduce and then engage in a conversation about a scientific topic of interest, discussing historical contexts and referring to recent research on the topic.[5] As the title suggests, the hosts focus on topics with elements of the extraordinary: the series comprises, at the time of writing, over 700 episodes since the launch of the podcast in 2010, with topics ranging from why whales beach themselves to the Bermuda Triangle, to why humans accessorise, to the relationship between music and mathematics, to the science of meditation.[6] Each individual episode can be read as is both a self-contained unit (consisting of a recorded episode, these having titles like 'The Science of Coincidence', 'Grand Theft Genome: Genestealers in the Wild', and 'Sex Cannibals of the Animal Kingdom') and a network of texts including overlapping and interlinked paratexts: supplementary material for each episode on the podcast website, like video and images; associated blog posts; user comments; user responses online; user reactions sent by email and read on the next episode. The format of *STBYM* is episodic (bi-weekly releases, approximately 55 minutes per episode) but not serial (you don't have to listen in order). While episodes occasionally reprise bits of older topics where relevant, listeners, as with most podcasts, can pick up virtually on any episode.

The register of *STBYM* can be described as drawing from conventions of talk radio, the (university) classroom, and casual chat in the relaxed American style.[7] This makes perfect sense: the podcast form descends from radio geneaology; research suggests that roughly 90 per cent of podcast listeners are university educated; and the parent company, How Stuff Works, is based in Atlanta.[8] The style of the podcast is casual; although the podcast is edited for time and flow, the dialogue is at least partly spontaneous, where the hosts work from notes rather than a script, and are sometimes hearing each other's findings and thoughts for the first time.[9] What results is a conversation delving into available research, writings, historical and cultural contexts for scientific issues, peppered with personal thoughts and reactions, occasional jokes and frequent tangents. None of the conversations that comprise *STBYM* offer—or seek to reach—conclusions; in fact, the narrative of each episode is typically based around posing open questions with multiple possible answers and/or approaches, giving a variety of views and opinions, giving interdisciplinary perspectives, highlighting myths and demystifying commonly misunderstood issues, but rarely posing final answers, chiming with the ethos of contemporary science. With hosts stepping into the role of casual, citizen scientists, the tone of *STBYM* tends toward the inquisitive, rather than the authoritative. The hosts frequently use qualifiers and deliver waivers to diminish their own authority, such as 'I'm not a scientist, but' or 'I think what this article is trying to say is …' McCormick describes himself and the other hosts as 'explanatory generalists': they have, he claims, expertise in none of the topics they cover, but they have become experts in the 'process of explaining': translating scientific research and cultural context into legible narrative dialogue, and making links between scientific ideas, and 'philosophical, historical, mythological and/or psychological' ones.[10] In not claiming expertise, they are free to make productive errors; the tone of the podcast is very much one of 'I'm not an expert, but what I think the analysis here is suggesting is that …' and bringing the suggested analysis into conversation with other, linked ideas and concepts.[11]

The podcast is conversant with other channels where supporting paratextual content is always arriving; this includes the official *STBYM* blog and YouTube channel, including user comments; exchanges on social media with official podcast accounts and individual hosts' social media accounts, using podcast-specific hashtags; fan-maintained wikis; live shows; other podcasts within the How Stuff Works network, where hosts collaborate; and a host of audio-centric social sharing sites, all of which allow user comments and sharing. In this sense a single episode, or even the whole podcast, barely exists as a discrete entity, being rather constantly intertextually linked to a variety of other texts, authors and producers, becoming part of what might be described as a sort of textual ecosystem.[12] Continuously arriving paratexts, as well as the shifting relationships between every part of the textual network of even a single episode, makes for unpredictable lines of narrative, not least because the podcast's producers are always responding to paratexts; producers cannot help but respond to paratexts; paratextual producers—or the awkwardly phrased 'pro-sumers'—naturally feed into the collective experience of the podcast.[13]

Ecological Form of the Podcast

Critically speaking, bringing the paratextual network into the sphere of the text itself is useful as a way of characterising what is different about online, or simply contemporary tech-enabled, texts. By situating these within particular feedback and feed-forward systems as they play out on the internet—where content is produced by many actors, often influenced in unpredictable ways by external factors such as the news headlines or trends in social media, and is continually new—it becomes easier to see the analogues we can draw between textual systems and biological environmental ones.[14] *STBYM* is a unique case within the broad category of shareable online media, as its hosts say they aim to embrace open conversations around scientific topics as a rule, and, like the other podcasts owned by its network, they actively encourage engagement across multiple platforms. As such, this podcast turns out to be an excellent forum for modelling the knowledge (eco)system, opening up fertile spaces for interchange, multiplicity and paradox. Like the ecosystem, this kind of text has a cumulative plot: as ecological philosopher Tim Morton argues, accurately expressive ecological thought is uncertain, sustained, even boring. That is, ecology has no climactic event—it just keeps churning itself out indefinitely, a sort of conversation between various living systems. This does away with the more marketable teleology of 'beginning-middle-end', the more dramatic arc that tends to characterise more prime-time scientific narratives, or those produced regularly by the mass media: the typical science-news headline or Hollywood blockbuster about environmental change tend to be full of climax and rupture, sensationalist in the extreme, but the reality is rather less exciting.[15] As any scientist will tell you, the environment—and relatedly, science itself—is a process of slow and continuous unfolding of questions and responses, feedback and feed-forward. *STBYM*'s approach is similar, interesting but not climactic, travelling from point to point, where every node of conversation and every episode exist conspicuously as part of what McCormick calls 'an intellectual ecosystem'.[16] Like Monbiot's approach to rewilding environments, *STBYM* is aimed at letting emerge over time what is 'relational, situational, flexible and multiple' in the conversational environment: a suitably complex approach to cultural forms that relies heavily on the open field.[17] To contextualise *STBYM* within the large and diverse category of science-related podcasts, its main differentiating points are a primary focus on conversation as a mode of inquiry within each episode, its lack of scientific 'experts' driving the conversation, and the conscious situation by its hosts and possibly its network within a knowledge ecosystem that is mostly self-determining. For example, *STBYM*'s hosts reject any imperative to address current events; this allows each episode, as well as the larger whole of the podcast, to develop according to operational rules of the textual system rather than based on market-driven strategies.[18]

Because this form of discourse does away with a number of controlling structures that frame other media, an episode of *STBYM* could be seen as more faithful to the reality of ecological processes than, for example, a news article, a scientific lecture in a university classroom, or a scientific paper. Matt

Tierney has argued that contemporary texts are more disruptive when they occur with a conceptual open field; the benefit is to open up any text to include new kinds of uncategorisable or ateleological content, which allows formal complexity to flourish.[19] This kind of interpretation is useful to approaching various forms of text in that it helps to frame their value in terms of systemic processes: (legible) complexity is a valid formal goal, in culture as well as nature. That this kind of approach exists in a fairly popular podcast forum, though this isn't yet how most people get their science news, still holds promise for public discourse around issues like climate change. This is because the open field format, with its invitation to unexpected configurations, allows everything that won't fit strategic talking points, and does away with insulating bureaucratic language and inaccessible scientific jargon.[20] In this sense the 'wild' podcast opens up space for disruptive knowledge production by removing what could be described as rhetorical barriers, those conventions of form that uphold structures of authority but don't necessarily produce new knowledge.[21] Environmental ecology is a good tool for imagining the complexity of other kinds of systems, so it's not surprising that a science podcast can work in this way: alluding continually to how things work in the natural world, the hosts of *STBYM* demonstrate reality to be 'plural and colliding, jumbled and constantly altered.'[22] In conversation as in natural environments, an alluvial muck is most fertile, an openness that doesn't occlude complex realities, and where fleeting contact can occur among elements that have yet to cohere into more permanent institutional and ideological forms. The approach of *STBYM* and that of those who carry out cultural and environmental rewilding efforts are in a large sense philosophically similar, in that each looks to the uncultivated or unmade space as both starting point and ending point: the ideal aesthetic in all cases is 'a kind of negativity that is elusive and relational rather than ideal or absolute,' a space of pure possibility.[23]

The very nature of open conversation allows the null hypothesis, the nonanswer, the unexciting conclusion or lack of a conclusion, to thrive and rule—which even peer-reviewed science publications do not; that is to say that papers with unexciting findings or a null result, however valuable, are far less likely to be published than papers which indicate a positive result or are headline-friendly. This has a major impact on what enters into the body of public scientific knowledge.[24] Not unlike the Hollywood blockbuster, proving an overarching high theory, i.e. producing a narrative climax, remains incredibly attractive as a way of marketing scientific research, despite how the nature of science itself conforms largely to the low theory: constant, fluid negotiation between a variety of possibilities. In addition, while the scientific method aims to dismantle any deep, prior model of causality as a rule, quite often the narrative modes of scientific communication confirm the politics of academic structures by adopting particular styles of rhetoric, typically that of the objective expert.[25] Furthermore, the technological format of podcasting is historically linked and extensively shaped by the philosophy of free and open sharing of data—something that puts it starkly at odds with the ethos of, for example, paywall-controlled scientific journals.[26]

Complex Listening

As a form of media that occurs, in the case of mobile listening, inside the body, the podcast form can be intimate and private in a way that textual forms rarely are.[27] The power of radio to 'involve people in depth', McLuhan wrote in *Understanding Media the Extensions of Man* (1964), 'is manifested in its use during homework by youngsters and by many other people who carry transistor sets in order to provide a private world for themselves amidst crowds.'[28] This is probably even truer of the podcast, which, not unlike the radio drama or symphony, creates an entire aural and imaginative experience within the confines of your head.[29] In the case of *STBYM*, that experience is one of a conversation in which you are, depending on how you listen, either a passive observer or an imaginary active contributor. While *STBYM* isn't an 'authoritative podcast' where listeners under pressure to pay attention, it's still present in the body in the form of sound vibrations, unlike, for example, a painting on an office wall that you pass on the way to your desk.[30] Texture also matters. The ear, McLuhan, 'is hyperesthetic compared to the neutral eye'; the auditory sense is delicate, sensitive, involved: '[i]f we sit and talk in a dark room, words suddenly acquire new meanings and different textures. … All those gestural qualities that the printed page strips from language come back in the dark, and on the radio.' The auditory experience also happens *in time*, involving on some level because, even when it's ambient noise, it still flows past like a river; it is something to be tuned into or ignored, but cannot be absent. At the same time, the radio 'gives privacy,' while producing what McLuhan calls 'the tight tribal bond of the world of the common market, of song, and of resonance. Radio, he wrote in 1967, 'restores tribal sensitivity and exclusive involvement in the web of kinship.'[31] This might explain something of why the style and tone of *STBYM* work so well; our 'tribal sensitivity' is awakened especially well by a format that is friendly, social, pleasantly intimate. This frames the podcast experience as a form of imagined community, where McLuhan's 'common market' is that of science, its community vastly networked.

The listening device, Jean-Paul Thibaud argues, creates an 'involvement shield, momentarily allow[ing] us to position ourselves outside of the social theatre' even as we move through it, mediating all relations to it.[32] The claim calls to mind a 'sound-shower' I witnessed in Oslo Airport circa 2007. This was a public installation wherein airport occupants could enter a space demarcated only by a circle on the ground and a large, shower head-like speaker above, to be immersed in a sonic environment: a rainforest, a thunderstorm, a meadow. The concept was simple and ideal, providing an oasis of sonic wilderness in an environment otherwise characterised by varying degrees of anxiety, and illustrates Thibaud's argument that sound can demarcate space and perform spatial interventions. In this case, the airport is a space characterised by continuous movement, where the sound-shower was a space of relative stasis; in the case of the mobile podcast listener moving through an urban environment, almost everything is mobile (the listener, the podcast microecology, and various moving elements of the city around), performing a more complicated theatre of moving parts. In moments where sound environments intervene upon each other, as when someone is listening to a podcast while moving through a city, the removal from the 'social theatre' is a powerful demarcation, a way to access the wild amid sometimes overwhelming civilisation.[33]

The sound-shower, and the podcast, only constitute a partial removal, however—we still see what's around us, we will probably remove our headphones if someone tries to ask us for directions—but perhaps this is where even more interesting interactions between spaces takes place, as these interventions can create fertile interchange. The urban subject receives, at any given moment, a vast amount of information: some of this information, like a street sign, is more likely to passively intervene into the stream of attention which is engaged with the podcast; some might directly interject, for example a car horn; some might be subconsciously received; all of this is drawn into the listener's purview, with multiple levels of associative linking, active and passive cognitive processes, happening at any given moment.[34] The listener is also engaged in a sort of noise-sifting exercise, parsing the useful patterns from noise, a normal state of living but also, again, heightened in intensity by the multiple streams of incoming information from overlapping experiences; there is more noise to sift, there are more patterns to notice. These patterns impinge upon each other, creating an altogether more complex experience of being somewhere—any place becomes more than one place. For the mobile listener, incoming information from either world can be included in the train of thought—now more accurately described not as a train but as a network, a system of thought.[35]

The 'wild' format of a podcast like *STBYM* links to this broader mobile listening experience in interesting ways. Thibaud argues that the screen of sound produced by the listening device simultaneously encloses and reframes the listener's experience of the environment around; as she moves through external space, the audio is like a mobile sound-shower, a moving biome constantly overlaying or intervening upon the administrated outer world—particularly because it wanders.[36] The ethos of the world inside the biome of the wild podcast is characterised by an un-administrated movement from point to undetermined point; it continues like any audio to intervene upon environmental experience, not unlike a sort of augmented reality layer. The micro-ecology of the wild audio serves to, as Thibaud describes it, 'derealize' urban space: being simultaneously within and outside it, its reality partially displaced, the mobile listener de-administrates and re-administrates the space based on the paths she may take, spatially and mentally. The city itself becomes more wild, as the listener is stimulated to a greater diversity of possible cognitive outcomes.[37]

The Value of Audio (Bio)Diversity

In characterising *STBYM* as a 'wild' podcast, the crucial element is its capacity for being extremely productive in terms of the variety of possible outcomes: the (bio)diversity of this particular ecology of discourse. To return to rewilding as an analogue, that strategy involves an informed roll of the dice in an uncontrolled environment: wolves are re-introduced into Yellowstone National Park, triggering an unfolding cascade effect that results in the flourishing of many species and habitats throughout the local environment (That actually happened).[38] For rewilding, the more complex an environment's existing ecosystems, the less predictable the outcomes; in the extremely biodiverse Great Barrier reef, for example, rewilding efforts may be more complicated. Rewilding creates a predictable burgeoning of fresh biodiversity of unpredictable type; while it's difficult to know in advance what exactly will happen, it is always likely that there will be a network effect that yields new ecological richness.[39] This is a creative ecological effort, and one that diverges significantly from what goes on in the highly controlled efforts of traditional conservation: '[r]ewilding has no endpoints, no view about what a 'right' ecosystem or a 'right' assemblage of species looks like. It does not strive to produce a heath, a meadow, a rainforest, a kelp garden, or a coral reef. It lets nature decide.'[40]

Compare this to *STBYM* host Robert Lamb's characterisation of their production process, which avoids a 'focus on creating a perfect, idealized expression' in favor of the spontaneous ecosystem, where the conversation is intentionally 'organic and unformalized.'[41] Like the rewilded landscape, this is a creative approach that sees production are an evolving system comprising myriad unpredictable interactions, and as such must welcome continuous restructuring.[42] In that sense either process seems half-structured, half-divergent, with discovery holding sway over intention in a way that underlines the speculative nature of the conversations. The hosts supply real-world examples, construct hypothetical scenarios to illustrate points, and make lateral moves across knowledge disciplines to produce insight about how and why particular findings might be worth noting; they seem to easily translate from one register to another (for example, from the academic to the lay, or from neuroscientific concepts to what's in your lunchbox). This mode of thinking-conversing results in a rhizomatic experience of scientific and cultural concepts, a formalism that implicitly supports a 'nuanced understanding of the many different and often disconnected arrangements that govern ... experience.'[43] The micro-ecology of the wild podcast space is thus necessarily always transitional, always unsettled; to limit a conversation to a particular moment or place would immediately impede the ability to place it within specifically vast networks of knowledge.[44]

This approach to production is driven by a rich and unromanticised realism, where the only qualifier of big wilderness is genuine (bio)diversity, without value judgments on what that diversity contains in particular: the aesthetic is relatively 'oozy', ambient, with no particular storyline and no definite background or foreground.[45] The epistemological function of all this ambience, or ooze, is to provide a space out of which knowledge can emerge—organically, so to speak—rather than being imposed; the knowledge equivalent of Benjamin's *flâneur*, without the necessity of an urban space to wander in (although it probably helps).[46] That is, *STBYM*'s particular aesthetic leaves space for a variety of gestures which are not obviously shaped by intention (read: ideology), and as a result a wandering ambience becomes a substrate for the low-key insertion of 'wild' elements into the relatively uncontrolled environment of the conversation, letting it simply unfold.[47]

Concluding Thoughts

The aesthetic of the 'wild' podcast is driven by changes in network-era culture, so it's not surprising that there are analogues in how science itself is performed, changes in how the scientific community actually carries out research. In recent decades there have been important movements in the direction of question-focused, flexible, intuitive approaches, an increasing trend toward discovery-driven (versus hypothesis-led) scientific research: enabled by computing technology in particular, discovery-driven research analyses data to undetermined ends, rather than imposing a hypothetical model, with its implicit biases, from the start.[48] *STBYM* could be seen as either reflecting, or responding to the same conditions as, scientific culture on the whole, whose implicit philosophies are in transformation, too. Perhaps by being positioned between the commercial and the grassroots, radio and internet, science and recreation, *STBYM* gives special access to a blended approach to science communication, favouring casualness, accessibility (and possibly reductiveness) over more authoritative styles; still, it has to be said that this particular podcast frequently and as a rule returns to scientific research, in a critical mode, for verification and inspiration of further discussions, so it is never divorced from the bureaucracy and politics of academic research, either. Rather than posing this kind of approach to science discourse as a definite alternative, it might be more constructively seen as another way—a particularly elegant way—to represent and problematise the state of humanness amid intractably complex environmental processes that determine our realities.[49] This is supported by how approximations of complex principles play out in the 'wild' podcast, elements such as nonlinearity, accumulation and diverse emergence.[50] In other words, the format takes as a premise and also actively demonstrates in a number of ways how humans (along with the conditions in which we exist) are ecological. Though it may not be precisely what Monbiot argues for when he insists on reviving wonder and excitement through confrontations with nature, it still works: engaging with this kind of audio experience is a form of rewilding in itself, a rewilding of the conception of knowledge structures, the nature of humanness, and the complexity of reality, through the interventions of an ambient ecology of knowledge.

'When you are sufficiently creeped out by the human species,' Tim Morton writes in *Dark Ecology*, 'you see something even bigger than the Anthropocene looming in the background'. He refers to the uncanny-ness of being human, when humanness is considered in the context of giant, looming, tiny, interconnected, neverending ecological systems.[51] This is a similar uncanny-ness to that which arises from listening to *STBYM*'s episode 'So Cute I Could Eat You Up', on the phenomenon of finding babies delicious-looking (for which there is a scientific basis), or 'Sexbots: From Objectification to Therapeutic Surrogates' on how sexbots are becoming scientifically compelling tools, and subjects.[52] Dealing with science and human culture simultaneously inevitably entails dealing with the deeply weird, the almost-unthinkable; blowing the mind, so to speak, in order to represent more complex and accurate models of human being in the world.[53] Lamb explains that giving fair treatment to particular topics requires, as a result, a certain willingness to confront intel-lectual discomfort, what he describes as 'reaching through the miasma of cul-tural revulsion to grasp the truth.' The creepiness, the uncanny-ness is an important part of the scientific picture. The show, says McCormick, 'is about helping people feel the weirdness of reality. The real world, … is reliably much stranger and more surprising than we imagine. Bringing people to that point of recognition is the core of what we do.'[54] Describing the conversational podcast as a 'wild' method of approaching science is perhaps just one way of drawing attention to the ways in which complexity can come to be repre-sented or performed by the media, within a larger argument that modelling complexity is necessary to understanding human and cultural processes, just as it's necessary to understanding natural processes. Modes of cultural and scientific rendering that draw both philosophically and aesthetically on post-computing movements in science and mathematics are extremely compelling, both conceptually and practically, if we hope to cultivate more effective ways of understanding how the world works; this is a point with resonance for every complex social and environmental issue that we face today.

Appendix

Interview with Joe McCormick and Robert Lamb

This interview was carried out by email in November 2016.

How do you identify a strong potential idea for a podcast? What topics (or kinds of topics) lend themselves well to the format? Why?

JM   When I suggest a topic, the most important thing is that it has to be interesting to me. If I wouldn't want to listen to a podcast on a subject, I don't think I should try to make one on that subject. One reason for this (in addition to the obvious) is that the audio presentation format of podcasting is one in which a lack of enthusiasm on the host's part will usually be palpable to the listener, making a boring and dreary final product. So the topics we choose are largely an extension of the hosts' personalities. I personally have a credo for the show that I like to keep in mind: Stuff to Blow Your Mind is about helping people feel the weirdness of reality. The real world, in a way that is to a great extent explicable by scientific investigation, is reliably much stranger and more surprising than we imagine. Bringing people to that point of recogni-tion is the core of what we do.

Also, I try not to chase news, big headlines or topics that seem like they 'should' be covered because of timeliness or societal impact. People don't come to us for science news. There's plenty of news coverage elsewhere. They come to us to have a thought-provoking experience grounded in a respect for science and an appetite for the weirdness of reality.

As for which topics lend themselves well to the format, one constraint is that there is no visual aid, so we also tend to skew toward topics that make for good conversation without the need for diagrams or illustrations. I think this does mean we end up talking about things like biology and the social sciences more often than things like chemistry or materials science. Sometimes there's just not an easy way we know of to have an interesting conversation about synthetic polymer research. But we do sometimes try to find interesting ways to talk about the 'dry' sciences – because I think the truth is that any of it can be interesting if you just find the right approach.

RL   Well, first and foremost *Stuff to Blow Your Mind* is a science podcast. In fact, it was known as 'Stuff From the Science Lab' in its earliest incarnation (I was joined by co-host Allison Loudermilk back then). So there always has to be a firm grounding in science or scientific thinking, though the show is at its best when it pulls in philosophical, historical, mythological and/or psychological concepts as well. I like to think of this as a triangulation of truth. Plus, I really try to stress the value of keeping one's mind open to varying and even conflicting worldviews and beliefs.

Is there anything you don't cover at all in terms of topics for podcast episodes? Anything you have categorically decided against?

JM   Not that I can think of. The core of the show is science, but if you've listened for a while, I'm sure you've noticed that we don't hesitate to range far and wide over history, religion, mythology, culture, literature, and of course all of the monster movies. I suppose we try to keep the show basically PG in that we avoid unnecessary vulgarity and foul language, but at the same time, we don't shy away from 'adult' topics. There are probably some topics that we would never cover, not because we have a rule against them, but simply because they don't fit our interests or the voice of the show. We're probably not going to be doing episodes about football or how to get a small business loan (as much as I'm sure some advertisers would like that).

I guess maybe one thing is that we try not to get too overtly political on the show. I think all three of us have fairly similar political viewpoints and our values probably do come through just in the topics we choose to talk about and how we treat them, but we usually try to avoid stuff like direct discussion of political candidates and so forth.

RL   As long as we're able to keep at least one foot firmly placed on the ground with a scientific/skeptical mindset, we can tackle just about anything. I try to keep in mind younger listeners more, especially as I have a young son now, but this hasn't prevented us from engaging some darker topics such as necrophilia. That's a great example of an episode that worked because we put a lot of effort into demystifying it – reaching through the miasma of cultural revulsion to grasp the truth.

Obviously your work as a writer/editor for HSW overlaps considerably with the development of podcasts. Could you characterize the ways in which it might differ?

JM   I don't write or edit for HSW all that often these days, though I sometimes write pieces for HowStuffWorks Now. Really, I think my approach to research is not especially different whether I'm writing an article or preparing for a podcast. Either way, I want to spend enough time with research materials that I have plenty of relevant facts in hand, but also so I can get a 'feel' for the subject. How do people in this subject area talk about their work? What questions are of interest to them? Etc. I think the main difference between preparation for a podcast and work on an article is that our podcasts are both collaborative and conversational. So on a podcast, I don't necessarily have to familiarize myself with everything that's going to be covered in the final product. Robert might read about one thing and I'll read about another, and then we sort of tell each other about it. With an article (or a video script, which I also write), you're pretty much on your own.

RL   In the early days of HSW podcasting (I started on this show 7 years ago), we were all writers and editors and the show topics were all, in theory, spinoffs from articles we wrote and edited for HowStuffWorks. com. Over the years, priorities have changed, but I still try to approach each topic as a writer. So the methodology is much the same, but generally with less of a focus on creating a perfect, idealized expression. The podcast product is a clay tablet etching.

Could you describe the development process for a single episode or topic? How much does the structure and content of an episode change, from the conception of the idea to the final moment of going live?

JM   Sure. Every episode is different, but most of the time the process is very uncomplicated and informal. I'd say the most common route looks like this: Robert and I email each other saying, 'Hey, have you ever read about X? I was thinking that could be interesting for an episode.' Then we bat the idea back and forth a little bit and weigh it against any other ideas we have in the queue. If we decide to move forward with it, we begin to collect and share resources for research: We create a shared Google document and paste in ideas, citations, links and so forth. We share any books or PDFs we have that the other might want to read. Then we go to work creating an outline for the episode in the shared document and filling it with notes from our research. The episodes are not scripted, but we do work from notes created in our shared document, so what you hear in the end is a mixture of comments we prepared ahead of time and spontaneous, free-flowing conversation.

The structure and content of the episode often changes a lot during the research phase. We're not always well-versed in the topic before we begin researching for an episode, so often we don't know what there is to know until we get into the weeds. Some new tangents and subtopics come into focus; some ideas we had in the beginning turn out to be dead ends. So the final structure and contents of the episode is really more an emergent product of our research and reading than anything else.

RL   A lot of it is organic and unformalised at this point. You just develop an idea for the general shape and flow of an episode and push for that. Then, discoveries in the research force you to restructure sometimes.

What various forms of feedback from listeners might feed into your development of topic concepts or episodes?

JM   Listener feedback from Facebook, Twitter and email can and does inform future episodes. We get a lot of great correspondence, and we have based episodes in the past on suggestions from listeners. The most common is probably from email, where people have room to express themselves at length. I think the quality of interaction we get on

Facebook is a little bit lower than what we get over email and Twitter – though I don't want to impugn the excellence of our very smart and gracious listeners who contact us through FB messenger. Facebook just seems to be the noisiest platform. There's a lot happening on it, and not all of it is incredibly coherent. Twitter is a great platform for connecting with fans, but a lot of our interaction on Twitter could be better characterized as appreciation and reference-sharing. I think we get our best topic suggestions over email. Not a lot happens in blog comments.

RL   All of it helps, though e-mail remains the best connection with listeners IMO.

Your podcasts have grown substantially in terms of audience in recent years. Do you have any opinions as to why? In other words, is there a societal reason for it?

JM   I would love to imagine that we're gaining subscribers from a wave of new interest in science and in the weirdness of reality, but I don't think I have any evidence to support that idea. I think the actual reasons might be more mundane, though still encouraging. A lot of people are buying mobile devices and stocking up their podcast apps with subscriptions to things that sound cool. Also, I think we make loyal subscribers, and that helps us as well – while we're adding all of these new subscribers, we've also still got lots of listeners who have been with us for many years, and we hear from them all the time. Beyond that, I honestly don't know exactly what is driving our growth. I hope it means we're doing something right!

RL   I can't speak for all podcasts, because you have so many varieties – tightly-produced radio show productions, casual conversational podcasts, music podcasts, etc. But I think the core HSW model for podcasting continues to resonate because it is an informed conversation that the user may listen in on – and then they can even engage in it, by spinning the content off into their own conversations, host interactions and artistic expressions.

In what ways do the various themes/podcasts in the HSW network work together, to achieve something bigger than the sum of the parts? You have a huge amount of content now – is this better?

JM   The full roster of HSW podcasts are differentiated by both approach and at least nominally by subject. So on *STBYM* we're probably not going to end up covering the same topic as a *CarStuff* episode, but being sort of scientific generalists, we often end up covering some of the same topics as Josh and Chuck on *SYSK*. However, whenever that has happened, I can't recall that we've ever had shared listeners complain about it – I think people seem to appreciate the two different perspectives. Podcast hosts at HSW sometimes go on each other's shows to talk about topics that are of particular interest to them. A while back I went on *Stuff They Don't Want You to Know* to talk about Gnosticism, which was a great fit. I was able to have another outlet for my interest in ancient religion, and Gnosticism has many elements in common with modern conspiracy theories. So hopefully stuff like this does help us bring listeners from one HSW show on board to others. It also does help create the sense that the HSW podcast universe is not just a list of shows, but sort of an intellectual ecosystem. Working in the same office, the hosts of different shows are going to be hearing and talking about many of the same ideas in editorial brainstorm meetings and interacting with one another a lot. Sometimes we hear from listeners of a surprisingly diverse set of different HSW podcasts. I'm sure one day soon we'll do an episode about fractal demonology or something and we'll get an email from a listener who says, 'This reminds me of something I heard on a recent episode of *Stuff Mom Never Told You...*' These types of interactions suggest that at least some people are tuning in rather omnivorously for the general HSW vibe, rather than just signing up for a show with a particular type of subject matter. Hopefully in the future we'll be able to add even more shows to the HSW podcast ecosystem – I know there's still plenty of room to grow.

RL   The HSW mission has always been to demystify, inform and entertain – and the podcasts as they stand today continue to reflect that.

Notes

1. Robert Lamb, Joe McCormick and Christian Saeger, *Stuff to Blow Your Mind* (Atlanta, GA: HowStuffWorks, 2010), www.stufftoblowyourmind.com
2. George Monbiot is a zoologist and environmental columnist for *The Guardian*, as well as author of a number of books on the subject of ecology and conservation. *Feral* won the 2013 Thomson Reuters Award for Communicating Zoology and the 2014 Society of Biology Book Award. Monbiot was also a recipient of the UN Global 500 award for outstanding environmental achievement, presented by Nelson Mandela. His influential 2013 'Manifesto for Rewilding the World' makes an impassioned argument for an approach to nature that is 'about abandoning the Biblical doctrine of dominion which has governed our relationship with the natural world' in exchange for what he terms 'positive environmentalism.' George Monbiot, 'My Manifesto for Rewilding the World,' *The Guardian* 27 May 2013, https://www.theguardian.com/commentisfree/2013/may/27/my-manifesto-rewilding-world
3. The philosophy of restoring ecological diversity to humans as well as environments is based on the writings of leading ecologists and anthropologists including E.O. Wilson and Spencer Wells. See also David Foreman, *Rewilding North America: A Vision for Conservation in the 21st Century* (Washington, DC: Island Press, 2004); Michael Soule and Reed Noss, "Rewilding and Biodiversity: Complementary Goals for Continental Conservation," *Wild Earth* 8 (1998): 18–28.
4. George Monbiot, *Feral: Searching for Enchantment on the Frontiers of Rewilding* (London: Penguin UK, 2013), loc. 202–255. Monbiot, 'Manifesto.'
5. For more on the 'conversational' science podcast, see Hayley Birch and Emma Weitkamp, 'Podologues: conversations created by science podcasts,' *New Media & Society* 12(6) (2010): 889–909. For a concise overview of the development of the genre of science podcasts, see Ilenia Picardi and Simona Regina, 'Science via podcast,' *Journal of Science Communication* 7(2) (2008): 2–4.
6. You can find the episode archive for *STBYM* at http://www.stufftoblowyourmind.com/podcasts/stbym-archive.htm. *STBYM* is one of a network of podcasts produced by the *How Stuff Works* website. At its time of inception in the early 2000s it was a fairly simple website with posts demystifying various topics; it is now a multimedia group owned by Biucora, Ltd. publishing the website as well as 16 podcasts and ten blogs, and covering various educational topics. The evolution of the organisation is a perfect example of changes in information culture more broadly: as our media diet has grown richer, so has the variety of ways in which we access and create information, with podcasting as a principal example of media which is conversational and user-driven.
7. Asif Agha, 'Registers of language', in *A Companion to Linguistic Anthropology* (2004): 23–45.

Jauert & Lowe argue that podcasting does not have the same well-defined listener position, tending to position listeners as interested in 'enlightenment', similar to traditional public service radio. Per Jauert and Gregory Ferrell Lowe, 'Public Service Broadcasting for Social and Cultural Citizenship', in *Cultural Dilemmas in Public Service Broadcasting* (Göteborg: Nordicom, 2005): 13–17.

8. Mariam Durrani, Kevin Gotkin, and Corrina Laughlin, "Serial, Seriality, and the Possibilities for the Podcast Format," *American Anthropologist* 117(3) (2015): 1–4.

9. McCormick differentiates the written from the spoken knowledge unit, claiming that

> the main difference between preparation for a podcast and work on an article is that our podcasts are both collaborative and conversational. So on a podcast, I don't necessarily have to familiarize myself with everything that's going to be covered in the final product. Robert might read about one thing and I'll read about another, and then we sort of tell each other about it.

Danielle Barrios-O'Neill, *Interview with Joe McCormick and Robert Lamb* (2017) (see Appendix).

10. Ibid., [Appendix].

11. Whether the hosts' assumptions about information explicated on the show are reductive (or even at times incorrect), interesting and worthwhile avenues open up. Notably, the hosts and producers are well aware of this fact, judging by the way that perception and interpretation of scientific materials are subjects that come up regularly, as an issue to be treated critically (see, for example, 17 January 2017 episode 'Scientific Reductionism,' *Stuff to Blow Your Mind* (7 February 2017), accessed at http://www.stufftoblowyourmind.com/podcasts/scientific-reductionism.htm).

12. For a discussion of how paratextual material influences contemporary forms across media boundaries with regard to the series format, see Alan Hook, Danielle Barrios-O'Neill & Jolene Mairs Dyer, "A Transmedia Topology of 'Making a Murderer'," *VIEW Journal of European Television History and Culture* 5(10) (2016): 124–139, http://ojs.viewjournal.eu/index.php/view/article/view/JETHC117/244

13. The term *prosumer* was coined by Alvin Toffler in *The Third Wave* (New York: Bantam books, 1981) and has since been adopted into discourses in marketing, media studies and a wide range of other disciplines. 'Prosumerism' describes the rise of do-it-yourself production and consumption, which have become increasingly normal in the post-computing era.

14. Hook et al., 'Transmedia Topology', 2016.

15. Levine, *Forms*, 23. Mackenzie Wark, also focusing on the lack of discernible teleology, argues that this style of narrativity ('as horizontal as a pipeline') is a precursor to capitalist realism: the story is 'about making something out of

this world, not transcending it in favor of another.' Mackenzie Wark, *Molecular Red: Theory for the Anthropocene* (London, UK: Verso Books, 2015): 185–7.

16. From *Interview* (2017): JM: 'It also does help create the sense that the HSW podcast universe is not just a list of shows, but sort of an intellectual ecosystem.' [Appendix].

17. Ibid., [Appendix].

18. For more on operational aesthetics in media, see Jason Mittell, *Complex TV: The Poetics of Contemporary Television storytelling* (New York, US: NYU Press, 2015), loc. 880–1192.

19. Matt Tierney, *What Lies Between: Void Aesthetics and Postwar Post-politics* (Lanham, MD: Rowman & Littlefield International, 2014): 10, 39.

20. The use of formal or technical language in relation to science and technology is a factor frequently cited as obfuscating information and alienating audiences; see for example Sebastian Krätzig & Bartlett Warren-Kretzschmar, 'Using Interactive Web Tools in Environmental Planning to Improve Communication about Sustainable Development' in *Sustainability 2014*, 6(1): 236–250.

21. Cheryl Geisler, *Academic Literacy and the Nature of Expertise: Reading, Writing, and Knowing in Academic Philosophy* (London: Routledge, 2013). Paul N. Edwards, *A Vast Machine: Computer Models, Climate Data, and the Politics of Global Warming* (Boston: MIT Press, 2010): 281.

22. Caroline Levine, *Forms: Whole, Rhythm, Hierarchy, Network* (Princeton, NJ: Princeton University Press, 2015): 81.

23. Tierney, *What Lies Between*, 20.

24. See for example: Kerry Dwan, Carrol Gamble, Paula R. Williamson, and Jamie J. Kirkham, 'Systematic review of the empirical evidence of study publication bias and outcome reporting bias—an updated review,' *PloS one* 8(7) (2013); Mark Peplow, 'Social sciences suffer from severe publication bias,' *Nature* (28 August 2014), https://www.nature.com/news/social-sciences-suffer-from-severe-publication-bias-1.15787

25. For specific enquiries into the politics of scientific writing, see for example Charles Leslie, 'Scientific racism: Reflections on peer review, science and ideology', *Social Science & Medicine* 31(8) (1990): 891–905; Malcolm N. Macdonald, 'Pedagogy, pathology and ideology: the production, transmission and reproduction of medical discourse', *Discourse & Society* 13(4) (2002): 447–467; Ding, Dan. 'Marxism, ideology, power and scientific and technical writing' in *Journal of technical writing and communication* 28(2) (1998): 133–161; Paul M. Dombrowski, 'Ethics and technical communication: The past quarter century' in *Journal of Technical Writing and Communication* 30(1) (2000): 3–29.

26. From Christie Wilcox, 'It's time to e-volve: taking responsibility for science communication in a digital age':

> Right now, science is almost entirely a monologue given to a very specific audience. As scientists, we pride ourselves on doing meaningful, cutting-edge research and publishing it in the top-tier journals of our field. The problem is, these publications only communicate science to other scientists. Articles are locked behind paywalls, and even those that are published in open access journals still lie behind jargon walls—the barriers that keep the people we want to become more scientifically literate from understanding what we do because they do not know the terminology.

Biological Bulletin 222(2) (2012): 86, http://www.journals.uchicago.edu/doi/full/10.1086/BBLv222n2p85

27. Margaret Bradley and Peter J. Lang, 'Affective reactions to acoustic stimuli,' *Psychophysiology* 37(2) (2000): 204–215.

28. Marshall McLuhan, *Understanding Media: The Extensions of Man,* New Edition (Cambridge, MA: MIT Press, 1994): 298.

29. Richard Berry argues:

> What has changed since podcasting began is that podcasters have developed aesthetics that are notably different to linear radio. ... podcasts have developed definite features that are distinct from ... podcasting ... offers, in many instances, a sense of 'hyper-intimacy'. Podcasts are listened to in an intimate setting (headphones), utilizing an intimate form of communication (human speech). Furthermore, in many cases, podcasts are presented by people from within a listener's own community of interest or by people she/he may already have a relationship with via social media and are frequently recorded in a podcaster's own personal or domestic space.

Berry, 'Part of the establishment: Reflecting on 10 years of podcasting as an audio medium', in *Convergence* 22(6) (2016): 666.

30. Lars Nyre found that subjects of a study found BBC podcasts difficult to listen to on the move, as they found they were 'too authoritative in tone' and 'this type of content requires enhanced concentration'. Nyre, 'Urban headphone listening and the situational fit of music, radio and podcasting,' *Journal of Radio & Audio Media* 22(2) (2015): 295.

31. McLuhan, *Understanding Media*, 303.

32. Marie-France Kouloumdjian, 'Le walkman et ses pratiques, rapport de recherché,' *Multigraphie* (Lyon: Center for National Scientific Research, 1985): 16.

33. Thibaud, Jean Paul, 'The Sonic Composition of the City', in M. Bull and L. Black (Eds) *The Auditory Culture Reader* (London: Berg, 2003): 329–342.
34. See for example Jatin Srivastava, 'Media multitasking performance: Role of message relevance and formatting cues in online environments', *Computers in Human Behavior* 29(3) (2013): 888–895.
35. The relationship between auditory processing and complexity is a compelling area spanning a number of disciplines, and much of this body of work suggests that this is a productive relationship; a 1999 study found, for example, that 'audio cues can provide useful information about processes and problems, and support the perceptual integration of a number of separate processes into one complex one.' William Gaver, Randall B. Smith, and Tim O'Shea, 'Effective sounds in complex systems: The ARKola simulation', in *Proceedings of the SIGCHI Conference on Human factors in Computing Systems* (New York: ACM, 1991): 85–90.
36. The phrase 'screen of sound' I borrow from McLuhan, who writes,

    So much do-it-yourself, or completion and 'closure' of action, develops a kind of independent isolation in the young that makes them remote and inaccessible. The mystic screen of sound with which they are invested by their radios provides … privacy … and immunity from parental behest. (303)

37. Jean-Paul Thibaud describes how

    Using a walkman in public places is part of an urban tactic which consists in decomposing the territorial structure of the city and recomposing it through spatio-phonic behaviors. Double movement of deterritorialisation and reterritorialisation. This new urban nomad is here and there at the same time, transported by the secret rhythm of his walkman and in direct contact with the place he's walking through.

    Thibaud, 'The Sonic Composition of the City' in *The Auditory Culture Reader* (London: Bloomsbury, 2003): 330.
38. William J. Ripple, Robert L. Beschta, Jennifer K. Fortin, and Charles T. Robbins, 'Trophic cascades from wolves to grizzly bears in Yellowstone,' *Journal of Animal Ecology 83*, no. 1 (2014): 223–233.
39. E. Borer, E. Seabloom, J. Shurin, K. Anderson, C. Blanchette, B. Broitman, and B. Halpern, 'What determines the strength of a trophic cascade?' in *Ecology, 86* no. 2 (19): 528–537.
40. Monbiot, *Feral*, loc 226.
41. As for preparation, McCormick describes it as 'very uncomplicated and informal':

    I'd say the most common route looks like this: Robert and I email each other saying, 'Hey, have you ever read about X? I was thinking that could be interesting for an episode.' Then we bat the idea back and forth a little bit …. If we decide to move forward with it, we begin to collect and share resources for research. We create a shared Google document and paste in ideas, citations, links and so forth. We share any books or PDFs we have that the other might want to read. Then we go to work creating an outline for the episode in the shared document and filling it with notes from our research. The episodes are not scripted, but we do work from notes created in our shared document, so what you hear in the end is a mixture of comments we prepared ahead of time and spontaneous, free-flowing conversation.

Interview, 2017, [Appendix].

42. Lamb explains how 'discoveries in the research force you to restructure.' Ibid., [Appendix].

43. Levine, *Forms*, 18. Lorri G. Nandrea, *Misfit Forms* (New York: Fordham University Press, 2015): 3. The incipient species or forms that Nandrea traces include, for instance, direct relationships between typology and affect in *Jane Eyre*, an alternative plotting structure in *Robinson Crusoe*, and the functions of wonder and negative capability in novels by Charlotte Brontë and Charles Dickens.

44. Timothy Morton, *The Ecological Thought* (Cambridge, MA: Harvard University Press, 2010): 26.

45. Morton argues for a very particular ecological innovation in the arts, a new aesthetic that is primarily ambient, 'oozes', 'drifts' and wanders relatively aimlessly, like a dust mote or a jellyfish. Morton, *Ecological Thought*, 102–7, 125.

46. Walter Benjamin, *The Writer of Modern Life: Essays on Charles Baudelaire* (Cambridge, MA: Harvard University Press, 2006).

47. Says McCormick,

We're not always well-versed in the topic before we begin researching for an episode, so often we don't know what there is to know until we get into the weeds. Some new tangents and subtopics come into focus; some ideas we had in the beginning turn out to be dead ends. So the final structure and contents of the episode is really more an emergent product of our research and reading than anything else.

Interview, 2017, [Appendix].

48. Importantly, this trend is linked to increasingly powerful methods for using and manipulating data in the sciences, which enables more effective intuitive modelling methods. In 'Equipping scientists for the new biology,' the authors describe 'discovery science,' as cataloguing the elements of a system without any hypotheses on how it works. Hypothesis-driven science is described as being smaller-scale, narrowly focused, and using a limited range of technologies. See Ruedi Aebersold, Leroy E. Hood, and Julian D. Watts, 'Equipping scientists for the new biology' in *Nature Biotechnology* 18, no. 4 (2000): 359–359. So-called 'Bayesian' or 'frequentist' systems of analysis arrived in the 1960s,

with the arrival of modern computing technologies. For a seminal description see Jerome Cornfield, 'Bayes theorem' in *Revue de L'Institut International de Statistique* (The Hague: SI World Statistics Congress, 1967): 34–49. A related change is the increasing use of Bayesian inference in statistical scientific analysis, which operates with the understanding that, unlike in a more orthodox view of scientific sampling, everything can be treating as a probability, and outcomes are always open to updating—effectively a statistical method that poses every conclusion as a draft. Again, this is an intuitive approach to data, where the model is created to fit the data rather than vice versa.

49. Morton, *Dark Ecology*, 42.
50. N. Katherine Hayles, ed. *Chaos and Order: Complex Dynamics in Literature and Science* (Chicago: University of Chicago Press, 1991): 25–27, 31–34.
51. Morton, *Dark Ecology*, 42.
52. Robert Lamb, Joe McCormick and Christian Saeger, 'So Cute I Could Eat You Up', *Stuff to Blow Your Mind* (Atlanta, GA: HowStuffWorks, 2015). http://www.stufftoblowyourmind.com/podcasts/so-cute-i-could-eat-you-up.htm. Robert Lamb, Joe McCormick and Christian Saeger, 'Sexbots: From Objectification to Therapeutic Surrogates', *Stuff to Blow Your Mind* (Atlanta, GA: HowStuffWorks, 2017). http://www.stufftoblowyourmind.com/podcasts/sexbots.htm
53. Morton, *Dark Ecology*, 42.
54. *Interview*, 2017, [Appendix].

Bibliography

Aebersold, R., Hood, L., & Watts, J. (2000). Equipping scientists for the new biology. *Nature Biotechnology, 18*(4), 359–359.

Agha, A. (2004). Registers of language. In A. Duranti (Ed.), *A companion to linguistic anthropology* (pp. 23–45). Oxford/Malden, MA: Wiley Blackwell.

Benjamin, W. (2006). *The writer of modern life: Essays on Charles Baudelaire.* Cambridge, MA: Harvard University Press.

Berry, R. (2016). Part of the establishment: Reflecting on 10 years of podcasting as an audio medium. *Convergence, 22*(6), 661–671.

Birch, H., & Weitkamp, E. (2010). Podologues: Conversations created by science podcasts. *New Media & Society, 12*(6), 889–909.

Borer, E. T., Seabloom, E. W., Shurin, J. B., Anderson, K. E., Blanchette, C. A., Broitman, B., & Halpern, B. S. (2005). What determines the strength of a trophic cascade? *Ecology, 86*(2), 528–537.

Bradley, M., & Lang, P. (2000). Affective reactions to acoustic stimuli. *Psychophysiology*, *37*(2), 204–215.

Cornfield, J. (1967). Bayes theorem. In *Revue de L'Institut International de Statistique* (pp. 34–49). The Hague: SI World Statistics Congress.

Ding, D. (1998). Marxism, ideology, power and scientific and technical writing. *Journal of Technical Writing and Communication, 28*(2), 133–161.

Dombrowski, P. (2000). Ethics and technical communication: The past quarter century. *Journal of Technical Writing and Communication, 30*(1), 3–29.

Durrani, M., Gotkin, K., & Laughlin, C. (2015). Serial, seriality, and the possibilities for the podcast format. *American Anthropologist, 117*(3), 1–4.

Dwan, K., Gamble, C., Williamson, P., & Kirkham, J. (2013). Systematic review of the empirical evidence of study publication bias and outcome reporting bias—An updated review. *PLoS One, 8*(7), e66844.

Edwards, P. (2010). *A vast machine: Computer models, climate data, and the politics of global warming.* Boston: MIT Press.

Foreman, D. (2004). *Rewilding North America: A vision for conservation in the 21st century.* Washington, DC: Island Press.

Gaver, W., Smith, R., & O'Shea, T. (1991). Effective sounds in complex systems: The ARKola simulation. In *Proceedings of the SIGCHI conference on human factors in computing systems* (pp. 85–90). New York: ACM.

Geisler, C. (2013). *Academic literacy and the nature of expertise: Reading, writing, and knowing in academic philosophy.* London: Routledge.

Hayles, N. K. (Ed.). (1991). *Chaos and order: Complex dynamics in literature and science.* Chicago: University of Chicago Press.

Hook, A., Barrios-O'Neill, D., & Mairs Dyer, J. (2016). A transmedia topology of *Making a Murderer. VIEW: Journal of European Television History and Culture, 5*(10), 124–139.

Jauert, P., & Ferrell Lowe, G. (2005). Public service broadcasting for social and cultural citizenship. In P. Jauert & G. Ferrell Lowe (Eds.), *Cultural dilemmas in public service broadcasting* (pp. 13–33). Göteburg: Nordicom.

Kouloumdjian, M.-F. (1985). Le walkman et ses pratiques, rapport de recherché. *Multigraphie.* Lyon: Center for National Scientific Research.

Krätzig, S., & Warren-Kretzschmar, B. (2014). Using interactive web tools in environmental planning to improve communication about sustainable development. *Sustainability, 6*(1), 236–250.

Lamb, R., McCormick, J., & Sager, C. (2010). *Stuff to blow your mind.* Atlanta: HowStuffWorks, Inc. www.stufftoblowyourmind.com [Internet]. Accessed 16 Dec 2017.

Leslie, C. (1990). Scientific racism: Reflections on peer review, science and ideology. *Social Science & Medicine, 31*(8), 891–905.

Levine, C. (2015). *Forms: Whole, rhythm, hierarchy, network.* Princeton: Princeton University Press.

Macdonald, M. (2002). Pedagogy, pathology and ideology: The production, transmission and reproduction of medical discourse. *Discourse & Society, 13*(4), 447–467.

McLuhan, M. (1994). *Understanding media: The extensions of man* (New ed.). Cambridge, MA: MIT Press.

Mittell, J. (2015). *Complex TV: The poetics of contemporary television storytelling.* New York: NYU Press.

Monbiot, G. (2013a). Accidental rewilding. *Aeon.* aeon.co/essays/why-humanitarian-disasters-are-good-for-nature [Internet]. Accessed 16 Dec 2017.

Monbiot, G. (2013b). A manifesto for rewilding the world. www.theguardian.com/commentisfree/2013/may/27/my-manifesto-rewilding-world [Internet]. Accessed 16 Dec 2017.

Monbiot, G. (2013c). *Feral: Searching for enchantment on the frontiers of rewilding* [electronic edition]. London: Penguin.

Morton, T. (2010). *The ecological thought.* Cambridge, MA: Harvard University Press.

Morton, T. (2016). *Dark ecology: For a logic of future coexistence.* New York: Columbia University Press.

Nandrea, L. G. (2015). *Misfit forms.* New York: Fordham University Press.

Norman, D. (2010). *Living with complexity.* Boston: MIT Press.

Nyre, L. (2015). Urban headphone listening and the situational fit of music, radio and podcasting. *Journal of Radio & Audio Media, 22*(20), 279–298.

Peplow, M. (2014). Social sciences suffer from severe publication bias. https://www.nature.com/news/social-sciences-suffer-from-severe-publication-bias-1.15787 [Internet]. Accessed 16 Dec 2017.

Picardi, I., & Regina, S. (2008). Science via podcast. *Journal of Science Communication, 7*(2), 2–4.

Ripple, W. J., Beschta, R., Fortin, J., & Robbins, C. (2014). Trophic cascades from wolves to grizzly bears in Yellowstone. *Journal of Animal Ecology, 83*(1), 223–233.

Soule, M., & Noss, R. (1998). Rewilding and biodiversity: Complementary goals for continental conservation. *Wild Earth, 8,* 18–28.

Srivastava, J. (2013). Media multitasking performance: Role of message relevance and formatting cues in online environments. *Computers in Human Behavior, 29*(3), 888–895.

Thibaud, J. P. (2003). The sonic composition of the city. In M. Bull & L. Back (Eds.), *The auditory culture reader* (pp. 329–342). London: Bloomsbury.

Tierney, M. (2015). *What lies between: Void aesthetic and postwar post-politics.* London: Rowman and Littlefield.

Toffler, A. (1981). *The third wave.* New York: Bantam Books.

Wark, M. (2015). *Molecular red: Theory for the Anthropocene.* London: Verso Books.

Wilcox, C. (2012). It's time to e-volve: Taking responsibility for science communication in a digital age. *The Biological Bulletin, 222*(2) 85–87. http://www.journals.uchicago.edu/doi/full/10.1086/BBLv222n2p85 [Internet]. Accessed 16 Dec 2017.

9

The Podcast as an Intimate Bridging Medium

Lukasz Swiatek

Who would have thought, not too long ago, that it would be possible to sit in regularly on a telephone conversation with a Nobel Prize-winner: but without a telephone, and at a time and place of one's own choosing? This scenario would have been a mere fantasy in the (not-too-distant) past. Yet this is the sort of possibility that podcasting offers: the chance to connect with others in different and distant places around the globe, to hear remarkable personal stories at entirely self-chosen times, and to gain new insights, all delivered in a way that feels intimate.

These are just some of the many benefits that podcasting has given publics around the world. The medium has been celebrated, and for good reason. As Berry (2006) points out, it has enabled individuals and groups to engage in new practices and deliver new types of audio content for listeners. It has also eliminated fixed listening schedules, complex broadcasting equipment, and the need for would-be content producers to receive specialised training (Berry 2015).

This chapter focuses on the way in which podcasts enable connectivity for diverse publics. Specifically, the chapter argues that the podcast can be conceived as an intimate bridging medium: a means of communication that generates a sense of intimacy (even though the podcast's participant(s) and the listener are not physically proximate) while enabling two types of boundaries to be crossed. The first are knowledge boundaries; the medium helps individuals and groups access new insights, from both inside and outside their

L. Swiatek (✉)
Massey University, Wellington, New Zealand
e-mail: L.Swiatek@massey.ac.nz

© The Author(s) 2018
D. Llinares et al. (eds.), *Podcasting*, https://doi.org/10.1007/978-3-319-90056-8_9

areas of expertise and interest. The second are boundaries between individuals and groups from different contexts; these contexts include diverse locations and socio-cultural backgrounds. Podcasting can also potentially help such individuals from diverse publics achieve particular goals. This bridging medium is distinct to others in the way it invokes the 'intensely personal and intimate' nature of listening (Brabazon 2016: 121) and 'return[s] the emotion, connection and community' (Brabazon 2012: 148) to the activities of publics around the globe.

At the same time, there are less egalitarian and democratising aspects of podcasting that the chapter also examines. It argues that, although the medium is generally equalising, the digital public sphere in which it exists is unequal, and this prevents podcasting's bridging function from being as successful as it could be. Many of the existing media hierarchies are replicated in the realm of podcasting.

To illustrate these ideas, the chapter provides an in-depth analysis of an episode from a representative podcast series: *Nobel Prize Talks* (produced by Nobel Media). This case has been chosen because it illustrates the chapter's key claims: that the podcast can be thought of as an intimate bridging medium, and that it is surrounded by inequalities that prevent it from functioning as effectively as it could. Analyses of specifically selected parts of the latest episode in the series—featuring a phone conversation with May-Britt Moser, one of the 2014 Nobel laureates in Physiology or Medicine—provide more than sufficient evidence to illustrate the key ideas.

The chapter contributes to our knowledge of podcasting by placing the medium within a social context, and by highlighting the challenges that it, and the producers using it, must confront. It also helps us understand its unique role within the wider media landscape and, in particular, its affordance, in Gibson's (1979) sense, as a highly portable medium that bridges temporal and spatial divides between social groups in a way that can strongly generate a feeling of intimacy between the podcast participant(s) and the listener.

Four sections make up the chapter. First, the notion of the podcast as an intimate bridging medium is discussed. Second, the medium's bridging of knowledge barriers is explored; third, its bridging of socio-cultural divides is examined. Fourth, the inequalities that surround it are canvassed. All four parts of the chapter draw on examples from the case study, whose details are outlined in the next section.

An Intimate Bridging Medium

The two ways in which the podcast can be conceived as an intimate bridging medium—in helping individuals cross contextual boundaries and knowledge boundaries—stem from the two key ways in which the notion of the 'bridging medium' itself has been discussed to date in scholarly literature. There is currently no accepted definition of the notion of the 'bridging medium' (in the area of media and communication), even though this term has been appearing now for years in relation to different topics.

The first way in which the notion has been discussed to date relates to education. In this area, the medium has been considered as a way to help individuals and groups learn effectively. For example, in their study examining the ways in which individuals learn about politics from the mass media, Chaffee and Kanihan (1997) have commented that television has been a key tool for educating newcomers about American politics. In particular, they note that it has been a bridging medium for immigrants and adolescents; television has helped both groups cross into this domain of knowledge. Another example is Bautista's (2000) examination of literacy work among minority language groups in the Philippines. She notes school administrators' resistance to the use of the vernacular as a bridging medium for early literacy. In both of these studies, though, the concept is not explicitly defined.

The second way in which the term has been examined concerns social connection. Here, the medium has been seen as a way to help individuals and groups forge links with each other. For instance, Singh (2012) examines teleconferencing as a bridging medium within the context of distance education. Specifically, he looks at the benefits (and challenges) of teleconferencing as a way to span, through technological mediation, the geographic and temporal distances among learners, teachers and institutions. Similarly, drawing on Downing and Husband (2005: 217), Brantner and Herczeg (2013) question whether a particular transcultural magazine can serve as 'a medium to bring differences together'. Boulianne (2007), to give one more example, has argued that the internet is a superior bridging medium to television, as it enables relational activities, such as social networking through discussion or forum sites. Again, such studies do not explore the specific characteristics of the bridging medium further.

A third way of understanding this type of medium relates to convergence. For instance, Bozeman (2004) argues that the internet, in melding various communication sources, is a multi-channel and bridging medium. Wei (2008) argues that the mobile phone is also a bridging medium, as it is able to bring together various media. However, this third approach is excluded from this chapter, given the fact that podcasting (as a sonic-only medium) does not subsume other media formats.

As mentioned in the introduction, the distinctive aspect of this bridging medium is its intimate nature. It is the sonically generated relationality of podcasting, in giving listeners the impression of directness and closeness, that makes it such a compelling way to bridge spatial and temporal divides. As Romero (in Greene 2016: 91) points out, 'most people are listening to it [podcasting] on their headphones. We are literally whispering in people's ears'. Indeed, the relational aspect of the medium is one of its key features. McQuillan (paraphrased in Walker 2011: 36–37) makes the observation that: 'Podcasting is intimate, and the most common mistake ... in amateur podcasters is the tendency to forget the relationship they have with their own listeners'.

This intimacy offers significant benefits to organisations creating podcasts, such as Nobel Media, which produces the popular series *Nobel Prize Talks*. Nobel Media (a commercially based, public limited company owned by the not-for-profit Alfred Nobel Memorial Foundation, which, in turn, reports to the Nobel Foundation) launched the series (available at www.nobelprize.org/podcast) in 2013. It features a range of different Nobel laureates in conversation with Adam Smith, the Editorial Director of Nobel Media. The Nobel Prize website promotes and describes the series as a way for audiences to:

> Get to know the individuals that have been awarded the Nobel Prize a little bit better. What gives them their drive and creativity? Which future challenges are they passionate about and how do they think we should tackle them? And what do they think about the Nobel Prize? Explore these conversations with host Adam Smith. (Nobel Media 2017)

Since the first episode in the series was released in 2013, 30 episodes have now been released; they feature Smith in conversation with a range of different Nobel laureates from across the six Nobel Prize-awarded categories (physics, chemistry, physiology or medicine, literature, peace and economics). The interviewees have included Edvard Moser (one of the 2014 laureates in physiology or medicine), Muhammad Yunus (the recipient of the 2006 Nobel Peace Prize), Eric Maskin (the winner of the Nobel Prize in Economic Sciences in 2007), and Alice Munro (the 2013 laureate in the literature category).

The *Nobel Prize Talks* podcast series has been constructed in a way that deliberately enhances intimacy. Each episode has a straightforward construction that underscores the nearness of the interviewee (and interviewer) to the listener, even though all three are physically non-proximate to each other. The episodes begin with a brief musical opening, featuring relaxed, modern-sounding, electronically composed music. After a few seconds, the voice of the interviewee (the Nobel laureate) appears and the music fades slightly; a choice comment from the laureate—a grab—is played, and then the volume of the music increases again for about two seconds, after which Smith gives his greeting of welcome. This salutation is designed to convey nearness and friendliness. It is evident, for example, in the most recent episode about May-Britt Moser. Smith says:

> Hello, and welcome to this episode of Nobel Prize Talks, in which we meet May-Britt Moser, one of the 2014 Nobel Laureates in Physiology or Medicine. My name is Adam Smith, Chief Scientific Officer at Nobel Media, and this is the podcast in which we get to know the Nobel Laureates a little better. (Nobel Media 2017)

The informal and conversational nature of the greeting, featuring the collective first person ('we'), underscores the relational, personal nature of the format. During the greeting, the music fades entirely. Next follows a short introduction about the laureate; the rest of the interview then comprises the phone conversation between the laureate and Smith. The phone conversation format also enhances intimacy, as it gives listeners the impression—especially if they are listening to the episode through headphones from a mobile device of some kind—that they are themselves part of the phone call. And not just any phone call: they are 'sitting in' on a conversation between a famous, award-winning individual and a representative of an internationally renowned organisation.

Bridging Knowledge Divides

Podcasting's bridging of knowledge barriers in an intimate manner is one of its key, and most readily apparent, properties. Thanks to the medium's wide accessibility—given its general affordability and portability—knowledge in diverse domains can be shared by individuals and groups around the world. Thanks, as well, to their intimate, personal and often-conversational natures, podcast episodes can help individuals of different educational levels cross disciplinary boundaries easily. Audience members need not be enrolled in an educational system in order reap their benefits. As Brabazon (2016: 122) writes: 'Podcasts—through sound—can move far beyond the limitations of bricks and mortar. A learning environment can transcend a physical environment.' Indeed, such environments—especially formal ones—often entail significant limitations, because: 'Too often, soundscapes are cheapened with monotonic verbal deliveries in lectures, interjected with stammering and confusion, and do not open our ears to the other rhythms, melodies, intonations and textures in the sonic palette' (127).

Listening, and relying on sounds alone, are the two key qualities that make this medium so effective as a way of traversing knowledge divisions. Brabazon (121) explains that: 'Listening is different from hearing. It is intentional, conscious and active. Listening is literacy for the ear. It is a social act and involves making choices in filtering and selecting sounds from our sonic environment.' Furthermore, she explains that: 'Sound is a mode of communication that slows the interpretation of words and ideas, heightens awareness of an environment and encourages quiet interiority' (127). These two aspects also enhance the medium's intimate nature.

The previous example, the interview with May-Britt Moser, again robustly demonstrates the way in which listeners can gain new knowledge in relatable and relational ways. Among the topics of discussion during the recorded phone call are the laureate's research achievements. At one point in the conversation, Smith playfully asks Moser, 'can you imitate the sound of a single-cell in the hippocampus?' (This is a sound that she discovered in the course of her research.) Moser laughs briefly, as does Smith. She explains that 'it's like popcorn', and then gives her impression, saying:

> it's: pop, pop, pop, pop, pop, pop. And then it comes into the field [of vision, presumably], and then it's [raising her pitch and pace]: pop! Pop! Pop! Pop! Pop! Pop! [Returning to her normal pitch and pace] And then it goes out of the field, and pop, pop, pop, pop. And then there's silence.

Moser then laughs again, as does Smith. Continuing to laugh, he says: 'That was a beautiful imitation. Absolutely loved it.' She, also continuing to laugh, exclaims: 'Thank you!' This highly humorous part of the conversation illustrates the way in which the podcast, due to its personal, intimate appeal, can help audience members gain new knowledge. In particular, it can help them connect with new, and even difficult, subjects beyond their regular areas of interest and expertise, by engaging them in easily digestible material through the intentional and conscious social act of listening. It reflects Brabazon's (2016: 121) observation that: 'When we listen, we learn.'

Bridging Socio-Cultural Divides

Connecting publics around the world, by bridging socio-economic divides, is the other salient aspect of podcasting. In particular, the medium allows individuals from different backgrounds to connect with the participants of the episodes to which they are listening. Meyerson (2010) and Reed (2012) note that the intimate nature of podcasting helps producers build loyal relationships with audiences; this can be vital from a commercial—and particularly marketing—standpoint. For both for-profit and not-for-profit producers, though, the ability to build bonds with listeners is vital. According to Platt and Truant (2013, n.p.), it is such an effective medium 'because listeners spend hours with your voice in their head and will come to feel like they know you in a way. It can make for fantastic bonding'. The authors also comment, from their experience, that 'we meet people all the time who say they feel like they know us and hence feel bonded. That's a hell of a thing in terms of building community around you' (Platt and Truant 2016, n.p.)

The technical and functional qualities of the medium enhance its ability to connect individuals with each other. As mentioned previously, episodes are portable and easily transferrable between devices, small in size, and nearly always very cheap to download, making it an effective way for individuals to encounter others at pretty much any time and place of their choosing. As a 'popular form of mobile entertainment' (King 2017: 159), the medium also enables listeners to make those connections while listening to the entertaining narratives of others. Focusing only on sound by listening carefully, again, makes this process of engagement and connection more intense. The *Nobel Prize Talks* series illustrates the way in which individuals from different socio-economic backgrounds can engage with a variety of different Nobel laureates from various fields and locations. They can connect with them, get to know them, and hear their unique career and life insights. Each episode offers precisely these opportunities.

However, podcasting offers listeners more than just connections to podcast participants through para-social interactions (Horton and Wohl 1956): one-sided, non-present (rather than co-present) social relationships (Hills 2015). The medium also offers opportunities for connection with other listeners and members of related social groups. Brabazon (2016: 121), writing about teaching and learning specifically, makes exactly this observation, commenting that: 'While hyper-personal, if teachers and librarians can find a way to share and enable sonic literacies and listening practices, then communities of interest – communities for learning – are made.' This is true beyond educational contexts, as well. When individuals can form such communities, share podcasts (as well as other resources), and generate dialogue with others, para-social relationships become multi-social relationships: ways for individuals to connect with others multiply by displaying and performing relationships within particular communities (Hills 2015).

In this respect, podcasting can help groups come together to achieve particular common goals. In terms of engaging others to realise political goals in particular, Graham and Hand (2017) note that, given the intimate nature of podcasting, 'many listeners expect to be able to reach you. An engaged audience also feels invested in your success, and part of the community you're building.' For instance, in recent years, LGBTQ communities have used the medium to unite and achieve educational goals. King and Sanquist (2008) found that LGBTQ organisations were able to use podcasts not only to educate publics, but also to strengthen community identities. They were also able to support adults and youth struggling with various issues, such as violence, homophobia and hate crimes. As the authors observed:

> podcasting has afforded a distribution and availability of GLBT perspectives spanning global dimensions from Australia, to USA, UK to Asia. This distribution is not just international, but also from the most urban to remote rural communities. Isolation of GLBT individuals is being eliminated by being able to hear a wide variety of GLBT lifestyles through a medium without mainstream media filtering and in listening and viewing modes which can be private. (King and Sanquist 2008: 6)

This is an excellent example of the multi-social relationships that podcasts enable: relationships that cross socio-cultural boundaries, as well as international time and distance divides. As the authors (6) conclude: 'Rather than isolation, this new media provides the variety of GLBT podcasters a global platform.'

In connecting individuals with each other, this medium helps generate 'bridging capital'. This refers to the building of weak ties between different social groups; by contrast, bonding capital connects smaller, denser networks together through stronger ties (Putnam 2000). Both types of capital are forms of social capital, which refer to individuals' interpersonal connections, including 'social networks and the norms of reciprocity and trustworthiness that arise from them' (Putnam 2000: 19). While some scholars—most notably Bourdieu (1977 [1972])—have argued that social capital perpetuates inequalities, others—such as Coleman (1988) and Putnam (2000)—view this form of capital as a positive, beneficial factor for strengthening civic life and social cohesion.

Nobel Prize Talks illustrates the way in which podcasting can help build bridging capital. It connects diverse listeners with each other, and allows them to listen to each other's ideas and narratives, in a way that seems close, direct and personal. It offers members of particular communities opportunities to share their stories. For example, members of scientific communities in the Nobel Prize-awarded scientific disciplines can hear the stories of other prominent, award-winning members of their disciplines. These narratives can also be heard by members outside of those epistemic communities; that is, they can also be heard by lay or non-academic audiences, whose members can gain new knowledge or be inspired by the laureates. These different individuals may not be strongly connected with each other, but they can benefit from the multiple connections that the medium helps generate. Indeed, Schuller, Baron and Field (2000: 10) point out that bridging capital helps build connections between heterogeneous groups: connections that are likely to be more fragile, but also more likely to foster inclusion. By contrast, bonding capital is less pervasive; it builds stronger, but bounded and more particular, connections (Wallace and Pichler 2007).

Nobel Prize Talks builds bridging capital in large part thanks to the multi-social relationships that the internet enables. Such podcast series can be re-published by other groups, which often use them to advance particular social causes. For instance, the interview with May-Britt Moser was shared on the website of the Rosalind Franklin Society (RFS n.d.). This interdisciplinary, international organisation 'recognizes the work of outstanding women scientists, fosters greater opportunities for women in the sciences, and motivates and educates by examples young generations of women who have this calling' (RFS 2017). The re-publication of the link to the episode on the society's website aligns with the organisation's goal of motivating and educating women in the sciences. Indeed, the organisation actively promotes the benefits of science in encouraging individuals to access the episode, by instructing them to: 'Listen to May-Britt Moser, one of few female Medicine Laureates, describing her life and work, and the pure joy of exploring the connection between behavior and the brain' (RFS n.d.).

Other social groups have also helped their members connect to the Nobel laureates, as well as each other, through the re-publication of links to the podcast series on their websites. For instance, the University of Wisconsin-Madison's Computer Sciences Department publishes a 'Scout' report featuring interesting and useful online information content. In one such report, it encouraged its readers to access *Nobel Prize Talks* (ISRG 2015). This was then re-published by other groups, including the Manchester Metropolitan

University Library, which noted the series in its online weekly researchers' bulletin (MMU 2015), and NC State University's Agriculture and Life Sciences News page (NCSU 2015).

Bridging in an Unequal Digital Public Sphere

While podcasting can help individuals and groups bridge knowledge and context-related barriers, its effectiveness is challenged by the unequal nature of today's digital public sphere. This notion is an extension of Habermas's (1989 [1962]) notion of a social arena for public, rational democratic debate. In its online form, the digital public sphere has been envisioned as:

> a communicative sphere provided or supported by online or social media, from websites to social network sites, weblogs, and micro-blogs, where participation is open and freely available to everybody who is interested, where matters of common concern can be discussed, and where proceedings are visible to all. (Schäfer 2015: 322)

In this digital public sphere, podcasting should serve as a means for such open and free deliberation to occur. It should enable the views and narratives of different individuals and groups to be made public, and should allow for listeners, in turn, to respond to those views. However, today's public sphere does not allow for such a high degree of egalitarianism and openness, in several respects.

The inequalities in existing forms of media and communication are replicated in the digital public sphere. Specifically, it is the large media organisations that tend to dominate the online realm. As Sousa, Pinto and Silva (2013: 10) point out: 'Structural organizational forms of the society, namely the mainstream media, continue to be central agents of communication and information, as well as the major producers of the content consumed online.' This inequality is borne out, for example, in the types of podcasts that climb to the tops of the podcast charts. At the time of writing (July 2017), the ten podcast series listed in Table 9.1 appear at the top of the *Podcast Chart* 'Top 200' page (available at www.podcastchart.com/categories/top-200-podcasts):

(With only two exceptions, this list is the same as another: the chart of the top 100 podcasts at podbay.fm; the exceptions are numbers five and six on the list above, with the two series being in reverse order on the podbay.fm list.) Seven out of ten series in the list above are produced by existing (and often large and well-known) organisations. Only three titles—numbers two to four on the list—are produced either independently, or by a small organisation dedicated to podcasting.

Table 9.1 The top 10 podcast series on the Podcast Chart 'Top 200' page in July 2017

Podcast	Producer
1. Revisionist History	Panoply Media
2. Live from the Poundstone Institute	Independent
3. Amazon Secrets With Matt Behdjou	Independent
4. Mogul: The Life and Death of Chris Lighty	Gimlet Media (a narrative podcasting company)
5. 30 For 30 Podcasts	ESPN Radio
6. TED Radio Hour	NPR and TED
7. S-Town	Serial and This American Life
8. This American Life	In collaboration with Chicago Public Media
9. Stuff You Should Know	HowStuffWorks.com
10. Invisibilia	NPR

The list above also reveals the fact that it is difficult for unknown podcasts to gain wide listenerships, again because of the inequalities in the analogue realm that are replicated in the digital public sphere. Specifically, it is difficult for podcasts without institutional affiliation, or brand recognition (or both), to achieve prominence. As Berry (2015: 301) notes, it is rare for new and unknown podcasts to achieve instant success; usually 'podcasts require an advantage, which often comes from being a brand, such as being associated with a familiar producer, brand or personality'. Numbers seven and eight on the list above originally drew on various established institutional advantages; as Berry (301–302) explains:

> Serial benefitted from a debut on *This American Life*, heavy promotion in the run-up to launch and several favourable reviewers keen to know what Ira Glass was doing. The podcast was also able to draw on the extensive human and financial resources of a large and well-resourced, experienced and extensive production team. This created a distinctive advantage which few podcasts could aspire to. Serial was narrated by Sarah Koenig (an experienced *This American Life* producer) and overseen by Executive Producer Ira Glass, who has been producing *This American Life* since 1995.

Also, the first podcast series on the list—*Revisionist History*—is presented by Malcolm Gladwell, a well-known journalist and author. Panoply Media, which produces the podcast, is also the audio arm of The Slate Group: a US publishing entity that produces several well-known online publications, including *Slate* and ForeignPolicy.com.

The *Nobel Prize Talks* series also benefits from existing institutional advantages. Above all, it leverages the symbolic capital—in other words, the accumulated prestige (Bourdieu 1989)—of the Nobel Prizes. These accolades are very well known around the world, and the Nobel brand (indeed just the name alone) are easily recognisable. Consequently, the prominence and popularity of the podcast series are enhanced from the outset by the high status of the world-renowned source from which they come. Given the fact that the phone conversations feature Nobel Prize-winners, the podcast series can also exploit the celebrity status of its subjects: something that many podcast series are unable to do. Given these challenges, as well as the others mentioned in this section, podcasting faces limitations in serving as an effective bridging medium in general.

Conclusion

Thanks to the close and personal nature of the listening that it enables, the podcast succeeds in crossing boundaries of knowledge, as well as time and space. As this chapter has demonstrated, it is an effective intimate bridging medium. It provides a way for listeners to access new insights in a direct, close way from others around the world; it also provides a way for individuals and groups from diverse backgrounds to connect with each other. The podcast succeeds as a linking mechanism in ways that other media do not.

While the case study of the *Nobel Prize Talks* series illustrates these qualities of the medium, it also highlights the tensions and challenges that podcasting faces in the digital public sphere. This sphere privileges existing, established media bodies. It also advantages well-known entities—both organisations and individuals—who can leverage their existing prominence and resources to attract listeners and increase their popularity. Less-well-known podcast producers must contend with these inequalities, which make the intimate bridging medium less effective than it could otherwise be.

Nevertheless, the case study highlights the podcast's superiority over many other types of media to act as an intimate bridging medium. While other media types—such as television, books, computer games and magazines, to name but a few—also bridge space and time, as well as boundaries of knowledge, few provide audiences with the nearness, directness, flexibility, portability and accessibility of the podcast. The *Nobel Prize Talks* series embodies all of these qualities, and particularly the direct, accessible nature of the content created for podcasts. The series breaks down complex topics and specific disciplinary jargon in a casual conversational format; it gives listeners the chance to venture beyond their areas of interest and expertise, by having Nobel laureates speak gently and familiarly into their ears.

This chapter opens many avenues for future research about this vibrant and growing means of communication. It has examined only one case study (related to academia); other case studies, from different areas (related to popular culture, for example) could be studied. It would also be beneficial to investigate listeners' reactions to podcasting series of different kinds, and to compare whether (or not) they found those series beneficial, in terms of bridging the two key areas mentioned in this chapter. Close, textual analyses of episodes from different series could also be undertaken to add to knowledge in this area.

Bibliography

Bautista, M. L. S. (2000). Bridging research and practice in literacy work among minority language groups in the Philippines. *Studies in the Linguistic Sciences, 30*(1), 203–218.

Berry, R. (2006). Will the iPod kill the radio star? Profiling podcasting as radio. *Convergence: The International Journal of Research into New Media Technologies, 12*(2), 143–162.

Berry, R. (2015). Serial and ten years of podcasting: Has the medium grown up? *Radio, sound and Internet.* Proceedings of Net Station International Conference, Braga, University of Minho (pp. 299–309).

Boulianne, S. (2007). *Connecting, informing, and mobilizing youth and the advantaged: The role of the Internet in political engagement.* PhD thesis, The University of Wisconsin-Madison.

Bourdieu, P. (1977 [1972]). *Outline of a theory of practice.* Cambridge: Cambridge University Press.

Bourdieu, P. (1989). Social space and symbolic power. *Sociological Theory, 7*(1), 14–25.

Bozeman, B. (2004). The internet's impact on policy evaluation: Information compression and credibility. *Evaluation Review, 28*(2), 156–174.

Brabazon, T. (2012). The sound of a librarian: The politics and potential of podcasting in difficult times. In T. Brabazon (Ed.), *Digital dialogues and community 2.0: After avatars, trolls and puppets* (pp. 137–162). Oxford: Chandos Publishing.

Brabazon, T. (2016). Press play. In T. Brabazon (Ed.), *Play: A theory of learning and change* (pp. 119–144). Cham: Springer.

Brantner, C., & Herczeg, P. (2013). The life of a new generation: Content, values and mainstream media perception of transcultural ethnic media—An Austrian case. *Communications, 38*(2), 211–235.

Chaffee, S. H., & Kanihan, S. F. (1997). Learning about politics from the mass media. *Political Communication, 14*(4), 421–430.

Coleman, J. S. (1988). Social capital in the creation of human capital. *American Journal of Sociology, 94*(Special supplement), 95–120.

Downing, J. D. H. & Husband, C. (2005). *Representing 'race': Racism, ethnicities and media.* London: Sage.

Gibson, J. J. (1979). *The ecological approach to visual perception.* Boston: Houghton Mifflin.

Graham, B., & Hand, C. (2017). *America, the owner's manual: You can fight City Hall – And win* (New ed.). Los Angeles: SAGE/CQ Press.

Greene, S. (2016). *Market domination for podcasting: Secrets from the world's top podcasters.* New York: Morgan James Publishing.

Habermas, J. (1989 [1962]). *The structural transformation of the public sphere: An inquiry into a category of Bourgeois society* (trans: Burger, T., & Lawrence, F.). Cambridge: MIT Press.

Hills, M. (2015). From para-social to multisocial interaction: Theorizing material/digital fandom and celebrity. In P. D. Marshall & S. Redmond (Eds.), *A companion to celebrity.* Hoboken: Wiley.

Horton, D., & Wohl, R. R. (1956). Mass communication and para-social interaction: observations on intimacy at a distance. *Psychiatry, 19,* 215–229.

ISRG. (2015). The scout report. *Internet Scout Research Group, 21*(39). Available at: https://scout.wisc.edu/report/2015/1009#13

King, K. P. (2017). *Technology and innovation in adult learning.* San Francisco: Wiley.

King, K. P., & Sanquist, S. R. (2008). Case study of empowerment through new media among underrepresented groups: GLBT adults gain dominant voice in the first wave of podcasting. *Adult Education Research Conference 2008: Conference Proceedings.* Kansas State University Libraries: New Prairie Press. Available at: http://newprairiepress.org/aerc/2008/papers/38

Meyerson, M. (2010). *Success secrets of social media marketing superstars.* Toronto: Entrepreneur Press.

Manchester Metropolitan University. (2015). *Researchers' weekly bulletin: The blog.* www.library.mmu.ac.uk [Internet]. Accessed 2017.

NC State University. (2015). *Agriculture and life sciences news.* www.news.lib.ncsu.edu [Internet]. Accessed 2017.

Nobel Media. (2017). *Explore the Nobel Prize Talks podcast.* www.nobelprize.org [Podcast]. Accessed 2017.

Platt, S., & Truant, J. B. (2013). *Write, publish, repeat: The no luck required guide to self-publishing success.* Published Online: Sterling & Stone.

Platt, S., & Truant, J. B. (2016). *Iterate and optimize: Optimize your creative business for profit.* Published Online: Sterling & Stone.

Putnam, R. D. (2000). *Bowling alone: The collapse and revival of American community.* New York: Simon & Schuster.

Reed, J. (2012). *Get up to speed with online marketing: How to use websites, blogs, social networking and much more.* London: Financial Times Prentice Hall.

RFS. (2017). About. www.rosalindfranklinsociety.org [Internet]. Accessed 2017.

RFS. (n.d.). *They saw that we were in love with science.* www.rosalindfranklinsociety.org [Internet]. Accessed 2017.

Schäfer, M. S. (2015). Digital public sphere. In G. Mazzoleni (Ed.), *The international encyclopedia of political communication* (pp. 322–328). Chichester: Wiley Blackwell.

Schuller, T., Baron, S., & Field, J. (2000). *Social capital.* Oxford: Oxford University Press.

Senior Women Web. (n.d.). Another scout report post: Comforts of a luxury cruise, grammarly, to live and dine in L.A., Privacy Palette. www.seniorwomen.com [Internet]. Accessed 2017.

Singh, G. (2012). Video teleconferencing as a bridging medium in open and distance learning (ODL): Making it more effective. *Malaysian Journal of Distance Education, 14*(1), 25–40.

Sousa, H., Pinto, M., & Silva, E. C. (2013). Digital public sphere: Weaknesses and challenges. *Comunicação e Sociedade, 23*, 9–12.

Walker, K. (2011). *How to get your message out fast & free using podcasts: Everything you need to know about podcasting explained simply.* Ocala: Atlantic Pub. Group.

Wallace, C., & Pichler, F. (2007). Bridging and bonding social capital: Which is more prevalent in Europe? *European Journal of Social Security, 9*(1), 29–53.

Wei, R. (2008). The convergent mobile telephone: An emerging bridging medium. In A. C. Harper & R. V. Buress (Eds.), *Mobile telephones: Networks, applications, and performance.* New York: Nova Publishing.

10

Inner Ears and Distant Worlds: Podcast Dramaturgy and the *Theatre of the Mind*

Farokh Soltani

Radio Drama and Audio Dramaturgy

In 1999, five whole years before the word *podcast* was even invented,[1] Tim Crook (1999: 22–29) opened his book on radio drama with a history of audio-drama, divided into six ages, in which he charts the beginning of the form not with the advent of radio, but from an indeterminate point in the ancient past; indeed, it is not until the fourth age that radio communication makes an appearance. The point of this rather counter-intuitive history is that sound drama is not limited to radio broadcasting, and that the terms *audio-drama* and *radio drama* are not intrinsically interchangeable. Currently, according to Crook, we are in the 'sixth age' (Crook 1999: 26) of audio-drama, when the internet's ability to act as a sonic medium has opened entirely new avenues of making, distributing and listening to audio-drama. Podcasting, as a technological means of maintaining and mediating a direct connection between the creators and the audience, is perhaps the key transformative development of this new age, as it detaches drama from the economic, insti-tutional, and political requirements of radio broadcast. Technically, any enthusiast in possession of a small set of resources—an idea for a drama, a personal computer, some actors (or a good voice changer software) and a decent microphone, which is currently available on any smartphone—has the

F. Soltani (✉)
Royal Central School of Speech and Drama, University of London, London, UK
e-mail: Farokh.Soltani-Shirazi@cssd.ac.uk

© The Author(s) 2018
D. Llinares et al. (eds.), *Podcasting*, https://doi.org/10.1007/978-3-319-90056-8_10

189

potential to access a rapidly expanding pool of listeners. In the UK, the number of podcast listeners increased by over 44 per cent between 2016 and 2017, from 3.8 million (RAJAR 2016) to 5.5 million (RAJAR 2017), while the proportion of Americans who listen to podcasts has increased from 11 per cent in 2006 to 40 per cent in 2017—an estimated 112 million potential audience members (Edison Research 2017). Drama podcasts have increased in number—enough for Neil Verma to explore 43 of them in his aesthetic survey (Verma 2017a: 2)—and in prominence: Gimlet Media's *Homecoming* (2017), for example, featured the talents of A-listers Catherine Keener and David Schwimmer. Two decades into this sixth age of audio-drama, the form has found a new home. Yet, one can ask, is the dramaturgy of sound drama also making itself at home? How are the practices, techniques, and aesthetics of previous ages changing to exploit the possibilities of new digital cultures and tools? Beyond extending its reach for both producer and audience, what is podcasting doing to audio-drama? In this chapter, I want to argue that the increasing prevalence of podcast drama provides an opportunity not just for making audio-drama more diverse and far-reaching, but an opening for a reconceptualisation of what it is to create drama with sound alone, which breaks from the radiophonic models of previous ages. I posit, however, that taking this opportunity first requires a radical rethinking of the philosophical framework through which the function of audio-drama is comprehended. In short, my goal is to show that by understanding the podcast in its own terms, can we move toward an audio-dramaturgy that looks beyond the boundaries of *radio* dramaturgy.

I should admit outright that claims of a complete rethinking of audio-drama are nothing new. Indeed, Verma observes that 'over the past half-century, the only thing more reliable than the constant revival of radio drama is the insistence that what ensues is not really a revival, but something utterly new, instead' (Verma 2017b: 5). Verma's survey of the recent uptick in podcast drama examines the developments of this new so-called-revival, asking the very question driving this chapter: 'What would the new audio-drama actually sound like?' (Verma 2017a: 5). He notes that unlike other dramatic artforms, radio has no canon to look back upon, and that 'the most prominent voices [in the field] describe radio drama in ways that seeks to distance it from audio-drama' (Verma 2017b: 5); the latter, instead, appears to look to film and television as a model. Highlighting parallels between radio dramaturgy and the aesthetic and textual features of podcast drama, Verma argues that in its move forward, audio-drama should in fact 'leave TV and film behind and 'come home' to radio drama' (Verma 2017b: 10). This sense of continuity, also echoed by Andrew Bottomley (2015) in his examination of the *Welcome to the Night Vale* podcast, could be considered an inevitability: after all, radio drama's defining feature is that it creates drama through sound alone, and this necessitates a particular approach to the form's aesthetics and practices. As podcasts share this feature, it is only natural that they look back to radio history, the site of the majority of experiments in audio-drama, where the distinctive principles of non-visual dramaturgy have developed through years of trial and error. Should one follow this logic, the pursuit I have outlined above is unnecessary: radio dramaturgy *is* the boundary of audio-drama. Hence, as Verma points out, attempts to break with the heritage of radio drama are eventually bound to repeat it.

In the next few sections, I want to unpick and critique the assumption that the unisensory nature of audio-drama is the determining defining factor of radio dramaturgy, and the subsequent conclusion that radio drama is a suitable blueprint or paradigm for podcast drama. I posit that the principles of radio practice instead emerge out of the particular modes of listening afforded by the medium of radio. Therefore podcasting, which offers a completely different manner of listening experience, requires its own mode of dramaturgy. I support this claim in two ways. Firstly, I critique theoretical accounts of the function of audio-drama—characterised by the term *the theatre of the mind*—and draw attention both to their influence on the practices of radio dramaturgy, and to their assumptions about dramatic experience. Secondly, I draw from the philosophical discipline of phenomenology to explore the listener's encounter with radio and podcast sound, positing that the two are radically different where dramaturgy is concerned. Through this, I hope to show that the path of audio-drama can diverge from, rather than follow, the radio past.

Audio Dramaturgy and the Theatre of the Mind

Let us begin with a clear working definition of audio-dramaturgy. According to Aristotle, a poem is *drama* if it is mimetic—that is, if it presents the 'characters as living and moving before us' (Aristotle 1898: 13). As Keir Elam elaborates, the mimetic mode provides its audience with an opening into 'a fictional dramatic world' (2005: 87); such worlds are 'presented to the [audience] as 'hypothetically actual' constructs, since they are ['perceived'] in progress 'here and now' without narratorial mediation' (2005: 98). Subsequently, we can understand dramaturgy, literally meaning 'putting into dramatic form' (Luckhurst 2006: 5) as the process through which a potential fictional world is actualised for an audience through specific methods of presentation and mediation. In this sense, dramaturgy does not deal with what happens in the dramatic world, but concerns, in the case of theatre, 'external elements relating to staging, the overall artistic concept behind the staging, the politics of performance, and the calculated manipulation of audience response' (Luckhurst 2006: 10). Audio-dramaturgy then, is the praxis that turns a fiction into a dramatic presentation in sonic form, to be experienced as the 'here and now' of a world by a listener: the practices and processes that construct and configure the sound structure, the technologies involved in its creation, aesthetic paradigms, hypotheses about the audience's response, and so on. The distinctive nature of audio-drama reveals itself within this very definition: a crucial aspect of the experience of the world, vision, is absent from the toolkit of audio-dramaturgy. Audio does not have direct recourse to the sense of sight, and much of our experience of real and dramatic worlds is visible, but inaudible. This quality of the medium of sound, whether labelled *blind, invisible, imaginative* or *dark*—following Andrew Crisell, Martin Shingler, Tim Crook and Alan Beck, respectively—requires the audio-dramaturg to take specific steps to make the dramatic world tangible for the listener by other means, regardless of the medium of distribution.

It is a common trope to describe the means of audio-dramaturgy in terms of its appeal to the mind, rather than the eye, of the listener. In theoretical discussions of audio-drama—which, one should note, almost all concern *radio*—one particular label is applied often: *the theatre of the mind*. Marin Esslin articulates the term clearly in *The Mind as a Stage* (1971):

> [The radio] play comes to life in the listener's own imagination, so the *stage* on which it is performed *is the listener's own mind*. He himself, by having to provide the visual component, which is undeniably present in any true dramatic experience transmitted by radio, is an active collaborator with the producer. (Esslin 1971: 7)

Andrew Dubber calls the term a 'useful cliché, repeated by practitioners and radio educators alike' (2013: 101). Indeed, the idea that radio drama occurs in the listener's mind is rather ubiquitous in the discourse around the artform: John Drakakis describes the listener creating 'mental pictures' (1981: 20). Crook argues that radio creates a multi-sensory 'imaginative spectacle' (1999: 64) for the listener. Crisell posits that the listener uses the sonic codes of radio to create a 'mental picture' (1994: 8). *Theatre of the mind* is more than a simple metaphor for the effects of radio drama on the listener; it implies a particular relationship between the drama and the radio listener—one in which the experience of the dramatic world is achieved not through the immediate, concrete channel of vision and space, but through the listener's mental activity and intention. Where theories of radio drama differ is on the mechanism through which the listener constructs the *theatre of the mind*. Crisell favours 'transcodification' (1994: 146) as an explanation, arguing that radio drama works by presenting the listener with an array of auditory codes and signs, replacing visible but inaudible elements of the dramatic world, that she interprets in order to reconstruct the world through mental representation. Beck sees the process as similar to cognitive mapping—'the sort of mental activity that one uses in travelling to a friend's house, having an internal picture of the route' (2000: 3.1), allows the listener to gain an abstract knowledge of the dramatic world. Esslin (1971) and Martin Shingler (in Shingler and Wieringa 1998) cite the power of sounds in evoking memories and images as the foundation of the *theatre of the mind*. These proposed explanations all lead more or less to the same conclusion: that the sounds of radio drama work to activate the listener's engagement, so that she can turn her mind into a theatre to contain the dramatic world. The prevalent theories of audio-drama, in other words, understand the listener's experience as intellectual and imaginary.

A look at the conventions of audio-dramaturgy in its most common form, radio drama, reveals how the sounds of drama are structured to address the mind. The briefest survey of practitioner accounts and educational guides shows that the emphasis in radio dramaturgy is on creating clear, meaningful sounds to replace the visual aspects of the world for the listener's mind. The spoken word becomes the most important dramaturgical element on the radio, providing a sonic stand-in for what is inaudible but should be seen; indeed, there exists a strong consensus among theorists and practitioners that radio is fundamentally dependent on speech (see Drakakis 1981: 6; Rodger 1982: 10; Crisell 1994: 6; Shingler and Wieringa 1998: 6; Crook 1999: 54; McInerney 2001: 4; Pownall 2011: 20). To avoid ambiguity in the process of mental interpretation, sound effects are drawn from a recognisable lexicon of 'not what is real, but what is understandable' (McLeish 2012: 259), and signposted with speech for more clarity. Musical elements, too, can be used in place of visuals by indicating mood, passage of time, or transition between scenes (McLeish 2012: 261). The practical process of producing this sonic construct, too, is geared toward the listener's mind. Due to the importance of speech, radio is frequently labelled a 'writer's medium' (Lewis 1981: 6; Drakakis 1981: 58; Willett 2013: 200; Hill 2015: 44; Smethurst 2016: 80); after all, if words are the key to the listener's mind, then the script contains a blueprint of all the information necessary for the reconstruction of the dramatic world. The process of producing the sound effects, whether background atmosphere or spot effects, is guided by the script, and is a 'search for clear associations between situation and sound' (McLeish 2012: 259). Frequently, this means resorting to conventional sounds that 'radio [producers] over the years have developed [...] with generally understood meanings' (McLeish 2012: 259). A sound structure thus produced is clear and meaningful enough to convey the dramatic world to the listener. Of course, with direct access to the mind also comes an expansion of the boundaries of possibilities in this world: after all, the dramatic world is not limited to what can be seen or recreated on a stage or on film, and bound only by what is imaginable. Addressing the mind rather than sight provides the audio-dramaturg ultimate control over the flow of the listener's awareness of space, time, positions, objects, identities, and other aspects that would be immediately manifest were she to experience the dramatic world visually. The modification and manipulation of the mind of the listener vastly expands the dramaturgical toolkit of audio-drama. As Verma points out, 'in radio there is no *mise-en-scène* in the traditional meaning. Instead, what we think of as *mise-en-scène* obeys the logic of contingency and expectation, of hint and hallucination.' (Verma 2017a: 15) The engagement of the mind rather than sight, then, defines both the limits and the possibilities of audio-drama. Podcast drama, as a subset of audio-drama and equally invisible, must logically follow the same path as its predecessor, the radio, and utilise the same dramaturgical toolkit.

This conclusion is one that I aim to contest; I want to argue that the *theatre of the mind* is tied to the medium of radio, rather than to the general properties of the sense of hearing. Podcasts, which are encountered in a radically different manner by the listener, can therefore go beyond a dramaturgy that appeals to the mind.

The Theatre of the Mind and the Perception of the World

Examined closely, the *theatre of the mind* does not stand up to scrutiny. After all, if audio-drama is the theatre of the mind, what kind of theatre is actual *theatre*? If it is presumed that the listener understands worlds, dramatic or real, through her mind—that is, a process of intellectualisation and imagination that requires an active process in addition to what is experienced through senses—then why not label all visual forms of dramatisation with the same moniker? The idea, then, implies that there are two modes of encountering dramatic worlds: one, accessible through sight, is immediate and tangible without significant mental interjections, and the other, the purely auditory, requires a mediation from the mind in order to become perceptible. This distinction, however, is problematic on two counts: firstly, it is predicated on the notion that the sense of sight is somehow more immanent and integral to the experience of the world than the sense of hearing, and secondly, it assumes that it is possible to experience the world through mental processing, rather than bodily engagement. It is the latter problem that, as I shall argue in this section and the next, has the most bearing on podcast dramaturgy—however, let us first address the former briefly.

Discussions of the *theatre of the mind* usually involve an examination of the different powers of the senses, in which a bias toward visuals is present. Crisell, for example, argues that 'the ear is not the most "intelligent" of our sense organs' (Crisell 1994: 5), whereas 'our primary means of understanding or interpreting the world seems to be visual' (Crisell 1994: 8). Esslin claims that 'man is, above all, a creature of the eye and [...] our minds automatically translate most information we receive into visual terms' (Esslin 1971: 5). Beck argues that the radio's auditory nature leads to 'considerable degradation of data' (Beck 1999: 1.4a). The sense of hearing, the argument goes, provides us with less information about the world, due to its ambiguity: while the eye sees objects as what and where they are, the sound of an object is somewhat detached from it; the sound of a car speeding could also be heard as the moo of a cow, or the roar of a broken trumpet, or a recording of the very sound of a car speeding, whereas the image of the same car does not open itself to this uncertainty. This binary distinction between the senses, however, can be questioned. Clive Cazeaux (2005) addresses this by shifting to a framework of phenomenology—the school of philosophy concerned with the nature of consciousness, which attempts to understand the experience of the world not by employing abstract, theoretical and reflective constructs– such as the concepts of mind, image, sense and thought—but by describing pre-reflective experience itself. The first-person experience of the world, Cazeaux argues by drawing from Maurice Merleau-Ponty's philosophy of perception, is primarily holistic, complete and synaesthetic: the world is experienced as a whole first, and the separation of sense experience into channels such as sight, hearing and touch requires deliberate, self-aware reflection; the sound of the speeding car, for example, is first heard not as a *sound* with multiple interpretations and requiring thought, but as the presence of a speeding car, a cow or a broken trumpet, within the context of experience before it can be divided reflectively into sounds, images (or lack thereof), and ideas. The world, in other words, is not primarily visual, but fundamentally experiential. As such, '[s]ound is not something that just happens to be emitted by our contact with objects, but part of the experiential fabric out of which the human being's engagement with the world is formed' (Cazeaux 2005: 162)—and sonic experience is therefore just as immanent and immediate as vision. The ambiguities arising from the sensory qualities of sound are, according to Cazeaux, not problematic for the presentation of the dramatic world, but instead 'invitational' (2005: 164): they allow the listener to encounter the sounds of audio-drama 'as a coherent whole through a series of "beckonings" and "openings unto" relationships *with other elements in the work and with the elements in the world*' (Cazeaux 2005: 167), opening up the aesthetic possibilities of the world.

Cazeaux's engagement with phenomenology is brief, but it can be extended here to address and critique the second assumption of *the theatre of the mind*: from a phenomenological perspective, it is impossible to encounter the world through the mind alone; as Merleau-Ponty puts it, 'the unity of the world, before being posited by knowledge in a specific act of identification, is 'lived' as ready-made or already there' (2002: xix). In other words, for the mind to be able to reflect, process, and interpret distinct elements that it encounters, the world must already be there in its interconnected totality. One's encounter with the world 'is not "a state of consciousness", or a "mental fact", and the experience of phenomena is not an act of introspection or an intuition […]' (Merleau-Ponty 2002: 66). If the listener is to encounter the *here and now* of a coherent, holistic world—in other words, if she is to experience drama— then the sound structure of audio-drama cannot be understood as an abstract series of concepts, ideas and codes addressed to the mind and subject to its acts of identification, but should instead be seen as an address to *perception*, in its holistic, multisensory, interconnected totality. Audio-drama, in other words, cannot be thought into existence by the mind, but is simply *perceived* in a primordial, pre-reflective manner.

Let us pause and consider the significance of this point. As mentioned earlier, the conventions of radio dramaturgy—which are presumed to emanate from the unisensory nature of the medium and thus extendable to audio-drama—are geared toward appealing to the interpretive and deliberative mind, providing it with the necessary clarity to perform its acts of identification on sounds, so that it can reconstruct the dramatic world in the form in which it was created, however realistic or imaginative, by the writer and producer. If, however, the drama is not encountered through the mind, then why should audio-dramaturgy follow this tendency?

This question becomes even more important once we take into account the fact that for Merleau-Ponty, the site of pre-reflective experience of the world is *the body*. This does not mean that the body is a source of information *providing* consciousness with content, or that it is a biological *tool* with which sensations are received or generated, to be put into a coherent understanding of the world in the mind—the division between body and mind is, for Merleau-Ponty, invalid; instead, experience fundamentally arises from the fact that one *is* a body: the world is *a world* to me because I have a bodily perspective on it. Here, 'the body' does not refer to the physical and biological descriptions of the human body as understood through science, physiology, or any kind of reflective comprehension, but to the pre-reflective, perceptual, experiential *lived body*: a primordial presence in the world, which makes perceptual experience possible through its pre-reflective abilities: looking, listening, moving, approaching, distancing, expressing and so on. Merleau-Ponty argues that such abilities constitute a *body schema*, which, as Taylor Carman explains, is 'the set of abiding noncognitive dispositions and capacities that orient, guide, and inform our bodily sensitivities and motor actions. [...] Our bodily skills and dispositions carve out a perceptual world' (2008: 132–133).

One can question, therefore, why audio-dramaturgy should be formulated to address the deliberative, semantic mind, rather than the holistic perceptual experience of the body. After all, the ability of the body schema to form deliberate thoughts, reflections and projections—in other words, the *mind*—allows for a perspective wholly different from one experienced through the body schema's auditory capabilities. Unlike one's thoughts, the sounds that one hears have a direct, antepredicative relationship with the body: they resonate with it physically—not through meaning and reference, but with rhythm, tempo, mood, volume, and other qualities found in sound. In the dramaturgy of the *theatre of the mind* however, as described earlier, these properties of sound remain subject to the condition of representational clarity. While the units of meaning represented by sounds can be as ambiguous to the mind as required and, to repeat Verma's phrase, 'obeys the logic of contingency and expectation' (2017a: 15), the sonic structure itself is constructed artificially, so as to be as unambiguous as possible to the body's perceptual experience. If it is the perception of the body, rather than the deliberation of the mind, that is responsible for the experience of the world as Merleau-Ponty observes, then why should audio-dramaturgy not optimise the dramaturgical toolkit to address the body schema's auditory abilities in perceiving the dramatic world? Orienting the sonic structure of audio-drama primarily toward its mental significance is valid only if we assume that the auditory possibilities of the body schema are insufficient in accessing the world—a position that, as elucidated by Cazeaux, is untrue from a phenomenological viewpoint.

Interestingly, this exact point was made in the early years of radio drama by arguably its first theorist, Rudolf Arnheim, who writes:

The most elementary aural effects [...] do not consist in transmitting to us the meaning of the spoken word, or sounds which we know in actuality. The 'expressive characteristics' of sound affects us in a far more direct way, comprehensible without any experience by means of intensity, pitch, interval, rhythm and tempo, properties of sound which have very little to do with the objective meaning of the word or the sound. (Arnheim 1936: 29)

Interestingly, although Arnheim was hoping for an audio-dramaturgy based on these 'expressive characteristics', the dramaturgical conventions of *the theatre of the mind*, which were taking shape around the time on the radio, were indeed formulated toward preserving the objective meaning of the word or the sound. Arnheim himself was aware of this development, and blamed it on radio practitioners who 'do not possess this simple instinct for sensuous qualities of their raw material, whether it is that they are simply incompetent or that they think they are doing a service to the meaning of the word' (1936: 28).

I want to posit an alternative explanation for this development: that the tendency to understand radio as the *theatre of the mind* arises from the specific properties of the qualities of the encounter between the listener and the audio-drama as mediated through conventional modes of radio listenership. To do this, I return to the body schema's auditory abilities, arguing that the bodily mode of engagement with the medium of radio is more conducive to a focused, attentive listening attitude, which can be addressed through the conventions of radio drama. Podcasts, on the other hand, facilitate a radically different engagement with the body, opening the way to a more immersive sonic experience which could be exploited dramaturgically.

Perception of the World and the Listener's Ear

To understand how the body engages with the dramatic world of audio-drama in its various manifestations, one must first ask: how does the body encounter the world through sound? This is a question that could be answered phenomenologically. For Merleau-Ponty, experience of the world is characterised by being located in a totality, rather than comprising of individual elements; indeed, any individual thing of which one becomes conscious only appears in perception because of its relationship to all other things. 'The perceptual "something"', he contends, 'is always in the middle of something else, it always forms part of a field' (Merleau-Ponty 2002: 4). It is this structure of *figure* and *ground* that, for Merleau-Ponty, underlies all experience of the world.

Such a structure can be observed in auditory experience, should one reflect phenomenologically on first-hand encounters with the world. Should I pause to reflect at any moment, I instantly notice that I am constantly surrounded by sounds; not only am I in the presence of constantly vibrating air, but the interior of my own body is never quiet. Silence, it seems, is theoretically impossible, as I am always immersed in sound. Yet, my usual sonic experience of the world is not of all that is audible, but specific sounds: the doorbell ringing, people speaking, and other sound *figures*. Other sounds, although audible, are not direct objects of perception, and could be said to be in the *ground*. In their exploration and classification of the everyday details of the experience of sounds, Augoyard and Torgue (2014) provide useful terminology with which to discuss this: they describe the ability to perceive some sounds out of the myriad of what is audible in terms of the two complementary *sonic effects* of 'asyndeton' and 'synecdoche'; the former is the 'deletion from the perception or memory of one or many sound elements in an audible whole' (2014: 26), while the latter is 'the ability to valorise one specific element [of the audible] through selection [...] produced by simple acoustic vigilance, by the determination of a predominant functional criterion, or by adhesion to a cultural schema establishing a hierarchy' (2005: 123–124). The two processes work in tandem: what is differentiated can only be understood by what is omitted; the sound of the speeding car, for example, can instead be perceived as a cow if set against the ground of the sounds of a meadow, although the latter is under asyndeton. The body schema, then, has the ability to experience figure and ground—and therefore, the world—through its pre-reflective ability to perform asyndeton and synecdoche.

Importantly, the relationship between auditory figures and grounds is rather more complicated than, for instance, in visual experience. As Ross Brown points out 'unlike the eye, the ear has no mechanical way of focusing' (2011: 5), and thus auditory perception relies solely on asyndeton and synecdoche to distinguish between figure and ground. After all, my body permits me to control my field of vision to a great extent, by turning my head, closing my eyes, focusing more closely, and a variety of other means that allow for new figures and grounds to emerge; in other words, I have the ability to pick what, out of all that is visible, can appear in front of my eyes. Conversely, my ear encounters all that is audible at any one moment, and so my field of audition is shaped through changes in figure–ground relationships between the same temporal continuity of sounds. In this field, any changes in volume, intensity, pitch, tempo or length—the same 'expressive characteristics' discussed by Arnheim—can lead to a complete change in the structure of figures and grounds: a sudden loudness, competing frequencies, or even the disappearance of a hitherto-constant background noise can shift the figures of perception rapidly and beyond the immediate control of the listener. In short, no synecdoche or asyndeton is ever complete or stable. For Brown, therefore, the figures perceived through auditory attention are always subject to the interruptions of the ground— 'actively "paid" or "given" attention is continuously tugged and grabbed by events in the heard environment [...] Sound must therefore be understood as ontologically distracting.' (2011: 6). Auditory experience of the world, then, is in constant oscillation between *engagement* with the figures of attention and *distraction* caused by new figures emerging out of the ground.

Let us now explore what happens in applying this understanding of the auditory world to audio-drama. If the aim of audio-dramaturgy is to create the experience of a dramatic world through sound, then its primary tool is to present a field of sonic figures and grounds to the listener, so that the auditory possibilities of her body schema allow her to perceive them in their totality as a world. The sound structure of the audio-drama distinguishes between the figure and ground within all that could be audible in the dramatic world; key sounds are heard at higher volume and with clearer dynamics, facilitating synecdoche, while other sounds are either eliminated or reduced in asyndeton in order to shape the ground against which figures appear. The dramaturgical toolkit of audio-drama, then, must be found in the effects created through skilful manipulation of the figure–ground structure of its sounds.

In the practices of the *theatre of the mind*, however, the tendency is to conduct this manipulation on a conceptual and intellectual, rather than sonic and, following Arnheim, *expressive* manner. While the structures of figure and ground can, on a conceptual level, change constantly and rapidly, to quote Verma once more, through 'hint and hallucination' (2017a: 15), the sonic structure focuses solely on the sound figures of speech and recognisable, codified sound effects and music, with all else in asyndeton; this stable structure is developed and maintained through dramaturgical acts and processes. As explored before, however, the stability of the sonic figure–ground relationship is not typical of auditory experience; indeed, to preserve the focus on specific sounds which refer to intended object or concepts, the aforementioned expressive characteristics of sound would need to be limited, as they might cause a reconfiguration of figure–ground relationships which obscures or alters the meaning of said sounds. In other words, the *theatre of the mind* creates the sonic structure of its dramatic world by moving away from the replication of auditory experience—in short, by treating sound as though it is not sonic, but conceptual.

As I have previously argued, this form of sonic structuring is not *the* theoretically-inevitable form of audio-dramaturgy, as some have claimed. Let us examine, however, a condition under which it might become necessary. If the listener encounters the dramatic world through the manipulations of the sonic figure–ground structures presented in the audio-drama, then she encounters this very structure, too, only through the auditory abilities of her body schema, as a figure within the perceptual structure of her own world, and similarly subject to the potential oscillation between distraction and attention. The dramaturgical manipulation of the sonic figure–ground relationships, then, does not necessarily translate into the perceptual experience of the same structure for the listener, as these relationships can be affected, disrupted or obscured by other figures and grounds in her field of auditory perception. This is not the case in visual forms of drama; a film director can frame a particular figure–ground relationship and present it to the viewer, who can take this as the sole content of her field of vision, whether by sitting in a dark cinema, or simply by looking at it and not any other visible thing. In contrast, an audio-dramaturg may set the characters' voices against musical accompaniments and a roaring sea that frequently obscures them, only for the listener to encounter it through her radio speakers, alongside the rest of all that is audible, which at any moment might become key figures of perception and create a different—and perhaps dramaturgically undesirable—experience of the dramatic world. In such a situation, the manipulation of figures and grounds is beyond the control of the dramaturg, and requires the listener to actively perform synecdoche on the sonic figures of the dramatic world, and asyndeton on the sounds of her own world; in fact, sonic complexity in the structure of the audio-drama would hinder, rather than facilitate, this process. A hypothetical strategy to counter this, then, may be to emphasise the stability of sound figures in order to allow the listener to focus and distinguish them from the ground of all that is audible—in other words, to structure a *theatre of the mind*.

Here, we finally have a theoretically valid justification for the dramaturgy of *the theatre of the mind*: it addresses the needs of the listener's active process of asyndeton and synecdoche by providing her with stable figures of sound against an otherwise unpredictable sonic background. This active process of listening, however, is only required if audio-drama is encountered merely as a part of all that is audible, competing for attention with other sonic figures emerging within the field of perception. If all other sounds fall silent and the listener encounters only the sonic structure of audio-drama without the distraction of what is audible but dramaturgically unintended, the need for active engagement in synecdoche and asyndeton is all but eliminated, and she is able to perceive the dramatic world based on the figure-ground relationships created and manipulated in the process of dramaturgy. Should the dramaturg have a great extent of control over the listener's auditory field, *the theatre of the mind* is no longer necessary.

We have arrived, therefore, at a point of radical variance between media: the level of dramaturgical control of the auditory field is not constant, nor is it somehow intrinsic to sonic experience; instead, it is determined by the sonic qualities of the listener's bodily encounter with it—for example, its fidelity, volume and location within the auditory field—which, in turn, are shaped by the medium that carries the audio-drama. A medium that projects audio-drama into the auditory field of the listener without filling it entirely would require the dramaturgical approaches of *the theatre of the mind*. Crucially, this is a property that has generally been associated with the conventions of listening to radio—which is why Crisell labels it a 'secondary medium' (1994: 162). The sounds of audio-drama emanate from the radio receiver or loudspeakers and are cast into the listener's space alongside all other sounds; the listener's body then has to direct itself toward the sound by performing asyndeton on all other sounds—a process that, as mentioned, is always subject to distortion and distraction. Furthermore, the radio listener's activities directly affect the experience of the sound: any movement around the space can change the volume of the sound and thus the figure–ground relationships, necessitating auditory reorientation, while simple actions such as washing up, driving, or even walking can cause a transformative disturbance in the auditory field. Moreover, the conventional radio listener has little control over when and how she encounters audio-drama, as programme schedules dictate the timing of the encounter; a moment's distraction may cause her to miss an important figure in the perceptual world that cannot be brought back, perhaps until the programme is repeated. Of course, a determined listener can alter her experience by changing the properties of the encounter—for example, by recording the drama, listening to it through headphones and ceasing other activities; this, however, would be an atypical use of the medium, and thus not the primary mode of listening to consider when devising dramaturgical methods for it. Overall, then, the conventional mode of bodily encounter with the radio demands the *theatre of the mind*. The implications of this point should be emphasised: the mode of dramaturgy that is generally assumed to emerge from the inherent properties of audio-drama has been revealed instead as arising from the qualities of *radio* drama.

Podcasts, on the other hand, engage the listener in a radically different way—to the extent that, as Richard Berry (2016) points out, it could be considered a new medium, sharing some aspects with radio but varying in others. Berry's thorough survey of a large amount of research into the two media reveals that unlike radio, podcast listeners select their schedule of listening, and have control over the flow of the audio-drama—in that they can pause, rewind, and repeat it—which allows them to be 'not only less distracted [than radio listeners] but also potentially more engaged in the experience' (Berry

2016: 12). Most importantly, podcasts are 'more often than not [...] [listened to] using headphones' (Berry 2016: 13). There is no distance between the listener and the source of sound: the audio-drama is plugged directly into the listener's inner ear, obscuring most day-to-day sounds; it does not occur within the auditory field – it becomes the field itself. Therefore, the sounds and activities of the podcast listener's actual space have little effect on the figure-ground relationships created through the process of dramaturgy: the dramatic world of the podcast becomes the entire content of the listener's world—experienced through direct perceptual encounter within the auditory field, rather than through deliberative focus. Indeed, performance and theatre already make extensive use of this phenomenon; Brown highlights how recent trends in theatre '[have] been for the sphere of sound to close in on the personal space of individual audience member, even into the "intercranial" sonic space between the ears. *Headphone theatre* and *theatre in the total dark* have become subgenres of "immersive theatre"' (2016: 175). As Misha Myers argues in her discussion of audio walks—another form of headphone-mediated dramatic experience—the listener's physical space and movements can combine with the sounds in her ear, leading to the emergence of an entirely new bodily space in the phenomenal field of experience. Myers argues that the audio walk is 'a theatre of intersubjective listening that both closes the distance and extends touch between two subjects within an interior bodily space, as well as within a landscape' (Myers 2011: 80). In podcast drama, the same space can emerge out of the listener's encounter not with another subject, but with a holistic perceptual dramatic world. The dramaturgy of the *theatre of the mind*, then, becomes redundant: the audio-drama can be addressed not to the mind, but to the ear, the body and the world around it.

The Listener's Ear and Podcast Drama

Let us return to the question that began the chapter: what should this new form of audio-drama, the podcast, sound like? In what followed, I critiqued the argument that it should follow the conventions and assumptions of radio drama, highlighting that contrary to its common theoretical characterisation, such conventions stem not from the unisensory nature of audio-drama, but the specifications of the medium of radio; simultaneously, I pointed to the expressive characteristics of sound—which, in the hierarchy of the *theatre of the mind*, rank below meaningful reference—as a possible avenue to be explored. The question, however, still remains: what should podcast dramaturgy be like, if not radio?

I posit that the answer does indeed lie in radio's past—but not the heritage of established modes of radio practice that Verma cites. Instead, podcast dramaturgy can find its blueprint or paradigm in radio experiments that did not survive to become part of the paradigmatic assumptions, practices, and conventions of radio drama. Radio dramaturgy, after all, emerged not from theoretical conjecture about *the theatre of the mind*, but out of a historical process: much like the podcast, the early year of the form in the 1920s was an era of experimentation. An unsigned 1928 article in the *BBC Handbook*—the corporation's public bulletin—indicates that 'the ends and forms of the new art of Radio Drama are hardly yet in sight' (1928: 116), and that 'the question of adapting and presenting [dramatic] material in that form which renders it capable of reception and appreciation by the listener' (1928: 115) continued to be explored. Interestingly, six short years later, the bulletin—now entitled the *BBC Yearbook*—argued that 'the first phase of development of radio drama has come to an end. The [...] special technique of presenting drama through the medium of the microphone has now crystallised as far [...] as its fundamentals are concerned' (1934: 57). Crisell's brief exploration of radio history (2000) characterises the interval between these two points as the period in which radio dramaturgs gradually became aware of what the possibilities and the limitations of the medium were, and adjusted their processes accordingly: they 'rediscover[ed] the verbal nature of drama' (Crisell 2000: 469), and discovered that 'mostly and primarily through speech, sound on the radio will tell us all the things we need to know' (Crisell 2000: 467)—in other words, the dramaturgy of the *theatre of the mind* took shape. Crisell, of course, ascribes this outcome to the intrinsic qualities of 'a sound-only medium' (2000: 471)—a position that has been critiqued extensively in this chapter. Should we consider, however, that these experiments may have ceased due to their incompatibility with the qualities of the medium of *radio*, perhaps returning to them through the new medium of the podcast can provide the opportunity for a productive revival.

A look back at the history of British radio, for example, reveals one such dramaturgical approach that did not survive the experimental era: the work of radio pioneer Lance Sieveking, whose treatise on radio drama, *The Stuff of Radio* (1934) understands the medium as a predominantly acoustic—and musical—medium, rather than a *writer's* medium. He proudly declares his play *Kaleidoscope* (1927) to be 'the epitome of the radio play: there is nothing to print!' (1934: 29) and is doubtful about publishing his scripts at all: 'a radio play being prepared for reading demands [...] that all the sound sequences shall be so described that nothing essential shall be lost. To do this completely is, I believe, an impossibility' (1934: 27). When discussing sound effects, he describes how the mixing of a variety of sound create a whole scene, and describes the mix not in terms of symbol and signification, but in terms of music: 'the exact *rightness* of its timing is everything [...] and this is not achieved with clocks, but with an instinct similar to a musician's' (1934: 39). Even the written scripts of his productions describe the sounds in expressive, rather than meaningful terms; his *Arrest in Africa* (1930), for instance, contains lines such as '*like a great wave gathering itself to its greatest height before it topples over and crashes on the beach, the howling, hooting, screaming, roaring jungle hovers, spreads, swoops, and in one final, deafening shudder, overwhelms the young men, and they are swallowed up*' (Sieveking 1934: 185). The stuff of Sieveking's radio dramaturgy, in short, was directed toward the ear, and not the mind.

This dramaturgical approach, however, did not continue past the experimental period. As a *Sunday Express* review remarked at the time, 'Most people hate [the experiments]. They are too bothersome for the ordinary listener' (Sieveking 1934: 404); one can hypothesise that the expressive characteristics of this mode of dramaturgy would have made it difficult for the early listener to grasp the dramatic world through the—still rather technologically basic—radio. Indeed, Sieveking advises his listener to listen to his work in silence, sitting still and in darkness (1934: 97)—a strategy to maximise control over the auditory field, but one which is atypical of the medium, and which would nevertheless be unsuccessful, as there still exists a physical and aural distance between the listener and the source of sound; thus, the sounds of the dramatic world would form only part of the auditory field. The listener would encounter Sieveking's musical combination of multiple sounds from a single point, and with acts of asyndeton and synecdoche as her only means of separating them from each other, and from the other sounds around her. There is also the matter of the theatrical sound of the day to consider: as Brown notes, 'whereas in the mid nineteenth-century, every theatrical moment had been filled with noise, sound and music, with scarcely a panting beat between verbal salvo or musical set-piece, the dawn of the twentieth-century saw dramatists actively seeking settings for their dramas where silence *was*' (2010: 77). Both the producers and listeners of radio drama, then, derived their knowledge of how drama should sound from the British stage, which in the preceding few decades had moved from the noisy and musical soundscapes of melodrama, and toward the quiet contemplation of the Shavian *drama of ideas*—itself a form of a *theatre of the mind*.

With the advent of podcast drama, however, a space has opened up for a return to such practices. The podcast dramaturg, exercising significant control over the listener's auditory field, can utilise the expressive characteristics of sound without compromising the listener's perceptual experience of the world. Furthermore, the listener, by virtue of seeking and obtaining the podcast and scheduling listening time, has already indicated that she is willing to listen to these experiments. Val Gielgud, the head of BBC Radio Drama during the experimental years, lamented in his reflections:

> It was the worst of luck for Sieveking that there was never an experimental laboratory available for British Broadcasting. [...] Experimental programmes had to be found a place in normal programme hours, and 'tried out' upon a patient, but necessarily largely uncomprehending public. And there was not infrequent expression of resentment that producers should apparently be learning their business at listeners' expense. (1957: 26)

The podcast listener, both by virtue of being a willing participant and through the specific mode of bodily engagement with the medium, is neither resenting, nor uncomprehending. Indeed, even niche interest such as soundscapes, comedy horror and 1940s American drama and variety radio can find a home, and an eager audience, in podcasts such as *Soundscape* (Harris and Harris 2015), *Welcome to Night Vale* (Night Vale Presents 2017), and *The Thrilling Adventure Hour* (Workjuice Corp 2014), respectively. In addition, the role of sound in drama, theatre and performance has become ever more prominent: from audio walks by the likes of Janet Cardiff and George Bures Miller to the experimental sounds of post-dramatic theatre,[2] and from the designed soundscape of horror films to various strands of sound art, radio dramaturgs and their audiences have access to wide range of aesthetic references and practices in sound. Podcast drama, then, provides the ultimate experimental laboratory in which follow Sieveking's lead away from conventional radio dramaturgy and toward more holistic, expressive, and musical forms, closer to the structures of bodily audition than mental interpretation. Whereas radio was the *theatre of the mind*, podcasts can move past the theoretical separation of body and mind, and become the theatre *in* the body.

Notes

1. The coining of the term is ascribed to BBC journalist Ben Hammersley (Berry 2016: 17).
2. For more on this topic, see Ovadija's (2013) survey of the role of sound in avant-garde theatre.

Bibliography

Anon. (1928). Production of radio plays. In *BBC handbook 1928* (pp. 15–117). London: The British Broadcasting Corporation.

Anon. (1934). Notes of the year. In *BBC yearbook 1934* (pp. 57–60). London: The British Broadcasting Corporation.

Aristotle (1898) *The Poetics of Aristotle* (trans. Butcher, S. H). London/New York: Macmillan.

Arnheim, R. (1936). *Radio* (trans. Ludwig, M., & Read, H.). London: Faber & Faber.

Augoyard, J. F., & Torgue, H. (2014). *Sonic experience: A guide to everyday sounds.* Montreal: McGill-Queen's Press-MQUP.

Beck, A. (1999). *Is radio blind or invisible? A call for wider debate on listening-in.* www.savoyhill.co.uk [Internet]. Accessed 11 Jan 2017.

Beck, A. (2000). *Cognitive mapping and radio drama.* www.savoyhill.co.uk [Internet]. Accessed 11 Jan 2017.

Berry, R. (2016). Podcasting: Considering the evolution of the medium and its association with the word 'radio'. *The Radio Journal – International Studies in Broadcast & Audio Media, 14*(1), 7–22.

Bottomley, A. J. (2015). Podcasting, Welcome to Night Vale, and the revival of radio drama. *Journal of Radio & Audio Media, 22*(2), 179–189.

Brown, R. (2010). *Sound: A reader in theatre practice.* Basingstoke: Palgrave Macmillan.

Brown, R. (2011). Towards theatre noise. In L. Kendrick & D. Roesner (Eds.), *Theatre noise: The sound of performance* (pp. 1–14). Newcastle-upon-Tyne: Cambridge Scholars Publishing.

Brown, R. (2016). Fix your eyes on the horizon and swing your ears about: Corwin's theatre of sound. In J. Smith & N. Verma (Eds.), *Anatomy of sound: Norman Corwin and media authorship.* Berkeley: University of California Press.

Carman, T. (2008). *Merleau-Ponty.* London: Routledge.

Cazeaux, C. (2005). Phenomenology and radio drama. *British Journal of Aesthetics, 45*(2), 157–174.

Crisell, A. (1994). *Understanding radio.* London: Routledge.

Crisell, A. (2000). Better than Magritte: How drama on the radio became radio drama. *Journal of Radio Studies, 7*(2), 464–473.

Crook, T. (1999). *Radio drama: Theory and practice.* London: Routledge.

Drakakis, J. (1981). *British radio drama.* Cambridge: Cambridge University Press.

Dubber, A. (2013). *Radio in the digital age.* Cambridge: Polity Press.

Edison Research. (2017). *The infinite dial 2017.* www.edisonresearch.com/infinite-dial-2017 [Internet]. Accessed 24 Apr 2017.

Elam, K. (2005). *The semiotics of theatre and drama.* London/New York: Routledge.

Esslin, M. (1971). The mind as a stage. *Theatre Quarterly, 1*(3), 5–11.

Gielgud, V. H. (1957). *British radio drama, 1922–1956: A survey.* London: Harrap.

Gimlet Media. (2017). *Homecoming.* gimletmedia.com/homecoming [Podcast]. Accessed 12 Jan 2017.

Harris, S., & Harris, W. (2015). *SoundScape: Hosted by Woody and Suzi Harris*. www.soundscapeprog.org [Podcast]. Accessed 21 Sept 2017.

Hill, C. W. (2015). *Writing for radio*. London: Bloomsbury.

Lewis, P. E. (1981). *Radio drama*. Harlow: Longman.

Luckhurst, M. (2006). *Dramaturgy: A revolution in theatre*. Cambridge: Cambridge University Press.

McInerney, V. (2001). *Writing for radio*. Manchester: Manchester University Press.

McLeish, R. (2012). *Radio production*. London: Focal Press.

Merleau-Ponty, M. (2002). *Phenomenology of perception* (trans. Smith, C., 1968). London: Routledge.

Myers, M. (2011). Vocal lanscaping: The theatre of sound in audiowalks. In L. Kendrick & D. Roesner (Eds.), *Theatre noise: The sound of performance* (pp. 70–81). Newcastle-upon-Tyne: Cambridge Scholars Publishing.

Night Vale Presents. (2017). *Welcome to Night Vale*. www.welcometonightvale.com [Podcast]. Accessed 21 Sept 2017.

Ovadija, M. (2013). *Dramaturgy of sound in the avant-garde and post-dramatic theatre*. Kingston: McGill-Queen's University Press.

Pownall, D. (2011). *Sound theatre: Thoughts on the radio play*. London: Oberon.

RAJAR. (2016). *MIDAS measurement of internet delivered audio services spring 2016*. http://www.rajar.co.uk/docs/news/MIDAS_Spring_2016_FINAL.pdf. Accessed 23 Mar 2017.

RAJAR. (2017). *RAJAR MIDAS audio survey*. http://www.rajar.co.uk/docs/news/MIDAS_Spring_2017.pdf. Accessed 24 Apr 2017.

Rodger, I. (1982). *Radio drama*. London: Macmillan.

Shingler, M., & Wieringa, C. (1998). *On air: Methods and meanings of radio*. London: Arnold.

Sieveking, L. (1934). *The stuff of radio*. London: Cassell.

Smethurst, W. (2016). *How to write for television: A guide to writing and selling TV and radio scripts*. London: Robinson.

Verma, N. (2017a). The arts of amnesia: The case for audio drama, part one. *RadioDoc Review, 3*(1). http://ro.uow.edu.au/rdr/vol3/iss1/5/. Accessed 10 May 2018.

Verma, N. (2017b). The arts of amnesia: The case for audio drama, part two. *RadioDoc Review, 3*(1). http://ro.uow.edu.au/rdr/vol3/iss1/6/. Accessed 10 May 2018.

Willett, A. (2013). *Media production: A practical guide to radio and TV*. Abingdon/New York: Routledge.

Workjuice Corp. (2014). *The thrilling adventure hour*. http://thrillingadventurehour.com [Podcast]. Accessed 21 Sept 2017.

11

A Feminist Materialisation of Amplified Voice: Queering Identity and Affect in *The Heart*

Stacey Copeland

The amplified voice through podcasting as an intimate aural medium carries with it the possibilities for a deep affective experience for both the creator and the listener. The sound of one's voice carries with it traces of age, sex, gender, sexuality, culture and many more facets of collective and individual identity. As feminist phenomenologist Adriana Cavarero reminds us 'when the human voice vibrates, there is someone in flesh and bone who emits it' (2005: 522). However, feminist media scholars have historically centred gender and sexuality on the visual form and written text, with the voice exercised as metaphor, immaterial or interpreted solely as the words spoken.[1] Representative of agency, the voice gets defined as solely what is being said rather than *how* one is saying it. Through this paper I intend to move away from the largely visualphilic tendencies of feminist media studies to explore a queering of gender and sexuality within podcasting through sound production and the material voice in the Radiotopia podcast *The Heart*. Radio scholars such as Frances Dyson (1994), Mitchell (2000), Anne Karpf (2007), and Christine Ehrick (2015) have gained considerable ground in the study of radio voice from a feminist perspective, yet growing interest in podcast studies raises new questions around the performativity and production of gendered voice and sound for the future

---

(tick Boom Boom—tick Boom Boom—tick Boom Boom) it's the universal sound of human life, of love… and of loves lost 'Welcome to the Heart'.

S. Copeland (✉)
Simon Fraser University, Vancouver, BC, Canada
e-mail: avcopela@sfu.ca

© The Author(s) 2018
D. Llinares et al. (eds.), *Podcasting*, https://doi.org/10.1007/978-3-319-90056-8_11

of this radiogenic medium. Technological changes in podcast listening toward screen based mobile devices and earbuds have contributed not only to a significant increase in podcast listening since *Serial*[2] but a shift in vocal performance and audio production practices for such a personal mobile listening environment. Through this case study of *The Heart,* I argue that podcasting, as an intimate aural medium, offers a powerful platform for a listening experience that can challenge visual-philic heteronormative and gendered expectations by engaging with the listener through the affective use of sound. Although the predominant voices presented on *The Heart* are aurally coded 'feminine', the podcast queers normative codes of gender and sexuality through the aesthetics of sound/art, the reconfiguration of conventional narratives, and the affective intimacy inherent of radio and podcasting.

The Heart, formerly known as *Audio Smut,* is a soundwork exploring intimacy and humanity. With Canadian roots out of Montreal's CKUT 90.3FM[3] as *Audio Smut,* the show has transformed into a podcast based in New York City as part of the Radiotopia/PRX network in 2014 under the new banner of *The Heart. Audio Smut's* 'Movies in Your Head' can be heard as the formation of a sonic aesthetic for *The Heart.* The 2014 radio documentary experiment with composer Shani Aviram won the 2015 Prix Italia Golden Award for New Radio Formats with their powerfully intimate approach to the question 'How does one's sense of reality fail when falling in love?'[4] As the show evolved out of *Audio Smut* and into *The Heart,* Season 1 'The Beginning' (2015) continued this exploration of feelings and love from the concept of 'firsts' in 'and 27 other firsts' to the reality of 'beauty is pain'. The following season titled 'Heatwave' released in Fall 2015, dug into a series of unreleased episodes of Audio Smut to take on the complicated and conflicting emotions around sex and intimacy. Whereas the 'make/break' (2015) series explored the personal stories of couples deciding whether to make it together or break it apart. Diving into the personal, this season begins with the two-part episode 'Kaitlin + Mitra – Wedding'. Kaitlin Prest, the most-often heard voice on the series, is the host and creative director. The show description oozes affective and queered experience,

> The things you whisper. The things you do in the dark... or light. The things you feel but you don't know how to name. This is a radio show about all of those things. It's about the triumphs and the terrors of human intimacy, the bliss and banality of being in love and the wild diversity of the human heart. (Radiotopia 2016)

Moving into 2016 and 2017, *The Heart* continues to push the limits of the hyper-intimacy of podcasting. From 'Diaries', life stories told using personal diaries and tattered notes, to the miniseries 'No', which takes the listener inside Prest's personal sexual journey from youth to adulthood. The 2016 season *Silent Evidence* was a finalist for the 76th annual Peabody Awards, further showcasing the podcast's cultural and creative impact.

This chapter focuses in on the creative sound production and unique vocalities within the aurally affective series *The Heart*. As these sonically rich soundworks[5] are discussed here through visual written text, you are encouraged to immerse yourself in a critical aural listening of the provocative works outlined in this study to further engage with the theories and analysis discussed here. The amplified voice through soundwork as an intimate aural medium carries with it the possibilities for a deep affective experience both for the presenter and the listener. Through the contrasting comparative analysis of select feminist scholarly work from the phenomenology of gender to modern work on identity technologies in the digital space, I focus here on the queering of gender and heteronormativity through the affective sonic experiences found in the Radiotopia soundwork series. This phenomenological approach in conversation with radio and sound studies enables an embodied exploration of music, spoken word, storytelling techniques and sound art used within select episodes to queer normative codes of gender and sexuality through the reconfiguration of conventional narratives, and the affective intimacy inherent in radio and podcasting soundwork.

Whispers of Intimacy

Before we can dive into the deep meanings hidden within the soundworks dramaturgical voice and the sticky language at play, we must first address the kind of affect that I am applying here. In *Affective Economies* (2004) Sara Ahmed repositions emotions within an affect theory that works like capital, continuously circulating yet coming to surface in large amounts only to be re-circulated again. Rather than a model of embodying emotion objectively and subjectively, Ahmed argues 'emotions are not simply "within"' or "without" but that they create the very effect of the surfaces or boundaries of bodies and worlds' (117). Although Ahmed's language is primarily focused on the body as surface for this affective 'stickiness', I argue that the theory of affective economy, this accumulation and redistribution of emotion holds potential power when discussing aural media. There is an inherent intimacy in voice-driven soundwork that seems to be soaking in affect. The listener puts on her headphones, presses play and becomes immersed in an affective discourse of human experience through listening and connecting.

The Heart, as imagined and material surface—a mediated intimate symbol—becomes sticky with affect through its social public circulation. That affect and its value will vary, dependent on the social and psychic relationships at play concerning the listener and the soundwork as a commodity. As Sara Ahmed explains, 'affect does not reside positively in the sign or commodity, but is produced only as an effect of its circulation' (120). Nevertheless, through voice, sound and narrative, the work brings forward 'the triumphs and the terrors of human intimacy, the bliss and banality of being in love.' (Radiotopia 2016). Season 2 of *The Heart*, carries the theme of 'Ghost'. The premise of being haunted by the ghosts that you love becomes soaked in affect for the listener as each episode entices both personal experience and imagined possibilities of love lost. This theme is taken to its highest point, as experienced in episode 11 titled 'You', tying together the haunting instrumental of *Claire de Lune* with feelings of love, of tragedy, of loss through the soft sombre and intimate voice of Kaitlin Prest, low whispers and echoed cries, as the piano floats in and out through the entire work. The lost love, never named, could be anyone. It could be anyone's anyone. The episode becomes a commentary more so on the collective emotional experience of lost love than on individualist experience and how sound–music carry memory through triggering affect. The instrumental *Claire de Lune* stirs the narrator's memory of this specific loved person, as they hear someone playing it in the downstairs apartment, they hear it in a film, they hear it in yoga class. The choice of *Claire de Lune* doesn't seem arbitrary. The famous third movement of *Suite Bergamasque* by Claude Debussy has been featured in over 80 different television and film works to date, including *Castaway* and the *Twilight* series, to convey love, loss and varying emotional responses from the audience.[6] There is undeniably something about sound–music and voice—as a commanding entity of connection and emotion it can so powerfully pull us backward and forward through our own memories, thoughts and feelings. The recorded voice, be it that of a piano or the human voice, carries a sense of permanence, a haunting of emotion that wells up at the strike of a chord or the uniquely *you* sound of a soft word spoken. Prest never gives a name to the 'you' within her work. 'You' becomes an open symbol for inscription, ungendered and unsexed, creating an open economy of affect between the work and the realised listener.

The Voice and the Body: Queering Performative Acts

This ungendered and unsexed 'you' for listener inscription is inherently intertwined with the queering of heternormativity that is central to *The Heart*. When discussing queer theory, Judith Butler has become a universally influential theorist to draw from. In her early *Performative Acts and Gender Constitution: An Essay in Phenomenology and Feminist Theory* (1988), Butler discusses gender as an unstable identity that is:

> tenuously constituted in time-an identity instituted through a *stylized repetition of acts*... the stylization of the body and, hence, must be understood as the mundane way in which bodily gestures, movements, and enactments of various kinds constitute the illusion of an abiding gendered self. (519)

As a dramaturgical or acted and produced soundwork without explicit material bodily form, *The Heart* doesn't at first seem to fit within Judith Butler's theory of gender performativity. As discussed in Annette Schlichter's *Do Voices Matter? Vocality, Materiality, Gender Performativity* (2011), Butler's theory of performativity neglects to theorise the mediation of interpellation and speech acts through the voice and its technologies, rather choosing to highlight the material body. Yet, the voice, although not 'tangible', can be withdrawn or projected at will as a product and as an immovable part of the body. In a way, as the hair or fingernails project outward, so does the voice. If we are to assume that the narrator, the voice of *The Heart* is an 'authentic' self as described and experienced by the listener through this intimate aural form as an expression of life rather than a theatrical façade, we must then apply Butler's phenomenological theories to comprehend the performative and unstable identities at work. Butler argues that 'one way in which this system of compulsory heterosexuality is reproduced and concealed is through the cultivation of bodies into discrete sexes with 'natural' appearances and 'natural' heterosexual dispositions' (524). These heterosexual cultivations are then performed day-to-day, incessantly, resulting in the creation of normative ideals, institutions and social expectations such as the institution of marriage between a man and a woman as commonly understood within most Western cultures.

The institution of marriage at present is the subject of heated political and religious debate, but it is through the performance of gender and sexuality as theorised by Butler that our society continues to both uphold and question this long-standing hetero-patriarchal institution and its surrounding socio-cultural traditions. In a two-part episode titled 'Kaitlin + Mitra – Wedding' (2015), a queering of the institution of marriage bound by love both as heterosexual tradition and religious and state contract takes place. The story is a story of their 'love', a five-year long sound/art/business collaboration. The episodes are guided by sonically artistic re-enactments and intertwined with narration by Kaitlin Prest and senior producer Mitra Kaboli. Driven primarily by their clear, 'feminine' coded, upfront yet conversational voices, the soundwork utilises whisper to represent inner thought and music cues such as the wedding song to stir affect and symbolism for the listener. The story is staged like a romantic comedy 'meet–cute' narrative—they both worked in the same Montreal restaurant. The episodes also include personal intimate anecdotes about each other that show just how close they are. Mitra vocalises, 'Kaitlin likes it when you play with her hair if she's sad'[7] while their inner anxieties bounce off-centre in light echoed whisper. Part 2 moves into the live-recorded 'wedding' with their editorial advisor Sharon Mashihi officiating the event. Her authoritative yet celebratory feminine voice states, 'We are gathered here today to celebrate love, business, partnership and radio' (Part 2), you can hear that she is smiling. As the episode comes to a close, the listener is left wondering whether or not the experience they have become a part of, the experience of a loving partnership and celebration of that love through the institution of marriage is one of fact or fiction. The simple fact that the story is told through sound invokes our sonic imaginary and plays with the cultural and social context of the time, as 2015 in the United States marks the Supreme Court ruling for the legalisation of same-sex marriage. We not only hear the 'feminine' voices of Mitra and Kaitlyn but that of the officiate as well. The queering and gender play of the wedding event from both a political and sonic angle creates a powerful soundwork, love story and commentary on the performativity of gender and sexuality intertwined with these traditional ideologies.

It may seem like an outdated notion in our proclaimed post-feminist culture but the number of female voices on radio continues to be greatly exceeded by the number of male voices heard on the air. Podcasting and digital soundwork offer a new platform for female voice, including those not traditionally 'warm' or 'low' enough for radio,[8] to not only be heard, but to speak out and 'exist' as representative of the female-identified half of the world's population. In a 2013 report by the UK based Sound Women network, one in five solo voices on the radio are female, that's just 20% per cent, copmpared with the 55 per cent female population of the United Kingdom. The report also states that 'you are nearly 10 times as likely to hear 2+ male presenters as you are to hear 2+ female presenters' based on 30 stations across the UK: all the main national networks/stations were analysed for this study. Similar research has been done for the Toronto market by Lori Beckstead for her 'Interactive Radio: Diversity on Air' project, an interactive radio which allows the 'auralisation' of data about diversity in radio to explore how many women and/or racialised persons host or present on the Toronto commercial airwaves.[9] However, the ecology and politics of the podcast industry from production to distribution and listenership, though radiogenic in nature, does indeed differ from traditional radio and requires further study into gendered representation on air. The podcast industry, much like it's radio mother, has yet to find gender balance. As explored by American radio producer Julie Shapiro for Transom.org, 'according to the widely-used podcast-delivery phone app *Stitcher*, in 2013 out of the top 100 podcasts in their system, 71 are hosted by men (many by two or three men), and 11 are hosted by women' and the remainder have a mix of hosts, both women and men, on a rotating or permanent basis (Shapiro 2013). After the 2014 podcast boom, the world of podcasting has, however, experienced a rise in the number of popular shows hosted by women, a consequence of the success of shows such as *Serial, Invisibilia, Guys We F****d, Limetown,* and of course *The Heart*.[10] Nevertheless, an exhibited gender bias of predominately male voice documented within radio's history as outlined by Michele Hilmes in *The Disembodied Woman* (1997), the potential for non-male coded voice within the digital podcast space to pull listeners in through niche interests and non-traditional formats becomes an enticing and very real shift in soundwork culture.

While the voices of Kaitlin and Mitra are aurally coded here as feminine and thus female, in the act of queered critical listening we must also bring awareness to the potential of a disruption in this reading, As Schlichter (2011) argues, 'the voice can become a site where gender is naturalized and denaturalized at the same time' (47). Gender differences in voice from pitch and timbre to resonance and variability are ultimately socially constructed rather than anatomically fixed. Drawing on popular scientific study of male and female biological difference in our vocal folds and oral system, Karpf and others explain how the thinner, tauter vocal folds of a human female vibrate more frequently to create higher frequency or pitch in sound production.[11] Despite these biological norms, it is the repetition of the performed combinations of voice and gesture that are coded and decoded as feminine or masculine. As scholarship, experience and knowledge of gender identity and performance move into the twenty-first century we see a crucial shift into the intersection with race, ethnicity, class and sexual identity. It is through this interdisciplinary intersectional lens that we must broaden the scope of the study of voice as noted by radio scholar Jason Loviglio (2007), 'to understand the complicated and creative performances that constitute radio's continued vital presence' in

North American culture (80). Through intersectional feminist scholarship and thoughtful sound production, we must work toward bringing a more fluid and malleable co-construction and queering of gender through continuous advocacy and theoretical work surrounding the material voice.

Voice(s) of Experience

Experience and story drive our knowledge and understanding of social and cultural phenomena, be it within the context of feminist theory, media production or simply day-to-day socialisation. I am spreading the value of experience and story throughout my analysis of *The Heart*, as these two terms play a key role in the understanding and affective economies that surround and stick to this soundwork. Joan W. Scott in *Evidence of Experience* (1991), argues that although it may be tempting to abandon it altogether 'experience is not a word we can do without'. She discusses the typical historian use of experience within scholarly works to write difference, of the experience of the 'other' without analysing how one's experience and thus identity is constructed. It is through this critique that Scott conceives that 'experience is at once always already an interpretation and something that needs to be interpreted... Experience is, in this approach, not the origin of our explanation, but that which we want to explain' (797). *The Heart* works toward this construction of experience and identity in season one episode three, 'Beauty is Pain'. Scott neglects to discuss the potential power of aurality and the amplified voice for the redefinition of experience, rather drawing on Donna Haraway's reflections on vision and eyes as perceptual systems (1988: 575) where, 'the vision of the individual subject becomes the bedrock of evidence on which the explanation is built... How one's vision is structured – about language or discourse and history – are left aside' (777). Although Scott uses a visually exclusive language of discourse that is deaf to the power of sound, her theories on the importance of a contextualised and structurally aware discourse of experience is utilised within soundworks to create powerful affective story for a public audience through multi-voice personal, historical and contextual sonic narrative.

Beauty is Pain begins with opening narration by Kaitlin Prest, her calm pristine voice paints imagery for the audience soaking in anxieties and reflected experience, 'I bet you've had one of those days you've woke up looked in the mirror and feeling like you want to cry... Trying to be beautiful is fun but it also fucking hurts.'[12] As internal anxieties vocalised whispers by Prest move left and right and she continues,

'It's hard to be a woman, yes. It's a lot harder to be a woman who's hairy, wide, big, tall, square instead of round, straight up and down—instead of curvy, with big hands, big feet, no vagina and maybe no breasts either. A woman who isn't quite looking like what some people think a woman should look like, but who is finding her way. To these women, the world can be downright cruel. More than cruel, but violent'. (Beauty is Pain 2015)

This story of universalised experience, of a lack of self-esteem, a lack of confidence in your feminine image moves into the anxieties felt by Rajee Narinesingh, a transgender woman whose voice follows Prest's. The change in voice brings us into a personal first-hand account of Rajee's experience receiving black-market plastic surgery and the roller coaster outcome that followed. The strategically sparing bed of sound effects, a metallic cut delayed in repetition moves into a light harp and electronic beat beneath Rajee's voice 'beauty is pain'. Fear moves to happiness back to fear and anxiety written in her voice, more nasal and sibilant than Prest's with a choice of conversational New York accented language and quickened speech to evoke intimate affect back and forth between the soundwork and the listener. When Rajee actively recounts, 'my face burst open, and all this green stuff splattered on the mirror... it was green and yellow and white pus mixed with blood, it just kept oozing out, it was the beginning of the nightmare...' and the music bed of the soundwork underlying Rajee's narrative with anxious slow tempo heart-beating instrumental, the imagined visuals project an uneasiness, a sickness, a sadness, a fear to create a weighted first-person context of Rajee's experience. The episode doesn't only recount Rajee's story as individual experience but pulls in scientific and multi-voice discourse on how this experience is constructed. Kaitlin invites Ril Goldstein, a nurse practitioner working to help medical providers be more LGBTQ-aware, into the sound-booth to give more structural context behind the experience of transgender surgery and dysphoria. Ril brings a new voice, an authority and appeal to logos into the episode, tying together Rajee's story and Kaitlin's closing narration soaking in experience and potential affect within and between the listener and the soundwork.

The Collective Voice: A Digital to Analog Multi-Self Presentation

As we move into a world where online and offline experience intertwine through daily online self-presentation, questions of 'authenticity' or 'realness' shake the affective and cultural value of podcasting and digital soundwork to the surface. Sidonie Smith and Julia Watson's *Virtually Me: A Toolbox about Online Self-Representation* (2014), discusses our fundamental human engagement and fascination with the lives of others, the continuous co-construction of the online self through story and interaction. Smith and Watson define the term 'self' as 'a pronominal marker of reflexivity, the shorthand term for acts of self-reference' rather than the humanist concept of self, it is 'the constructed self not as an essence but as a subject, a moving target, which provisionally conjoins memory, identity, experience, relationality, embodiment, affect and limited agency' (72). Through a mix of personal story and collective or universalised notions of human affective experience, *The Heart* plays with this notion of the self as experienced in our malleable and co-constructed modern digital/analog identities. Smith and Watson indicate, 'we do not take up oral storytelling such as co-produced stories told in offline workshops and then mounted online' (73). This phonophobic rejection of the oral tradition from its crucial place in the co-construction of self-presentation ignores the growing and widespread popularity of autobiographical and experience driven podcast listening and creation. As theorised by Walter S. Gershon in the *Vibrational Affect: Sound Theory and Practice in Qualitative Research* (2013), 'sounds are methodologically valuable as they sit at the paradox of human experience' (258). Sound, particularly the human voice, is simultaneously individualistic and collectively socio-culturally universal. It is through a vocal ontology of uniqueness in which voice 'radically contests the metaphysical tradition that silences the 'I' in flesh and bone' (Cavarero 2005: 176). Like Schilchter (2011), Cavarero calls out the feminist philosophers of the past on the way in which speech and voice are often construed to be interchangeable rather than symbiotic. There is speech because there is a living, breathing, feeling human from which these words extend through sound in a given space. The voice is a powerful tool not only because of its relation to speech but because human voice as sound (online and offline) connects us, like nothing else.

The Heart plays with this notion of offline/online through temporally unfixed digital/analog story, with recorded 'live' performances mixed with studio recording and post-production. What differentiates podcasts like *The Heart* from what Smith and Watson perceive as online self-presentation is the inclusion of the oral sound-art driven narrative that pushes the self-presentation put forward into the collective realm of digital identity work, somewhere between a personal blog post and a high-art artistically made autobiographical film. The online presence of *The Heart,* primarily aural-focused with simplistic–complementary web design and visual content, cannot exist fully without the orally produced soundworks that hold centre to the identity creation of the entire digital brand. The podcast and particularly the voice of Kaitlin

Prest, are both metaphorically and literally the heart of the work. Michele Hilmes in *The New Materiality of Radio: Sound on Screens* (2013), discusses the formative new materiality of radio's as well as podcasting's present era, and its new place as a screen medium. There is potential for shows to include visual branding and accompanying imagery to enhance the listening experience, a facet reserved exclusively for radio's visual-based siblings until recent years. As seen in Fig. 11.1, *The Heart* website creates a visually pleasing yet simple design to showcase the featured episodes without reducing the potential for self-produced imagery or imagined possibility and memory-recall for the listener when engaging with the chosen soundwork.

The simple design effectively creates a centring around the affective intention and circulation around the soundwork. This centring on affect creates a streamlined universe for *The Heart* driven by co-constructed presentation from a collective team always listening and engaging with their audience.

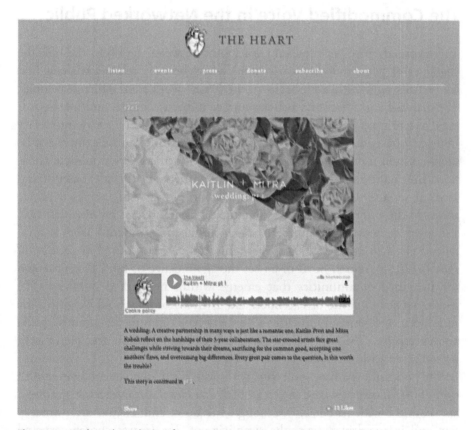

Fig. 11.1 Web and art design for 'Kaitlin + Mitra: A Wedding' pt 1. (*The Heart*, October 2015, http://www.theheartradio.org/season2/kaitlinandmitra-pt1)

From each episode's image to the sound effects that underline each amplified voice, it is a continuous, visceral work in progress. As Kaitlin Prest divulged to CBC's *DocProject* 'we work with an incredible designer named Jen Ng who makes everything we do look the way the show sounds when it's presented online. Jen and I spend afternoons in coffee shops creating inspiration boards and thinking about titling conventions' (2016). Through personal stories of a first kiss and 23 other firsts, along with queered stories of love and loss, the creators of *The Heart* bring their personal continuous self-presentation to each episode, blurring the edges of drama and autobiography. Driven by the intimacy of the sound medium that continues to hold in the digital present, *The Heart* circulates within affective and cultural economies as a commodified form available through the encompassing and expanding webs of our digital networked publics.

The Commodified Voice in the Networked Public

The recorded voice, as aural junction point between the body, the self, the character of performance and listener, cannot be fully realised without first contexualising it within the socio-cultural framework from which it belongs. The material voice becomes a sticky surface to be stuck with multiple decodings, re-workings and affect. Yet the affective value, and of course monetary value, of the commodified voice through soundwork can only increases its socio-cultural influence and affective political worth through public circulation. The increased possibilities for circulation offered by digitally based sound archival services like iTunes and Soundcloud along with increased public access to the internet, makes possible the on-demand sharing of experience, self co-construction, and intimate human connection unbound from temporality that is so central to *The Heart*. In *Social Network Sites as Networked Publics* (2011), danah boyd discusses the significance of both the space and the imagined communities that emerge within networked publics.[13] The global network publics of Facebook and Twitter not only hold weight in the social relations between individuals but between communities, brands, media and enterprise. *The Heart* is no exception to the inclusion and digital self-presentation within these network publics.

The podcast has a Facebook page with over 5700 'likes' and a Twitter with over 7900 followers, where the creators of *The Heart* can interact, experiment and connect with listeners.[14] Although Facebook and Twitter are primarily text and image-driven sites, the simplicity of *The Heart*'s chosen text and image echo the aural importance and its centring in voice, continuously driving visitors to the soundworks through engagement with fans and potential listeners within these networked publics. For the announcement on Facebook of their final episode of *Ghost* series, *The Heart* creators simply post, 'our final episode on the #ghost series and it's...You' with a link to the episode playing back to the notion of plurality in identity and the affective value of sound within the work. But it isn't just updates on new episodes, *The Heart* Facebook page also acts as a member of the public, sharing online news articles of interest or events relating to the constructed multi-self and affective branding of the series. danah boyd (2011) notes, 'as social network sites and other genres of social media become increasingly widespread, the distinctions between networked publics and publics will become increasingly blurry' (55). It is through the interactions and engagement within these publics that *The Heart* can circulate and grow not only as a digital work but also as an intimate, personal and affective plurality of voice.

Although networked publics and social interaction increase the distribution of *The Heart*, it is the branding through online circulation that calls into question the authenticity, political value and intimacy of amplified voice within soundwork if perceived as a simply a commodifed and thus produced or fabricated media object. In *Remediating Politics: brand(ed) new sexualities and real bodies online* (2013), Fotopolou examines two feminist porn production companies with a focus on the sites as media texts in relation to authenticity, real bodies and diversity discourse through a queer feminist lens. Fotopolou is concerned with the ways in which queer and feminist sexual politics and codes become themselves branded, commodified material objects in online porn culture. This article is of particular interest in conversation with *The Heart*, in the ways in which it problematises the notion that the bloggers sexuality becomes a commodity transforming political values into commercial value. Rather Fotopolou suggests 'that genderqueer and women's porn is permeated by the logic of making the medium disappear—strangely enough by appealing to "reality"' (257). We can easily exchange 'genderqueer and women's porn' for 'podcasting' in the ways in which Fotopolou is speaking of queered porn online in relation to changing perception of reality and technology; soundworks like *The Heart* experience and play with this changing perception through the raw intimacy of the amplified voice. Yes, this may seem at first like a stretch but the affective value of soundworks rely heavily on this blurring of reality, this intimacy and trust that is inherent to the whispers, coos and laughter of the human voice shared through the act of listening.

Reflections of the Aural Heart

The study of digitised material voice has become more crucial now than ever. As our daily lives fill with digital image and text-based interactions via social media and instant messaging, it's hard not to notice how meaning, emotion and personal coalition can so easily become lost in translation as words become disconnected from their unique material voiced expression. However, the voice cannot be fully comprehended or studied exclusively detached from the extended body and socio-cultural circumstances of its unstable performative being. The human voice—in particular here, the publicly amplified and digitised voice—as an extension of the body binds it to our understanding of the self and our performative identities from a phenomenological and existential perspective. Its political and affective value remains dependent on the social and aural relationships at play concerning the listener and the soundwork as a commodity. The human voice is a powerful tool and a bodily extension for our presentation and understanding of one another, but the voice amplified, the voice carefully and thoughtfully moulded through sound–art holds dramatic intimacy, affect and power. When the electronics and digital distribution models are stripped away, the voices of radio and podcasting are embodied human beings/ persons sharing their unique perspectives and personalities with the public. The English word 'person' shares roots with the Latin term 'personare' meaning 'to sound through', expressing the human understanding of the sound of the voice as an indisputable part of both an embodied self and performative identity.[15]

The voices presented on *The Heart* are aurally coded 'feminine' yet through the adoption of Butler's phenomenologies it is clear that the podcast queers norms of gender and sexuality through the use of voice, narrative form and aesthetics of sound–art within the affective soundwork. Experience and story play a key role in the understanding and the affective economies that surround and stick to this soundwork. The political and social mediation and commodification of the amplified voice within soundwork in the digital space is a subject that requires further exploration as more concrete frameworks for the discussion of the material voice and further discourse on the materiality of radio and soundworks are written. Although this chapter focuses on the soundwork and voices of women in English-speaking Western media, many of the ideas discussed here can be used for the inspiration and growth of intersectional community and the cultivation of diverse and historically underrepresented voices within soundwork. *The Heart* podcast is just one of many soundworks which embodies this power. With this reflection, I urge you to go forth with open ears, listen to your breath, feel your chest rise and fall reading for the extension and performance of your unique voice. Go forth, create, and listen in to the sounds of humanity.

Notes

1. In 'Do Voices Matter? Vocality, Materiality, Gender Performativity', Annette Schlichter examines the ramifications of Judith Butler's notion of gender performativity that ignores the performatives aspects of the material voice. From a feminist phenomenological perspective, Schlichter asks what it means to theorise a body without a voice.
2. The success of the American podcast *Serial* in 2014 has been framed as a significant moment in podcast history as argued by Richard Berry (2015) with '*Serial* reaching five million iTunes downloads in record time' (Dredge 2014).
3. CKUT is a non-profit campus-community station based at McGill University in Montreal, Canada. Audio Smut still exists as a show on the station with new producers as a monthly sex-positive, queer-positive radio show.
4. In 'How podcasting is changing the audio storytelling genre' (2016), radio scholar Siobhan McHugh notes 'Movies in your Head' as a groundbreaking work in experimental audio storytelling (72). Quote pulled from *The Heart* Website: http://www.theheartradio.org/audio-smut/moviesinyourhead
5. I use the term 'soundworks' put forward by media scholar Michele Hilmes in *The New Materiality of Radio* (2013), as 'creative/constructed aural texts that employ the basic sonic elements of speech, music and noise; this excludes the field normally encompassed by the term "music," though of course the boundaries are anything but clear. Typically speech is the dominant aspect of soundwork, with music and noise secondary' (60).
6. The discussion of Claire de Lune used in films comes from the IMDb online database of Claude Debussy (1862–1918) by calculating the number of films in his filmography as of 10 April 2016 that note the compositions use on their soundtrack.
7. The quote is taken from a critical listening of 'Kaitlin + Mitra – Wedding', *The Heart* podcast.
8. In *Sound effects: Gender, voice and the cultural work of NPR*, Jason Loviglio discusses the aural attributes common to the female radio voice, 'The voices of women hosts, presenters and correspondents on NPR's most widely heard programmes are uncommonly low in pitch. There is a pronounced lack of pitch variance, a kind of disciplined, flat monotone delivery, with few pitch shifts' (67).
9. I discuss the status and content of Lori Beckstead's Diversity on Air project as experienced attending a presentation of her work at Podcamp Toronto 2016 held at Ryerson University.
10. Data from: iTunes. Apple Canada, 2015. Accessed 11 December 2015. http://www.apple.ca/itunes/

11. In addition to the biological differences in male and female vocal organs, Karpf as well as Loviglio (2007) indicate a sonic shift in women's voices over the past fifty years in the Western world. With a focus on broadcast voices in particular, they claim that women's voices are getting deeper.

12. Season 1 episode 3 of *The Heart* opens with Prest's narrative voice speaking to us as if the anxiety, the lack of self-confidence is her own. The use of explicit language and conversational tone draw the listener into her intimate 'authentic' voice.

13. danah boyd describes networked publics simply as 'publics that are structured by networked technologies' (39).

14. These numbers from Facebook and Twitter were last reviewed and updated on 24 November 2017.

15. Although the Latin term 'personare' is mentioned here in text, Greek roots have also been noted by Sendlmeier (2013), as seen on p. 32 in the 'Introduction' to *Electrified voices: Medial, social-historical and cultural aspects of voice transfer.*

Bibliography

Ahmed, S. (2004). Affective economies. *Social Text, 22*(2 79), 117–139.

Berry, R. (2015). A golden age of podcasting? Evaluating serial in the context of podcast histories. *Journal of Radio & Audio Media, 22*(2), 170–178.

Boyd, D. (2011). Social network sites as networked publics: Affordances, dynamics and implications. In Z. Papacharissi (Ed.), *A networked self: Identity, community, and culture on social network sites* (pp. 39–58). London: Routledge.

Butler, J. (1988). Performative acts and gender constitution: An essay in phenomenology and feminist theory. *Theatre Journal, 40*(4), 519–531.

Cavarero, A. (2005). For more than one voice: Toward a philosophy of vocal expression, trans. Paul A. Kottman. Stanford: Stanford University Press.

Claude Debussy. (n.d.). From http://www.imdb.com/name/nm0006033/, [Internet]. Accessed 10 Apr 2016.

Dredge, S. (2014). Serial podcast breaks iTunes records as it passes 5m downloads and streams. www.theguardian.co.uk, [Internet]. Accessed 2017.

Dyson, F. (1994). The geneology of the radio voice. In D. Augaitis & D. Lander (Eds.), *Radio rethink: Art, sound and transmission.* Banff: Walter Phillips Gallery.

Ehrick, C. (2015). *Radio and the gendered soundscape: Women and broadcasting in Argentina and Uruguay, 1930–1950.* New York: Cambridge University Press.

Fotopoulou, A. (2013). Remediating politics: Brand(ed) new sexualities and real bodies online. *Journal of Lesbian Studies, 17*(3–4), 253–266.

Gershon, W. S. (2013). Vibrational affect: Sound theory and practice in qualitative research. *Cultural Studies & Critical Methodologies, 13*(4), 257–262.

Haraway, D. (1988). Situated knowledges: The science question in feminism and the privilege of partial perspective. *Feminist Studies, 14*(3), 575–599.

Hilmes, M. (1997). *Radio voices: American broadcasting, 1922–1952.* Minneapolis: University of Minnesota Press.

Hilmes, M. (2013). The new materiality of radio: Sound on screens. In M. Hilmes & J. Loviglio (Eds.), *Radio's new wave: Global sound in the digital era.,* Chap 3. New York: Taylor and Francis.

Ihde, D. (2007). *Listening and voice: Phenomenologies of sound* (2nd ed.). Albany: State University of New York Press.

Karpf, A. (2007). *The human voice: The story of a remarkable talent.* London: Bloomsbury.

Loviglio, J. (2007). Sound effects: Gender, voice and the cultural work of NPR. *Radio Journal: International Studies in Broadcast & Audio Media, 5*(2), 67–81.

McKay, A. (2000). Speaking up: Voice amplification and women's struggle for public expression. In C. Mitchell (Ed.), *Women and radio: Airing differences.* London: Routledge.

Mitchell, C. (2000). *Women and radio: Airing differences.* London: Routledge.

Prest, K. (2016). Lessons in getting an indie podcast off the ground. www.cbc.ca, [Internet]. Accessed 10 Apr 2016.

Radiotopia. (2016). Description of *The Heart* podcast. http://www.radiotopia.fm, [Internet]. Accessed 10 Apr 2016.

S1E3: *Beauty Is Pain.* (2014). https://www.theheartradio.org/season1/beautyispain, [Audio Podcast]. Accessed 10 Apr 2016.

S2E1: Kaitlyn & Mitra. *Parts 1&2.* (2015). https://www.theheartradio.org/season2-episodes-makebreak, [Internet]. Accessed 10 Apr 2016.

S2E11: *You.* (2016). https://www.theheartradio.org/season2-ghost/you [Audio Podcast]. Accessed 10 Apr 2016.

Schlichter, A. (2011). Do voices matter? Vocality, materiality, gender performativity. *Body & Society, 17*(1), 31–52.

Scott, J. W. (1991). The evidence of experience. *Critical Inquiry, 17*(4), 773–797.

Sendlmeier, S. (2013). Introduction: Voice – Emotion – Personality. In D. Zakharine & M. Nils (Eds.), *Electrified voices: Medial, socio-historical and cultural aspects of voice transfer.* Göttingen: Niedersachs.

Shapiro, J. (2013). Women hosted podcasts. www.transom.org, [Internet]. Accessed 8 Dec 2015.

Smith, S., & Watson, J. (2014). Virtually me: A toolbox about online self-presentation. In *Identity technologies: Constructing the self online.* Madison: The University of Wisconsin Press.

Sound Women. (2013). Sound women on air report. http://www.soundwomen.co.uk/research/, [Internet]. Accessed 10 Apr 2016.

The Heart Facebook page. (2011). www.facebook.com/theheartradio/, [Internet]. Accessed 10 Apr 2016.

The Heart Podcast. (2014–). www.theheartradio.org, [Podcast].

The Heart Podcast. (n.d.). About. http://www.theheartradio.org/about/, [Internet].

Twitter. (2011). @TheHeartRadio. https://twitter.com/theheartradio/, [Internet]. Accessed 8 Apr 2016.

12

Comedian Hosts and the Demotic Turn

Kathleen Collins

> Listen to enough episodes and you begin to consider the wild biographies of
> writers and artists in relation to your own attempts to pursue your dreams.
> *Larson (2015)*

Introduction

Over the course of the past decade, the digital medium of audio podcasting
has become a robust enterprise. According to numbers in the US, Edison
Research and Triton Digital survey data in 2017 reveal that four in ten
Americans aged 12 or older have listened to a podcast, and 24 per cent have
listened to a podcast in the past month, up from 9 per cent in 2008 (Edison
Research 2017). The report claims there are 57 million US monthly listeners.
Ear Buds: The Podcasting Documentary (Elwood and Mancini 2016), estimates
some 350,000 podcasts in existence. The surge in the relatively new medium
can be attributed to three main factors: a confessional culture, the triumph of
experience over expertise, and accessible technology. Over the course of the
twentieth century, the United States experienced a marked trend toward public confessional behaviour as well as an embrace of the pro-am (professional–
amateur) approach in multiple sectors of society (Leadbeater and Miller
2004). In the domain of psychology and mental wellness, especially, experience (vs. expertise) has shown marked increased cultural impact, as evidenced

K. Collins (✉)
John Jay College of Criminal Justice, CUNY, New York, NY, USA
e-mail: kcollins@jjay.cuny.edu

© The Author(s) 2018
D. Llinares et al. (eds.), *Podcasting*, https://doi.org/10.1007/978-3-319-90056-8_12

by comments to programmes and documented in *Ear Buds*. Finally and relatedly, the emergence of a panoply of podcasts extending to a long tail of topics since roughly 2004 exists in large part because of democratisation—podcasts are cheap and easy to create—allowed by the form's technology.

The focus here is on 'born' or 'native' podcasts as differentiated from downloaded radio programmes, which conform to effectively different parameters. Nevertheless, it bears acknowledging that podcasting is a descendant of traditional radio and as such shares a number of salient attributes. While many traditional radio programmes (music programmes being a noted exception) necessitated appointment listening and podcasts are accessed on demand, the state of intimacy remains a constant characteristic given, in part, the physical aspects of audio, enhanced further by the use of earbuds or headphones and the feeling of a one-to-one relationship with the speaker(s). The intersection of the distinctive intimacy of the podcast form (Berry 2006, 2016) the prevalence of comedian-hosted podcasts, and a flattening of the celebrity layperson hierarchy are characteristics of a sub-genre of the format under consideration here. Podcasting is a showcase for the term that cultural studies scholar Graeme Turner (2010a) coined 'the demotic turn', that is, the increasing visibility of the 'ordinary person' in today's media landscape. These characteristics are interdependent and operational in creating a new form of self-help broadcasting. A historical comparison of the early days of podcasting and of radio is also instructive in placing the newer medium in perspective.

Off-Label Use

Not surprisingly, given the self-reflexive and independent nature of podcast construction and the intimacy of its format, many self-help oriented podcasts have arisen in this new content creator's hothouse. Topics range from meditation, language learning and spirituality to happiness, physical health and financial coaching. Celebrity-hosted and celebrity or artist interview programmes have also emerged as a popular podcast category. A phenomenon can be observed here wherein many of the latter have evolved into an oblique form of the former, i.e. the self-help type, adopting what I have come to term an 'off-label' use, meaning the use of a programme for a purpose other than that for which it is ostensibly intended. In addition to the increased accessibility of podcast creation, this sub-genre is an apt illustration of the aforementioned confessional and pro-am evolution in modern media. Comedian Marc Maron's *WTF* is the best and most widely recognised of this genus which began in 2009 and boasts hundreds of thousands of downloads per episode.

WTF set the bar for and inspired others to create similar shows. The formula, popularised by Maron, tends toward host monologue followed by guest interview (comedians, actors, musicians, directors, writers, even the president of the United States) that emphasises conversation between host and guest replete with intimate, personal subject matter, rather than rote, or the publicity-style interview banter seen and heard in other broadcast venues. Vincent Meserko describes *WTF* as 'the go-to site from which a more authentic self can emerge' (Meserko 2015: 807). Emotions are apt to run high, and the effect for the listener can approximate that of eavesdropping. This style of podcast has grown significantly since 2010, and though not all such programmes exhibit the 'off-label' characteristics in each episode or with the same intensity, other examples of comedian-hosted programmes include *You Made it Weird* hosted by Pete Holmes, *Girl on Guy* hosted by Aisha Tyler and *Nerdist* hosted by Chris Hardwick. For brevity's sake, this genre will heretofore be referred to as CHIPs (Comedian Hosted Interview Podcasts).

Self-Help History

Self-help via broadcasting has a long history, dating back to radio advice shows that made their appearance with the US advent of the medium in the 1920s. Such programmes provided and still provide proxy counselling on personal matters for those writing or calling into a show and, vicariously, for listeners. While other early radio genres such as cooking instruction and home-making tips eventually found a more effective home on television aided as they were by the visual component (Collins 2009; Douglas 2005; Hilmes 1999), with the exception of a few celebrity psychologists like Joyce Brothers and Ruth Westheimer, media psychology has maintained a comfortable niche in the audio realm where intimacy is elemental to the therapeutic mission of the programmes. John Langer deconstructed the talk show format in 1981, describing its 'carefully orchestrated informality, with its illusion of lounge-room casualness and leisurely pace' (Langer 1981: 360). He exposes the chat between host and guest as an 'advertising forum' promoting the guest's commodities, not—as the format ostensibly offers—an occasion of personal disclosure and rare glimpse of the guests' 'real selves' (quotes in original) (Langer 1981: 360–361). In the pre-podcasting years, some comic talk show hosts, such as radio's Howard Stern (Kurtz 1997) and television's Steve Allen (Collins 2016) and David Letterman (Schaefer and Avery 1993) cultivated a style and environment that occasionally prompted guests to reveal intimate or emotional information. The modern talk show iteration in the form of CHIPs differs in many ways, the least of which include the larger number and variety, the presence of conversation, and personally revealing content, but also in the self-awareness and psychological savvy of the audiences and creators. What notably persists is listeners' ability to benefit from vicarious counsel. In the radio days, learning what other people were experiencing and taking in what the doctor (or psychic or fortune-teller or whoever the host may have been) advised allowed uncertain individuals or their spouses, parents, employees or friends in the listening audience to heed similar counsel. At the very least a listener feels less alone in his situation and, ideally, the indirect advice might spark in an attentive listener a different way of looking at a painful or immobilising situation.

Because podcasting is free from oversight, unlike US Federal Communications Commission regulated radio, creators have no need to argue for their existence or defend their content. I will, however, argue for the benefits of podcast listening to bolster the 'off-label' theory. In the 1920s, the FRC (Federal Radio Commission, the forerunner to the FCC) regulators felt that one-to-one communication exhibited on programmes featuring psychologists and fortune-tellers (then grouped into the same eyebrow-raising category) was of no benefit to incidental listeners. They may have come around to seeing that it was entertaining and loosely advantageous as such, but there was little discussion of it being actually helpful and therefore quite literally in the public interest, as mandated by the FRC (Goodman 2012: 196). Historian David Goodman, in his description of the obstacles faced by fortune-tellers, psychics and other early radio advisors, observes that the 'entertainment' card may have quelled the FRC and the FCC in some cases (Goodman 2012: 198). The entertainment aspect or benefit is undeniable, as much of the appeal of these instruments derives from the innate human desire for eavesdropping. But even at the time listeners, then television viewers, and now podcast listeners lavishly avow that hearing other people's problems helps them in their own lives. 'Banishing the fortune-tellers was an affirmation,' writes Goodman, 'of what radio should have been—civic, improving, local, encouraging of self-government and of critical self-reflexive listening' (Goodman 2012: 201). But to that very point, many television scholars have written about the neoliberal service provided by reality TV (e.g. Ouellette 2009; Turner 2010a; Vered and McConchie 2011). Entertainment, empathy and vicarious counsel co-exist in each of these formats, allowing an à la carte menu of 'benefits,' convenient and often legitimate for consumer, citizen, regulator, parent or producer.

Solace-seeking for personal problems was no stranger to mass media, and radio was a haven for mental health issues. Several programmes in the first two decades of radio offered distance counselling. All had varying degrees of bona fides as well as a heavy reliance on moralising. Among them, Lee Steiner, a psychologist and marriage counsellor hosted *How's Your Mental Health* in 1934 and *Psychologically Speaking* in the 1950s. Steiner, a rare woman on the air, was clear about radio's limited role in personal psychology. She believed that it 'should be geared specifically to that part of the population that can utilize a *point of view* [her emphasis] about the solution of personal problems, rather than that part of the listening audience that needs "therapy"' (Steiner 1954: 205). *The New York Times* wrote of the *Call Dr. [Joyce] Brothers* show in 1966, 'Aside from taking telephone calls from listeners, the psychologist… will answer letters that represent a cross-section of the problems bothering people the most. If you have a problem, try to make it fit in a cross-section' ('Dial Dr. Brothers' 1966). Here is another distinct departure from early radio on through network television, when general advice was favoured over specific in order to appeal to the broadest possible audience. Podcasting, however, thrives on specificity and niches because it can, and audiences attest to the fact that no problem or situation is so specific that a listener cannot relate in some way.

In radio broadcasting, the 'clients' who called or wrote into shows were regular, non-famous people. This pattern exists today in some podcasting programmes whose explicit purpose is to provide psychological or spiritual guidance. One example of a podcast that conforms to the traditional trappings of an early radio show is the *Dear Sugar Radio* podcast, hosted by well-known, 'celebrity'-status writers Cheryl Strayed and Steve Almond. It appears to intentionally pay nostalgic homage to the aesthetic and mission of old-school radio advice shows in its name, in its introduction, (as Strayed says, they are there for the 'heartsick, lost, and lonely') and in their answering letters and addressing correspondents as they signed their letters, such as 'Heartbroken.' Its existence galvanises the idea that even though the technology has advanced beyond imagination since broadcasting's early days, the simple need of succour for the human spirit remains steadfast. Strayed describes the show as 'therapy in the town square' (Strayed 2015). *Sex with Emily* is another well-established and popular podcast hosted by relationship/sex expert, Emily Morse. Likewise, a new generation podcast, *Beautiful Stories from Anonymous People* (aka *Beautiful/ Anonymous*) hosted by comedian Chris Gethard, usually features guests who are laypeople, and, usually, anonymous. Notably, these hosts are not licensed clinical mental health professionals. In the pre-podcasting era, especially in the early radio days, credentials were valuable in gaining audience trust. In the modern era, especially in the podcast realm, a host who is not an authoritative expert and who is more similar to a layperson might be perceived as more approachable by listeners. Experts do not have the strong foothold in the world of podcasting as they do in radio or television or real life. This bolsters the demotic theme and exemplifies a modern trend toward an anti-intellectual, experience-as-authority trend (Collins 2016).

Since the psychic and fortune-teller days, the credentials of broadcasting advisors have been greeted with suspicion due, among other reasons, to a distrust of psychology and 'the sin of popularity' (Miller 1980: 1). There has always been a mix of purveyors of psychological, emotional or general life advice, only some of whom are professionally credentialled. Broadcasting allows for this flexibility since hosts are not technically providing therapy to their listening audiences. In 1969, as a climate of revolution and change was affecting nearly every aspect of society, American Psychological Association president George Miller enjoined practitioners to engage in a 'public psychology' in the spirit of educating people freely so that psychology and psychotherapy—which was growing in acceptance and popularity but suffering from a shortage of professionals—could theoretically be available to everyone. Though he didn't specify broadcast psychology in his speech, the practice dovetailed perfectly with his 'give it away,' do-it-yourself sentiments. His intention was not directed to media psychologists (a nascent recognised subset at the time), but those who practised via TV and radio did just that, providing a free service to a populace that might otherwise be unable or unwilling to access traditional and often costly professionals. A passive, indirect, democratically-spirited counselling over the airwaves was a sign of the times (Miller 1969: 1066).

In his analysis of the function of phone-in radio programmes, Andrew Crisell observed three categories that callers might fall into: expressive (sharing opinions), exhibitionist (performing personality), and confessional (sharing a problem) (Crisell 1986). Current podcasts display similar motivations. In addition to the fact that host and guest are usually sitting in the same room together and podcast interview guests have more 'air time' than a radio caller, the most significant difference between the two formats is that both host and guest proactively encourage behaviour in all three categories.

Tone and Content of CHIPs

The informal conversations on podcasts tend to be far less structured or planned and more spontaneous, intimate and confessional than traditional broadcast interviews. Open and honest conversation on the part of host and guest is now almost de rigueur for this genre of podcast, so much so that small, superficial talk is not tolerated for long by habitual listeners. Some guests confess, in the interview, to being nervous—this is especially true on

Maron's *WTF* as he has become known for opening people up in ways that surprise all involved. This phenomenon leads to a self-selecting guest cohort who choose or agree to be on such shows. Those who are willing or eager to talk about personal matters will be more likely to engage, and those who keep a tight rein on their public personas will stay away. As one testament to this expectation of openness, a comment on the *WTF* blog (wtfpod.com) criticised Maron's conversation with comedian Tommy Davidson for being 'too certain' in his self-presentation. Quite unlike the time-tested protocol of late-night talk shows where celebrities entertain audiences with packaged, publicist-endorsed stories, podcast listeners look forward to celebrities talking candidly about their insecurities. In a tidy summation of these ideas, on *Distraction Pieces*, a podcast similar in tone and format to Maron's *WTF*, host poet/musician Scroobius Pip invited radio presenter Geoff Lloyd for an episode (November 1, 2016, Ep. 122), where Lloyd shared revealing stories of his own mental health issues and discussed the value of sharing personal feelings via radio and podcasts. Lloyd also confessed that podcasting seems to be the way of the future and indeed left radio several months later and began a podcast, *Adrift*, described as 'A comic tragedy for anyone flailing in the sea of their own inadequacy. [The hosts] steer a life-raft through the choppy waters of being a functional human' (https://www.acast.com/adrift).

While CHIPs occasionally feel like mere overhearing a rather banal conversation, for instance, comedians talking shop, trading comments on a particular club, or annoyances of life on the road, the effect is similar to that of a documentary or reality TV show in their departure from the PR-regulated interviews on TV talk shows. That quality alone renders the conversations compelling. The skilled or unconventional interviewer will elicit something other than the repeated answers and stories that listeners have heard from the same guest in other venues. As in any interview situation, the better listener the interviewer is, the more spontaneous the conversation and the more interesting the product. Classic interview protocol, where hosts ask questions about their current projects, eliciting interesting stories about working on the set or interactions with other actors, allow guests to shine. They—or their agents—may even have fed questions to producers in advance, so the host can ask something seemingly spontaneous. This style, while it is often part of a CHIP interview, would be too flat and restrained to evoke a more genuine conversation. The seductive power of celebrities revealing information about themselves coupled with the sometimes raw and personal issues themselves makes for a potentially rich and absorbing entertainment format. A listener may become engaged because she feels she is learning 'secrets' about famous people or gaining support, commiseration or insight into her own problems (as the issues discussed are inevitably universally shared to some degree), or both. With substantial anecdotal evidence supporting the idea that CHIPs provide access to a host of shared human angst, it is reasonable to wonder why these comedian hosts and their similarly honest guests are willing to reveal these human foibles on behalf of listeners. 'Stars articulate what it is to be a human being in contemporary society,' writes Richard Dyer, 'that is, they express the particular notion we hold of the person, of the "individual"... they articulate both the promise and the difficulty that the notion of individuality presents for all of us who live by it' (Dyer 1986: 8). Likewise, Tolson, who describes celebrities as nowadays often giving interviews in the context of personal problems, such as addictions, says, 'Celebrities personify contemporary beliefs and concerns about the human condition and their talk, in this context, is designed to construct them as representative of this.... As representative human beings, celebrities today (when they are not being ironic) are much more likely to reproduce a motivational, even moral, discourse of personal achievement' (Tolson 2006: 155).

Horton and Wohl's pioneering research in the para-social relationship—the false sense of intimacy fostered by someone on the TV screen talking directly to individual viewers—can be applied to the effect of podcasting (Horton and Wohl 1956). Marc Maron recognises the emotional benefits of his podcast on listeners: 'I get a lot of gratitude from people who felt alone, who are depressed, who didn't understand their creativity, or had a drinking problem. [They tell me:] 'You know, you really helped me through stuff" (Campion 2015). Paul F. Tompkins, comedian and host of multiple podcasts (also a guest who discussed his own depression on other CHIPs) says he gets emails from listeners who say, 'You guys help me do my job because I'm stuck at a desk all day and I'm looking at a monitor and without these shows I would go crazy. It's like you guys are my friends' (Tompkins 2016).

Echoing similar statements by Maron and others, Aisha Tyler, whose guests and callers also share experiences of earnest personal problems, has said, 'When I share myself with the world, typically what I get is a positive response with people who've gone through something similar and feel more connected with me and maybe by association feel their burden is lighter because of it. So if I can help somebody by sharing my experiences that's really my goal and that makes all the revelation and the divulgence worthwhile' (Tyler 2015). Comedian Paul Gilmartin provides a succinct description of the effect of listening to other people talk about their problems when he says to a guest on his *Mental Illness Happy Hour* podcast, 'I love when somebody else has the exact same fear I do... There's something so soothing to me when somebody can articulate a fear that is just a grey ball inside me that I've never been able to specifically articulate what it is that is scaring me' (Gilmartin 2012). Marc Maron is known for his compulsive confessions in each prologue to his guest interviews. *Dear Sugar* co-host Steve Almond reveals a previous problem with shoplifting. What might constitute 'over sharing' in another setting is an advantage for a certain stripe of podcaster. As Meyrowitz writes: '…a revelation that would destroy heroic aura may only deepen the sense of intimate connection with a media friend' (Meyrowitz 2007: 101).

Comedy and Psychology

On 10 November 2016, pop culture critic Nathan Rabin wrote a piece for the comedy website *Splitsider*, where he openly lamented the hours-old election of Donald Trump to the US presidency. He wrote, 'I decided that doubling down on my obsessive love of podcasts would be among the survival tactics I would employ to help me survive.' In the same piece, he describes the emotional role podcasts play in his life, calling them 'cathartic' and 'almost a form of free therapy'. He explains that the therapeutic effect can come from the companionship and solidarity as well as the escape into 'pure silliness and joy' (Rabin 2016). This is a role that comedy has long served, in this two-pronged (though the cathartic and entertaining prongs are sometimes difficult to differentiate) fashion.

Melanie Piper discusses the 'humour–honesty discourse' (Piper 2015: 54) prevalent in comedy podcasts. Her focus is on the type of programme that features comedians being themselves (conversing, monologuing, but not necessarily interviewing) and whose performances 'shed light on the cultural position of comedians more generally' (Piper 2015: 43). The 'off-label' podcasts discussed here consist of conversations between celebrities. Given that CHIP guests discuss their creative work, the exchange often gives rise to issues of self-image and self-doubt, overcoming obstacles, and the impact of early life experiences. *WTF* guests have openly discussed depression, suicide, addiction, and relationship issues. One comedian came out as gay on the show and another legendary episode details a suicide attempt. Media and culture critic James Wolcott suggests an 'off-label' use when he describes podcasts this way: 'They were and remain confessionals, healing exercises, bonding experiences, one-on-one Gestalt therapy sessions, and *WTF* doesn't so much find an audience as its audience finds something it didn't know it was looking for' (Wolcott 2016). For social theorist Michel Foucault, confession is a truth-producing technique and is so ingrained in Western culture that if a truth fails to surface it is because 'the violence of a power weighs it down… Confession frees, but power reduces one to silence' (Foucault 1980: 60).

On almost every *WTF* episode subjects arise that are appropriate fodder for a licensed therapist's office. Maron's monologue might focus on a traditional worried-well psychological topic—for instance, how to avoid being like your parents. Or he might discuss the recent tragic death of a fellow comedian (Garry Shandling, Robin Williams). Topics range from guests talking about early career and rejection and failures to work ethic and procrastination, the meaning of comedy, tormented family relationships and mental health. On his podcast, *You Made It Weird*, comedian host Pete Holmes gets dark with guests, too. Comedian and writer Harris Wittels talked frankly with Holmes about his addiction in 2014, and sadly died of a heroin overdose at the age of 30 the following year; Aisha Tyler also has a substantial collection of heavy and intimate *Girl on Guy* episodes. When she interviewed comedian and talk show host Chelsea Handler in 2016, the two women engaged in a candid and spontaneous discussion of their body image issues in Tyler's regular 'self-inflicted wounds' segment with Handler revealing facets of her life that she said she had never divulged before.

CHIPs are, in essence, an alternative form of media psychology—the more traditional being a call-in radio show or a programme such as *Dr. Phil* where guests present their problems in a public forum with the deliberate goal of seeking help from a professional. These podcasts can provide oblique access to the same sort of resolution. It might be that this private form of vicarious listening and relating is effective due to its off-label, unintentional usage. Because it is categorised as entertainment it reaches people when their guard is down—while washing dishes, taking a walk, relaxing on a non-psychiatrist's couch. Listeners may encounter self-realisation or insight that would be more difficult to access or accept in a formalised setting. While this can be true of radio programmes, the greater informality of podcasts is able to provoke even more intimacy and loosening of boundaries. The social world of podcasting, too, as evidenced in the *Ear Buds* documentary and online discussion sections of individual podcasts, engenders a perceived 'safe place' where like-minded listeners gather and create a sense of a virtual community. As Berry writes, 'The podcast listener relates to the podcast producer on a more intimate level because the listener may feel that the producer is 'one of them,' a member of their community, whether defined by geography, ethnicity, culture, or social group' (Berry 2006: 148). Meserko responds to this by saying, 'I have argued that this intimate discourse constitutes an audience of mental illness sufferers that are invited to relate to performers in less artificial, less transparently performative ways' (Meserko 2014: 467).

At the start of one *WTF* episode, Maron affirms that his podcast is not about his political opinions (he was a co-host of several Air America Radio programmes beginning in 2004 where he regularly railed against conservative politics). 'I deal with sadness, existential anger, the frustrations of just being alive, trying to be a compassionate person and know yourself in the world…' (Maron 2016). Likewise, *WTF* was described by one journalist as 'the patron saint of those that live in their heads – the emotionally needy, insecure and distraught' (Campion 2015). Maron as host is forthcoming about his own past suicidal thoughts, substance abuse, and insecurities and thereby encourages his guests to talk freely about their inner demons. In his book *Sick in the Head*, writer, producer and comedian Judd Apatow provides a transcript of his own *WTF* interview with a brief introduction wherein he refers to Maron as 'an insightful interviewer and empathizer and therapist of sorts, and we connected in a deep way about so many aspects of our journey' (Apatow 2016: 303). In addition to the aforementioned trepidation to which some have confessed about venturing into the garage where Maron records his interviews, he receives volumes of gratitude in emails from listeners as well as directly from guests. Playwright and composer Lin-Manuel Miranda said to Maron, 'Thanks for getting so much honesty out of so many people we love. I think of so many of your interviews and I think, I never saw that person in that way before. If the beginning of art is empathy, you give us a master class in it every time you get someone in this crazy garage of yours' (Miranda 2016).

The 'crazy garage' referred to by Miranda is not incidental. Maron often refers to the garage as being a special place to him and by extension for his guests, as deep, sometimes difficult but ultimately rewarding conversations take place there. It is filled with numerous personal artifacts that guests often comment on, therefore reflecting a personal side of the interviewer. Maron not only makes his home and his belongings part of the talking space, but he shares a great deal of his own personal experiences, feelings and confessions in every episode, both in the monologue preamble and then while conversing with his guest. The garage is viscerally symbolic. It is both the place where Maron confesses to having considered suicide years earlier and is the place where he saved himself and revived his career by starting the podcast there. The garage and the man are therefore intertwined so that the combination increases the intimacy of the conversations that take place there. Even when Maron does gladly mention a guest's newly released book, album or movie (he is explicit about selectively inviting people back to the show for short segments to help them promote a project), the conversation still lacks a standard PR-driven gloss.

There is already a charged nexus where comedy and psychology meet, but adding that to the demotic trend (Gamson 2011) in the celebrity realm (portraying 'real' or 'honest' selves in the media), a new connection is formed that deserves attention. In addition to the performative aspect of podcast hosting, there is a link between comedy and the emotional intimacy prevalent in audio formats and podcasting in particular. As truth-telling and personal revelation are basic elements of contemporary CHIPs, it should come as little surprise that so many comedians are taking advantage of the format. Comedians are perpetually creating new material, are well-versed in verbal expression, and, in general, are comfortable speaking extemporaneously and honestly. It is the latter quality that has forged a perhaps unforeseen path in an uncategorised type of programme. While many radio interviews and CHIPs—for instance, the venerable *Fresh Air* with host/ interviewer Terry Gross—carry out conventional interviews with actors, writers, musicians, and other creative people, it is by and large those podcasts hosted by comedians where this increased emotional intensity is found. Comedian and filmmaker Kevin Smith relates an interaction with a suicidal friend who turned a corner after starting his own podcast, and Smith told him, 'As long as you're always candid with them, it's a win–win. The audience will stick by you' (Pollak 2015). Both host and guest stand to benefit from such conversations.

The link between comedy and emotional health goes back at least to the 1950s (communications scholar Ethan Thompson writes about the dual post-war American obsessions of mental health and humour), manifest in performers like Shelley Berman and Lenny Bruce (Thompson 2011: 15), and comedians have long been stereotyped as sad clowns. 'Comedians are sensitive instruments', as comedian Dana Carvey said to Maron on *WTF* (Carvey 2016). In 2015, actor and comedian Kevin Pollak produced a documentary, *Misery Loves Comedy*, wherein a number of contemporary comedians address this assumption. In the film, Maria Bamford, a comedian who has been open in her stand-up about her mental health, describes a show where she revealed that she had accidentally and tragically caused her dog's death. After the bit, audience members shouted out their own similar experiences, such as 'I sat on my rabbit!' Bamford found great comfort in such instances, she says, 'so it doesn't become this private horrible thing.' The oft-quoted humourist Mark Twain has, of course, an appropriate adage for this current off-label phenomenon long before it became one: 'The secret source of humor is not joy but sorrow' (Zall 1985: 70).

New York Times cultural reporter, Lee Siegel, writes, '…there is a schizoid dimension to comedy now. As fiction merges into autobiography, and movies based on actual events proliferate, the compulsion for comedians to smash through the artifice of comedy and tell the unadorned truth without humor is becoming stronger and stronger…Comedy is becoming an occasion to abandon humor for the exposure of unsoftened truth….' While this characteristic of comedy is not a new development, there is a perfect cultural storm in the early twenty-first century entertainment and media ecosystem. Siegel identifies it: 'Now, when our awareness and self-awareness are reaching meta-levels of intensity, we need to be entertained in new ways. That is why comedy bracingly hovers just at the edge of tragedy' (Siegel 2015).

Several comedians in the Pollak film reference the recognition of common, collective humanity as an element in their work. Actor and comedian Steve Coogan, for instance, comments that comedians '[shine] a light on what it is to be human'. And in response to the notion that perhaps comedians or other performing artists are more miserable than regular folk, comedian and magician Penn Jillette concludes, 'People in show business have the same pain, the same suffering, the same angst, the same tortures. They're just showing the angst of humanity that we all share…. If you had a comic that truly had experiences that were outside of the realm of the general humanity, no one would go see them.' Indeed it can feel to the comedy consumer that comedians are wearing their hearts and guts on the outside, literally baring their souls, and taking risks that most people would be too timid to take or too ashamed to even admit to themselves. But it is the universality and relatability of their material that appeals and a fundamental reason why these types of podcasts are so popular. Comedians are already truth tellers and revealers and are willing to express it. They are attracting a following to what feels like a more private world where listening on earbuds to emotionally vulnerable content is safer even than going to a comedy show and recognising that you relate to these issues in a public place.

And so, bringing this angst to podcasting in an entertainment shell—while simultaneously broadening a comedian's recognition and fan base—is a natural progression and an alluring, organic brand of self-help. 'Ultimately what we're all doing is trying to turn our psychological problems into a paycheck,' comedian Bob Odenkirk told a reporter. 'You want to be broken in just the right way to make the most amount of money' (Cox 2016). In Pollak's documentary, Kevin Smith refers to podcasting as 'the talking cure' and likewise writer and creator of the TV sitcom *Community*, Dan Harmon, in the documentary *Harmontown* refers to podcasting as 'the best kind of therapy I could get' (Harmon 2014). Maron has said that he simply set out to create his own show because his career had stalled and that his first 100 shows consisted of inviting celebrities over to help him with his problems, namely eradicating his professional bitterness. But because of his uncensored style and desire to express and share his true feelings, he creates a fertile space for his guests to share similarly and consequently allows listeners to relate. His interviews often intentionally aim to encourage guests to share experiences that might be of value to himself and his listeners. Terry Gross, in a rare self-revealing interview by Maron at a public event in 2015, admitted she does the same: 'You know, people always say they want to find out what makes other people tick. I always feel like, I want to find out what makes me tick. [I've] learned about a lot about myself and about people in general by having the liberty of asking people very personal things' (Gross 2015).

The timing of a growing alternative comedy scene, an established confessional media culture and the new form of podcasting worked well in Marc Maron's favour. *WTF* set the standard for CHIPs and as a result, the expectations for self-revelation in podcast interview shows are high because of his pioneering. But still, it is the culmination of the three points—confessional, experience and democratisation—that made his show so galvanising in this respect. *WTF*'s popularity spawned imitators thus strengthening these factors and furthering the confessional form and emotional and psychological access via arts and cultural programming rather than through strictly psychological channels hosted by professionals or experts.

The Confessional Factor

Audio broadcast technology has evolved as a psychological self-help tool, reflecting changing values regarding voyeurism and the ethics and effectiveness of 'vicarious therapy.' Privacy, stigma and shame about personal problems have largely given way to exhibitionism. On most call-in type programmes, callers can maintain anonymity if desired. Despite this evolution, anonymity is still prevalent, as evidenced in part by Chris Gethard's *Beautiful/Anonymous*. Notably, anonymity is reserved for the non-famous for the obvious reasons that voice recognition would obliterate the anonymity of a celebrity, and laypeople have not made the choice to 'out' their problems with the world and may simply be actually looking for free emotional help and wish to maintain their privacy. Guests are either desperate enough to voice their problems on a widely available broadcast medium or they are steeped enough in the confessional culture that such a venture does not seem daunting or unusual.

Several other podcasts hosted by comedians that are not of the 'off-label' type but that are explicitly intended for discussions of mental health or personal problems illustrate instances of help-seeking in podcasting, for the most part featuring anonymous laypeople rather than celebrities. Gilmartin's *Mental Illness Happy Hour* is a vehicle for guests talking about their personal issues, where Gilmartin stresses the use of humour as a beneficial coping mechanism. On one episode, for instance, Gilmartin talks with a guest by the pseudonym Noemi, a young woman dealing with chronic disordered eating (November 28, 2014, Ep. 201). *Fixing Joe,* hosted by comedian Joe Matarese wherein he talks on each episode about a specific problem he is dealing with, is likewise explicit in its intention. The *Hilarious World of Depression*, hosted by public radio host John Moe, joined the celebrity confession podcast community in late 2016 where guests talk at length about their experiences with clinical depression (Moe himself has suffered from it and talks about it openly). Maron tells Gilmartin when he is a guest on MIHH: 'My podcast sort of functions in the same way [as MIHH] without it being about that [mental illness]. It's just knowing that this is something a lot of people struggle with and at some point, you shouldn't be alone, but you should try to take some responsibility for your disposition... just knowing that people that have these problems, do ok, and can do ok is important' (Meserko 2014: 464). Whereas *WTF* does not present as a self-help podcast, these programmes are designed for just the purpose of an individual guest receiving help but also relieving many individual listeners of their feelings of isolation with similar problems. Depression, in particular, has seen an uptick in 'popularity,' for lack of a more appropriate term, in both published memoirs and on podcasts in the modern confessional environment. Whether or not the increase is perceived or real, there are more outlets for people to share their experiences and more willingness to share and more opportunities for decreasing stigma.[1]

Podcast listeners' level of sophistication and preoccupation with self-understanding and awareness in 2017 is in stark contrast to what one learns about listeners of psychology-oriented early radio shows, noting the relatively naïve questions from listeners and the simplistic, jargon-free language used by the hosts (Collins 2016). The contrast reveals the educational and cultural sea-change that has occurred over the twentieth century, motivated by a popular keen and ever-increasing desire to know oneself—a trend that blossomed in the 1960s and 1970s (Collins 2016; Herman 1995; Pfister and Schnog 1997). Technology has both stimulated and reflected this change in the form as well as the protocol presented in media psychology.

The Demotic/Democratisation Factor

Four decades later, broadcast psychology is carrying on APA president George Miller's democratic call to arms, with a few significant addenda. The demotic turn is evidenced by recognisable verbal styles now heard on much of talk radio. A 2015 *New York Times* article describes the 'NPR Voice,' the casual speaking mannerisms on the airwaves now prevalent which the author attributes to the massive number of people involved in broadcasting and the perception that "amateurs have now taken over the airwaves and Internet"' (Wayne

2015). This simultaneously supports the notion of the reign of experience over expertise and highlights the striking approachability of those voices heard on podcasts. The notion of demotic is not as optimistic as it might sound, however, and Turner is keen on it not being equated with democracy. As he writes, 'It is important to remember that celebrity still remains a systematically hierarchical and exclusive category, no matter how much it proliferates' (Turner 2006: 157). Likewise, an economic digital divide still prevents the availability of even relatively low-cost technology for everyone. The development of the term 'podcasting,' write a group of communications and art history scholars, 'followed the pattern… where new information technologies are uncritically championed as embodying a Jeffersonian democratic ideal' (Sterne et al. 2008). A moral assessment of 'demotic' is therefore subjective—it depends on whether or not the diverse display of people having access to creating or consuming culture is seen as good or bad or somewhere in between.

The increased awareness and openness with which well-known people publicly discuss private tribulations is also a demotic characteristic. In Andrew Solomon's review of writer and cultural critic Daphne Merkin's memoir, *This Close To Happy: A Reckoning with Depression*, he writes, 'Famous people use such disclosures to persuade you that they are just like you, perhaps even more vulnerable; it's a way of compensating for the discomfort attached to their glamour. Indeed, in an increasingly stratified world, people with any modicum of privilege may reveal their depression as an assertion of their common humanity. Clinical misery has taken over from death as the great equalizer. Vanity of vanities, all is depression' (Solomon 2017). For comedians, then, covering such issues is the natural order of things, as their content is almost always focused, albeit with a unique perspective ('point of view' is a key feature of both comedy and psychotherapy [Piper 2015: 43]), on the mundane and the ordinary. To separate themselves from their audiences by exhibiting any privilege would damage their credibility and likeability. Perhaps comedy's current high value provides a new public relations blueprint for other artists to follow.

Similarly, comedy critic Jason Zinoman sums up the climate of a particular moment in the 2010s when the comedy boom seemed at its peak and perhaps not incidentally showcased a number of comedians contending with the darkest of human experiences. As he writes, '[T]he trend toward comedy that confronts personal experiences with death is also a result of a culture that encourages confession and that has cut the distance between artist and audience… We trust stand-up comics in a way that we don't for almost any other artist, and it's part of the reason they have such stature in our culture now. That's why when they joke about death, it can come across like a friend's sharing intimate secrets. And that allows them leeway to express themselves without euphemism' (Zinoman 2016).

The Expertise Factor

The traditional authority hierarchy has flipped or has at least been flattened in the digital age. A surge of political populism in the 2016 US elections may have seemed to be a peak expression of this, but it had shown itself with as much fanfare on daytime television talk shows in the 1980s and 1990s, with programmes such as *Geraldo*, *The Jerry Springer Show* and *The Jenny Jones Show*. The message from each of these sectors was that expertise gained from experience is valued above that which is gained through traditional academic channels. A peer-to-peer model has usurped a top-down model in many sectors of modern life, including psychological information and counselling. Vincent Meserko observes how Paul Gilmartin's *Mental Illness Happy Hour* (and its ilk) exemplifies such a postmodern version of the original radio advice shows, focusing on the host *consubstantiating* (shared experience or identification) with their fans (Meserko 2014: 457). Gilmartin is a comedian, not a professional psychologist, but the show operates in many ways like a therapy session and, according to listeners' testimonies, is effective in providing emotional relief.

Similarly, Pete Holmes regularly dives into topics of sexuality and spirituality with his guests. When asked about the comedy boom and why comedians seemed so fitting for the media landscape, including podcasting, Holmes responded: 'We're looking for insight. We raise some people up and [are] like, "Louis [C.K.], he talks the truth about parenting and divorce." And he's become an authority in an authorityless society. We all have maps and Google, and we all have ways to get to fucking Nevada on a Southwest flight, but the thing that we can't all do for ourselves or get from our phones or get from just reading something on the Internet is perspective and authenticity and a direct, soulful communication with somebody' (Fox 2015). Here again, Foucault is invoked, along with one of the long-held claims by many comedians: the comedian is the confessor who speaks truth to power (Gimbel 2017; Jeffries 2017).

When Gilmartin says to a guest, 'You want my opinion?' it is valued not because he has professional credentials but because he has been through a similar experience. CHIPs hosts have relatability because they are baring their souls and they have credibility because they are somewhere on the continuum of celebrity, which, given a cultural bestowal of imprecise authority, renders them doubly credible and trustworthy. When writers Cheryl Strayed and Steve Almond—who are open about their own struggles—freely give advice on their *Dear Sugar* podcast, likewise they are seen as legitimate help-givers. This reflects both the heightened value of fame as well as that of experience. When Dr. Joyce Brothers began giving advice over the airwaves in the 1950s and 1960s, many APA members roundly criticised her for a lack of ethics in her populist method, despite the fact that she had a doctoral degree in psychology. Such outcries are virtually non-existent in the twenty-first century. Put another way, in her book *The Art of Memoir* Mary Karr writes, '[W]hile formerly sacred sources of truth like history and statistics have lost ground, the subjective tale has garnered new territory' (Karr 2015: 16). This was written even before the 'fake news' fervour took the United States into its clutches in 2016, and now evokes an even stronger intensity.

Converse, or perhaps consequential, to the demotic turn, as sociologist Joshua Gamson who also observes 'the turn toward the ordinary' writes, '[C]elebrity culture is increasingly populated by unexceptional people who have become famous and by stars who have been made ordinary' (Gamson 2011: 1062). It is the stars being made ordinary that garners less attention in a fame-seeking world. The internet, Gamson argues, has had a large hand in pushing 'ordinariness into the cultural forefront' (Gamson 2011: 1062) and this is true for podcasting as an internet product. In the early twentieth century, the advent of visual media technology triggered the cult of celebrity, but paradoxically, in this flourishing subculture of the relatively simple mechanism of podcasting, we have come back around to audio as the technology that allows us the greatest access to the deepest secrets of our celebrities. In the mid-1990s, Gamson cited the 'dissemination of the face' as replacing the 'dissemination of ideas' thanks to visual technology (Gamson 1994: 21).[2] But thirty years earlier sociologist Leo Lowenthal observed that, in the first half of the twentieth century, 'idols of consumption' gradually replaced 'idols of production,' so radio entertainment evidently also played a part. In podcasting, we are seeing not one or the other but an amalgam. The intimacy of audio (versus visual) turns on its head Gamson's and others' theories that it was the advent of visual media that engendered the culture of celebrity. We're finding celebrities' most intimate details not on TV or in magazine articles, but via image-free podcasts.[3]

So while there is an unprecedented groundswell of desire for fame among the general population, celebrities are increasingly choosing to exhibit their quotidian selves. CHIPs are, in expression, a rejection of the pedestal version of stardom. As an example, Chris Gethard says podcasts serve comedy careers by encouraging fans to 'opt into your cult.' Ironically, however, he has discovered that one secret to *Beautiful/ Anonymous* is keeping his comic personality in check. 'For these phone calls to work,' he says, 'I need to be the less interesting person in the conversation' (Jurgensen 2016). Gethard is, according to one description, 'part interlocutor, therapist and comic commentator' (Jurgensen 2016). This continuum or dichotomy is seen in podcasting overall: hundreds of podcasts are created by relative unknowns hoping for massive, life-altering followings, and more and more famous people are hosting and being interviewed on podcasts with a seeming intention to reveal their authentic selves via unscripted conversation. The idolatry and the demotic are both at work. If everyone is meeting in the middle, as this syllogism set up might suggest, it would theoretically result in a level field and celebrity would lose its lustre. But certainly, that is not the case. Just as reality TV has little to do with reality, perhaps we are too easily seduced by the authentic-sounding veneer of interview podcasts. After all, the voices being interviewed are still those of bona fide celebrities, a small percentage of the population who has achieved exceptional status. 'The podcast provides,' writes Meserko, referring to WTF, 'a vehicle through which these comics exercise a *perceived freedom of control* [emphasis added] over their public identities and where contestations of authenticity are foregrounded through revealing conversation' (Meserko 2015: 782). *New Yorker* writer Sarah Larson refers to this genre (CHIPs) as 'the portrait-in-greatness podcast' with its 'dual presentation of culture and character, the insight into both art and its creation' (Larson 2015), where the curtain is pulled back on an artist to reveal their humble beginnings, numerous life challenges, and the like, that preceded their current level of success.

Nevertheless, testimonies from listeners make it difficult to deny the emotional benefit of vicarious relating—even Judd Apatow and a procrastinating graduate student have something in common. As the subjects in Pollak's film emphasise, their comedic craft is about sharing their humanness which is what is being promulgated on these podcasts as well, and one could argue quite convincingly that they are honest and representative of the experiences of people without a voice. Perhaps podcasting is the platonic ideal of the optimistic expression of the demotic turn where a status hierarchy fades into the background. As Meserko writes, 'While it may be impossible to determine authentic selves from unauthentic selves, especially given how 'authentic' performances are themselves performative, authenticity nevertheless exists as an aspirational ideal, and these comics are quick to attribute their perceptions of authentic expression and conversation to the podcast medium' (Meserko 2015: 805).

Conclusion

Beyond the implications for the evolution of celebrity theory and the changing culture of comedy, investigation of this phenomenon has potential value for the psychological professions. How effective is this type of ersatz vicarious therapy, for instance, and how does it differ than other types of more conventional call-in radio or advice programmes? At the very least, the development of this form sheds light on Western attitudes about personal and group identity and about alternative approaches to mental health issues.

While there is a burgeoning scholarship on the topic of podcasting,[4] observing the historical evolution contributes to the larger discussion of the glories and pitfalls of modern technology. By looking at the antecedents to such a popular medium, our recognition of what has remained and what has been discarded illuminates the static and dynamic values in global Western culture as reflected in popular culture. The evolution of our first world attitudes toward the reception and treatment of serious psychological content, especially via non-traditional and often nonprofessional methods, can reveal significant clues about a set of human values at this particular moment in time.

Notes

1. See for instance Hidaka (2012) 'Depression as a disease of modernity: Explanations for increasing prevalence', *Journal of Affective Disorders*, 140(3): 205–221; and Pratt et al. (2011) 'Antidepressant use in persons aged 12 and over: United States, 2005–2008', *NCHS Data Brief*, 76: 1–8.
2. The 'dissemination of the face' in this context perhaps has its origins in Leo Braudy's *The Frenzy of Renown: Fame and its History* (1986). Graeme Turner discusses the evolution of the concept, including Gamson's reinterpretation, in Turner (2010b: 10).
3. For intimacy in radio, see the work of Atkinson and Moores (2003), Chignell (2009), Loviglio (2005), McLuhan (1964), Meyrowitz (2007), and Kirkpatrick (2013); For intimacy in podcasting see Berry (2006, 2016), Florini (2015) and Lindgren (2016).
4. In addition to the authors cited herein, see for instance the work of Andrew Bottomley, Kris Markman and Jeremy Wade Morris. As an illustration of the scholarship accumulation, as of October 2017, the Communications and Mass Media Complete database, which indexes more than 770 journal titles, contains more than 160 articles (as identified by the term 'podcast' included in the abstract or as an author-supplied keyword) with the first appearance in 2005.

Bibliography

Apatow, J. (2016). *Sick in the head: Conversations about life and comedy*. New York: Random House.
Atkinson, K., & Moores, S. (2003). 'We all have bad bad days' attending to face in broadcast troubles-talk. *Radio Journal: International Studies in Broadcast & Audio Media*, 1(2), 129–146.

Berry, R. (2006). Will the iPod kill the radio star? Profiling podcasting as radio. *Convergence: The International Journal of Research into New Media Technologies, 12*(2), 143–162.

Berry, R. (2016). Podcasting: Considering the evolution of the medium and its association with the word 'radio'. *Radio Journal: International Studies in Broadcast & Audio Media, 14*(1), 7–22.

Braudy, L. (1986). *The frenzy of renown: Fame & its history.* New York: Oxford University Press.

Campion, C. (2015). How comedian Marc Maron got legions of fans muttering WTF. www.theguardian.com [Internet]. Accessed 2017.

Chignell, H. (2009). *Key concepts in radio studies.* Los Angeles: SAGE.

Collins, K. (2009). *Watching what we eat: The evolution of television cooking shows.* New York: Continuum.

Collins, K. (2016). *Dr. Joyce Brothers: The founding mother of TV psychology.* Lanham: Rowman & Littlefield.

Cox, A. M. (2016). Bob Odenkirk thinks other comedians are lousy critics. www.nytimes.com [Internet]. Accessed 2017.

Crisell, A. (1986). *Understanding radio.* London: Methuen.

'Dial Dr. Brothers'. (1966, September 4). *The New York Times.*

Douglas, S. J. (2005). *Listening in: Radio and the American imagination.* Minneapolis: University of Minnesota Press.

Dyer, R. (1986). *Heavenly bodies: Film stars and society.* New York: St. Martin's Press.

Edison Research. (2017). *The infinite dial.* www.edisonresearch.com [Internet]. Accessed 2017.

Elwood, G., & Mancini, C. (2016). *Ear Buds: The Podcasting Documentary.* Comedy Film Nerds.

Florini, S. (2015). The podcast chitlin' circuit: Black podcasters, alternative media, and audio enclaves. *Journal of Radio & Audio Media, 22*(2), 209–219.

Foucault, M. (1980). *The history of sexuality, volume I: An introduction.* New York: Vintage Books.

Fox, J. D. (2015). Pete Holmes on how the comedian became the modern-day philosopher. www.vulture.com [Internet]. Accessed 2017.

Gamson, J. (1994). *Claims to fame: Celebrity in contemporary America.* Berkeley: University of California Press.

Gamson, J. (2011). The unwatched life is not worth living: The elevation of the ordinary in celebrity culture. *PMLA, 126*(4), 1061–1069.

Gilmartin, P. (2012). Episode #43: Meghan P, *Mental Illness Happy Hour.* www.mentalpod.com [Podcast]. Accessed 2017.

Gimbel, S. (2017). *Isn't that clever: A philosophical account of humor and comedy.* New York: Routledge.

Goodman, D. (2012). Making early American broadcasting's public sphere: Radio fortune telling and the demarcation of private and public speech. *Historical Journal of Film Radio and Television, 32*(2), 187–205.

Gross, T. (2015). Terry gross to Marc Maron: 'Life is harder than radio'. '20 May. Recorded at Brooklyn academy of music, www.npr.org [Internet]. Accessed 2017.

Harmon, D. (2014). *Harmontown*, dir./prod. Neil Berkeley, Future You Pictures.

Herman, E. (1995). *The romance of American psychology: Political culture in the age of experts, 1940–1970*. Berkeley: University of California Press.

Hilmes, M. (1999). *Radio voices: American broadcasting, 1922–1952*. Minneapolis: University of Minnesota Press.

Horton, D., & Wohl, R. R. (1956). Mass communication and para-social interaction. *Psychiatry, 19*, 215–229.

Jeffries, M. P. (2017). *Behind the laughs: Community and inequality in comedy*. Stanford: Stanford University Press.

Jurgensen, J. (2016). Chris Gethard finds a new form for the comedy podcast. *Wall Street Journal*. www.blogs.wsj.com [Internet]. Accessed 2017.

Karr, M. (2015). *The art of memoir*. New York: HarperCollins.

Kirkpatrick, B. (2013). Voices made for print. In J. Loviglio and M. Hilmes (Eds.), Radio's new wave: Global sound in the digital era. (pp. 106–25). New York: Routledge.

Kurtz, H. (1997). *Hot air: All talk, all the time*. New York: Basic Books.

Langer, J. (1981). Television's 'personality' system. *Media, Culture & Society, 3*(4), 351–365.

Larson, S. (2015). Better living through podcasts. www.newyorker.com [Internet]. Accessed 2017.

Leadbeater, C., & Miller, P. (2004). *The pro-am revolution: How enthusiasts are changing our society and economy*. London: Demos.

Lindgren, M. (2016). Personal narrative journalism and podcasting. *Radio Journal: International Studies in Broadcast & Audio Media, 14*(1), 23–41.

Longform. (2015). Episode #144: Cheryl Strayed. www.Longform.org [Podcast]. Accessed 2017.

Loviglio, J. (2005). *Radio's intimate public: Networking broadcasting and mass-mediated democracy*. Minneapolis: University of Minnesota Press..

Maron, M. (2016). WTF. www.wtfpod.com [Podcast], Episode #689: Michael Rapaport (2016) Accessed 2017, Episode #759: Lin-Manuel Miranda (2016) Accessed 2017, Episode #765: Dana Carvey (2016). Accessed 2017.

McLuhan, M. (1964). *Understanding media: The extensions of man*. New York: McGraw-Hill.

Merkin, D. (2017). *This close to happy: A reckoning with depression*. New York: Farrar, Straus and Giroux.

Meserko, V. (2014). Going mental: Podcasting, authenticity, and artist–fan identification on Paul Gilmartin's *Mental Illness Happy Hour*. *Journal of Broadcasting & Electronic Media, 58*(3), 456–469.

Meserko, V. (2015). The pursuit of authenticity on Marc Maron's WTF podcast. *Continuum: Journal of Media & Cultural Studies, 29*(6), 769–810.

Meyrowitz, J. (2007). From distant heroes to intimate friends: Media and the metamorphosis of affection for public figures. In S. J. Drucker (Ed.), *Heroes in a global world* (pp. 100–128). Cresskill: Hampton Press.

Miller, G. A. (1969). Psychology as a means of promoting human welfare. *American Psychologist, 24*(12), 1063–1075.

Miller, J. G. (1980). Margaret Mead. *Behavioral Science, 25*(1), 1–8.

Ouellette, L. (2009). Take responsibility for yourself: Judge Judy and the neoliberal citizen. In S. Murray & L. Ouellette (Eds.), *Reality TV: Remaking television culture* (pp. 223–242). New York: NYU Press.

Pfister, J., & Schnog, N. (1997). *Inventing the psychological: Toward a cultural history of emotional life in America*. New Haven: Yale University Press.

Piper, M. (2015). Little big dog pill explanations: Humour, honesty, and the comedian podcast. *Philament, 20*, 41–60.

Pollak, K., dir. (2015). *Misery Loves Comedy*, prod. Barry Katz Entertainment.

Rabin, N. (2016). How comedy podcasts can help you get through these nightmarish times. www.splitsider.com [Internet]. Accessed 2017.

Sampler. (2016). Episode #25: P.F. Tompkins. www.gimletmedia.com [Podcast]. Accessed 2017.

Schaefer, R. J., & Avery, R. K. (1993). Audience conceptualizations of late night with David Letterman. *Journal of Broadcasting & Electronic Media, 37*(3), 253.

Siegel, L. (2015). Welcome to the age of the unfunny joke. www.nytimes.com [Internet]. Accessed 25 Apr 2018.

Solomon, A. (2017). Diving into hell: A powerful memoir of depression. www.nytimes.com [Internet]. Accessed 25 Apr 2018.

Steiner, L. R. (1954). The use of radio as a medium for mental health education. *International Journal of Group Psychotherapy, 4*(2), 204–209.

Sterne, J., Morris, J., Baker, M. B., & Freire, A. M. (2008). The politics of podcasting. *The Fibreculture Journal, 13*(87). www.thirteen.fibreculturejournal.org [Internet]. Accessed 2017.

Strayed, C. (2015). Longform, episode #144, 3 June, longform.org.

Thompson, E. (2011). *Parody and taste in postwar American television culture*. New York: Routledge.

Tolson, A. (2006). *Media talk: Spoken discourse on TV and radio*. Edinburgh: Edinburgh University Press.

Tompkins, P. F. (2016). Sampler, episode #25. 22 August, gimletmedia.com.

Turner, G. (2006). The mass production of celebrity: 'Celetoids', reality TV and the 'demotic turn'. *International Journal of Cultural Studies, 9*(2), 153–165.

Turner, G. (2010a). *Ordinary people and the media: The demotic turn*. Los Angeles: Sage.

Turner, G. (2010b). *Understanding celebrity*. London: Sage.

Tyler, A. (2015). Episode #209: Omar Benson Millar. www.girlonguy.net [Podcast]. Accessed 2017.

Vered, K. O., & McConchie, J. (2011). The politics of third way TV: *Supernanny* and the commercialization of public service TV. *Camera Obscura, 26*(77), 65–90.

Wayne, T. (2015). 'NPR voice' has taken over the airwaves. www.nttimes.com [Internet]. Accessed 2017.

Wolcott, J. (2016). So, like, why are we so obsessed with podcasts right now? www.vanityfair.com [Internet]. Accessed 2017.

Zall, P. M. (1985). *Mark Twain laughing: Humorous anecdotes by and about Samuel L. Clemens*. Knoxville: University of Tennessee Press..

Zinoman, J. (2016). A year when death loomed in laughter. www.nytimes.com [Internet]. Accessed 2017.

13

Using a Humour Podcast to Break Down Stigma Around Illness

Pille Pruulmann-Vengerfeldt
and Johanna Willstedt Buchholtz

Introduction

This chapter concerns how the *Sickboy* podcast series uses comedy to present discussions around illness. To introduce the topic and focus of the chapter, we present a short transcript from the podcast:

- *The podcast you're about to listen to deals with some pretty intense subject matters, and we sometimes have a potty mouth, so listeners' discretion is advised.*
- *Welcome to* Sickboy, *a podcast where we talk about what it's like to be sick. My name is Jeremie Saunders, and I live with cystic fibrosis. So let's talk about it.* [Coughing]
- *Should I be coughing directly into the mic?*
- *Yeah, every time.*
- *Every time…* [More coughing]
- *Whoa, dude! That sounded exactly like the intro!* [Laughing]
- *Why the fuck do we even have that cough on the intro when we have a professional in our midst?*
- *Yeah, Jeremie, what is CF?*
- *Nice transition!*
- *Flawless*
- *Yeah, alright. Hi everyone! You are listening to* Sickboy, *and I'm your host, Jeremie Saunders. First off, let me just thank all of you for tuning in and thank you guys for sitting in. I'm pointing at you and no one can see that! Yeah, so, this*

P. Pruulmann-Vengerfeldt (✉) • J. Willstedt Buchholtz
Malmo University, Malmö, Sweden
e-mail: pille.pruulmann.vengerfeldt@mau.se

© The Author(s) 2018
D. Llinares et al. (eds.), *Podcasting*, https://doi.org/10.1007/978-3-319-90056-8_13

is a podcast where in each episode, we cover a different disease. (*Sickboy*, 'Cystic Fibrosis'. 2015)

What Is *Sickboy*?

This excerpt from the first episode of *Sickboy* was initially shared via a Kickstarter page in August 2015, and it immediately attracted media attention for doing something extraordinary. *Sickboy* can be seen as a cross-media production with a podcast series at its centre, which is complemented by a website and social media elements, like a blog, Patreon page and Facebook, Twitter and Instagram accounts. *Sickboy* is a collaboration between Canadian-based friends Brian Stever, Jeremie Saunders and Taylor Macgillivary. The three men, all of whom are in their late twenties, record funny and inspiring conversations about living with sickness, with the aim of showing illness as something that can affect people in their youth. They relate their stories to the personal experiences of being young North Americans, and while Brian and Taylor are healthy, Jeremy lives with cystic fibrosis (CF). The weekly podcast was born after 153 people contributed more than 12,000 Canadian dollars on Kickstarter. *Sickboy* airs every Monday on Libsyn, iTunes, Soundcloud and Google Play. At the time of writing this text, there were 111 tracks in total. The podcast has 151 donors, who contribute over a 1000 Canadian dollars per month on the collaborative funding site Patreon. Further, they have more than 2000 followers on Twitter, over 6500 followers on Facebook and just under 6000 followers on Instagram.

The aim of this chapter is to discuss the *Sickboy* podcast series and the accompanying cross-media production from the perspective of cultural studies, using Richard Johnson's (1986) 'circuit of culture' concept. Johnson (1986) proposes a heuristic model to unite the different branches of cultural studies and show how they fit together while seemingly examining very different aspects of cultural products. His model offers an approach for systematising the different angles of podcast production, to evaluate the impact that a show like *Sickboy* can have on cultural change. According to Johnson (1986: 46), the circuit of culture consists of the moment of production and the circulation and consumption of cultural product; each element is dependent upon others and indispensable to the whole. Johnson (1986: 46) stresses that each moment is distinct and involves characteristic changes of form, and such changes of form have crucial implications when we discuss the ideas of podcasting. In this chapter, we utilise the circuit of culture model to discuss the production, text and readings of the *Sickboy* podcast, as an avenue to understanding the potential cultural effects of podcasting more generally. After discussing the theoretical concepts related to podcasting as social media and why we think that investigating podcasting from the perspective of civic agency is important, we will tackle each circuit of culture element one by one, discussing the peculiarities of podcasting production from the perspective of collaborative media. Then we will continue by looking at the podcast as a text, and discuss how the podcast utilises social media affordances to support people living with illness. After that, we will look at audience reactions and feedback to the podcast, and finally consider the podcast as part of larger cultural change, drawing together the circuit of the culture. Thus Johnson's model will help us to both frame the case study and to take a holistic view of podcasts more generally as cultural productions with the potential to bring about societal change.

Podcasts as Social Media

Berry (2006) clarifies some of the changes in form that the emergence of the podcast has effected by looking at how podcasts challenge the tradition and format of radio. However, to understand the podcast phenomenon, we argue that it must be considered from a cross-media perspective, where various social media technologies are integrated and, through that convergence, the affordances of the podcast and audio broadcasting more generally are expanded. Thus, regarding the podcast merely as a new form of radio would be severely limiting; instead, we investigate it from the perspective of social and collaborative media. The concept of affordances comes from psychologist James J. Gibson (1979) and refers to the potential for taking action with material objects or technologies. Norman (2013: 145) adds that 'affordances refer to the potential actions that are possible, but these are easily discoverable only if they are perceivable: perceived affordances'. In their review of social media affordances relating to chronic disease management, Merolli, Gray and Martin-Sanchez (2013: 961, 965–966) identify five types of affordances: identity, flexibility, structure, narration and adaptation. These affordances are specific to social media and chronic illness management, but as *Sickboy* focuses on illness, the applicability of these affordances is considered later in the chapter. Focusing on affordances allows us to consider the role that podcast-focused cross-media production can play in effecting cultural change.

Podcasting at the Intersections of Public and Private Sphere

We investigate *Sickboy* as an example of the 'microdynamics of democracy' (Dahlgren 2006: 282). According to Dahlgren (2006: 272), 'there is no gap between civic agency as a traditionally-conceived political activity in the public sphere, and the culture of the everyday: people in daily life may self-create themselves into citizens'. This means that while the *Sickboy* podcast is not part of any political movement, the presenters' passionate and engaged speech about their own and their guests' daily lives allows certain aspects of their experiences to become political.

We seek to locate the *Sickboy* podcast project at the intersection of the private experience of health/illness and public advocacy around issues of empowerment and inclusion. We are interested in the potential of *Sickboy* and similar podcasts to democratise the understanding of being ill, an outcome which we see as a non-political act of citizenship. We investigate *Sickboy* as a way to discuss mundane and everyday practices through the prism of humour, to activate and engage the audience by raising awareness and changing normative attitudes towards people facing health-related challenges. In the podcast series, humour is used to join together mundane and often silly talk with activism and awareness-raising. Dahlgren (2006: 275) discusses the challenge of understanding how actions in private space can be seen as migrating to public space, as the private and public spheres have been characterised traditionally in very different terms. According to Dahlgren (2006: 275),

> the idea of 'public' is associated implacably with reason, rationality, objectivity, argument, work, text, information and knowledge (and, de facto, one might add, discursively dominant, masculine and Caucasian). 'Private' resonates with the personal, emotion, intimacy, subjectivity, identity, consumption, aesthetics, style, entertainment, popular culture and pleasure.

Therefore, the content and style of the *Sickboy* podcast are inherently private, but the public medium of the podcast and the activist intentions of the hosts take the discussions to the public sphere and become part of 'doing' citizenship.

In discussing the emergence of the podcast as a new medium, Berry (2006: 144) identifies it as a converged medium of audio, the Web and portable media devices, as well as a disruptive technology that is forcing traditional radio to reconsider its position. Over a decade after this analysis, the convergence of the podcast medium can be understood as having intensified. In light of Kaplan and Haenlein's (2010) classic definition, podcasting, as part of social media, can be seen as an internet-based application that adopts the collaborative and participatory platform of Web 2.0 and supports user-generated content. From this perspective, discussions about social media affordances are applicable to podcasts as well. While Kaplan and Haenlein (2010) do not explicitly mention podcasts, the properties of the podcast format closely resemble the properties of blogging, which they proffer as a general example of social media. Furthermore, Berry (2006) claims that the technologies for creating podcasts are easily available to interested parties. Similar to blogging, entering the world of podcast production does not necessarily require advanced skills or expensive equipment. Since the technological barriers are low, the product can be made accessible to an array of listeners through readily available Web channels.

In the case of *Sickboy*, the medium—the podcast—is central, but it would be limiting to discuss it only from that perspective. To understand it as a cultural product through Johnson's (1986) ideas of production, text, audience and lived cultures, we must treat *Sickboy* as a cross-media production, where different media platforms produce a variety of entry points to the central medium of the podcast. According to Ibrus and Scolari (2012), cross-media can include intellectual property, a service, a story or an experience that is distributed across multiple media platforms. Thus, contrary to Jenkins (2003) or Scolari and Ibrus (2014), who emphasise the intertextual and intersemiotic idea of transmedia storytelling, where one narrative spread across various media holds the experience together, cross-media can employ different platforms to support a central platform (e.g. the podcast) to share a story. The podcast is the central empowering medium for the *Sickboy* team, but they use a plethora of other media to compensate or enhance the affordances of the podcast. In this chapter, we also analyse the use of elements of other media to complement our understanding of the podcast.

In the analysis below, *Sickboy* is discussed in relation to the elements of the circuit of culture—namely, production, text, readings and lived cultures (Johnson 1986)—to shed light on the phenomenon of humour podcasts about illness and how they might contribute to changing norms and how people do citizenship (Dahlgren 2006). Our reading of *Sickboy* is partially inspired by a fascination with the hosts' unconventional approach and an attempt to question whether their way of discussing mundane and everyday topics relating to illness can indeed make a difference. To discuss the different elements of the podcast, we use media interviews with the podcast producers; transcripts of five episodes; listening experiences of the podcast as a whole; blog posts, to understand the views of guests; and comments from *Sickboy's* Facebook, iTunes and Instagram pages to reflect on the views of the audience. The aim is to give a broad view of the issues discussed from diverse perspectives, rather than to dive deeply into any single dimension of cultural production.

Production of the *Sickboy* Podcast

Jeremie Saunders, the host with CF, explains his motivations for producing this podcast as a co-occurrence of interesting conversations with his friends as well as accepting the realities of his own illness:

> People don't want their illness to define them. But I have now let it define me, but on my own terms. CF has become [a] powerful source of inspiration, it drives me. I only have a short time left, I want to use it to my advantage. I was using this 'fault' to my advantage. What is the reaction of others? Overwhelmingly positive. We did not... Let's sit down and record this goofy conversation. We had stumbled on this profound thing. The conversation we were having, we realized other people had not had them. It was refreshing, finding humour in an otherwise dark situation. Lots of people will be inspired about the way you approach things. That's my goal—to inspire people, to stop taking life and breath for granted. I want to make people laugh, to share inspiration. (CBC News Toronto 2016)

The affordances of the conversations on the podcast reflect Piper's (2015: 42) explanation of comedy podcasts, where she sees the rise of an increasingly successful form of introspective comedy that 'cut[s] the jokes'. Piper (2015) analyses an episode of *Walking the Room*, hosted by two stand-up comedians, where they discuss the drug addiction of one of the hosts. Piper (2015: 43) deploys ideas from Freud: '[H]umour is the triumph of ego and the pleasure principle: in joking about adversity, humour creates distance from it and allows one to minimise the adversity's power.' Similarly, Jeremie uses *Sickboy* to overcome his own adversary, CF, and turn it into a tool of empowerment.

The first five episodes were produced in the city library of Halifax, Nova Scotia, Canada, using publicly available podcast equipment. However, after a successful Kickstarter campaign, the technical production and recording equipment were financed by donations. In her analysis of a Kickstarter-funded Web series, Ellcessor (2017: 32) stresses that these new funding models allow 'new forms of access and participation blurring distinctions between media production and reception'. This initially collaborative start to the podcast inspires us to look at the podcast through the notion of collaborative media (Löwgren and Reimer 2013a, b), referring to an emerging cultural form of digital media that is characterised by several different traits. These traits offer perspective on the format and affordances of podcasts as collaborative media. Löwgren and Reimer (2013a) argue that collaborative media are *forms for practice*, oriented towards action and open for interaction. For *Sickboy*, this means that the key aim of this comedy podcast is social change and action for better recognition and understanding of the sick. As Saunders explains, 'We want to eliminate the awkwardness and discomfort that sometimes comes with speaking about illness. It just adds to stigma and shame and embarrassment' (quoted in Clarke 2015). Löwgren and Reimer (2013a: 88) continue, 'Collaborative media offer a framework with components to combine and appropriate in different ways [...] Collaborative media are cross-medial and increasingly material, catalyzing convergence between traditional media channels and extending into the physical world beyond screens and loudspeakers'. In the case of *Sickboy*, the podcast gained recognition in traditional media, and Saunders became a local celebrity. The framework of the podcast allows for live shows, public speeches and merchandise supporting the hosts' message. The properties of collaborative media 'entail close links between media infrastructures and media texts, essentially blurring the traditional media distinction between means of production and distribution on one hand and content on the other' (Löwgren and Reimer 2013a: 88). Piper (2015: 45) refers to Meserko (2010) and highlights that, 'The comedian podcast gives comedians, as both podcast hosts and interview subjects, a forum that allows direct and intimate communication with audiences in ways unmediated by content regulations, advertiser requirements, or the politics of the comedy club bookings'. This refers to the affordances of the podcast, which enable direct and intimate conversations. In the case analysed by Piper (2015) and with *Sickboy*, this intimacy is used to discuss difficult topics and bring them closer to the audience. Co-hosts Brian and Taylor stress the authenticity and down-to-earth nature of the podcast and the need to create a light-hearted and safe space for their guests.

Löwgren and Reimer (2013a) stress that collaborative media prioritise *collaboration*, and thus actively promote the engagement of the people traditionally known as the audience in not only consumption, but also in production and design. In the case of *Sickboy*, there are two important ways in which the collaborative ideal is realised. First, *Sickboy* follows what Ibrus and Scolari (2012) discuss as 'open collaborative innovation', which, at the micro level, has a feasible business model, as it was initially funded through a Kickstarter campaign and is currently sustained through continuous support via Patreon. While in the early stages, the *Sickboy* hosts expressed a desire for possibly obtaining funding from a larger sponsor, they later decided against this and pursued funding that would allow them to remain independent producers. Sarasohn-Kahn (2008) discusses different business models for online social media and warns that, for instance, health bloggers writing about their own conditions walk a fine line between accepting advertising and appearing as though they are 'selling out' to corporate interests. There is also a perceived threat to the privacy of data when using corporate funding. Therefore, it is easier to maintain independence by using crowdfunding initiatives.

Second, the collaboration with guests is central to *Sickboy*. The hosts realise their activism and spread awareness through various guests sharing their stories. While the hosts clearly dominate the production and organisation of the podcast, the success or failure of their platform is clearly dependent on the guests, as this mix of humour and illness is uncommon in public discourse and it can be difficult to find people who are willing to share the story of their sickness in this particularly challenging format. In the Kickstarter campaign, the (un)availability of guests was illustrated as the greatest risk: 'One of our challenges is securing sick people that are willing to sit down and have a chat. So far we've been really lucky in that we know a few sickos in our own lives. We also had a number of people reach out to us after an article about Sickboy Podcast was featured in Metro' (Kickstarter 2015). As the website was developed, the *Sickboy* team added a registration form to manage people seeking to tell their stories. The form asks, among other things, 'What cool disease/illness/infection/virus/physical disability do you have?!' and 'Tell us why you should be on the show? Example: How does your illness affect your life? Any cool stories to share? Etc.' (*Sickboy* 2017). These questions stress the importance of humour and the perceived 'cool factor' of the illness. A guest named Andrew Henderson (quoted in Clarke 2015) reflects as follows:

> You rarely hear this young voice… talking about illness in a fun, positive way [...] I just want a pamphlet that says, 'Live your f****** life. Go to the club, party.' [...] We don't have the same comfort level with illness as we do with other social topics. 'People panic', Henderson says, thinking of the times he shared his diagnosis with friends. 'What I got a lot of the time was pity, which is really isolating'.

This highlights a valuable dimension of the podcast series—namely, the ability to share stories in a frank, open manner, without pity or disgust. The collaborative dimension means that guests have a significant amount of control over how their stories are told and what aspects they will discuss.

The variety and diversity of guests is also used to balance the gender representation in the podcast. With three male hosts, the style, jokes and topics address issues that can be seen as heteronormatively masculine by nature. Yet, by the end of 2016, there had been 78 episodes with a guest discussing their illnesses. Of those guests, 40 were female (including a transgender woman) and 38 were male. As the format has developed, a pattern of alternating between guests of different genders has become increasingly clear. While one could argue that the podcast is still male-dominated in voice and has a distinctly laddish style, it is also evident that the hosts make a clear attempt to be conscious and aware of gender representation.

In numerous episodes, the hosts stress that the stories are produced and told from the perspective of the individual, rather than that of a patient. This sets them apart from what Sarasohn-Kahn (2008), Moorhead et al. (2013) and Merolli et al. (2013) review as the use of social media by patients, where the focus is on diagnosis, medication and treatment. In *Sickboy*, there is little to no focus on clinical details; the emphasis is on the issues and ideas relating to lived experiences ('Brian and Taylor: Live from Studio 5'). This is similar to internet forums or blogs where patients use therapeutic affordance through narrative (Merolli et al. 2015) to share their experiences and learn from others, as the guests are given an opportunity to discuss their experiences openly. While Merolli et al. (2015) offer another affordance related to structure, where the physician's guidance can be seen as part of the affordance, *Sickboy* uses structure only in the moderation of the narratives, setting it apart from a radio phone-in show, where the medical authority or the host's authority provides the structure. Since the show is mainly led by the guests, its approach to illness is not necessarily always medically accurate. The podcast gives its guests a voice and allows them to discuss their experiences and, in some cases, the hosts return to the topic in a subsequent intermediary episode to update some of the medical information. But as they allow the quest voice to lead the story, they also take a clear stance in discussing the illness from the perspective of the person experiencing it. To balance the discussions with guests, there are occasionally episodes with no guests, labelled 'Just a Routine Check Up' (Sickboy Libsyn 2017a) making a reference to the medical discourse and using it against itself in a humorous turn. Usually, these are short intermediary episodes where, without claiming authority, the hosts dive deeper into the subjects discussed by their guests, adding their own voices in a more opinionated manner. In these episodes, the collaborative element comes in the form of addressing people's questions, comments, feedback and e-mails, as feedback from listeners often contradicts the lived experiences of guests aired in previous episodes. In such episodes, the ethos of *Sickboy* becomes more visible, as they discuss the makings of the podcast and tackle the challenge of discussing trickier topics with as much neutrality and respect for their guests and listeners as possible.

The production of the podcast has been fraught with challenges. Using collaborative media as an analytical framework has allowed us to demonstrate the importance and challenges of collaborative funding and guest-led storytelling. As an all-male team, the hosts have demonstrated awareness of the need to pay attention to gender issues by inviting a range of guests. They have also largely succeeded in balancing the often overly-medicalised discourse around health and illness by focusing on personal and humorous stories to empower both guests and listeners. The format of the podcast and the structure of the content affords control over the content by the guests. We will discuss the elements of this content in the next section.

Content of the *Sickboy* Podcast

Seriality

Sickboy differs from the podcasts mapped by Sarasohn-Kahn (2008) by being patient-led, but not necessarily focused on illness or medical issues. However, the podcast shares numerous similarities with health blogging, which can be seen as a popular health-related social media platform (McCosker 2008; Sarasohn-Kahn 2008; Moorhead et al. 2013). Borrowing the concept of technology of the self from Lovink (2008), McCosker (2008) points out that blogs written about, and in the context of, personal illness are examples of an inclination to speak one's truth in the confessional mode of modern culture borne of the Church, science and talk show television. While the confessional mode of blogs is individual, serial and develops over time, as in Piper's (2015) comedy podcasts, in the case of *Sickboy*, there is little or no attempt at seriality. When paying tribute to the passing away of an earlier guest, the episode is, like in many other podcast formats, reposted with an extra introduction rather than just referencing or linking to it (Sickboy Libsyn 2017b). Thus, while there are recurring themes and back-and-forth referencing different episodes, each story can be listened to as a one-off; the listener need not have followed the whole series to feel sympathy, be energised or understand the jokes.

Elements of seriality are added through the aforementioned episodes involving the hosts alone. At the same time, this allows for establishing links between and across themes. The episodes without guests provide space for meta-level reflection on the role of the podcast in the hosts' lives and the links between the different podcasts. These intermediary episodes are not regular reflections but are sporadically spread across the hundred episodes. *Sickboy* also has non-medical guests, who themselves may not have a condition, but are sharing their lives with people with medical conditions (e.g. Jeremie's wife and parents, as well as some doctors and activists). However, overall, such guests are infrequent. In discussing the affordances of the show, we focus on the 'regular podcasts', where hosts Jeremie, Brian and Taylor speak with guests with medical conditions.

Structure

The initial episodes of *Sickboy* are fumbling and explorative, as the hosts are searching for a functional structure to talk to each other as well as the guests. The very first episode features Jeremie as the guest, due to his CF. The podcast was Jeremie's idea and, originally, he was going to be the only host. Thus, his two good friends were supposed to be temporary hosts interviewing him; however, the three-host format took off. In examining subsequent episodes, regular patterns of conversation between the hosts and their guests emerge. Their focus on specific topics and exclusion of others lead up to what we consider 'constructions of normality.' The *Sickboy* team also establishes a reoccurring mechanics of humour, which they use to support the same construction of normal. We explain this in greater detail in the next paragraphs and draw parallels to the five types of social media affordances outlined by Merolli, Gray and Martin-Sanchez (2013: 961, 965–66).

Typical episodes include an introduction, where the illness and its implications are presented by the guest from a personal and lived perspective. This is followed by what can be labelled as 'care talk'—elaboration on a diagnosis and how it emerged, including struggles and turns towards better medical knowledge, and the goal of receiving suitable healthcare.

The timing of the diagnosis and the emergence of problems, for example, might steer the conversation towards childhood, and the hosts might enquire how the guest's illness and condition influenced life at home and at school. Merolli et al. (2013: 965) distinguish the affordance of identity showing that social media users feel more in control of how they present themselves and how much they want to discuss their condition. The hosts allow their guests to choose the level of detail, and terms they want to use, to discuss their situations.

If the guest's diagnosis is more recent, the conversation will move away from care talk and focus on the practical implications of sickness, typically surrounding how one copes with everyday productivity issues, like university studies or work life. Discussions about the emotional and private consequences of sickness, like managing friends or romantic relationships, also play a major role on the *Sickboy* podcast. In general the different ways in which *Sickboy* allows people to share their stories fits well with the social media affordance of narration (Merolli et al. 2013: 966) as guests have control over their own stories and use storytelling for the emotional management of their illnesses. The ways in which sharing information on social media brings the private domain to the public, and allows users to build an identity around taboo topics, inevitably brings the discussions to the notion of activism, being a role model and showing others that the guests are more than their diagnoses. This section of the podcast connects *Sickboy* to 'citizenship making' through everyday talk (Dahlgren 2006) and combatting the stigma around illness. *Sickboy* hosts and guests talk about illness as an inevitable part of everyday life and how it would help them if the general public could simply acknowledge that people with diverse abilities should all feel themselves to be valued members of society. While there are elements in the discussion that celebrate the extraordinary ways in which people cope with living with illness, most of the podcast focuses on the mundane elements of living with challenges the best one can. The activism or citizenship making is not made explicit, but rather becomes an implied part of sharing the stories. When wrapping up the show, every guest is offered the opportunity to add further thoughts or observations. In other words, guests have the final say and can dictate the conclusion, thus reaffirming their control over the story that is told.

The Mechanics of Comedy in Relation to Severe Illness

The balance between different forms of humour and more serious and emotional content has some patterns that link to the above-described topical structure. Humorous situations generally appear when discussing the experience of everyday sickness in relation to personal or romantic relationships or coping with work life. This is less common in the care talk or diagnosis segments, although they contain their fair share of humour and embarrassing stories. This allows for what Berger (2014) calls redeeming laughter, where the jokes do not diminish the gravity of the situation but suspend the weight of it temporarily. What is considered funny is generally picked up and commented on by Jeremie, as he connects a guest's event to his own lived experience, ridiculing himself and thereby inviting further laughter in the studio. This technique is used for comic relief, when permitted, regarding heavy or serious subject matter, or when the situation is already light. The comedy appears in two ways. It is physical and related to bodily functions' misbehaving outside of accepted contexts, leading to social embarrassment in various situations both within healthcare institutions and in daily life. In parallel, it appears in and through the jargon of provocative and teasing interplay among the three hosts, who are clearly comfortable enough with each other to push themselves towards complete humiliation before returning to the conversation's original track. What is noticeable is that the jokes consistently start with the hosts, who carefully invite the guests to choose whether or not they want to take part. Hence, in the end, the joke is never on the guest unless they explicitly invite laughter; to maintain a light-hearted and humorous tone, the joke is largely on the hosts. This technique also allows for bringing light-heartedness to situations where the guests have difficulty expressing themselves lightly, thus providing what can be perceived as an emotional catharsis for everyone.

To elicit personal views from guests, beyond symptom descriptions, a short life story and some embarrassing episodes, the hosts get into conversations around rough topics by addressing those topics directly. In many episodes, 'What is the worst thing that has happened?' is a recurring question that leads the story away from a more superficial or sometimes technical narrative. Once they have ventured into those deep waters, the hosts often lay out their own preconceptions and ignorance around the specific illness or try to relate some symptoms to their own experiences before letting guests elaborate on their emotions and experiences. This makes the relationship more equal than in the case of a professional and a patient, as the hosts and the guests share their experiences and thoughts in a reciprocal way. On occasion, Jeremie uses his CF and the fact that he himself is living with chronic illness as a gesture to put things in perspective and to clarify that the guest is safe and not alone. Thus, personal connection is used as a specific narrative affordance (Merolli et al. 2013: 2015) to allow people to elaborate on their personal experiences and, at the same time, to experience emotional catharsis.

Clearly stating that the guest can terminate a topic is another a tool for establishing comfort if a line is crossed, letting guests know that nothing will be aired if they are not entirely comfortable with the result. This creates a safe space, which might otherwise be difficult to find in normative mainstream culture (Tiidenberg 2014). At other times, Brian and Taylor, pursue sensitive topics by simply and curiously asking guests to tell them more, instead of leaving it to the guests to let details slip into the conversation. Asking questions one normally would not ask due to stigma or fear is an express purpose of the whole podcast's concept, and it inevitably leads to the audience learning about more aspects of living with illness. This coincides with the idea that social media, collectively written by a large mix of patients and authorities, are becoming health information sources (Moorhead et al. 2013).

Through using humour, stressing that the guests are in control of their own stories and drawing on their own experiences and examples, the hosts of *Sickboy* create safe spaces where laughter becomes a coping mechanism. Humorous interludes help the guests and the listeners to overcome some of the more grave and emotional moments. Sharing stories of everyday life allows the humour in different coping techniques to show through, and adds a level of normalcy to the stories of people whose health situations are not usually discussed.

Constructing Normalcy

As the podcast is intended to overcome stigma and normalise the experiences of young people living with illness, a contextual definition of what is considered *normal* is needed. As we use secondary sources, and participants never really express what they consider to be normal, we listened closely to the episodes to understand some constructions of normalcy underpinning *Sickboy*'s discussions. After listening to five episodes, it appears that normality must be defined by the given context—in this case, the backdrop of Canada, the codified cultural values and the preconception of what might constitute a 'regular life' for a young person in that time and space.

The feeling of deviating from that 'regular life'—that is, what is 'normal'— shows in how *Sickboy*'s guests of all genders, who are mostly in their twenties, describe their lives and, primarily, their experiences of school and early romantic relationships, which clearly stand out as areas where conforming is difficult when dealing with physical and sometimes mental challenges. Growing up immersed in particular cultural understandings of relationships and social behaviours, guests, due to their illnesses, could not always take part in these areas of life. Situations vary from missing social events due to stomach problems, to becoming overweight due to medication, to being excessively tired and sleeping throughout a whole year of university studies.

From the texts of the podcasts, in which guests discuss growing up and their experiences of adolescence, it is clear that they have experienced being different and consider their experiences to be deviations from the norm. In discussions about how they cope with feelings, relations and physical restrictions, they also reveal their relationship to 'normalcy'. Two opposite approaches can be distinguished here. The first is the self's disassociation with the illness and the second can be called 'owning the illness'. Both allow for the different types of identity work afforded by social media (Merolli et al. 2013).

'Fighting and conquering and surviving the disease' and 'refusing to let it define you' are statements typical of *Sickboy*, which hint at a disassociation with the part of the self that does not conform to what is accepted socially or culturally. From this perspective, it is more socially acceptable to disown one's disease than to embrace it. Some episodes reflect striving for normality by fighting the illness, living life to the fullest and (for those with physical ability), for example, exercising or looking better than a healthy person. The advantages of being sick that are discussed in some instances concern appearance. It is apparent that there is a normal baseline constituting social acceptance, according to popular Western notions of physical beauty, where illness is linked inherently to unattractiveness and physical weakness. Hence, there are linkages to body normative mainstream culture (Tiidenberg 2014) and the guests or hosts endeavouring to fit in. In this approach, participants fight stigma by focusing on the individual's efforts to work around the challenges of their particular illness.

The second approach is embracing the illness, owning it fully, taking it along and forcing it to be a part of life, whether this is socially acceptable or not. Proponents of this approach make deviations seem natural and advocate that they be incorporated into everyday life through accessibility and acceptance, thus pressing for a collective de-stigmatising of illness, regardless of its form. We can locate many guests on a sliding scale between the two approaches depending on the situation, and ultimately, it is the fact that they deviate and feel the need to cope with that deviation that constitutes the construction of normality in the discussions.

At all times, there is a cultural norm baseline that is negotiated in a constant relation to the guests' experiences of their illnesses, rather than medical facts or diagnoses, which are frequently at the centre of other health-related social and traditional media or mainstream depictions of disability. Ellcessor summarises the challenge of accessing traditional media despite its barriers, and sees online media as a way to overcome historical barriers and institutionalised voices:

> For people with disability, this [loss of institutional barriers] has meant increased access to the range of media texts, tools and communities. Blogs, Twitter and other social networking sites provide a necessary antidote to stereotypical media representations of disability by allowing individuals with disability to have a public voice with what to 'tell the world about their own stories and life experiences'. (Haller 2010: 20; Ellcessor 2017: 37–38)

Thus, the podcast becomes a medium where hosts and guests tell their own stories in their own voice and can make their everyday experiences public. Publicness allows participants to raise awareness, but also broadens understandings of human experience writ large.

Readings: Audience Reactions to the *Sickboy* Podcast

When discussing the audience's reading of the podcast we rely solely on secondary sources. We examine the reactions of people on social media or in the interim episodes sharing reflections, where the hosts discuss the feedback they have received. As regards reactions on social media, we cannot always be sure whether commenters have listened to the podcast or whether they are reacting to others' reflections on it. On Facebook, it is easy to react to a post about a new podcast episode even before listening to it, and users do often react to the ongoing conversation. At the same time, the cross-media aspect of the podcast brings audience reactions and the collaborative dimension of the podcast reading to the forefront.

The relevance of looking at social media platforms is reflected by McClung and Johnson (2010: 89), who use online surveys to uncover motivations for downloading and listening to popular podcasts, and reveal that activities grouped as 'social aspect', like sharing and discussing podcasts with friends, play the most significant role in determining podcast use. This 'social aspect' of interacting with podcasts is also visible in *Sickboy*. Looking at the activity on its Facebook, Twitter and Instagram pages, the commenters often tag friends to bring podcast episodes or images to their attention. Posts also have quite a large number of shares (in comparison to the number of likes), indicating that this medium is where many people participate in conversations. For instance, at the time of writing this, the most recent guest episode post about a paramedic, Josh, who was suffering from post-traumatic stress disorder, had 165 likes, 21 shares and 5 comments.

Overall, the audience reactions are positive. The podcast is rated highly on its Facebook page (68 out of 70 reviews have given the podcast the maximum of 5 stars). The actual number of listeners is difficult to trace, as the embedded Libsyn platform does not display the number of listeners. Furthermore, podcasts in general are shared across several platforms and, in most cases, as in the case of *Sickboy*, are free services, which do not require registration or payment to access them.

The comments support Radio Advertising Bureau's (2004 quoted in Berry 2006) notion of two ways of listening: habitual and discretionary. While Berry (2006: 147) reads all ways of listening to be in the discretionary category, as listeners must make deliberate choices to subscribe to and transfer content, the affordances of mobile phones, etc., indicate a rise in habitual listening, where regular Monday podcasts are awaited and celebrated.

> I laugh, I cried once, and a Patreon supporter! Literally the first thing I think about when I get into work is where's my coffee and SICKBOY. Mondays at work are definitely not boring. *cough cough*. (*Sickboy* Facebook rating, April 2017)

Others describe different practices, where they become compelled to binge-listen to several episodes in a row.

> Sometimes I don't listen to sick boy for a couple months (six months has been my record) just so I can binge listen to it and hear all the inappropriate jokes my little heart desires for hours (days) on end. (*Sickboy* Facebook rating, April 2017)

The development of the *Sickboy* podcast follows Berry's (2006: 147) idea of the original radio communication, initially used for point-to-point communication, becoming a means to talk to the masses when crowds started tuning in. Similarly, the hosts of *Sickboy* initially ventured to record a conversation among themselves, with little interest in sharing it with others, but they realised the comedic potential of the show and the prospect of having this larger role. The podcast as a medium could be seen as the ideal of radio expressed by Bertolt Brecht (quoted in Berry 2006: 147), where people may speak as well as listen to the medium. However, instead of taking the view of Berry, who applauds the possibility of everyone becoming a producer of a podcast, thus blurring the roles of producers and the audience, we use the concept of 'produser' (Bruns 2006), as the podcast becomes a multi-communication medium which takes advantage of the affordances of cross-media. As discussed above, *Sickboy* is available on several platforms and through tagging, sharing and commenting, the audience plays an active part in the discussions.

There are clear moments in these discussions with the audience where the idea of empowerment is tapped into and people explicitly address the motivations of the podcast producers in their comments. For example, a tweet from April 2017 states, 'Thank you for this ep. I dont [sic] know anyone else who was born with this condition and it gets a bit lonely, it helped my self-esteem a lot' (Twitter 2017). Here, empowerment comes from learning about others suffering the same disease, and the feeling of recognition supports self-esteem. Another reviewer from the Facebook page stresses the importance of learning about new diseases:

> This has been a kick ass podcast to listen to each day (to get caught up on all episodes) and is the first thing I turn on in the morning! It is such a fantastic way to learn about diseases, disorders and medical issues that would otherwise remain foreign to me. It helps remove stigma and shows a different perspective that has been fascinating! Keep up the amazing work guys!! (*Sickboy* Facebook rating, December 2016)

Here, the writer does not self-identify as belonging to any of these stigmatised groups but, rather, talks in general terms about the empowering potential of the podcast. Through the three hosts and the guests, *Sickboy* offers the audience two different ways to identify with the podcast. On one hand, there is the identification of a fellow sick person—either the guest or Jeremie. On the other hand, Brian and Taylor both afford general identification as healthy but compassionate listeners as well as their individual, specific identifications. If one listens to only a few episodes, it is difficult to tell the hosts apart; hence, the identification can mostly be done through the healthy–sick binary. However, based on our experience, as regular listeners we learned to distinguish between the three hosts, and the textual analysis of the podcast transcripts shows that they tend to have their own individual roles in the discussions. Brian is the one who saves the uncomfortable moments, whereas Taylor is the one who is unafraid to ask even silly-sounding questions. This allows the audience to identify not only with the content of the discussions but also with the hosts and their personal stories (Piper 2015).

In our investigation of audience reactions, we can see different kinds of listening practices—people who are habitual listeners, those who binge-listen to several episodes in a row or those who get introduced to individual episodes through their own conditions. The podcast is shared, commented on, and celebrated via the supporting social media platforms (Facebook, Twitter, Instagram) and these platforms allow the hosts to maintain contact with their listeners.

Conclusions: Can Podcasts Impact Lived Culture?

As Piper (2015: 58) summarises, 'I have argued that the comedian podcast offers a platform for comedians to perform the state of being themselves, bringing what would typically be regarded in a mainstream comedy club contest as a backstage identity to the front, allowing the comedian to present a comedian-as-person identity'. Similarly, the identities of Jeremie, Brian and Taylor are performed to create a sense of closeness and authenticity. The hosts of *Sickboy* make jokes about themselves, their health, their habits and their lives in order to create an inclusive and intimate space for guests to share their personal stories. *Sickboy* manages to use (fairly) unedited versions of their podcast discussions to convey a sense of intimacy and immediacy for their guests and the audience.

The collaborative production—with both collaborative forms of funding and the collaborative format with regular guests—allows the podcast to remain open and avoid being tied to specific issues. The affordances of the social media linked to this collaborative production, as well as the open innovation business model, allow for a fairly democratic and open podcast. This openness and a rather predictable format allow for addressing a wide variety of topics. To balance the discussions on the borders of activism around the stigma of illness and humour, the hosts have developed a set of interventionist tactics to bring comedy to the platform. These interventionist tactics focus on jokes around the mundane that tend to target the hosts more than the guests. The format of the podcast shows that the interviewees balance between two coping mechanisms—owning and disowning their illness—both of which can be seen as relating to the identity related affordance to which the podcast affords a safe space for discussion. The audience can also identify with the sick and/or the healthy (hosts or guests), making discussions about health-related stigma outside patient–patient interactions possible. The public feedback on the podcast across different platforms seems to be uniformly positive and confirms many of the ideals the *Sickboy* team set out to fulfil. It appears that *Sickboy* occupies a unique place at the corner of health, comedy and activism. Coming back to Dahlgren's (2006) notion of doing citizenship, the *Sickboy* podcast seems to be doing exactly that. Employing everyday talk on private issues through the public medium of a podcast, and through a fairly ordered public format (Johnson 1986), building on identity construction of living with sickness, can, according to Dahlgren (2006), assume political relevance quickly and mobilise civic engagement. Therefore, investigating such media is interesting and relevant not only from the perspective of the medium of the podcast but also from the perspective of larger societal and cultural change.

Bibliography

Berger, P. L. (2014). *Redeeming laughter: The comic dimension of human experience.* Berlin: de Gruyter.

Berry, R. (2006). Will the iPod kill the radio star? Profiling podcasting as radio. *Convergence: The International Journal of Research into New Media Technologies, 12*(2), 143–162.

Bruns, A. (2006). Towards produsage: Futures for user-led content production. In F. Sudweeks, H. Hrachovec, & C. Ess (Ed.), *Cultural attitudes towards communication and technology* [Proceedings of the fifth international conference on cultural attitudes towards technology and communication, Tartu].

CBC News Toronto. (2016). Finding the funny in Cystic Fibrosis. www.cbc.com [Internet]. Accessed 1 May 2017.

Chung, D. S., & Kim, S. (2008). Blogging activity among cancer patients and their companions: Uses, gratifications, and predictors of outcomes. *Journal of the Association for Information Science and Technology, 59*(2), 297–306.

Clarke, K. (2015). Sickboy podcast tackles illness with humour. www.thestar.com [Internet]. Accessed 1 May 2017.

Dahlgren, P. (2006). Doing citizenship: The cultural origins of civic agency in the public sphere. *European Journal of Cultural Studies, 9*(3), 267–286.

Ellcessor, E. (2017). Kickstarting community: Disability, access and participation in my gimpy life. In E. Ellcessor & B. Kirkpatrick (Eds.), *Disability media studies* (pp. 32–55). New York: NYU Press.

Facebook. (2017). Sickboy Facebook ratings page. https://www.facebook.com/pg/sickboypodcast/reviews/?ref=page_internal [Internet]. Accessed 20 Oct 2017.

Gibson, J. (1979). *The ecological approach to human perception.* Boston: Houghton Mifflin.

Haller, B. A. (2010). *Representing disability in an ableist world: Essays on mass media.* Louisville: Advocado Press.

Ibrus, I., & Scolari, C. A. (Eds.). (2012). *Crossmedia innovations: Texts, markets, institutions.* Frankfurt: Peter Lang.

Jenkins, H. (2003). Transmedia storytelling: Moving characters from books to films to video games can make them stronger and more compelling. www.technologyreview.com [Internet]. Accessed 2017.

Johnson, R. (1986). What is cultural studies anyway? *Social Text, 16,* 38–80.

Kaplan, A. M., & Haenlein, M. (2010). Users of the world, unite! The challenges and opportunities of social media. *Business Horizons, 53*(1), 59–68.

Kickstarter. (2015). Sickboy Kickstarter page. https://www.kickstarter.com/projects/1674002261/sickboy-podcast [Internet]. Accessed 1 May 2017.

Lovink, G. (2008). *Zero comments: Blogging and critical internet culture.* New York: Routledge.

Löwgren, J., & Reimer, B. (2013a). The computer is a medium, not a tool: Collaborative media challenging interaction design. *Challenges, 4*(1), 86–102.

Löwgren, J., & Reimer, B. (2013b). *Collaborative media: Production, consumption, and design interventions.* Cambridge, MA: MIT Press.

McClung, S., & Johnson, K. (2010). Examining the motives of podcast users. *Journal of Radio & Audio Media, 17*(1), 82–95.

McCosker, A. (2008). Blogging illness: Recovering in public. *M/C Journal, 11*(6). http://journal.media-culture.org.au/index.php/mcjournal/article/view%-20Article/104/0 [Internet]. Accessed 20 Oct 2017.

Merolli, M., Gray, K., & Martin-Sanchez, F. (2013). Health outcomes and related effects of using social media in chronic disease management: A literature review and analysis of affordances. *Journal of Biomedical Informatics, 46*(6), 957–969.

Merolli, M., Gray, K., Martin-Sanchez, F., & Lopez-Campos, G. (2015). Patient-reported outcomes and therapeutic affordances of social media: Findings from a global online survey of people with chronic pain. *Journal of Medical Internet Research, 17*(1), e20.

Meserko, V. (2010). *Upright citizens of the digital age: Podcasting and popular culture in an alternative comedy scene.* MA Thesis, Kansas University. https://kuscholarworks.ku.edu/bitstream/handle/1808/7702/Meserko_ku_0099M_11108_DATA_1.pdf;sequence=1 [Internet]. Accessed 1 May 2017.

Moorhead, S. A., Hazlett, D. E., Harrison, L., Carroll, J. K., Irwin, A., & Hoving, C. (2013). A new dimension of health care: Systematic review of the uses, benefits, and limitations of social media for health communication. *Journal of Medical Internet Research, 15*(4), e85.

Norman, D. (2013). *The design of everyday things: Revised and expanded edition.* New York: Basic Books (AZ).

Piper, M. (2015). Little big dog pill explanations: Humour, honesty, and the comedian podcast. *Philament, 20,* 41–60.

Sarasohn-Kahn, J. (2008). The wisdom of patients: Health care meets online social media, *California HealthCare Foundation.* wwwchcforg [Internet]. Accessed 1 May 2017.

Schrøder, K. C., & Larsen, B. S. (2010). The shifting cross-media news landscape: Challenges for news producers. *Journalism Studies, 11*(4), 524–534.

Scolari, C. A., & Ibrus, I. (2014). Transmedia critical: Empirical investigations into multiplatform and collaborative storytelling. *International Journal of Communication, 8,* 2191–2200.

Sickboy. (2017). Contact. www.sickboypodcast.com [Internet]. Accessed 1 May 2017.

Sickboy. (n.d.) Brian and Taylor: Live from studio 5. www.sickboypodcast.com [Podcast]. Accessed 1 May 2017.

Sickboy Libsyn. (2015). Cystic fibrosis. www.sickboy.libsyn.com [Podcast]. Accessed 1 May 2017.

Sickboy Libsyn. (2017a). Definition of Sickboy in memory of Matthew Amyotte. www.sickboy.libsyn.com [Internet]. Accessed 1 May 2017.

Sickboy Libsyn. (2017b). All episodes. http://sickboy.libsyn.com [Internet]. Accessed 1 May 2017.

Tiidenberg, K. (2014). Bringing sexy back: Reclaiming the body aesthetic via self-shooting. *Cyberpsychology: Journal of Psychosocial Research on Cyberspace, 8*(1). https://cyberpsychology.eu/article/view/4295/3342 [Internet]. Accessed 20 Oct 2017.

Twitter. (2017). Sickboy Twitter page. www.twitter.com/sickboypodcast [Internet]. Accessed 1 May 2017.

14

Welcome to the World of Wandercast: Podcast as Participatory Performance and Environmental Exploration

Robbie Z. Wilson

Introduction

Although the very existence of this volume implies a degree of cohesion across what are known as podcasts, the editors' framing of this field as a *new aural culture* indicates its far-reaching heterogeneity. Within any culture there are sub-cultures: this chapter attends to aural cultural creations that diverge from podcasting's mainstream tendencies by necessitating the listener's physical interaction with their environment. I provide a performance studies perspective on podcasts, which contrasts with, but hopefully complements, the others of this volume. Although this chapter's main subject, *Wandercast*, conforms to the definition of podcasts as digital audio files downloaded via the internet, not all the works cited here do; however, all could be encoded and distributed in this way. As the editors note in their introduction, we must ask how much more than a means of distribution is the podcast medium? Analysing podcasts in comparison with closely related cultural offerings can offer valuable insights, as I hope to show. The works discussed in this chapter certainly fulfil Lukasz Swiatek's notion—posited in this volume—of the podcast as an 'intimate bridging medium' that provides intimate connectivity, and arguably blurs the boundaries, between artist and listener. These works invite consideration of what happens at the fringes of a 'liminal medium' such as the podcast and at its points of interaction with other innovative

R. Z. Wilson (✉)
University of Kent, Canterbury, UK
e-mail: rzw3@kent.ac.uk

© The Author(s) 2018
D. Llinares et al. (eds.), *Podcasting*, https://doi.org/10.1007/978-3-319-90056-8_14

aural forms. They also raise questions around whether podcasts themselves constitute a new aural culture or are examples of increasing cultural engagement with aurality in the digital age.

In addition to the dominant form of what might be called discursive podcasts, i.e. one or more people discussing one or more topics, there are narrative podcasts. These narratives are either fictional, as in *The Truth* and *Welcome to Night Vale*, or non-fictional, as in *Radiolab* and *Serial*. Narrative podcasts have been variously described as 'changing' (McHugh 2016) or 'remediating' (Bottomley 2015) earlier forms of narrative audio; nonetheless, they arguably possess dramatic structure. In live drama (i.e. theatre) in the twentieth century, the development of site-specific (Pearson 2010; Wilkie 2008; Kaye 2000) and participatory (White 2013; Bishop 2012, 2006) performance led to radical new approaches and a wide diversity of forms. (I use the term *performance*, since this work often draws from both theatre and visual arts traditions.) The work addressed within this chapter, which is participatory in nature and deals with issues of site, suggests that the podcast medium possesses versatility and creative potential similar to theatre/performance, the extent of which is only beginning to be explored.

Wandercast

Wandercast is a podcast that invites listeners to take it on a wander. It employs podcasts' portability and aural intimacy to unearth playful affordances[1] inherent in our surroundings and to encourage enaction of those affordances as a means of rediscovering one's environment. *Wandercast* also provides opportunities to investigate the nature of both playful interactions and the 'play of listening' (Home-Cook 2015: 168) common to all aural experience. The podcast form is therefore harnessed simultaneously as both a mode of participatory performance and a knowledge-producing research tool;[2] I aim to elucidate its value on both fronts, thus indicating what podcasts can achieve.

This chapter takes the form of a case study. I present a multi-layered account of the *Wandercast* series, beginning by positioning it within a field of similar work, before framing it theoretically, then analysing listener feedback. The theoretical framing encompasses Batesonian ecology, performance studies, and phenomenology. Throughout the discussion, I will address the challenges, opportunities, and potential impact associated with these kinds of podcasts, and how they relate to other podcast forms. In order to engage fully with this chapter, which posits the reality of embodied knowledge, the reader may wish to experience *Wandercast* first-hand.[3]

Each *Wandercast* encourages a particular modality of playfulness from listeners. After an introductory first episode (Ep. 1), which seeks to establish the podcast's aural aesthetic and detail its rules of engagement, the second, *Headphone Adventure Playground* (Ep. 2), targets physical play,[4] and the third, *Attenborough's Imaginarium* (Ep. 3), foregrounds playful imagination.[5] A fourth, which seeks to instigate social play, is currently in the planning stage. *Wandercast* combines elements of popular performance, such as direct address and jokey delivery, with others common to radio drama, such as realistic soundscape and representational sound-effects. As such, it manifests the informality (McHugh 2016) and radio heritage (Bottomley 2015; Berry 2006) that have shaped podcasting, but renders these so as to invite active participation.

Wandercast requires movement through, and invites interaction with, an environment; *Wandercast* remains inchoate without this dynamic physical engagement. As I shall discuss, this puts the work in dialogue with Clive Cazeaux's argument that '"calling for completion" [is] a vital component of artistic expression,' of which aural work is an 'exemplary form' (2005: 157–8). Created using only a handheld digital voice recorder and a laptop, *Wandercast* could further be seen as an expression of the democratisation of media production (cf. Berry 2006), though this is far from an unproblematic notion, as I briefly address below.

The Practical Terrain

As digital technologies have made recording and editing sound more practicable and, latterly, more affordable, increased numbers of artists from theatre, performance, and visual arts backgrounds have begun making audio-works, with podcast platforms offering means of making this work globally accessible. *Wandercast* is an example of a subset of audio-works that invite or demand physical action from their listeners; I therefore term *Wandercast* a performative podcast.[6] Though this is an issue that I will not explore in detail here, it is pertinent to point out that whilst I, as a funded researcher, have the means and inclination to produce free podcast content, the free-to-download aspect of the form presents a significant barrier to its adoption by freelance artists. This undoubtedly troubles simple notions of the podcast as an agent of media democratisation, a recurrent theme throughout this volume. As neither supposedly emancipated 'prosumer[s]' (Toffler 1980: 11), nor entities which host, and/or profit from, user-generated cultural artefacts (nor necessarily wishing to closely associate with those entities), artists can find it doubly difficult to negotiate the social media ecology/economy.[7]

Whereas discursive and narrative podcasts seek to foster participation and create 'a sense of "liveness"' largely through the use of social media (Markman 2015: 241), performative podcasts, like other performative audio, necessitate the listener's physical, cognitive, and affective participation in the co-creation of an unambiguously live event. *Wandercast* listeners play a double role as participants both in the performances and the research. Doubling character-ises performative audio in general, since it necessitates a double performance in order to (fully) exist: firstly, when the artist produces the audio and, sec-ondly, when the listener accepts the invitation to perform. It is not sufficient that performative podcasts merely be listened to, as we shall see. Listener feed-back on *Wandercast* indicates that this multimodal engagement, and the approaches used to effect it, can overreach the characteristic podcast intimacy and create a sense of palpable co-presence between artist and listener.

The variety of styles and approaches evident across performative audio is considerable, though many implicate walking as a mode of environmental interaction. This can be seen in the event Sound Walk Sunday, which seeks to 'globally celebrate' audio that instigates walking (Museum of Walking n.d.: [online]). Here, I briefly sketch the relations that three selected pieces bear to *Wandercast*, each of which prompted significant discoveries during the series' development. I also include a selection of notable examples at the end of this chapter. (Details of any pieces mentioned can be found there.)

Linked (2003–Present)

Linked, by Graeme Miller, though not a podcast, is certainly a broadcast. Audio is broadcast from a series of analogue radio transmitters along a route through north-east London to a portable radio receiver borrowed by the walker or 'witness,' as Miller terms his listeners (2005: 162). In *Linked*, listen-ers are witnesses to the upheaval visited upon the communities of Hackney and Wanstead in the name of progress.

Linked was created in response to the changes wrought by the construction of the M11 link road, which involved the compulsory purchase and demoli-tion of 400 homes. It was through participating in *Linked* that I first perceived the potential of audio to reconfigure individuals' relationships with their envi-ronment; in this case, by animating multiple histories and instantiating them in the present, producing an eerie overlay of a past in which the neighbour-hood was complete, without the roaring chasm of the motorway.

The recordings that make up *Linked* have been cut and layered to pro-duce an effect often more akin to soundscape than story—a far cry from the suspenseful, episodic structure that made *Serial* so successful. Nonetheless, *Linked* is powerfully affecting, engendering in the listener an acute awareness of, and emotional response to, the environment through which they walk. Miller likens *Linked* to a climbing frame onto which people interweave their own narratives as they play upon and interact with it.[8] This became somewhat of a guiding principle as I sought to establish *Wandercast's* methodology. The idea even influenced the title of Ep. 2: *Headphone Adventure Playground.* In contrast to *Linked*, however, a podcast cannot be bound to a singular physical location if it is to find a significant audience.

Wondermart (2009)

Since I am keen to maximise the variety of environments that listeners can rediscover through *Wandercast*, as opposed to *Linked's* 'moments of the past [that] haunt the present' of a very particular place (Linked n.d.: [online]), I came to realise that an instruction-based production was most suited to the task. This is also the technique employed by Silvia Mercuriali and Matt Rudkin in *Wondermart*, in which listener duos undertake surreptitious tasks in order to rediscover the banal bizarreness of the supermarket environment.

Covertness is a key aspect of *Wondermart*; listeners' activity is explicitly framed as clandestine. At the outset, one is instructed to 'make sure you don't stand out' and 'act natural.' Although this approach provoked an experience of furtiveness and dislocation in me, I do not imply that *Wondermart* is intended, nor bound, to engender such feelings in its listeners; I earlier posited the co-created nature of performative audio, so cannot speak of a piece being determined by its aural qualities. Nonetheless, the character and content of the production necessarily influences listeners' subsequent performances to a considerable extent. Paradoxically, rather than opening out my perception beyond the normative, *Wondermart* seemed to narrow it. I experienced a lesser degree of presence than I usually feel while shopping.

The potential for performative audio to close down perceptions is something that I have therefore paid particular attention to when developing *Wandercast*. I aim to open perceptions in order to engender a perceptual shift that allows playful affordances to appear alongside the normative and functional, thus enabling listeners' rediscovery of their environments. Yet there remains a distinct tension within *Wandercast* when it comes to encouraging the enaction of those affordances, as these often go against social norms. In contrast to my *Wondermart* experience, my research seeks aural structures and atmospheres which enable listeners to find the confidence to interact overtly playfully with their environment without feeling furtive or self-conscious. The intimacy of the podcast medium is key to this; however, as I will note, feedback suggests that *Wandercast* has not been completely successful in this regard.

Guide to Getting Lost (2010–Present)

My decision to utilise the podcast medium was partly motivated by a desire to make the research accessible to as wide a range of people as possible. This aim also influenced my choice to make my work site non-specific, which is to say that a listener should be able to take *Wandercast* anywhere and still be able to fully engage with it. Berry (2006) deems freedom of listening location to be podcasts' most significant operational feature; since *Wandercast* necessarily places a constraint on listeners' engagement in that they must be walking, it is important to minimise further constraint. A piece with similar site-non-specificity is Jennie Savage's *Guide to Getting Lost* (GTGL).

Savage invites listeners to walk a familiar environment and to get lost in it, seeing the place anew as the familiar is overlaid with a 'fictional sonic landscape' (Savage n.d.: [online]) knitted together from field recordings made in many countries. This work too is instructional; Savage directs listeners to turn left or right, replicating the route she followed in the moment of recording. In this sense, there is a playful character to GTGL as one makes essentially arbitrary twists and turns.

The major drawback with the GTGL format is that the environment often will not afford turning left or right when that instruction is given. When this happens, one finds oneself either having to ignore the instruction, or, like me, attempting to hold in mind the last instruction (and sometimes multiple instructions) for some time before being able to execute them. Naturally, both outcomes limit a listener's potential engagement with the work and thus its effectiveness.

GTGL thereby revealed the utmost importance of open, widely applicable instructions with broad interpretative potential when designing performative, site-non-specific podcasts. In fact, I aim for *Wandercast* to be perceived as involving invitations, rather than instructions. A further discovery from my experience of GTGL was the crucial nature of technical considerations when producing performative podcasts. There were many instances in GTGL where I simply could not hear Savage's voice and consequently may have missed certain instructions. *Wandercast*-listening also occurs outside, so may have to compete with significant background noise. Therefore, I have endeavoured to ensure that both the technical aspects of my performance (articulation, pace of speech, tone of voice, etc.) and my manipulation of the requisite technology (digital voice recorder and audio editing programs) are acquitted so as to minimise the possibility of inaudible content.

The aesthetic form of GTGL has been influential also. Envisaging the environments through which Savage was moving resulted in the overlay of, and juxtaposition between, imagined and physical environments. This provided an intriguing affective experience, which I have sought to explore further. Investigating the potential of aural overlay and juxtaposition (present also in *Linked*) became an important aspect of *Wandercast*'s methodology.

To summarise, the works discussed above have, jointly and severally, had a considerable impact on the ongoing development of the *Wandercast* series and my understanding of performative podcasts. Key discoveries have been that: *Linked* established the idea of creating structures which are sufficiently open and indeterminate to allow listeners to co-author their experience; *Wondermart* revealed the potential for performative audio to reduce listener presence; and GTGL demonstrated the necessity of devising invitations that, as far as possible, do not depend upon specific environmental affordances. Having now situated *Wandercast* within the terrain of related work, I move to sketch out its theoretical framework.

Theoretical Framing

Ecological Lens

Since *Wandercast* addresses listeners' environmental interactions, ecological theory forms a key element of its framework; I further suggest that an ecological lens would prove fruitful for all performative podcasts—as all performances take place within an environment—and perhaps podcast studies generally. I draw on the work of Gregory Bateson,[9] for whom 'All biological and evolving systems (i.e., individual organisms, animal and human societies, ecosystems, and the like)... share certain formal characteristics' ([1972] 2000: 447).

The characteristic of most importance here is Bateson's assertion that such systems must be considered in strongly holistic terms. Consequently, this view does not admit of unilateral control; that is, no part of a system can unilaterally control the system nor any other part (2000: 315). The same also holds for coupled systems, such as two interacting individuals, which, for Bateson, create a single, two-person system (2000: 267). I argue that the parallels between ecological systems as strictly holistic and my notion of performative-podcast-art as entities co-created by artist(s) and listener(s)—which remain inchoate without podcast-listener interaction—are fairly striking. One could even say that performative podcasts exemplify this ecological principle.

Though artists' and listeners' performances each constitute complex systems in their own right, it is only in their coupling that the artwork can potentially achieve completion, thereby freshly illuminating notions of the podcast as an 'intimate bridging medium' (Swiatek, Chap. 9, this volume). This is not to suggest, however, that it is an easy or frictionless process. As the above examples and *Wandercast* feedback discussed later demonstrate, there are many factors which can lead to only partial (or potentially zero) meshing between podcast and listener systems. These factors could originate from either side, but will only be realised in interaction. For example, a podcast's formal, conceptual, aesthetic, or technical aspects can limit system-meshing, as can individual differences in listeners, as well as things such as disposition and mood.

Schechner argues that 'people are increasingly finding the world not a book to be read but a performance to participate in' (2013: 25), implying (perhaps unknowingly) the system-meshing of person and world, and also evoking the interactivity and conversationality of Web 2.0 that has shaped podcasting's development. Since they predominantly take place in everyday spaces, I argue that performative podcasts are particularly well-placed to structure explorations of contemporary being in ways that embrace the digital but also root us in our physical environment. Podcast-listener coupling within a performance exemplifies, and thus reveals, the deeper coupling of listener and world.

Ecological Performance

Ecology has become an established framework within performance studies, of which Baz Kershaw is a key proponent. Kershaw argues that people can be 'performed by' certain performance structures. For Kershaw, this phenomenon exemplifies, and can help humanity to recognise, the way in which our species is performed by Earth's ecologies, puncturing the belief that we possess unilateral agency with which to control them (2015: 115). Again, by siting these experiences within everyday situations (supermarkets and streets, for example) performative audio reveals that our agency is always-already embedded within, and contingent upon, larger systems.

Kershaw further argues that, due to global forms of change within politics, economics, media, and technology, the twentieth century saw humanity develop into 'performative societies,' which are 'crucially constituted through performance,' such that performance pervades every instance of human action and experience (2007: 11–12). This second point Kershaw tethers to the current ecological crisis, characterising the processes by which performative societies arose and are perpetuated as manifesting a 'performance addiction,' which establishes endemic vicious circles that both reinforce their performative underpinnings and compound their effects, for instance climate change (2007: 12–15).

One might wonder, then, what difference artistic performance—via podcast or otherwise—can make to a species defined and trapped by this phenomenon. Is it not like trying to change the ocean by pouring water into it? Not so, says Kershaw (2015). He does not claim that identifiable artistic performances (that is, those which are more or less objectively framed as performance by virtue of association with particular traditions) effect instantaneous recalibration between individuals, communities, or societies and the environments they inhabit. Rather, such performances afford recognition of relations between humans and their environments (which, from an ecological perspective, are not strictly separable), forming the precursor necessary for potential recalibration (Kershaw 2015: 119).

As with cognitive behavioural therapy, thinking about how one acts can beget change in how one acts, begetting change in how one thinks. Similarly, engaging in, and being performed by, carefully structured performance activity can promote the recalibration of one's performative existence. This recalibration can be described as effecting a new meshing between self and environment, such that new modes of perceiving, performing, and being can obtain. If humanity is suffering from performance addiction, perhaps performative behavioural therapy is called for. Indeed, though unintended, listener feedback indicates a therapeutic aspect to *Wandercast*. Owing to the medium's global reach and extensive accessibility, performative podcasts present a potentially useful contribution to this pernicious situation.[10]

Phenomenological Lens

According to Cazeaux's 'calling for completion' thesis, performative podcasts may provide a particularly effective artistic form for fostering personal creativity, which is 'manifested in the intentions and motivation to transform the objective world into original interpretations, coupled with the ability to decide when this is useful and when it is not' (Runco 1996: 3–4). Cazeaux's thesis positions performative podcasts' inchoateness—until performed by a listener—as a 'highly significant aesthetic property' (2005: 158), which strongly invites original interpretations of the objective world through the coupling of podcast and listener.

Cazeaux (2005) phenomenologically counters the negative claim that radio drama is an incomplete medium, drawing primarily on Merleau-Ponty to positively reformulate said claim. The negative claim asserts that, due to its representational nature but lack of visual images, radio drama suffers from an absence of the visual sensory modality. This criticism, of course, applies similarly to *Wandercast*, the works discussed above, and all narrative podcasts.

Cazeaux counters this position by refuting the 'orthodox, empiricist conception of the senses' as 'discrete channels' (2005: 160).[11] He takes a phenomenological stance, according to which the senses are interdependent elements of the holistic way in which our consciousness opens onto and grasps the world. In this view, our synaesthetic sensory experience and the world co-constitute one another, since one's sensory capacities determine the aspects of the world that may be experienced (2005: 160), which reflects the ecological perspective taken here. Perception both shapes and is shaped by our active coupling with the world (cf. Noë 2004).

For Cazeaux, though it is possible to distinguish between the senses, this is only so because of their commonality as 'interlocking and corresponding world-openings,' which '[beckon]' toward both one another and the world, jointly creating the conditions for perception through individual modalities (2005: 163). Thus, performative and narrative podcasts should not be seen as negatively incomplete, but rather as valuable exemplars of perceptual process, since they invite, or beckon forth, interaction between numerous modalities in the listener, including visual and kinaesthetic. Crucially, Cazeaux argues that aurally manifested art possesses greater potential for exemplification than visually focused forms because of sound's ambiguous, quasi-autonomous ontology:

> Whereas sight is comparatively 'transparent' in giving us reality, sound hangs or endures as a transformation between subject and object and, as such, is the region of sensory experience we can turn to in order to appreciate the invitational relationship in which we stand to the world. (2005: 173)[12]

Sound, Phenomenology, and Performance

Phenomenologically, the designation of something as art requires that the work reveals or exemplifies the 'cognitive, world-organising processes' just described; artworks thus express meanings above and beyond those of presentation and representation (Cazeaux 2005: 164). Theatre does this, according to George Home-Cook, since it is a 'place where the playfulness of perception is phenomenally presenced by and in the attentional enactments of its participants' (2015: 8). Characterising perception as inherently playful is of especial interest in the context of *Wandercast*, since it suggests that *Wandercast*'s playful focus opens up another exemplary register in addition to its aural orientation, implying a layering of exemplification. For game designer and philosopher Ian Bogost, play is 'a tool to discover and appreciate the structures of all [that]... we encounter' (2016: 12), echoing the notion of ecological recalibration. From Home-Cook's perspective, play reveals the perceptual processes by which we encounter these structures; taking Cazeaux's (2005) and Home-Cook's (2015) views together, *playful aurality* exemplifies perception twice over.

Home-Cook attributes playfulness to perception from a phenomenological position similar to Cazeaux's and also focuses on aurality, but in staged theatre. This presencing of perception's posited playfulness occurs through interplay both between the senses and the phenomenal elements of the artwork, as well as within these two groups, during one's active constitution of experience. Whilst I agree with Home-Cook's analysis with regard to theatre, it strikes me that performative audio generally, and *Wandercast* in particular, reveals and exemplifies this process especially clearly, since it does so within environments not designated as arenas of aesthetic experience and also invites a greater degree of active engagement than does staged theatre. When I ask listeners to slalom through environmental objects, as if they're on *Ski Sunday*, in Ep. 2 and to imagine any people or animals in their vicinity as undersea creatures in Ep. 3, *Wandercast* instantiates a complex web of invitational relations. As Home-Cook observes, 'To be in sound is not to be straightforwardly, spherically and passively "immersed", but rather consists of an ongoing, dynamic and intersensorial bodily engagement with the affordances of a given environment' (2015: 3).

Crucially, performative podcasts invite listeners to physically enact the affordances of their immediate environment in a way that far outstrips the invitational structures of staged theatre. Furthermore, podcast performances take place in environments where modes of behaviour not associated with aesthetic experience are likely to dominate. Whereas staged theatre could be described as a laboratory for aural-perceptual investigation, podcasts could be said to take this endeavour into the wild. This may reinforce any potential impact on listeners, since the work's expressiveness is rooted in a quotidian environment, thus signalling more clearly the universality of the processes exemplified.[13]

Presence, Performative Podcasts, and Audio-walks

Home-Cook's notion of presencing also re-raises the issue of artist-presence in performative podcasts. As Misha Myers observes, it is not appropriate to characterise artists as absent in performative audio (2011: 76). Myers argues that the bodily presence of the speaker may be 'conjured within the imagination of the listener' (2011: 76), such that intersubjective contact occurs between the two, which resonates with the notions both of system coupling and of podcasts dissolving barriers between artist and audience, as posited in this volume's introduction. Their oft-noted intimacy implies that intersubjective contact may be characteristic of podcasts, yet performative podcasts take contact into another register, and arguably intensify it, as the speaker brings the listener into contact also with their surroundings. Though it can be, this conjuring need not be visual, since 'contact' implies an affective, even tactile, phenomenon. This conjured contact feeds into the work's web of invitational relations aurally, kinaesthetically, and perhaps visually in the mind's eye of the listener.

Audiowalks, of which *Wandercast* is an example, possess a particularly potent expressiveness for Myers, since the practice of perambulation whilst engaging in artistic aurality instantiates direct and dynamic kinetic connectivity which 'interanimates and shapes landscapes' for the listener (2011: 79), revealing with particular clarity the way in which perception opens onto the world. Thus, they may also be particularly effective in facilitating ecological recalibration. In an age when many people navigate the world whilst magnetised to the visual interface of their smartphone and/or encased in 'solitary experience in the shrunken and isolated space' of their personal collection of audio (2011: 79–80),[14] audio-walks aim to use the medium of sound to open listeners out into their environments. In audio-walks, as Myers observes, 'self, body and landscape are shaped and enmeshed through voicing and listening bodies in motion' (2011: 80); the artist is presenced in the experience of the listener and the listener in their environment.

Recalling Home-Cook's argument that being 'in sound' is dynamic engagement with affordances, *Wandercast* takes Myers' enmeshing process further by both drawing attention to playful affordances, thus revealing them, and directly inviting the enaction of these affordances. In so doing, *Wandercast* doubly reveals and exemplifies the perception-action cycles by which self and world are co-constituted through both its calling for completion and its playful orientation (since perception itself is deemed playful [Home-Cook 2015: 7–11]). The enaction of affordances through performance also provides the possibility for personally creative original interpretations to be made manifest. For Sally Banes and Andre Lepecki 'any body in a performance situation… is an inexhaustible inventor of sensorial-perceptual potentials and becomings' ([2007] 2012: 4). With staged theatre, the realising in overt action of these potentials is usually restricted to performers. With performative audio, the possibility of creativity-in-action is extended also to the 'audience.'

This is not to suggest that performative podcasts can render listeners creative, only that they create the conditions for the generation, and possible realisation, of creative potential. Recall that, from an ecological perspective, no part of a system can unilaterally control any other. Now that the theoretical framing has been sketched, I flesh it out by positioning *Wandercast* as a model that manifests the themes discussed above, teasing out how they are reflected in listener feedback. I also delineate when reality approaches the ideal of what performative podcasts can achieve and when meshing between podcast and listener systems approaches zero. I address the themes in the above order, treating some together, as they overlap, and expanding upon others.

Wandercast Listener Feedback[15]

System Coupling

I address listeners directly, which is a hallmark of popular performance (Double 2017: 8) and imperative for participation, as well as being a common approach for podcasts with a single host. In Ep. 2, I also engaged in the same actions as listeners 'simultaneously'—for example, jumping and swinging on things. Both of these tactics appear to have positively influenced system coupling:

> The fact that I believe [the perfilitator] was doing the moves as he spoke facilitate doing it more as you feel like it's a shared experience and it teaches you to be a bit more carefree.

Intertwined with this is the concept of presencing, since these listeners appear to have felt that I was somehow with them. One even commented that I 'did not have a physical form [yet] appeared as a presence,' which demonstrates that performative podcasts can overreach traditional podcasts' bridging between artist and listener to effect Myers' (2011) notion of intersubjective contact that is felt as well as thought. The fact that I was undergoing a similar experience was important:

> The sense that the narrator was also learning at the same time mimicked the thought process I had at some key moments – such as encountering other people – where it kept me from returning too much to my own thoughts. It also created a feedback process which was surprising given that there is no actual way to ask questions in the moment.

The notion of a 'feedback process' is particularly interesting, since it is not possible to have feedback without contact, which Myers (2011) relates to presencing. This also suggests that performative podcasts can give a semblance—in the moment of listening—of the feedback that traditional podcasts seek through social media. Coupling is evident in the above quote in the way that the listener felt no longer in complete control of their thought process; they were 'performed by' (Kershaw 2015: 115) the *Wandercast* structure. This reflects the ecological denial of unilateral control and also Bogost's conceptualisation of play as the '[subordination of] agency to a larger system' (2016: 92). Ecologically, we might say that *Wandercast* exemplifies the way in which all interaction involves the integration of systems' relative agencies.

Coupling was almost zero for some Ep. 3 listeners, however, who found my energetic and expressive tone (used in support of the podcast's imagination-orientation) 'pretentious and patronising':

> It's very hard to relate and enjoy something like this when you feel like you are being spoken to like a child.

Another listener commented that 'it's very hard to relate to something that you dislike.' It is possible that these listeners' dispositions toward the work may have been negatively influenced by their being required to experience it as part of a module (see note 15). Nonetheless, this demonstrates an important constraint on performative podcasts' possible effectiveness, as noted earlier. Since the artwork only completes in the meshing of podcast and listener, performative podcasts' effectiveness is contingent upon the extent to which meshing occurs. Judgements made by the artist (such as my vocal aesthetic) and listener preferences can conspire to radically increase or decrease system meshing. Additionally, this demonstrates that the speaker's style is equally, if not more, important in performative podcasts as it is in traditional forms (cf. McHugh 2016).

Performative-Behavioural Therapy

A common thread throughout feedback on all episodes attributes calming or meditative qualities to them. Words such as 'relaxed,' 'happy,' 'calm,' 'soothing,' and 'chilled' appear numerous times as listeners describe their experience. Many listeners note that the work reduced their stress-levels. Some listeners specifically likened the experience to meditation, one describing Ep. 3 as 'reminiscent of mindfulness techniques,' with another saying that Ep. 2 made them 'feel quite Zen.' This, again, ties in with the notion of being more present in one's environment through performance and also through play, suggesting that this might be a general quality of environmentally and/or playfully focused performative podcasts. As I intimated earlier, these responses were unanticipated and unsought.

Thich Nhat Hanh defines mindfulness as 'keeping one's consciousness alive to the present reality' (1976: 11), which resonates with listeners who 'concentrated on the immediacy of the surroundings' (Ep. 2), or for whom their environment 'became more visible' (Ep. 3). In seeking an operational definition of mindfulness, Bishop et al. argue that the practice is characterised by 'openness and acceptance of experience.' Nonetheless, the means by which this is achieved is 'self-focused attention' (2004: 236); I find this problematic, since it promotes individualism and acts to obscure the invitational nature of perception.

Like Bogost, *Wandercast* instead seeks a 'commitment to *worldfulness*,' which turns one's attention outward, rather than inward (2016: 224, emphasis original). Myers perceives a similar ambition in all audio-walks, as noted above. However, *Wandercast* is not always successful in this; many Ep. 3 listeners reported that the experience largely took place 'within' their minds. As I have expressed, many subtleties pertaining to podcast production and listening can lead to the lived experience feeling inwardly or outwardly oriented. Each orientation has value, phenomenologically, since both subject and world are interdependent. However, I suggest that within contemporary consumer culture, consumption being a profound and pervasive metaphor of inwardness, it is necessary to seek to foster outwardness in order to rebalance perspectives, especially in light of the fraught state of global ecologies. Notably, Bogost associates this sensitivity to worldly structures with creativity (2016: 146–153), a personal quality that is becoming ever more valuable as job automation increases.

Personal Creativity

A significant number of listeners explicitly characterised their experience as 'creative,' one going so far as to say that they were in a 'state of heightened creativity for some time afterwards' (Ep. 3). Listeners' self-reports, however, do not necessarily comply with the standard definition of creativity: 'originality and usefulness' (Runco and Jaeger 2012: 95). The play of perception and performance is more closely associated with original interpretations than with evaluation of their extrinsic usefulness (Bateson, P. 2010: 45). Nonetheless, one Ep. 3 listener wrote that they would use *Wandercast* as a means of generating a creative frame of mind before embarking on a creative task, such as writing, thus expressing a usefulness-evaluation not of the original interpretations themselves, but of the mental processes arising from their performance. Notwithstanding that 'intrinsic and ... instrumental impacts of arts participation are fundamentally interwoven' (Reason 2017: 47), usefulness is a problematic notion in art (and play) contexts, since it often overshadows vital, subjective elements such as recalibration of personal ecologies. It is also worth remembering that '(H)uman well-being is a justifiable end in itself' (Bateson, P. 2015: R16), which is strongly associated with both play (Lester and Russell 2008) and art-engagement (Mowlah et al. 2014), as well as evidenced by the responses in the previous subsection.

The original interpretations of seeing one's environment 'in a new way' recur across Eps 1–3, with one listener even noting that a familiar environment became '(T)o some extent, a place where I had never walked before' (Ep. 1). The focus on imagination in Ep. 3 lends itself to visualisation, such as when 'clouds became coral,' which is an imaginative overlay of the visible world beckoned into being by the aural overlay of the podcast. *Wandercast* evidently facilitates these original interpretations manifesting in action, as when (for this same listener) 'buildings became rocks to hide behind' (Ep. 3). These examples clearly demonstrate performative podcasts' capacity to perform listeners into new meshings with their environments.

Exemplification of Perception

The vividness of some listeners' imagistic experiences shows that *Wandercast* has considerable expressive potential, which I argue evidences performative podcasts' significant artistic worth. Even after the podcast, one listener 'could see monkeys jumping from car to car,' leading to the apprehension of meaning beyond the representational:

> For every person that walked past, I found myself wondering what they were thinking, or imagining, and what it'd be like to get into their head too. (Ep. 3)

This kind of behavioural change continuing, or even beginning to occur, after *Wandercast* was over indicates that performative podcasts have considerable potential to recalibrate listeners' relationships with their environment.

Earlier, I argued that performative podcasts' explicit or implicit invitations to interact with one's surroundings extend Cazeaux's (2005) notion that audio has a particular propensity to exemplify perception's invitational structure. This is borne out by listener testimony:

> Every little sound invited me to explore that immense world it possess [sic]. I submerged myself into the nature seeing different birds in the farm and aquatic creatures under the sea. (Ep. 3)

The first sentence here evokes the work's expressiveness, which arises from the complexity of its invitational relations. All podcasts, especially narrative podcasts, exemplify perception's invitational structure, as podcasts' aurality beckons forth other perceptual modalities, yet performative podcasts manifest particular relational complexity, since they also exemplify the intimate interrelations between perception and action (Noë 2004).

Listeners often described *Wandercast*'s sound as drawing them into their surroundings, making them more 'aware of sounds in real life, blurring what sounds came from the podcast and what came from the real world' (Ep. 1). The use of different sonic elements seems to have been particularly effective, which positions aural overlay as a key element of performative podcasts' structure:

> the change of audio environment through the use of voice, and ambient sound made it easier to engage with the imaginary landscape of the real world. (Ep. 2)

Again, this last phrase suggests apprehension of meaning that exceeds the content of the work, pointing toward the listener's construction of reality.

Listeners reported experiencing change to the global character of their perception, for instance inhabiting 'a more child-like perspective,' leading to the rather intense experience of having been 'swooped into a fairy tale' (Ep. 3). These changes in global perception necessarily throw into relief one's default mode: 'it...made me more aware of my surroundings where usually it's like I have blinders [sic] on and I am not really paying attention to anything' (Ep. 3). I contend that this increased awareness indicates the revealing of perceptual processes through the work. Additionally, listeners often reported increased intensity of experience across all sensory registers, which supports the synaesthetic phenomenological thesis and my argument for performative podcasts' artistic value.

Active Engagement

A major challenge for podcasts seeking to instigate overtly playful behaviour as *Wandercast* does, or any behaviour not within social norms, is to alleviate listeners' concerns about being observed by non-listeners. As noted earlier, my practice of engaging in physical play whilst recording Ep. 2 seems to have helped in this regard. I suggest that a light-hearted vocal performance is also useful. Listeners tend to find imaginative or unobtrusive play less daunting, yet I propose that performative-audio-artists should not shy away from encouraging more involved environmental interactions. It is also possible that the structure of Eps 1–3, which invites solo listening, contributed to listeners' reticence for overt playfulness exceeding social norms; group podcast performance might mitigate concerns about being observed. Though not an example of a podcast, this was certainly my experience of *Remote London* (see list of Performative Audio Artworks).

Curiously, however, many listeners' testimonies indicate a feeling of empowerment arising from their private experience:

> I enjoyed the fact that people were walking past me not knowing that I was in a world of my own. It was also interesting knowing I was the only one doing this type of thing and no one had any idea of what I was imagining them as/how I was looking at my surroundings. (Ep. 3)

Although this listener describes being in a world of their own, the latter part of the quote clearly indicates that they were connected to their surroundings. As well as empowerment, for some, a reassuring feeling of partnership was engendered: 'I felt not alone it was as if 'Wandercast' was really with me in the experience' (Ep. 3). Again, this resonates strongly with the notion of artist presence explored above and indicates that performative podcasts may outstrip other podcast forms in the intensity, vividness, and palpability of the connection effected between artist and listener. As I mentioned, presencing cuts both ways; one listener experienced being 'transported by sound to your playgrounds' (Ep. 2). Though, of course, in reality this listener manoeuvred themselves through their own co-constituted playgrounds whilst the sound participated in the revealing and exemplification of perception-action processes.

One listener put their feeling of immersion, implicit in the experience of transportation, down to

> the ambiance [sic] sounds that were playing throughout, as it sort of tricked your mind into thinking you were in a different place and that this was the way you should be responding to it. (Ep. 3)

Here, the use of the word 'responding' indicates their active engagement. As the podcast progressed, another listener even felt as though non-listeners could also hear the *Wandercast* soundscape, which became 'a normal thing,' commonly shared. This is a clear example of the podcast's aural environment extending into the objective world.

Conclusion

Performative audio constitutes a valuable sub-set operating at the fringes of the podcast medium. I argue that these participatory artworks exploit and increase the exemplifying potential of sound by inviting dynamic interaction between listener and environment that extends and complexifies the set of connections inherently established by listening. Home-Cook asserts that 'Whilst the listener resides *in* the medium of sound, equally this medium must be attended, explored and travelled through' (2015: 169, emphasis in original).

Yet, whilst this can be achieved with the minimum of physical movement in the case of staged theatre or traditional podcasts, performative podcasts require more robust environmental interaction. Whether this leads to bizarre, furtive acts in a supermarket during *Wondermart*, '[hopping] on and off some tiny speed bumps' and 'swinging on every lamp post' during *Wandercast* (Ep. 2), or simply taking a left turn during GTGL, the interaction involved is decidedly more kinetic. For Home-Cook, '(I)n 'paying attention', whether in the theatre or the world at large, we must...'grasp', and this act of grasping requires effort' (2015: 3). Clearly, though performative podcasts involve, and can reveal, this attentional grasping, they also make concrete movement demands, thus requiring additional effort. With additional effort, I argue, additional value can be generated, enabling the podcast to perform listeners into recalibration of their personal ecology. In other words, performative podcasts offer performative-behavioural therapy for performative societies.

If 'when we listen, we *shape* meaning: in attending sounds, we set sounds in play' (Home-Cook 2015: 169, emphasis original), then when we simultaneously set ourselves in motion and physically interact with the world, I suggest that we tether this meaning-shaping more closely to our corporeality, which may make the effects of performative podcasts more durable than those of traditional forms. Furthermore, though the impact of engaging with one performative podcast is necessarily modest, the embedding of the experience within 'the world at large' enables meaningful outcomes to directly impact listeners' views of their environment after the event:

The colours and objects seemed to jump out at me, I felt more in tune and aware. I started thinking about what things could be rather than what they actually were. (Ep. 3)

Such outcomes clearly exhibit the novelty-generation necessary for personal creativity and indicate the potential development of worldfulness. Although most listeners reported such phenomena occurring only for a modest period, the fact that this effect began or persisted post-*Wandercast* again demonstrates the potential recalibration of listener-environment relationships.

Wandercast's recalibration towards worldfulness arguably has ontological implications. By performing listeners into states of increased presence, *Wandercast* helps listeners recognise that they are 'in and toward the world' (Merleau-Ponty [1945] 2012: lxxiv), thus revealing their ecological embeddedness. It is reasonable to posit that further engagement with *Wandercasts* or similar podcasts would result in further, perhaps longer-lasting, recalibration. Upon retracing their steps once Ep. 3 was over, one listener had the 'fascinating' experience of 'changing my walk as I came back through my farm' and went on to 'Wonder whether from now on this particular spot in this field will always be underwater for me?'

In characterising listening as fundamentally playful, Home-Cook (2015) implicitly states that all instances of performative audio, and all podcasts, involve aural play. Not all will exemplify this process equally, however. *Wandercast* binds the perceptually exemplary 'play of listening' (2015: 168) to complex, manifestly playful environmental interaction, such that play across multiple modalities occurs, thus multiplying the potential for perceptual exemplification and ecological recalibration. The above listener experienced increased propensity for playfulness and altered perception pertaining even to their own ontology, the latter of which arguably increases the likelihood and potential extent of recalibration, as the listener's being is directly implicated. Post-*Wandercast*, they were 'still playing,' feeling 'smaller than normal.'

Although my particular research focuses on playfulness, I contend that participatory performance mediated through podcasts has considerable potential in many areas. Performative podcasts' portability, global reach, and embeddedness within Web 2.0 frameworks means that they have the capacity to artistically and actively address issues of global significance such as the ecological crisis and gender equality. Furthermore, as *Wondermart* demonstrates, the ubiquity of headphone-wearing in contemporary metropolitan society means that the podcast medium provides an opportunity for the incursion of art into almost any sphere of life without arousing suspicion. Normative patterns of behaviour may thus be disrupted from inside. However, a major issue requiring further research and innovation is how to assuage listener-performers' self-consciousness.

Whether or not performative-audio-artists choose to harness the magnification of exemplification that playfulness offers, I have shown that performative podcasts can have significant worldly impact. Given their aesthetic value, performative podcasts also present a sizable reservoir of research potential, into which only a toe has been dipped. In this endeavour, I suggest that ecological and phenomenological lenses will be invaluable. Performative podcasts effect coupling between artist, listener, and environment, as well as exploiting both performativity and the sonic medium to exemplify the invitational nature of perception. As Banes and Lepecki observe, 'transmissibility of the senses is one of performance's most powerful performatives' (2012: 4). Why not give *Wandercast* a try and you too might '[befriend] an elephant and [flirt] with a mermaid' (or merman—Ep. 3).

Notes

1. Affordance is a technical term coined by James J. Gibson (1966) to denote the range of actions permitted by environmental elements relative to a particular organism.
   An example of a playful affordance would be that a bollard affords vaulting:

Photo 1: Dad vaults bollard.

2. Specifically, *Wandercast* constitutes practice-as-research (PaR). PaR refers to research whereby (predominantly artistic) practice is the chief methodology. See Nelson (2013) for a key reference text.

3. Before reading this chapter, you might want to undertake a *Wandercast* (or more than one) for yourself, as there are significant aspects of any fundamentally embodied, kinetic experience which cannot be put into words. You will find more details and download information here http://ludicrouspilgrim. co.uk/wandercast-2/, or search 'Ludicrous Pilgrim' on iTunes.

4. *Headphone Adventure Playground* is more or less self-explanatory. I guide listeners through various tactics for playful environmental interaction whilst conducting those same tactics myself and recording my endeavours. The tactics have ludicrous names such as 'The Kerb-Hop' and 'The Swing-King.' There are also interjections from me 'in the studio,' which give extra information and context.

5. In *Attenborough's Imaginarium*, I accompany listeners on a journey through three environments within David Attenborough's imagination, inviting imaginative and physical interaction between: listeners, the sonic environment (created through soundscape), and the environment through which listeners wander.

6. The concept of performativity is a mutable and vexed one (see Shepherd and Wallis 2004: 220–224). Here, I use the term performative in its general sense of instigating action or performance. There is also the sense, with which listeners might identify, of engaging in action which connotes performance. Whether or not any action associated with *Wandercast* can be objectively categorised as performance is less important than whether it bears some of the hallmarks of performance.

7. For a discussion of the oppositional forces at work in digital media ecologies, see Jenkins and Deuze (2008); for a view on the implications of social media for professional artists, see Manovich (2009); and for an analysis of prosumer capitalism, see Ritzer and Jurgenson (2010). I propose that an investigation into factors limiting the uptake of the podcast form by participatory performance artists would make a valuable research project.

8. This was at a ResCen Research Seminar at the University of Middlesex, 3 February 2015. Miller presented on the life of *Linked* since 2003.

9. For more detail on this expansive epistemology, see Bateson ([1972] 2000, 1979, 1991) and Bateson and Bateson (1987).

10. I am being a little playful here; just to be clear, I am not suggesting that performative podcasts constitute therapy, only that they may be viewed as therapeutic within the specific context that Kershaw (2007) outlines.

11. For a more lyrical account of the mingling of the senses, see Serres (2008).

12. Though not mentioned by Cazeaux (2005), this links also to the 'centering' and 'unifying' nature of sound, as described by Ong ([1982] 2002: 69–72).

13. For the avoidance of doubt, I reject the drawing of a distinction between any event and 'real life,' since reality encompasses all events. Therefore, I do not describe *Wandercast* as taking place in the real world, whilst staged theatre takes place somehow outside of it.

14. Ironically, this could include 'traditional' podcasts, as well as music mp3s or streaming services.

15. Many more listeners fed back on Ep. 3 than either other episode, since Ep. 3 was included as an independent performance task in a first-year core module on which I taught within the Drama and Theatre Studies BA at the University of Kent. As previously argued, all listeners have dispositions that affect the degree to which they engage with performative podcasts; in the first-years' case, perceiving *Wandercast* as 'work' may well have negatively affected their engagement. It is also worth mentioning that the relative foci of the episodes (Ep. 3's focus being imagination), entails that, overall, more feedback addresses themes pertaining to imaginative than to physical interaction, yet this does not mean that *Wandercast* as a whole bears this orientation.

Selected Performative Audio Artworks

And While London Burns, Platform (2007–present)
Operatic thriller in the form of an audiowalk.
Listener-participants: 1
Site-specific: City of London
andwhilelondonburns.com (download available)

Guide to Getting Lost, Jennie Savage (2010–present)
Instruction-based audiowalk incorporating aural overlay of field-recordings.
Listener-participants: 1
Site-non-specific
www.jenniesavage.co.uk/ (no download, but hosted on Soundcloud)

Linked, Graeme Miller (2003–present)
Analogue radio audiowalk in the form of a treasure trail.
Listener-participants: 1
Site-specific: route of the M11 link road
www.linkedm11.net/ (no download, but facilitated by Artsadmin)

Memory Points, Platform 4 (2012–2015)
Participatory promenade theatre piece dealing with Alzheimer's.
Listener-participants: up to 6
Site-specific: various performance venues
www.platform4.org/ (no download)

Remote X, Rimini Protokoll (2016)
Instruction-based, responsive, cinematic audiowalk, which develops in each new city.
Listener-participants: up to 50
Site-specific: various major cities
www.rimini-protokoll.de/ (no download)

The Quiet Volume, Ant Hampton and Tim Etchells (2010–present)
Instruction-based exploration into the act of reading.
Listener-participants: 2
Site-specific: various libraries
www.anthampton.com/ (no download)

Walking Stories, Charlotte Spencer Projects (2013–present)
Choreographic audiowalk designed for green open spaces.
Listener-participants: up to 22
Semi-site-specific: parks
charlottespencerprojects.org/projects/walking-stories/ (no download)

Wondermart, Silvia Mercuriali and Matt Rudkin (2009–present)
Instruction-based investigation into the supermarket environment.
Listener-participants: 2
Semi-site-specific: supermarkets
silviamercuriali.com/ (no download)

Bibliography

Banes, S., & Lepecki, A. ([2007] 2012). *The senses in performance*. Hoboken: Taylor and Francis.

Bateson, G. ([1972] 2000). *Steps to an ecology of mind*. Chicago: University of Chicago Press.

Bateson, G. (1979). *Mind and nature: A necessary unity*. New York: Dutton.

Bateson, G. (1991). In R. E. Donaldson (Ed.), *A sacred unity: Further steps to an ecology of mind*. New York: HarperCollins.

Bateson, G., & Bateson, M. C. (1987). *ANGELS FEAR: Towards an epistemology of the sacred*. New York: Macmillan.

Bateson, P. (2010). Theories of play. In P. Nathan & A. D. Pellegrini (Eds.), *The Oxford handbook of the development of play*. Oxford: Oxford University Press.

Bateson, P. (2015). Playfulness and creativity. *Current Biology, 25*(1), R12–R16.

Berry, R. (2006). Will the iPod kill the radio star? Profiling podcasting as radio. *Convergence, 12*(2), 143–162.

Bishop, C. (2006). *Participation (documents of contemporary art)*. London/Cambridge, MA: Whitechapel Gallery/MIT.

Bishop, C. (2012). *Artificial hells: Participatory art and the politics of spectatorship.* London: Verso.

Bishop, S. R., et al. (2004). Mindfulness: A proposed operational definition. *Clinical Psychology: Science and Practice, 11*(3), 230–241.

Bogost, I. (2016). *Play anything: The pleasure of limits, the uses of boredom, and the secret of games.* New York: Basic Books.

Bottomley, A. J. (2015). Podcasting, Welcome to Night Vale, and the revival of radio drama. *Journal of Radio & Audio Media, 22*(2), 179–189.

Cazeaux, C. (2005). Phenomenology and radio drama. *The British Journal of Aesthetics, 45*(2), 157–174.

Double, O. (2017). Introduction: What is popular performance? In A. Ainsworth, O. Double, & L. Peacock (Eds.), *Popular performance* (pp. 1–30). London: Bloomsbury Methuen Drama.

Gibson, J. J. (1966). *The senses considered as perceptual systems.* Boston: Houghton Mifflin.

Hanh, T. N. (1976). *The miracle of mindfulness: A manual on meditation.* Boston: Beacon Press.

Home-Cook, G. (2015). *Theatre and aural attention: Stretching ourselves.* Basingstoke: Palgrave Macmillan.

Jenkins, H., & Deuze, M. (2008). Convergence culture. *Convergence: The International Journal of Research into New Media Technologies, 14*(1), 5–12.

Kaye, N. (2000). *Site-specific art: Performance, place and documentation.* London: Routledge.

Kershaw, B. (2015). Performed by ecologies: How *Homo sapiens* could subvert present-day futures. *Performing Ethos: International Journal of Ethics in Theatre & Performance, 4*(2), 113–134.

Kershaw, B. (2007). *Theatre ecology: Environments and performance events.* Cambridge: Cambridge University Press.

Lester, S., & Russell, W. (2008). *Play for a change summary report.* London: National Children's Bureau.

Linked. (n.d.). Available from: http://www.linkedm11.net/index2.html. Accessed 24 Mar 2017.

Manovich, L. (2009). The practice of everyday (media) life: From mass consumption to mass cultural production? *Critical Inquiry, 35*(2), 319–331.

Markman, K. M. (2015). Considerations – Reflections and future research. Everything old is new again: Podcasting as radio's revival. *Journal of Radio & Audio Media, 22*(2), 240–243.

McHugh, S. (2016). How podcasting is changing the audio storytelling genre. *Radio Journal: International Studies in Broadcast & Audio Media, 14*(1), 65–82.

Merleau-Ponty, M. ([1945] 2012). *The Phenomenology of Perception* (trans: Landes, D. A.). Abingdon: Routledge.

Miller, G. (2005). Walking the walk, talking the talk: Re-imagining the urban landscape. *New Theatre Quarterly, 21*(2), 161–165.

Mowlah, Andrew, et al. (2014). *The value of arts and culture to people and society: An evidence review*. Arts Council England [Online], Available from: http://www.artscouncil.org.uk/sites/default/files/download-file/Value_arts_culture_evidence_review.pdf. Accessed 20 Mar 2017.

Museum of Walking. (n.d.). *Sound Walk Sunday*. Available from: http://www.museumofwalking.org.uk/events/sound-walk-sunday/. Accessed 14 Aug 2017.

Myers, M. (2011). Vocal landscaping: The theatre of sound in audiowalks. In L. Kendrick & D. Roesner (Eds.), *Theatre noise: The sound of performance* (pp. 70–81). Newcastle Upon Tyne, Cambridge Scholars.

Nelson, R. (2013). *Practice as research in the arts principles, protocols, pedagogies, resistances*. Basingstoke: Palgrave Macmillan.

Noë, A. (2004). *Action in perception*. Cambridge, MA: MIT Press.

Ong, W. J. ([1982] 2002). *Orality and literacy*. New York: Routledge.

Pearson, M. (2010). *Site-specific performance*. Basingstoke: Palgrave Macmillan.

Reason, M. (2017). Intrinsic and instrumental impacts in participatory arts. In N. Rowe & M. Reason (Eds.), *Applied practice: evidence and impact in theatre, music and art* (pp. 37–47). London: Bloomsbury Publishing.

Ritzer, G., & Jurgenson, N. (2010). Production, consumption, prosumption: The nature of capitalism in the age of the digital "prosumer". *Journal of consumer culture, 10*(1), 13–36.

Runco, M. A. (1996). Personal creativity: Definition and developmental issues. *New Directions for Child and Adolescent Development, 72*, 3–30.

Runco, M. A., & Jaeger, G. J. (2012). The standard definition of creativity. *Creativity Research Journal, 24*(1), 92–96.

Savage, J. (n.d.). *A guide to getting lost*. http://www.jenniesavage.co.uk/Guide to getting lost/guide to getting lost.html. Accessed 16 Feb 2015.

Schechner, R., & Brady, S. (2013). *Performance studies an introduction* (3rd ed.). London: Routledge.

Serres, M. (2008). *The five senses: A philosophy of mingled bodies* (trans: M. Sankey & P. Cowley). London: Continuum.

Shepherd, S., & Wallis, M. (2004). *Drama/theatre/performance*. London: Routledge.

Toffler, A. (1980). *The third wave*. New York: Bantam Books.

White, G. (2013). *Audience participation in theatre aesthetics of the invitation*. Basingstoke: Palgrave Macmillan.

Wilkie, F. (2008). The production of "Site": Site-specific theatre. In N. Holdsworth & M. Luckhurst (Eds.), *The Blackwell companion to twentieth century British and Irish drama* (pp. 87–106). Oxford: Blackwell.

15

An Interview with Richard Herring

Neil Fox

Introduction

Richard Herring is a writer, stand-up comedian and podcaster. In recent years he has found sustained success as a podcaster, particularly through the podcast *Richard Herring's Leicester Square Theatre Podcast* (RHLSTP), on which he interviews a renowned comedian, broadcaster or celebrity guest in front of a live studio audience. RHLSTP is released in both audio and video versions. He also uses the podcast form to explore improvisational aspects of his writing and stand-up through the *As It Occurs To Me* (AIOTM) and *Richard Herring's Meaning Of Life* (RHMOL) projects. Then there's the surreal performance art of *Me1 vs Me2 Snooker* that finds Herring playing himself at snooker and taking on the persona of both players and also commentating on the frame as it happens, in audio form. Due to the variety of podcast forms he engages with and his high profile through them, Herring is an appropriate practitioner to provide a case study interview for this book. His work cuts across several types of podcast—live, pre-recorded, comedy, interview/ chat etc. and podcasting is central to his work. It is the area where he gains the most recognition of the varied work he does and also, as he discusses in the interview, podcasting provides the opportunity to drive audiences and consumers to the other areas such as his stand-up shows. He is also a reflective practitioner, taking the

N. Fox (✉)
School of Film & Television, Falmouth University, Penryn Campus,
Penryn, Cornwall, UK
e-mail: neil.fox@falmouth.ac.uk

© The Author(s) 2018
D. Llinares et al. (eds.), *Podcasting*, https://doi.org/10.1007/978-3-319-90056-8_15

opportunity to discuss podcasting as a form on his RHLSTP podcast when a suitable opportunity arises, for example with fellow podcaster Adam Buxton on episode 138.[1]

This interview was conducted via email in two exchanges in March and April of 2017. This is the full transcript, edited only for typographical errors. In it Herring explores his feelings regarding the podcast medium, his myriad approaches to the form, how podcasting relates to the rest of his output and where he feels the medium, and his relationship with it, is headed. This interview is intended to showcase and critique the role of podcasting in contemporary British media culture from the perspective of a practitioner whose work in the medium has crossed over into wider public consciousness. This was the case with the episodes featuring Stephen Fry and Stephen Merchant that are discussed in the interview, which were featured in and on a variety of mainstream media outlets. Arguably, Herring has brought knowledge and discussion of podcasting in the UK to a wider audience than was previously the case.

The interview presented here explores a number of the themes arising throughout the varied academic contributions to this book, including form, funding, creative practice and the audience. The majority of the interview is concerned with RHLSTP, which at the time of going to press was in its fifth season. Episodes are released fortnightly and seasons run a couple of times per year.

Interview

Interviewer: The RHLSTP podcast is released in audio and video versions. Do you class them both as a podcast? What is a podcast to you?

Richard Herring: I don't think it really matters what you call them. They are self-generated audio or video shows. Podcast covers it quite well but aside from having no outside interference or executives to commission them I don't see them as any different from radio or TV shows that just happen to go up on the internet – as many real ones do nowadays anyway.

Does podcasting tap into a particular desire for catharsis and communication for you that can't be reached in stand-up or your other writing, and if so how?

Podcasts are like stand-up in that they are self-generated works. I like both as a medium for comedy as I have autonomy, am uncensored, can try out anything I like and reach consumers directly [Herring's podcasts are free but act as drivers for purchase of tickets to his stand-up tours and merchandise]. With stand-up you have to persuade people to come to a venue and give you some money but podcasts are more direct and have a bit more scope in what you can do with them. My attraction to them initially though was that they were an immediate way to get ideas to an audience without interference or censorship.

How liberating has the freedom afforded by podcasting been for you? I'm thinking particularly around the ability to discuss the process within the form and the potential for commentary and/or self-reflection?

It's very liberating to not have to wait to be commissioned or be in fashion, and also to have an idea and be able to get it out to people as soon as you wish rather than wait for a gap in [the] schedule. It gives me control over when something starts and finishes, has no time limit and lets me do stuff that no broadcaster would ever commission – *Me1 vs Me2 Snooker* being a prime example. So for expression and 'art' these [aspects] are more valuable that anything. Of course you don't directly get paid either but that was not a concern for me. Or at least, getting stuff out there was more important to me.

As someone who has worked across radio, television and podcasting what are the differences between the forms in terms of what is permissible, and might be termed 'political correctness'?

You obviously have freedom to do what you want at any time with podcasts but your audience can still express discomfort or anger with material so it's not a carte blanche. It's exactly the same as with stand-up [where] only you and the audience decide what is acceptable. Comedy is partly about being incorrect in all different kinds of ways and I think TV and radio allow for a certain amount of this stuff but obviously it depends [on the] time and place [that] work is available. Just as in life. A joke that would work with your mates in a pub might not go so well at your Grandma's funeral. The good thing about podcasts is that the audience choose to download them and they aren't beamed into people's homes [without their permission]. So it's fair that you have more liberty. [With] stand-up too, generally, the audience know what they are letting themselves in for, but that does not give you blanket permission to say *anything* [*emphasis added by interviewer*]. Your audience lets you know if you have overstepped a mark and if you do it too much or too often then you won't have an audience. Political correctness is a pejorative term and I don't think it's something that exists in the way that people who use it seem to think it does. You are, as the success of many politicians show, allowed to say what you like. The idea that you're not is what fuels that kind of politics [and] it's just bullshit.

To what extent do you feel that podcasting is secondary to television in terms of aspiration and artistic satisfaction? Do you think podcasting has the ability to ever change this?

It depends what you want. If you need fame and adulation and affirmation from the mainstream then you need to be on TV, but if you are interested in the 'art' of it then it doesn't matter where you are performing. The downside of podcasting is that you're unlikely to be able to achieve the kind of budgets that mean you can have the production values or scope of TV. But you have autonomy and your own channel. So if money and fame are less important than self-expression and the ideas, podcasts are not secondary at all. You have a potential audience of anyone in the world with Internet access. I think in a few years there will be little distinction, as people will just download the content they want and the only advantage of a broadcaster or Production Company is the budget and PR that comes with that. But make something that's good and people will hear about it. The quality of TV comedy in general is not so brilliant that it eclipses what the best people are doing online.

It has been said, by comedians amongst others, that there is a distinct relationship between comedy and podcasting, especially stand-up. Is this something you concur with? How would you explain the attraction for comedians within podcasting?

Autonomy again. Not being told what to do, or hammered into a different shape to fit a certain hole. These are the things that should appeal to any decent stand-up [comedian].

Why do you release audio and video versions of RHLSTP? To what extent is it easy to do because of the form the podcast takes, and to what extent is it to cater to different types of audiences?

Partly [I do it] to see what's possible within the medium. If we can film these and learn from what we're doing we can move on to bigger things. But, seeing what's going on provides another aspect to it and gives us potentially more scope to expand – get the show on Netflix or [an]other platform.

Basically we give people the choice. We can do the audio for free, if they want the video they can Kickstart [Kickstarter – a crowd-funding service] it. So far they have Kickstarted [paid for it through the crowd-funding service] it. But we've moved on to more ambitious stuff like *RHMOL* and *AIOTM* and I'd like to push on to film sitcom[s] and movies too if we can get the necessary backing from the people who like it.

How does podcasting play into your creative identity? To what extent do you feel you are regarded as, and/or see yourself as a podcaster?

I think it works for me and my 'character' of wanting to be on the telly and being a bit of a nearly man. So to do it myself works on a couple of levels. I think I have had most of my successes within podcasting and many people view me as primarily that. I still view myself as a writer/stand-up though. Occasionally I wonder if it's counterproductive to these careers. The podcasting stuff has to be a bit improvised and slapdash by necessity as I do need to earn some money and so can't put too much time into the stuff I do for free. My stand-up shows are much denser and more sophisticated than the riffed opening monologue of *RHLSTP* [at the opening of each episode Herring can be heard doing a short 'bit' for the live audience]. Does that lead people to underestimate me as a stand-up? Perhaps. But also my stand-up audience has grown as a result of the podcasts, so it's probably a positive overall.

How interested are you in pushing the limits of the podcasting form? For example, *Me1 vs Me2* Snooker feels more like surrealist art than anything else.

Very much so. I think the sky is the limit both in terms of surreal ideas and ambition of scope. I hope to be able to explore more stupid ideas and bigger production values over the next twenty years of my career.

Are guests aware prior to recording that the recordings are generally edited minimally and go out as if 'live' to a certain degree? Have there been instances of guests wishing to considerably edit the recording?

[I am] aware that the long-form interview can lead to people saying stuff they don't necessarily mean to reveal [so] I give every guest 100% control beforehand, letting them know we will edit out anything they want and indeed not put the podcast out if they don't want us to. Because of this they speak freely and rarely ask for any cuts.

Where does the decision to leave so much in come from? For example, in the Stephen Merchant episode[2] [where an uncomfortable tension grows between Herring and his guest during the interview], were you ever tempted to cut around it or edit it to relieve the tension?

We did edit a little bit out of that one actually, for that reason, but I'd rather leave everything in because it's real, and also for the occasional awkward and failed bits there are much more in the way of hits. By keeping everything in you are showing the people at home how high the standard of this show actually is. I think the increasingly sophisticated viewers of TV know how much editing and filming goes into making a tight 30 minutes. So I prefer not to patronise them and show it warts and all. I have only ever taken stuff out at request of guest[s] and there are more awkward bits than that one that I'd happily have put out.

There is a strong degree of honesty and frankness on the *RHLSTP* podcast. I'm thinking here of the now infamous Stephen Fry episode[3] [where Fry admitted publicly for the first time that he had in the past tried to commit suicide]. In your opinion to what extent does the liveness of the recording facilitate this?

It's not just the live-ness, it's the trust in me and the audience and the fact that the guest knows stuff is not going to be edited down to sound-bites and that they're going to get to tell the whole story. The live audience in the Fry one certainly contributed to him opening up. The love in the room was palpable and he felt comfortable, and justifiably so. None of those 400 people even tweeted what had happened in the room before broadcast. No one went to the papers to break it.

How do you regard those moments when the recording captures something primarily visual – for instance Simon Munnery[4] taking to the auditorium, then engaging you in an arm wrestling match – knowing that those moments will feel very different when listened to? This goes back to the idea of the surreal mentioned earlier.

Don't mind. Like it. You can watch it if you want of course too. Or come and see it live. Only way to be certain you see everything.

Could you discuss your feelings on funding for podcasting. The relative freedoms you've discussed seem to be offset by a precarious funding

model and you are constantly seeking financial support to keep the show going. It seems that greater funding could be possible but would come with compromises that would restrict the freedoms and change the identities of what you do? Is this a fair assessment or is it simply that podcasting hasn't yet proven its worth in the same way that radio or television has?

I was never bothered about making money from this, just [in] getting ideas out there. I didn't want to lose tens of thousands of pounds, so with the more ambitious ideas we ask for money and then if people don't want those ambitious ideas they won't happen. But accidentally the regular free podcasts are a good business model providing you can cope with not being paid directly. It's publicity for tours and DVDs. Producers and executives hear you. You build up a loyal audience – all these things help. In an attempt to be able to afford the more ambitious stuff I do ask for occasional or monthly donations. In an ideal world my 150,000 listeners would all give me a pound a month and I would make a feature film a year (or whatever). In reality it's so far a much smaller hit rate, but we raised £100,000 for AIOTM via Kickstarter and we do make some money selling tickets [and so on]. If we can convince more people that we're using their money to make more content and not to make ourselves rich then that would be amazing.

But personally, through increased ticket sales on tour and maybe a bit more interest from radio and TV, I am making as good a living now as I ever did. So like I say, I am not a businessman, but through my desire to get ideas and good comedy out there I have chanced across a good business model. And most people will at some point want to put their hands in their pockets to thank me for all they've had, especially if they are getting more content out of it. On the Internet a lot of people giving a small amount could [result in] amazing things. But I like the fact that my [podcast] stuff is free for everyone and that those who can afford to pay [generally] choose to do so, so that those who can't afford to pay can still enjoy it.

Since you started writing and publishing everyday you've kept it up despite the increase in popularity and presumably workload of the podcast, plus your Metro column, stand-up career and family life. Are you similarly committed to podcasting? For example, should a return to television happen would you continue with your podcasts?

It's hard to balance everything, but as you say, I've managed to keep up the blog through some very busy times. At the moment *Me1 vs Me2 Snooker* is on hiatus [because] there is too much going on and I want to make sure that I get enough time to enjoy my family and be around for my wife and daughter. But I can't see me giving up podcasting entirely if I get more success elsewhere. In fact why do something like *RHLSTP* on TV if you're a success? I can keep doing it myself and retain control over what it is. *RHLSTP* is so easy to do. It takes a day out of my week – though booking guests is a bit of a hassle – that I think I would keep doing it. And if I were a 'TV name' too then it would mean we'd sell more tickets and it would be worth doing financially anyway.

It's like the Edinburgh Fringe. In the 1990s some journalists suggested I would only do it until I was on TV and then leave it behind, but through all the ups and downs of my career I have only taken 4 years off since 1992 and am about to go back there with my 40th show for my 30th anniversary Fringe.

I do things because I think they will be good, or will teach me something or help me get better at what I do, not for the money or fame. I am happy to make money if it comes along, though less keen on being famous as I'd like to retain my relative anonymity so I can go out with my family and listen in to people's conversations in cafes without them noticing me!

Podcasting has been good for me, and good to me, and I think it has more potential for me than TV anyway. But if a good TV job meant I could spend six months with my family doing not too much else then I'd have to think about that too. I think I probably need to keep working and would be a pain in the arse if I stopped, so it might be good for my family that I will always have this outlet.

Have you noticed people coming to your work via podcasting and staying for all the other, different outputs, particularly your stand up?

Yes definitely. My live audiences more or less doubled in the first couple of years I was podcasting and plenty of people tell me how much the podcasts mean to them after the shows. So it's one of the things that has helped me keep on doing the live work – though I employ a multi-pronged attack so also get some sales from newspaper articles, radio shows [and so on]. I think if you've enjoyed 50 or so hours of free stuff a year, you will probably want to give a bit back, but also if you've enjoyed them you will seek out more.

You could argue that your work is very much steeped in a UK context. To the best of your knowledge do you get much of a non-UK audience? Would you ever think about doing something that might be more suited to a specific international audience, say the US?

There are certainly listeners all over the world and I get emails from Afghanistan, Antarctica, Africa and other places that don't begin with A. I don't know if it's enough to sustain work out there. There's certainly a core of US fans. I am not that interested in cracking the world before I have cracked the UK. I like the fact that the podcasts can reach everyone on the planet, but I don't really target any specific demographic with my work so wouldn't really fancy doing something specific in this regard.

Your podcasts, particularly *AIOTM* and *RHLSTP* feel like they have a very British sensibility. Do you see any differences between US and UK podcasts that to an extent could be said to mirror differences between US and UK comedy?

America is much bigger with more potential listeners which I think makes it easier for a niche podcast to get loads of downloads. I don't really think of my stuff that way. I am just doing what I think is funny. US podcasts seem to be more professionally produced and more targeted to sponsorship, but I don't listen to enough to be able to give you much [more] of an answer.

In closing, do you have a sense of how podcasts might expand – for example will they become mainstream or will people see them as just a derivative of radio and other media?

I think the Internet gives us all the chance to be our own production company and broadcaster. I think soon we will consume all our media from the same basic device, selecting what we fancy and having a big name like BBC or HBO might make people gravitate to those things, but they will also be able to pick out podcasts or radio and TV shows made online. I'd ultimately like to use the platform to make my own sitcoms and films. I don't think I have quite enough time to make this happen, but out there somewhere is the Charlie Chaplin of the internet who will be both able to produce the material and galvanise enough people to give him or her a dime a throw and become a millionaire.

Conclusion

This interview has provided an introduction into how a podcast practitioner thinks about the form in relation to their career and other forms of creative and professional output. It also engages with the key area of funding for and revenue from podcasting and from Herring's answers it is clear that it can be an expensive and precarious business even at what might be termed the elite, or most visible at least, level.

It is difficult to engage in detailed discussions around listenership and impact of the podcast when the main podcast platform, iTunes, refuse to release data on listenership to either creators or consumers. As a result any discussion will be missing vital data. Discussions around revenue for the podcaster and how the revenue from podcasts compared to say, stand-up comedy touring, are complicated given the self-employed nature of Herring in this case, and those in a similar position. No doubt this will change if and when data on listenership becomes more transparent and podcasting as a viable commercial endeavour become more commonplace. Despite these limitations, this interview case study has provided important insight into the thought and creative processes that go into podcasting practice, into podcasting in terms of funding, brand and product building and into the value and worth of podcasts and podcasting to one of the form's most successful UK practitioners.

Notes

1. Richard Herring's Leicester Square Theatre Podcast, 'Episode #138 Adam Buxton', https://www.comedy.co.uk/podcasts/richard_herring_lst_podcast/rhlstp_138_adam_buxton/, [Podcast] July 5, 2017.
2. Richard Herring's Leicester Square Theatre Podcast, 'Episode #33: Stephen Merchant', https://www.comedy.co.uk/podcasts/richard_herring_lst_podcast/episode_33_stephen_merchant/, [Podcast] November 12, 2013.
3. Richard Herring's Leicester Square Theatre Podcast, 'Episode #18: Stephen Fry', https://www.comedy.co.uk/podcasts/richard_herring_lst_podcast/episode_18_stephen_fry/ [Podcast] June 6, 2013.
4. Richard Herring's Leicester Square Theatre Podcast, 'Episode #132: Simon Munnery', https://www.comedy.co.uk/podcasts/richard_herring_lst_podcast/rhlstp_132_simon_munnery/ [Podcast] February 1, 2017.

Bibliography

Herring, R. Richard Herring's Leicester square theatre podcast. www.comedy.co.uk/podcasts/richard_herring_lst_podcast/ [Podcast]. Accessed 18 Nov 2017.
Herring, R. Me1 vs Me2 snooker. www.comedy.co.uk/podcasts/richard_herring_snooker/ [Podcast]. Accessed 18 Nov 2017.
Herring, R. As it occurs to me. https://www.comedy.co.uk/podcasts/as_it_occurs_to_me/ [Podcast]. Accessed 18 Nov 2017.
Herring, R. Richard Herring's meaning of life. https://www.gofasterstripe.com/cgi-bin/website.cgi?page=rhmol [Podcast]. Accessed 18 Nov 2017.

Index[1]

---

[1] Note: Page numbers followed by 'n' refer to notes.

© The Author(s) 2018   **309**
D. Llinares et al. (eds.), *Podcasting*, https://doi.org/10.1007/978-3-319-90056-8

Printed by Books on Demand, Germany

Printed by Books on Demand, Germany